State and Local Finances under Pressure

STUDIES IN FISCAL FEDERALISM AND STATE–LOCAL FINANCE

Series Editor: Wallace E. Oates, *Professor of Economics, University of Maryland and University Fellow, Resources for the Future, USA*

This important series is designed to make a significant contribution to the development of the principles and practices of state–local finance. It includes both theoretical and empirical work. International in scope, it addresses issues of current and future concern in both East and West and in developed and developing countries.

The main purpose of the series is to create a forum for the publication of high quality work and to show how economic analysis can make a contribution to understanding the role of local finance in fiscal federalism in the twenty-first century.

Titles in the series include:

State and Local Finances under Pressure

Edited by

David L. Sjoquist

Georgia State University

STUDIES IN FISCAL FEDERALISM AND
STATE–LOCAL FINANCE

Edward Elgar
Cheltenham, UK • Northampton, MA, USA

336.013
S797

© David L. Sjoquist 2003

All rights reserved. No part of this publication may be reproduced, stored in a
retrieval system or transmitted in any form or by any means, electronic,
mechanical or photocopying, recording, or otherwise without the prior
permission of the publisher.

Can

Published by
Edward Elgar Publishing Limited
Glensanda House
Montpellier Parade
Cheltenham
Glos GL50 1UA
UK

Edward Elgar Publishing, Inc.
136 West Street
Suite 202
Northampton
Massachusetts 01060
USA

A catalogue record for this book
is available from the British Library

Library of Congress Cataloguing in Publication Data
State and local finances under pressure / edited by David L. Sjoquist.
        p. cm. — (Studies in fiscal federalism and state–local finance)
    1. Finance, Public—United States—States. 2. Local finance—United States. 3.
Intergovernmental fiscal relations—United States. I. Sjoquist, David L. II. Series.

HJ275.S677 2003
336'.01373—dc21

2003044098

ISBN 1 84376 011 8

Typeset by Manton Typesetters, Louth, Lincolnshire, UK
Printed and bound in Great Britain by MPG Books Ltd, Bodmin, Cornwall

Contents

University Libraries
Carnegie Mellon University
Pittsburgh PA 15213-3890

Figures

Tables

Contributors

James Alm is Professor of Economics and Chair of the Department of Economics in the Andrew Young School of Policy Studies at Georgia State University. He has held faculty positions at the University of Colorado at Boulder and Syracuse University. His research has ranged widely on public finance issues, particularly the marriage tax and tax compliance.

Kelly D. Edmiston is an assistant professor of economics at the Andrew Young School of Policy Studies, Georgia State University, where he teaches public finance and urban-regional economics. His research interests fall predominantly in the areas of state and local government finance, regional economic development, and intergovernmental relations. He has published in journals such as the *National Tax Journal*, *Municipal Finance Journal*, and *Public Finance Review*.

Ronald C. Fisher is Professor in the Department of Economics and the Department of Accounting at Michigan State University, where he also serves as Director of the Honors College. He specializes in the study of government finance and taxation, particularly regarding state and local governments, and has authored the leading textbook in the field, *State and Local Public Finance*. He has also served as Deputy Treasurer for the State of Michigan and as Visiting Fellow at the Federalism Research Centre at the Australian National University.

William F. Fox is Professor of Economics and director of the Center for Business and Economic Research at the University of Tennessee, Knoxville. He is active in the National Tax Association, serving as President in 1997. He has consulted on fiscal policy issue with the Tennessee state government and has worked with many states and developing countries in structuring and analysing tax systems. He is the author of numerous publications on state and local taxes, especially sales taxation, and on economic development.

W. Bartley Hildreth is the Regents Distinguished Professor of Public Finance in the Hugo Wall School of Urban and Public Affairs and the W. Frank Barton School of Business at Wichita State University. His research focuses on municipal bonds, state and local finance, and electric industry restructuring. His recent co-edited books include the *Handbook on Taxation* and *Performance-Based Budgeting*.

Jill Ann Holman is Assistant Professor of Economics at the University of Wisconsin – Milwaukee. She has held previous positions at the Federal Reserve Bank of Kansas City and the University of Georgia. Her research has ranged widely on open-economy macroeconomic issues, particularly the growth effects of tax-financed versus inflationary-financed government spending, the transmission of inflation across countries, and current account sustainability.

Daphne A. Kenyon is principal of D.A. Kenyon & Associates, a public finance consulting firm. Prior positions include president of the Josiah Bartlett Center for Public Policy, professor and chair of the Economics Department at Simmons College, senior economist with the U.S. Department of the Treasury and the Urban Institute, and assistant professor at Dartmouth College. Her research has focused on, among other topics, intergovernmental fiscal relations, including mandates and tax competition.

Therese J. McGuire is at Northwestern University where she is Professor in the Kellogg School of Management and Faculty Fellow in the Institute for Policy Research. Her areas of expertise are state and local public finance, fiscal decentralization, property tax limitations, education finance, and regional economic development. She was President of the National Tax Association in 1999–2000, and is currently co-editor of the NTA's academic journal, the *National Tax Journal*.

Daniel R. Mullins is Associate Professor in the School of Public Affairs at American University. His research focus is state and local fiscal issues with major interests in intergovernmental fiscal relationships and local fiscal structure. He is managing editor of *Public Budgeting and Finance*, has experience in executive level local government administration and has worked extensively on international fiscal reform.

Rebecca M. Neumann is Assistant Professor of Economics at the University of Wisconsin-Milwaukee. Her research focuses on open-economy macroeconomic issues, including the form of international capital flows, the transmission of monetary policy across countries, and international effects of taxation.

Lawrence O. Picus is Professor in the Rossier School of Education at The University of Southern California. His research focuses on school finance and issues related to educational productivity and the design of state school finance funding formulas. He is a former President of the American Education Finance Association.

Ross Rubenstein is Assistant Professor of Public Administration and Urban Studies in the Andrew Young School of Policy Studies at Georgia State University, with a joint appointment in the College of Education. His research focuses on public budgeting, education policy and public finance, specifically funding equity and adequacy in education, performance measurement, and merit-based financial aid.

Bruce A. Seaman is Associate Professor of Economics and Associate in the Fiscal Research Program in the Andrew Young School of Policy Studies at Georgia State University. A former president of the Association for Cultural Economics, International, with interests also in industrial organization, regulation and antitrust, he has written and testified regarding severance taxes, local option sales taxes, franchise fees, and special excise taxes. He has written widely on economic impact methodologies and also in arts economics.

David L. Sjoquist is Professor of Economics and Director of Domestic Programs and of the Fiscal Research Program in the Andrew Young School of Policy Studies at Georgia State University. His research focuses on state and local fiscal issues and urban poverty, and he recently published *The Atlanta Paradox* (Russell Sage Foundation). He is on the Board of Editors for the *National Tax Journal*.

Sally Wallace is Associate Professor of Economics and Associate Director of the Fiscal Research Program in the Andrew Young School of Policy Studies at Georgia State University. She has served as a Financial Economist at the US Treasury Department and Resident Advisor for the AYSPS Tax Reform Project in the Russian Federation. Her research focuses on domestic and international taxation, with a particular focus on the impacts of tax policy on individual behavior.

Acknowledgements

The development of this book grew out of conversations I had with Bob Ebel when he was executive director of the National Tax Association. His insights were extremely helpful and his encouragement and support are greatly appreciated. It goes without saying that he bears none of the responsibilities for any deficiencies in the implementation of the concept. I also want to thank Dorie Taylor and Arthur Turner for their valuable assistance in the preparation of the manuscript.

David L. Sjoquist

1. Introduction

David L. Sjoquist

In the history of the United States there have been numerous forces that have had profound effects on the structure of state and local government finances. For example, the Great Depression led many states to implement a sales tax; during the 1930s, 24 states adopted the sales tax. The adoption of the Great Society programs in the 1960s resulted in new and expanded state and local government expenditure programs and a substantial increase in reliance on federal grants. Comparisons of the structure of state and local government finances before and after bear witness to the impacts of these events.

Today, state and local governments face numerous pressures, not just one major force. The chapters in this volume explore the nature of these pressures, discuss their implications for the finances of state and local governments, and explore how these forces play out in terms of changes that state and local governments will and should undertake in response to these pressures. These forces stem from technological advances, court rulings, federal government policies, changes in population demographics and in the nature of the economy, and political pressures.

Each of these forces by itself is not likely to have the impact that a Great Depression or Great Society had, but taken together they confront state and local governments with the need to make substantial changes in their fiscal systems. These pressures represent a diverse set of forces. Thus, rather than having to react to one event or force by, for example, adopting a new tax source, state and local governments are being pressured to adjust along multiple dimensions.

Unlike the Great Depression, the pressures that state and local governments face today do not require immediate adjustments to their fiscal systems. Failure to act in the short term will not be devastating to state and local governments. But longer term, the failure to act is likely to result in substantial adverse effects and increasing pressures that will require more substantial changes, changes that are more difficult to implement and changes that are more politically unpalatable. Without change, state and local fiscal systems will grow increasingly out of sync with economic reality. It will be death by a thousand pin pricks, not by a gun shot.

Because the effects in the short run of not acting in response to these pressures will be small, state and local governments will be inclined to avoid making the necessary changes. Over time, some state and local governments will likely realize that their fiscal systems do not match the environment and will begin to make changes. But other governments will wait it out until a fiscal crisis occurs. Thus, governments will change at different times and at different rates, and the responses are therefore likely to be evolutionary, not revolutionary. The response to some of these pressures will be noticeable in the short run, but for other pressures, we will see only small changes within five or ten years. However, in, say, 25 years we will witness the fact that substantial changes have occurred in how state and local governments conduct their fiscal affairs.

Compared to the previous 20 years, the past 20 to 25 years can be categorized as ones of stability in state and local finance. Ronald Fisher in Chapter Two sets the stage with an overview of how state and local government fiscal affairs have changed over the past 20 years in contrast to the changes during the previous 20 to 40 years. The size of the state and local sector relative to the size of the economy has remained essentially constant. In terms of the composition of expenditures and revenue sources and the importance of states relative to local governments, there has been little change. Expenditures on health and criminal justice have increased while transportation spending has decreased as a share of total expenditures. Charges for services have increased relative to other revenue sources and state governments have become somewhat more important relative to local government. But in contrast to the 1960s and 1970s, these changes are modest.

In Chapter Three, Sally Wallace discusses the changes in the demographic and economic profiles of the US, how they are likely to change in the future and the potential effect these changes will have on state and local government finances. There are many changes occurring to the demographic profile of the US population, to the nature of the output of the economy, and to the sources of household income. The aging of the population is one trend that has received considerable attention, particularly as to how it affects the future of social security. But the changes in the age distribution also have implications for state and local government finance, both on the revenue and expenditure sides of the budget. In addition to the aging of the population, the US is experiencing an increase in the share of the population that are immigrants and in the share of families without children. In terms of economic changes, the relative importance of manufacturing has declined while services have increased, and the sources of income have changed, with wages and salaries comprising a smaller share of income.

Wallace explores how these trends will exert pressures on the current revenue and expenditure patterns of state and local governments. For example, since the elderly are taxed differently, have different consumption patterns, and obtain their income differently, the growth in the elderly population could have profound effects on the level of state and local revenue and the nature of public expenditure patterns. Thus, as the relative size of the different demographic groups changes, state and local government will face pressures to change their tax systems and their public expenditure patterns. Changes in the structure of the economy and the sources of income have important implications for the growth of the various tax bases. Wallace concludes by offering suggestions for how state and local governments might deal with the pressures they face from these demographic and economic trends.

For the past quarter of a century, the courts have exerted strong influence on state and local government finances, particularly on the provision of education. But the courts are not the only pressure that is likely to have major effects on how education is provided and financed. In Chapter Four, Ross Rubenstein and Lawrence Picus point out that primary and secondary education is going through a transformation as a result of a set of diverse forces. The courts have had a significant effect on the financing of education, and the recent court decisions are having even more profound effects than earlier rulings. But in addition, there are calls for greater autonomy for individual schools and the adoption of new accountability systems which tie funding levels to performance. There are also several market-based alternatives that are creating competition for traditional public (that is, publicly funded) schools. These forces will likely drive major changes in how education is financed and delivered.

In early cases the courts established standards for school finance equity, measured in terms of available resources, for example, equal property tax base per student. Rubenstein and Picus describe the effect that these cases have had on school finances, particularly the equity of school funding. However, for school finance lawsuits that have been decided within the past decade or so, the courts have become more aggressive in specifying remedies and have focused on output, requiring states to ensure that school districts have the level of resources necessary to provide an adequate education. This focus on adequacy represents a substantial alteration in how states will have to think about school finance systems.

While states have responded to equity cases by allocating additional funds to resource-poor school districts, adequacy cases pose the threat of requiring even greater increases in resources, with the amount of resources and their allocation dependent upon how adequacy is measured. The basic foundation program used by many states for education funding determines adequacy in terms of what revenue can be made available from the state budget, while the new standard will be driven by what resources students need. Rubenstein and Picus point out that satisfying issues of adequacy most likely means that current standards for equity cannot be achieved.

Many of the pressures facing public primary and secondary education, namely, accountability systems, market-based alternatives and the demands for change from teachers and parents, focus on the individual school and not the school district. Thus, there is a disconnection between how education is funded, which is district-based, and where the responsibility for the delivery of education is being laid, which is at the individual school level. Rubenstein and Picus discuss these pressures and their implications for the future education finance systems, including how a funding system focused on schools rather than districts might work.

While Fisher (Chapter Two) notes that the last 20 years have been a period of relative stability in state and local government finance, there have been many changes, but as Daniel Mullins suggests in Chapter Five, the changes have been very subtle. Over the past quarter of a century various restrictions have been imposed on state and local governments that limit the use of certain taxes and expenditure levels. Mullins attributes these revenue and expenditure limitations as a major cause of this restructuring, and argues that the limitations will continue to expand, particularly at the state government level.

Mullins argues that the effects of fiscal limitations are not benign and have unintended consequences. The limitations can significantly affect the capacity of governments to provide the public services demanded by citizens. In order to adapt to this imbalance, local governments have had to distort the fiscal and service delivery structures, with the result being a more fragmented and complex state and local public sector and a less responsive one.

Fiscal limitations substantially alter the structure of local finance (for instance by an increase in non-tax sources of revenues) and create shifts in the distribution of service responsibilities between units of government (for instance through the increased role of special service and finance districts). Limitations have reduced the relative role of the property tax, and yielded a property tax that is often at considerable variance with tenets of equity and efficiency, and they are likely to produce a local public sector which is less redistributive in its effects and lead to increased pressures to use privatization and service contracts. Mullins notes that the effects of limitations vary by type of government and service subgroups, and by the demographics of resident populations. He also suggests that the increasing need to adapt to new limitations will likely result in additional fiscal innovation, additional losses in transparency and additional initiatives for reform.

Outside of the role of federal grants, little attention has been paid to the role that federal government policies exert on state and local government finances. Daphne Kenyon (Chapter Six) begins her analysis with a discussion of the many ways that the federal government influences state and local government finances. Federal grants are probably the most significant federal influence on state and local governments. Kenyon notes that while the relative importance of federal grants has not changed in recent years, there has been a major shift to grants that are directed to individuals rather than to places. But there are several other ways in addition to direct assistance through grants that the federal government influences state and local governments. These influences include indirect assistance through the tax code, for example, through the deductibility of taxes and interest on government bonds.

The federal government also has a major effect on state and local government finances through its influence over the national economy, through mandates and via the 'rules of the game'. In the case of the latter influence, the federal government can affect state and local governments not only by passing legislation, but also by choosing to not intervene, for example, by allowing states to compete for economic development activity through tax subsidies and by not addressing the nexus issue associated with sales taxes on internet sales.

How the federal government responds to the return of large federal budget deficits could have major effects on state and local government finances; for example, will the federal government make major changes in grants to subnational governments? There is also the question of whether Congress will enact fundamental tax reform. If it does, it will have major effects on state income tax systems, particularly those that are tied to the federal income tax.

Kenyon goes on to discuss how the role of the federal government has changed and how the 11 September terrorism could alter the relationship between the national and subnational governments. During the 2000 Presidential campaign one news magazine suggested that the candidates appeared to be running for the local school board. But as a result of 11 September, the federal government changed its focus from domestic affairs to international affairs. One possible reaction is that the present focus of the federal government will result in a modification of the current 'fend for yourself' federalism and that we will enter a period of either cooperative federalism or coercive federalism; there is evidence to suggest that either outcome is a possibility.

Advances in information technology have had significant effects on our lives. These same advances are also having substantial effects on government. In Chapter Seven, Kelly Edmiston and William Fox explore how information technology is affecting the provision of public services and changing the tax landscape. Information technology has allowed improved access to many government services. For example, the provision of education, particularly specialized courses and education in more rural areas, has been enhanced by new technologies. And just as information technology has improved efficiency in business, it has the capability to do the same for government. Edmiston and Fox describe the many ways that governments are using new technologies to improve the efficiency of service delivery, for example, by allowing online applications. And the internet has the potential to increase democracy, for instance by providing greater access to information about government and improved access to public decision makers. But Edmiston and Fox suggest that governments are only at the early stages in their use of information technology, and that there are several obstacles, including funding, that have to be overcome in order for state and local government to fully utilize the new technologies.

Information technology has also altered many aspects of business, putting pressures on state and local tax systems. The range of products that can be provided has changed and the physical characteristics of some products can be altered, both of which have consequences for taxes. For example, while a printed version of a book is subject to a sales tax, a digitized version generally is not, and with the ability to order online, a growing percentage of purchases escapes sales tax. In addition, information technology has changed the relative importance of some of the factors associated with business location decisions, perhaps increasing the sensitivity of factors such as taxes. These have consequences for the size and mobility of tax bases such as for the property tax, and for the tax rate that can be imposed without worry that the base will evaporate. Edmiston and Fox point out that these factors will force state and local governments to consider new ways to tax and discuss how state and local governments might respond.

The changes in technology that Edmiston and Fox discuss are part of the reason why state governments face serious challenges regarding the tax and administrative burdens associated with changes in the provision of electricity, natural gas, and telecommunications services. Historically, the three industries operated as regulated monopolies for almost an entire century. But as W. Bartley Hildreth and Bruce Seaman point out in Chapter Eight, the technological change, demand growth, and other developments in the respective industries made this structure inadequate. The deregulation of energy has changed the nature of competition in the industry. In the telecommunications industry the product has evolved into many alternative products provided by many competing firms. The result of these changes in industry structure is a need for states to re-evaluate their tax and public finance systems as they relate to these previously monopoly businesses.

Hildreth and Seaman note that elected officials face considerable complexity as they try to adjust both regulatory and public finance policy to these structural and technological changes. For example, moving toward greater equality in the overall industrial tax burden would require lowering the previously high tax burdens for the newly competitive energy and telecommunications industries. However, without offsetting increases in the overall tax base, or politically unpopular increases in the tax burdens of other sectors, overall tax revenues will decline. Further complications arise since public officials must design legally acceptable taxable relationships (nexus) with newly emergent out-of-state service providers following deregulation. Furthermore, there is no presumption that deregulation of natural gas and electricity, and the technological and structural change in the telecommunications sector, raise exactly the same fiscal issues for all state and local governments.

Hildreth and Seaman suggest labeling states as either 'reform' states or 'coping' states, depending upon whether they adopt policies that represent either a forward-looking (efficiency) or a backward-looking (distribution) focus. A backward looking focus highlights the winners and losers of deregulation, with efforts to design compensatory relief that will redistribute the results along a desired path. This can lead to small policy changes, rather than more fundamental ones. A forward-looking efficiency approach requires the establishment of a 'level playing field' to neutralize taxes as a factor in the competitive interaction among the newly expanded providers of services.

Hildreth and Seaman discuss how various states have responded to this new environment, and do so in the context of a fiscal stress hypothesis, that is, that states facing greater fiscal stress from utility deregulation will be more likely to adopt reform tax policy strategies. The bottom line, however, is that states are taking multiple roads to deregulation and the associated tax reform, and that there is much reform left to be carried out.

Much has been made of the globalization of business and its impact on US businesses. But globalization of the economy also has the potential to have profound influences on state and local fiscal systems. In Chapter Nine, James Alm, Jill Holman and Rebecca Neumann explore this force. As they point out, state and local tax systems were originally designed in an era in which firms produced tangible goods using factors of production that were largely immobile and in which the sale and consumption of these goods were generally performed in the same location. Economic globalization has changed that. Alm, Holman and Neumann describe the various ways that globalization might affect state and local governments and use a stylized model to highlight the probable consequences of the increased mobility that is implied by globalization.

One of the principal characteristics of globalization is the increased mobility of businesses and factors of production. The authors explore how that change affects state and local governments. Greater mobility probably means that competition for the tax base will be more intense. The result is that state and local governments have less autonomy in the design of the fiscal systems they adopt. Alm, Holman and Neumann discuss the likely patterns that might result from this increased mobility, describe how state and local governments will have to adjust their fiscal systems in light of the pressures from globalization and search for any trends that suggest that these patterns are occurring. For example, with increased mobility of some factors of production, we should expect to see a shift away from taxes on more mobile sources.

The more rapid expansion of urban land than of urban population has become a major issue in many urban areas. While sprawl is a topic that has been widely written about, there has been little attention paid to the implications of sprawl for the finances of state and local governments. In Chapter Ten, Therese McGuire and David Sjoquist explore the causes of sprawl, the consequences of sprawl for state and local government finances, and options that state and local governments might adopt to deal with the issue.

As the authors point out, there is no commonly accepted definition of sprawl. However, in designing appropriate policy concerning the geographic expansion of an urban area it is important to separate causes that lead to an economically efficient expansion of the urban boundary from the causes that result in an economically inefficient expansion. Thus, an expansion of an urban area is not necessarily undesirable, but an economically inefficient expansion is. Among the causes that do not necessarily lead to inefficient expansion are increases in population and income, both of which cause the demand for land on the urban fringe to increase. McGuire and Sjoquist identify a host of policies and forces that lead to inefficient expansion of urban areas, including underpricing of the use of roads, property taxation, and the system for financing the expansion of infrastructure.

The expansion of urban areas, whether they are efficient or inefficient, has several consequences for state and local finances, both in terms of the cost of providing public services and in the geographic distribution of tax bases. McGuire and Sjoquist list many of the ways that expansion of the urbanized area can affect the cost of public service delivery and discuss the existing empirical evidence. Finally, they present an extensive discussion of policies for addressing the causes and consequences of the economically inefficient expansion of urban areas. Many of the causes of sprawl are a result of inappropriate market signals, so one set of solutions is to impose proper prices or user fees, an approach which is the standard fare of economists. But McGuire and Sjoquist also discuss other options, including growth management programs such as urban growth boundaries.

There are undoubted other forces and pressures that are driving changes to state and local government fiscal systems, for example the state of the macro economy. But the ones discussed in this volume are certainly some of the most important and persistence pressures forcing structural changes in state and local government fiscal systems. As a result of these pressures, there will likely be substantial changes in the next 25 years in the nature of state and local government fiscal systems.

2. The changing state–local fiscal environment: A 25-year retrospective

Ronald C. Fisher

THE STATE–LOCAL SECTOR: AN OVERVIEW

There was substantial and remarkable stability of state–local finances in the last 20 years of the past century (that is, since 1980) especially compared to the prior 30 years (1950 to 1980). State–local expenditure and revenue remained around 12 per cent of gross domestic product (GDP), with no real trend. There was certainly no dramatic change in the distribution of state–local tax revenue among the various revenue sources. And even with important revisions in the mechanism of provision and finance for some services, notably welfare and education, there were very few large changes in the shares of state–local expenditure for various services. Thus, a period of remarkable turbulence in the world of state and local government, essentially from 1950 to the middle or late 1970s, was followed by a period of remarkable fiscal stability.

A key issue for state and local government analysts and leaders is whether the new century is likely to see a continuation of the recent experience in the area of state–local finance or a reversion to a time of dramatic change reminiscent of the 1950s and 60s. Certainly some people believe that a confluence of circumstances – including economic and demographic trends, new technologies, and the evolving political landscape – may foster important and substantial changes in state and local government fiscal practices over the next several decades. In large measure, that issue is the topic of this book. In subsequent chapters, other authors will explore the likely implications of expected changes in demographics, economic conditions, technology, and political attitudes. The purpose of this chapter is to provide a baseline so that these investigations may be put into proper context. Knowing where you are and how you arrived at that point can be helpful in determining where you will go next.

Size and Growth of Subnational Government

The state–local sector accounts for a very substantial segment of the national economy. In 2000 state–local governments spent about $925 billion of resources collected from their own sources, which represents slightly more than nine per cent of GDP (Table 2.1). When spending financed by federal grants is included, state–local expenditures represent nearly 12 per cent of GDP. For every dollar collected from its own sources and spent by the federal government in 2000, state–local governments collected and spent about $0.51. In per capita terms, state–local governments collected and spent about $3360 per person in 2000 from own sources and about $4250 per person including federal aid. If comparison is limited to spending for domestic programs by all levels of government, state–local governments collected about 42 per cent of those funds and were responsible for spending about 53 per cent.

Table 2.1   The relative size of federal and state–local government, 2000

Type of expenditure	Federal government		State and local government	
	Amounts (billions)	Percentage of GDP	Amounts (billions)	Percentage of GDP
Expenditures from own sources	$1813.9	18.2	$926.2	9.3
Expenditures after grants	1569.3	15.8	1170.5	11.7
Domestic expenditures: own sources	1283.6	12.9	930.7	9.3
Domestic expenditures: after grants	1039	10.4	1175.3	11.8

Note: Domestic expenditures include nondefense purchases, transfer payments to persons and governments, and net subsidies of government enterprises.

Source: Department of Commerce, Bureau of Economic Analysis.

The current substantial relative size of the subnational government sector arose from a roughly 25-year period of sustained rapid growth between 1950 and 1975, as depicted in Figures 2.1 and 2.2. Using National Income Accounts data, state–local expenditures grew from about six per cent of GDP in 1950 to about 12 per cent in 1975, implying that state–local spending increased at roughly twice the rate of the national economy. Since 1975, however,

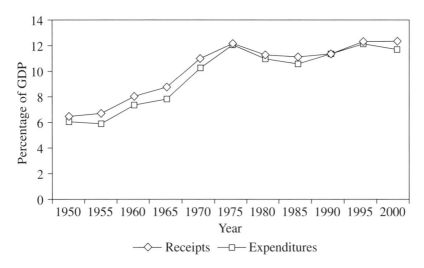

Sources: US Department of Commerce, Survey of Current Business, various years; *Economic Report of the President*, 2001.

Figure 2.1   State–local receipts and expenditures relative to GDP, 1950–2000

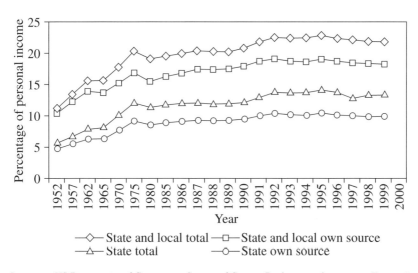

Sources: US Department of Commerce, Survey of Current Business, various years; *Economic Report of the President*, 2001.

Figure 2.2   State–local expenditures relative to personal income, 1952–2000

state–local spending has remained in the neighborhood of 12 per cent of GDP. Figure 2.1 illustrates another important feature of state–local finances. Generally, the state–local sector has operated with a fiscal surplus, as receipts have been greater than expenditures. (Deficits can occur in individual years of course, but the data at five-year intervals underlying Figure 2.1 illustrate the overall trend.)

A similar perspective is revealed if one uses US Census Bureau data and compares relative to personal income, as in Figure 2.2. In 1952 total state–local spending from all sources represented about 11 per cent of personal income, but by 1975 state–local spending had grown to more than 20 per cent of income. Even excluding federal grants, state–local spending from own sources increased from about ten per cent of income in 1952 to about 17 per cent in 1975. Since 1975, however, state–local spending has continued to grow relative to personal income, but at a much more modest pace. Over this period, state–local spending has increased from a little more than 20 per cent of income to 22 per cent, hardly a dramatic change over a 25-year period. Importantly, also, the pattern of changes in spending by state governments alone parallels the pattern for the entire state–local sector rather closely. Thus, the past 25 years have seen little substantial change in the relative fiscal magnitude of state and local government, at least at the macro level.

State and local governments also account for nearly 79 per cent of all government employees, a share that continued to increase over the last half of the past century. For instance, state and local governments accounted for only about 60 per cent of public employees in the middle 1960s. And as depicted in Figure 2.3, over a period when federal government employment (both civilian and military) has declined relative to population, employment by both state governments and local governments increased faster than population. Not surprisingly though, given the patterns of spending, the last 20 years have also not seen a dramatic change in state–local employment relative to population, but clearly a dramatic change relative to federal government employment.

The substantial relative growth of the state–local sector from 1950 to the middle 1970s is usually explained by three main factors. First, income in the United States increased rather substantially in this period, causing an increase in demand for many different types of goods and services, some of which were provided largely by subnational governments. Second, a variety of demographic factors especially new family formation and the resulting creation of new suburban communities and the 'baby boom' in the postwar period led to an increase in demand for state–local services (especially education, highways and other transportation services, public safety, and so on). Third, substantial increases in manufacturing-labor productivity and thus manufacturing wages during this period created pressures to increase wages

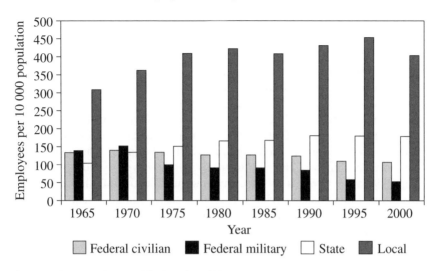

Source: *Economic Report of the President* (2001).

Figure 2.3   Government employment relative to population, 1965–2000

of state and local employees as well. This caused an increase in the relative cost of providing state–local services. In essence, spending rose faster than the economy grew because the population to be served (especially children) was rising relatively fast, because the costs of providing state–local services were rising faster than average, and because consumers were demanding new or improved services from subnational governments.

The relative size of the state–local government sector has not changed nearly as substantially since the middle 1970s, however. In general, the reduction in the relative growth of the fiscal size of state and local government during the last quarter of the past century simply reflected a reversal of all those factors that had been operating since 1950. Income did not grow as fast in those years as previously, as the economy experienced two substantial recessions between 1974 and 1983. Demand for educational services lessened as the 'baby boomers' completed school and delayed starting their own families. State–local government costs, especially wages, did not increase relatively as fast in this period as previously, in part due to slower growth of private productivity nationally. It has also been suggested that a change in the tastes or preferences of consumers for government services, reflected by coordinated opposition to state–local taxes in the late 1970s and 1980s, led to a change in the political environment.

Interstate Variation

Although the relative fiscal magnitude of the state–local sector did not change substantially in the past 25 years, there have been important changes in fiscal variation among the states. During the past 20 years there was a very substantial narrowing of fiscal differences among the states. The changes in the distribution of state–local per capita general expenditure are shown in Table 2.2. If all states and the District of Columbia are considered, the coefficient of variation for per capita spending fell by half between 1982 and 1999, from 0.47 to 0.23. Similarly, the ratio of the highest to lowest spending state fell from 5.9 to 2.9. Even if the two outlying jurisdictions of Alaska and the District of Columbia are excluded from the analysis, an important decline in interstate variation in spending is still apparent. Not surprisingly, there has also been a similar decrease in interstate variation in per capita revenue.

Table 2.2   *Variation in per capita state–local general expenditure, 1982–1998*

Year	States	Mean	Coefficient of variation	Max.	Min.	Max. to min. ratio
1982	All states	$1992	0.47	$7958	$1345	5.9
1992	All states	$3900	0.30	$9893	$2751	3.6
1998	All states	$5224	0.23	$11 502	$4037	2.9
1982	Excl. AK & DC	$1841	0.19	$3157	$1345	2.3
1992	Excl. AK & DC	$3708	0.17	$7788	$2751	2.1
1998	Excl. AK & DC	$5025	0.12	$7351	$4037	1.8

Source: Department of Commerce, Bureau of the Census.

Interstate variation in per capita revenue is slightly greater than the variation in per capita spending, which reflects the equalizing role played by federal aid. So some of the narrowing of fiscal differences over this period is the result of growth and changes in the structure of intergovernmental grants. The other major factor is the narrowing of regional economic differences (in other words, convergence of state personal income), which has translated into a corresponding narrowing of fiscal differences as well.

Is 'Whitewater' to Follow?

Given these patterns, the natural question, referred to at the start of this chapter, is whether a new period of substantial and sustained growth of state local spending should be expected. There are a number of factors identified or suggested by a variety of people that could bring this about.

1. At the time this is being written, the nation has just completed an excep-tionally long period of sustained economic growth, characterized again by substantial productivity growth and resulting income growth. This economic growth, although tempered now by a modest downturn, could be expected to increase demand for services provided by state–local governments and could increase wages nationally and thus unit costs for government.

2. Changes in demographic trends also are potentially important. As a result of 'baby boomer' families, the number of students in both the K-12 and public higher education systems has been increasing and is expected to continue to do so for at least several more years. In addition, of course, the aging of the 'baby boom' population may create new issues and resulting demands for state–local government services.

3. The expansion of state–local government in the 1950 to 1975 period included a major effort to build public facilities, especially schools, colleges, highways, and airports. Of course, those facilities depreciate and require maintenance and eventual replacement. As those facilities age, maintenance costs are expected to increase. Many of those facili-ties have already come to the end of their useful lives and have or are being replaced. Many others may need to be replaced in the next 20 years.

4. Changes in technology are creating both new investment requirements for state and local governments, but also possible opportunities to reduce production costs. Governments have and are investing in new technology for their own service production, which creates both a new and continu-ing expenditure item (as technological facilities and equipment need to be acquired and then replaced or updated). In many cases, state and local governments also may have a role in creating and maintaining the infra-structure necessary for new information technology, including that necessary for internet connectivity and public access facilities (such as are often in public libraries). Technology changes in both information and biological science are creating new demands for research funded by states and localities, often done through public universities and thought of as an economic development initiative. Each of these forces contrib-utes to greater spending.

On the other hand, technology may also allow states and localities to provide traditional services with different production methods. To the extent that technology can substitute for other productive inputs at lower cost, spending may be restrained. The hope, of course, is that technology may permit the public sector to enjoy productivity increases similar to those that traditionally have been easier to achieve in the production of goods than services. If so, then the link between private sector wage increases and public sector unit cost increases may be mitigated. In some areas of state–local government (involving records and registration activity), the potential cost saving seems to have been realized. In other areas, notably education, the net effect so far seems to have been an increase in expenditure.

STATE–LOCAL SERVICES AND EXPENDITURES

Trends in Spending

About half of state and local spending in aggregate goes to provide education or public welfare services, as shown in Figure 2.4. Over the period since the early 1960s, the share of spending for education has declined slightly while the share for welfare increased substantially (particularly in the late 1960s and late

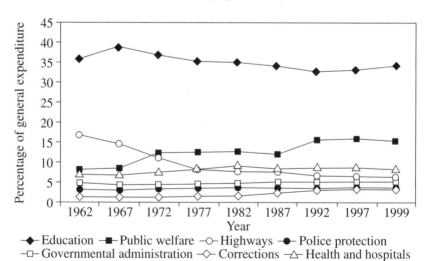

Source: US Department of Commerce, Bureau of the Census (various years).

Figure 2.4   Distribution of state–local general expenditure, 1962–1999

1980s). Thus, the share of spending on education and welfare combined has increased modestly over the long run (from 45 to 50 per cent), although it remained essentially constant in the 1990s. Among other major spending categories, the share of expenditures for highways declined dramatically until the late 1970s and modestly since; the shares of spending on health and hospitals and police protection have remained relatively stable (around nine and four per cent respectively); and the share of spending for corrections, while still low, has more than doubled from 1.3 to 3.3 per cent. In summary, over the past 30 years, spending for education and highways has become a smaller fraction of state–local expenditure in aggregate, while the share of expenditure for public welfare and corrections has risen. As with state–local expenditures in aggregate, changes in spending patterns were much more dramatic prior to 1980 than after. The most substantial changes since 1980 involve welfare and corrections, which are considered in greater detail below.

Welfare: Health Costs and Spending Escalate Throughout the Economy

Most of the increased share of state–local spending on 'welfare' can be attributed to a single factor – increasing health care spending funded largely though the Medicaid program. Over the past 30 years when welfare expenditures rose relative to total state–local budgets, the share of spending on cash assistance programs (such as Aid to Families with Dependent Children and Supplemental Security Income) actually declined (see Figure 2.5). The increasing relative expenditure in the welfare category has been due to programs providing direct services in kind rather than cash, and the overwhelming bulk of that type of welfare is Medicaid. Between 1980 and 1990, Medicaid expenditures rose by about 178 per cent; from 1990 through 1999, Medicaid spending increased at an even greater rate – 188 per cent. By 1999, total Medicaid spending was about $187 billion, or about $670 per person.

Medicaid provides health care to individuals and families who have low incomes and resources and is jointly operated and financed by the federal government and the states. States are required by federal regulations to cover certain individuals and certain types of health care services, but states also have options to expand both eligibility and coverage beyond those mandated by federal policy. States receive open-ended federal matching grants to help finance their Medicaid expenditures, with the federal matching rate determined by state per capita income relative to the national average. The federal government reimburses states for a larger fraction of Medicaid expenditures in lower income states than higher income ones. In 1999, these federal grants covered about 58 per cent of Medicaid expenditures in aggregate, varying among the states from a minimum of 50 per cent (in ten states) to a maximum of nearly 77 per cent (in Mississippi).

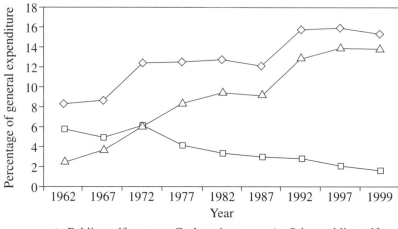

Sources: US Department of Commerce, Bureau of the Census (various years); US Department of Health and Human Services, Social Security Administration (2000).

Figure 2.5   Welfare expenditures relative to general expenditure, 1962–1999

Increases in state spending on Medicaid (and also in the federal grants for this program) arise from (1) increases in the number of mandated covered individuals; (2) increases in the prices charged by vendors for medical care or drugs; and (3) policy decisions by states to expand eligibility or coverage beyond that mandated by federal law. Although the number of individuals receiving benefits through Medicaid has continued to increase (more than 60 per cent since 1990), that rate of growth is clearly substantially less than for total Medicaid expenditures. A number of states have explored alternatives to the traditional Medicaid structure and mechanisms to reduce or restrain health care prices. But obviously, the magnitude and growth of Medicaid expenditures continues as a major issue facing both the federal government and state–local government.

It is especially important to recognize that the growth of Medicaid expenditures is part of a national trend of increasing relative expenditure on health care generally. Total private and public health care expenditures increased by 183 per cent in the 1980s, but by only 74 per cent from 1990 to 1999. Health care spending rose from 8.8 per cent of GDP in 1980 to 12 per cent in 1990 and 13 per cent in 1999. The slowdown in the growth rate in the latter half of the 1990s has been attributed to the shift toward more managed care systems. But recent evidence suggests that the rate of growth of health care spending is again returning to the double-digit rates common in the 1980s. A major factor is that growth in spending for prescription drugs continues to outpace growth of spending for health care services in general. Thus, while Medicaid expenditure remains a major policy issue for state–local government, health care spending in general remains a major issue in the economy affecting essentially all individuals and industries, both private and public. As such, this seems a much broader issue than a limited state–local fiscal matter, but one that will continue to occupy state–local officials.

Growing Importance of Criminal Justice Activities

One service or expenditure category showing substantial and important recent change concerns public safety and corrections. Per capita expenditure by state and local governments on corrections increased from $36 in 1982 to $167 in 1999, an increase of more than 350 per cent. Over the same period, spending on corrections increased from 1.9 per cent of general expenditure to 3.3 per cent. Focussing on spending in the 'corrections' category understates the impact on state and local government finances of public safety issues and policies, of course. In 1999, state and local governments spent an additional $54.4 billion on police protection and $25.3 billion on the judicial and legal system. If these are combined with spending on corrections, the total amounts to nearly nine per cent of general expenditure. In 1982, these three areas together represented about six per cent of state–local spending.

The immediate or direct reason for this increase in spending for corrections and public safety is that many more individuals are now incarcerated or supervised by the justice system than in the past. In 1999, nearly 1.9 million inmates were being held in federal or state prisons and local jails. Another 700 000 people were on parole (and being supervised) and about 3.8 million people were serving probation. In 1980, there were about 215 people in federal and state prisons and local jails per 100 000 people in the population; by 2000, this number had risen to over 700 per 100 000. Because about 94 per cent of all inmates are held in state prisons or local jails, the incarceration rate for state prisons and local jails alone was about 650 inmates per 100 000 population. This direct relationship between the incarceration rate in state or local jails and state–local per capita expenditure on corrections is shown in Figure 2.6.

The fact that relatively more people are in prison may reflect an increase in the amount of criminal activity, more effective or stringent law enforcement, higher conviction rates in court, or changes in sentencing practices. In fact, some combination of all of these is likely involved. It is important to recognize, however, that three of these four factors reflect direct policy choices by state and local governments. For instance, between 1988 and 1998 there was about a 40 per cent increase in felony convictions in state courts. But the share of those convicted of felonies in state courts who were sentenced to

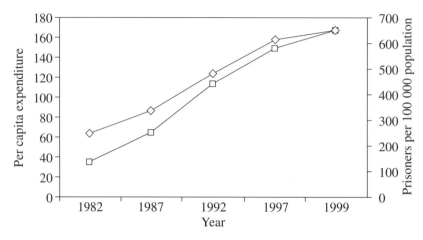

-□- Per capita S-L expenditure -◇- State–local incarceration rate

Source: US Department of Justice, Bureau of Justice Statistics, *Correction Statistics* (2000) and *Prison Statistics* (various years).

Figure 2.6   Corrections population and spending, 1982–1999

state prisons remained constant (at 44 per cent) in both years. These data suggest that it has been one of the first three factors, rather than sentencing changes, that have been important since 1988.

Drug-related offenses continue to account for much of this change, as about 32 per cent of felony convictions in state courts were related to drug offenses in both 1988 and 1998, four of ten of which were related to possession rather than trafficking. The percentage of those convicted of drug offenses who are sentenced to prison is slightly less than for all felons (42 compared to 44 per cent) and average sentence length is a bit less also. As a result, the US Department of Justice reports that about a fifth of state prison inmates were sentenced for a drug-related crime. In comparison, about one fourth were sentenced for a property crime (burglary, larceny, fraud, and so on) and a bit less than half for a violent crime (assault, robbery, rape, murder).

STATE–LOCAL REVENUE SOURCES

Trends in Taxes and Other Sources

Five major sources, all of roughly equal importance, account for approximately 84 per cent of state–local general revenue in aggregate, as shown in

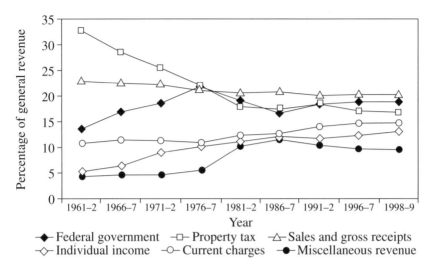

Source: US Department of Commerce. Bureau of the Census (various years).

Figure 2.7   Distribution of state–local general revenue, 1961–62 to 1998–99

Figure 2.7. These five, in order of importance, are sales taxes (20.3 per cent of general revenue), federal grants (18.9 per cent), property taxes (16.7 per cent), current charges (14.7 per cent), and individual income taxes (13.2 per cent). Between 1962 and 1982 there was a dramatic narrowing of the differences in degree of reliance upon these revenue sources. The share of general revenue from property taxes, for example, declined from about 33 per cent of general revenue to less than 22 per cent, while the share from individual income taxes rose from about five per cent to more than 11 per cent. Similarly, but less dramatically, reliance on sales and gross receipts taxes declined while reliance on fees and charges increased. In contrast, reliance on grants from the federal government was more variable, first rising substantially before subsequently declining and then stabilizing in recent years.

Compared to the period before 1980, the period since has certainly been characterized by substantial stability in revenue reliance for the state–local government sector. Reliance on charges and individual income taxes did continue to increase, though modestly, as shown in Figure 2.8. As a result of this continuing trend, by 1999 current charges had become the second largest provider of revenue from own sources to state–local governments. Current charges accounted for nearly 15 per cent of general revenue in 1999, more than general sales taxes (14 per cent), individual income taxes (13 per cent), and excise taxes (about six per cent). Only property taxes (at about 16.7 per

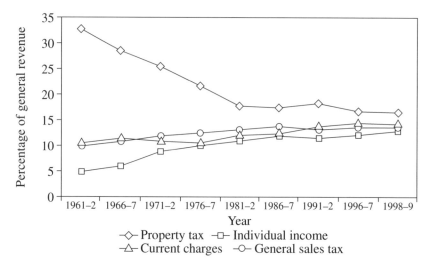

Source: US Department of Commerce, Bureau of the Census (various years).

Figure 2.8   Distribution of major own source revenues, 1961–62 to 1998–99

cent) were more substantial than charges, although that difference continues to narrow.

Increasing Reliance on Charges

The importance of 'prices' in state–local finance – charges and fees for specific services – continued to increase over the last quarter of the past century. By the narrowest traditional definition of user charges, they amounted to $210.9 billion for 1999 and accounted for 15 per cent of general revenue. This category includes such charges and fees as those related to education, hospitals, sewerage and solid waste disposal, transportation and parking, parks and recreation, among others. Within this definition specific types of charges include prices for services at public hospitals, college and university tuition and fees, sewer charges, airport fees (including PFCs), fees for refuse collection, highway tolls, school lunch sales, fees for the use of parks and recreational facilities, parking charges, and so forth.

Other substantial forms of revenue that have the character of 'prices' are not included in this narrow definition, however. Possible additional types of charges include license taxes ($30.4 billion), special assessments ($3.6 billion), interest earnings ($65.9 billion), sales of property ($1.6 billion), revenue from utility sales ($81.9 billion), liquor store sales ($4.2 billion), and other miscellaneous nontax general revenue including revenue from gambling ($66.1 billion). If all of these are counted as fees and charges, then this category of revenue represents more than 25 per cent of the total revenue received by state–local governments. By this definition, 'prices' or charges and fees are the largest single source of revenue for subnational government by a wide margin. (I have not included insurance trust revenue, including unemployment and workers' compensation taxes and retirement contributions, in this total. One might argue that the UI and worker's comp components are insurance premiums and also represent prices. But one also might think of these as taxes earmarked for income support services.)

Increasingly, then, it is difficult to escape the conclusion that in many ways states and localities look and operate like private businesses. Even with growing interest in privatizing the production of some services traditionally provided through state and local governments, the importance and relative magnitude of state–local fees and charges have continued to increase. To some extent, this reflects a growing demand for certain services, such as recreational facilities, that traditionally have been provided by subnational governments. The trend toward substantial reliance on fees and charges is unlikely to be reversed, and there also may be opportunities to increase that reliance even more both by substituting charges for taxes in some service areas and by changing the character or structure of charges in other areas where they are currently used.

Changes in the Nature of Federal Grants

The last half of the 20th century saw dramatic changes in the role of the federal government in assisting in the financing of services provided directly through state–local governments. In aggregate, federal grants rose greatly in relative importance to states and localities until the late 1970s when, for about a ten-year period, federal grants grew slower than state–local revenue overall. In the past 15 years federal grants have grown only modestly as a share of state–local revenue, as shown in Figure 2.9. By the end of the century, federal grants accounted for nearly 19 per cent of state–local general revenue in aggregate, still below the peak of more than 22 per cent reached in 1977.

The change in the purposes of federal grants has been even more dramatic and important than the change in the aggregate amount of those grants. The greatest changes have come in two areas, which are depicted in Figure 2.10. Grants for health purposes – more than 95 per cent of which go for Medicaid – represented more than 43 per cent of federal grant dollars in 2000. In contrast, grants for health represented only 17 per cent of the total in 1980 and only five per cent in 1950. Grants for income security programs, such as

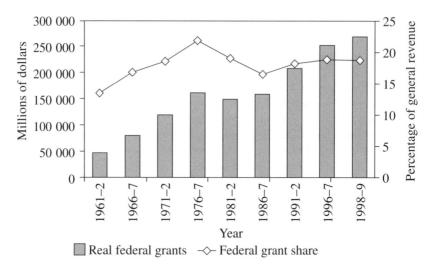

Source: US Department of Commerce, Bureau of the Census (various years).

Figure 2.9   Federal grants to state–local governments, 1961–62 to 1998–99

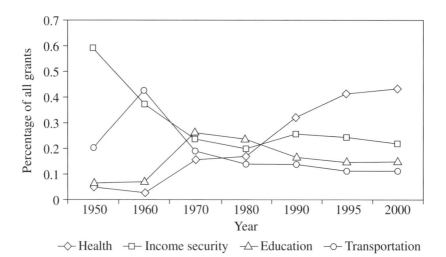

Source: US Department of Commerce, Bureau of the Census (various years).

Figure 2.10   Changes in the distribution of federal grants, 1950–2000

food stamps or Temporary Assistance to Needy Families (formerly Aid to Families with Dependent Children), now account for about 22 per cent of federal aid compared to 26 per cent in 1990 and 59 per cent in 1950. Among other changes, grants for education and training increased in relative import- ance until the mid 1970s and have since declined. Grants for transportation, the great bulk of which support highway construction and maintenance, increased dramatically in relative importance in the 1950s, but have declined relatively since.

The only broad federal grant category for which the share of federal aid increased since 1990 is health, reflecting the very rapid growth of Medicaid (as noted previously). Because federal grants to states for Medicaid are open-ended matching grants, the substantial relative increase in these grant amounts resulted from increases in state spending on Medicaid. And those increases in spending seem to have been driven mostly by two factors – increases in the number of eligible persons (including many elderly) given existing program rules, and increases in health care prices, especially for prescription medications. One should not conclude that the substantial in- creases in federal grants for health programs have eliminated state budget pressures in this area. Indeed, only a portion of increased state government expenditures on Medicaid is offset by additional federal grant funds, so the increasing demand for and cost of health care continue to create serious budget difficulties for states. As state Medicaid expenditures rise, the amount needed to cover the state share does also, creating fiscal pressures for the federal government as well.

REFOCUSING RESPONSIBILITIES: THE EXPANDING ROLE FOR STATES

Perhaps the most significant change over the past 25 years in the world of state and local government finance is the increasing importance of state governments relative to both localities and even the federal government. This change is not readily apparent from aggregate fiscal statistics about spending or employment, as shown in Figures 2.2 and 2.3, partly because the increased state role manifests itself more through control of policies, procedures, and regulations than direct spending. Yet this increased state role is most signifi- cant and substantial in the two largest categories of spending by state–local governments – for education and welfare. In the case of education, the in- creased role for the states was in large measure thrust upon them by the courts, while the increased role in welfare programs came at the request of the states, believing that state choice and differentiation would lead to better results than national standards. Each is discussed below.

States have also taken an increasingly aggressive yet cooperative approach in attacking issues that inherently are not limited by boundaries. Regulation of and litigation involving the tobacco companies, discussion and deliberation regarding internet taxation, and aggressive antitrust enforcement all represent examples of this evolving state influence. In these instances, the state governments as a group are becoming an important, and sometimes even dominant, force in influencing national public policy. In essence, the states have become more substantial challengers of the federal government.

Education Finance, Production, and Evaluation

Two distinct factors have led to the increased state role in providing education. First, as a result of a number of legal challenges to the system of financing education, courts have ordered states to substitute financing systems that are less driven by differences in local wealth than the traditional provision by local school districts relying on property taxes. In other legal challenges to the traditional system, courts have recognized the responsibility of state governments to ensure not just equal, but 'adequate' education for all children. Consequently, a number of states have revised both the sources of revenue for education and the distribution of those funds among local schools. In the 1950s and 60s, states provided about 40 per cent of the funds for public elementary and secondary schools. By the late 1980s, the state government share had risen to nearly 50 per cent. Although that share declined a bit in the first half of the 90s, it increased again in the last half of that decade so that states again provide about half of the funding for primary and secondary education.

The other important factor through which the state role has grown is the renewed focus on measurement and evaluation of both schools and educational results. The emphasis on accountability is in many ways the natural result of those legal decisions that have forced states to take more fiscal responsibility for the distribution of educational resources and for ensuring adequacy of educational production. The state emphasis on accountability has also arisen from the now well-documented long-run trend in public education finance. Over the past 35 to 40 years, real per student spending by public schools increased continuously and average class sizes declined, but student performance as measured by a wide variety of tests – both comparing among students in the US as well as comparing US students internationally – either declined or did not improve nearly as fast as spending grew. This fact has induced states to want to improve the results of public education systems and to find ways to ensure that the increasing state spending is being used in the most effective manner.

Hanushek and Raymond (2001: 369) note that 'The basic skeleton of accountability systems involves goals, standards for performance, measurement, and consequences … .' They further report that while few states have set clear goals for their accountability systems, essentially all states have established standards for performance and test students in some form. In addition, most of the states also evaluate and report on the performance of schools, but perhaps only about half of the states have explicit consequences for poor performance by either students or schools. Three issues about educational accountability seem to have been most contentious: (1) who should be evaluated – students, schools, or school districts; (2) how should the evaluation be structured – in other words, what are the relative advantages of various testing methods; and (3) what level of government should be primarily responsible for setting standards and conducting the evaluation – states or the federal government. For instance, Ladd (2001: 398) argues that 'schools are the most logical starting point for a top-down accountability system …', although that view remains controversial. There are a host of controversial and well-known issues about student testing, and debate continues about the relative merits of federal as opposed to 'local' standards. But what is inescapable is the increased focus by states on educational performance and the important new role that this focus represents.

Welfare and Work

The states' role in providing basic welfare services also changed dramatically in the 1990s, not financially, but in terms of control and objectives. The Aid to Families with Dependent Children (AFDC) program provided cash payments to families with children, an absent or unemployed parent, and low income and assets and was financed by open-ended matching grants to the states. Although state governments operated this program, state authority to establish eligibility requirements and benefit levels was severely constrained by federal requirements and limitations. In the early 1990s, several states sought waivers from the federal government so that they could implement experimental welfare programs with eligibility standards and benefit structures different than those prescribed. Of particular interest were requirements that recipients had to go to school, participate in job training, or go to work to continue to receive benefits and the setting of overall time limits on benefits. In this way, states were seeking authority to have increased responsibility for welfare programs and the right to experiment with dramatically different objectives.

   This culminated in the adoption of a new system of welfare programs in 1996 that formally transferred substantial program responsibility to the states. AFDC was reconstituted as Temporary Assistance to Needy Families (TANF). Under TANF, states were given broad flexibility to set eligibility standards and benefit levels, with the condition that they maintain spending of at least

80 per cent of the amount of nonfederal funds spent in 1994, and states receive block grants based on past spending to cover part of the welfare program cost. Importantly, TANF includes work requirements, financial incentives for states to move recipients from welfare to work, provisions to provide childcare and health benefits in support of work decisions, as well as a maximum five-year life welfare time limit for families. As noted, state governments now have substantial flexibility in deciding how to move toward achieving the broad work goals of TANF. For instance, TANF funds can be used for expenditures other than direct cash payments to recipients (such as education, job training, or child care), and states can set lower maximum time limits.

As a result of these changes, the total number of persons receiving TANF/ AFDC benefits has fallen dramatically, from a peak of 14.2 million recipients in five million families in 1994 to 7.2 million recipients in 2.6 million families in 1999. Increasingly, states are spending resources on mechanisms to assist and encourage these individuals and families to work in the private sector or accept public sector or volunteer assignments. Clearly the ability of states to move former welfare recipients to forms of work was aided by the long, sustained period of substantial economic growth in the 1990s. So one issue is the degree to which these changes can be maintained through the business cycle. Another issue concerns the economic well being of former welfare recipients, as participating in work does not guarantee a level of support sufficient to escape poverty.

These two cases of education and welfare reform illustrate important ways that the policy influence of state governments has grown in the last decade. The states' role has expanded from merely a source of funds (in the case of education) and a delivery agent (in the case of welfare). In the case of education, states traditionally provided financial support and general guidelines to localities, which had the primary responsibility of producing and evaluating education. Clearly today, states are deeply involved in assessment, evaluation, and production as well as finance of education. In the case of welfare, states traditionally served as implementation agents of the federal government in providing the day-to-day operation of programs that were largely federally mandated, but jointly financed. Today, states have a direct policy role in determining goals and methods, as well as generating financial support.

SUMMARY

After a period of dramatic growth following World War II until the middle 1970s, the state and local government sector continues to be a very substantial component of the national economy. But the issues facing state and local governments are very different now than fifty years ago. On the expenditure side of budgets, states are pressured fiscally by rising health care costs and the resulting effects on Medicaid spending, and the sector continues to face rising expenditures to ensure public safety, especially related to incarceration and corrections. Both trends may be exacerbated by demographic changes. On the revenue side of budgets, the mix of funding sources is much more balanced than in the past, but states and localities continue to seek additional nontax sources of funds. Finally, states are actively seeking to insure that subnational government is as effective as possible in achieving society's objectives. On the one hand, this had led states to explore ways that new technology can be used in providing state–local services, and on the other, it has led states to become more involved in assessing the outcomes of public expenditures and in developing alternative policies to utilize funds more efficiently and effectively.

BIBLIOGRAPHY

Advisory Commission on Intergovernmental Relations (1993), *Significant Features of Fiscal Federalism,* Washington, DC: author.
Economic Report of the President (2001), Washington, DC: US Government Printing Office.
Fisher, Ronald C. (1996), *State and Local Public Finance*, Chicago, IL: Richard D. Irwin, Inc.
Hanushek, Eric A. and Margaret E. Raymond (2001), 'The confusing world of educational accountability', *National Tax Journal*, 54(2): 365–84.
Ladd, Helen, F. (2001), 'School-based educational accountability systems: the promise and the pitfalls', *National Tax Journal*, 54(2): 385–400.
Ladd, Helen F. and Janet S. Hansen (eds) (1999), *Making Money Matter*, Washington, DC: National Academy Press.
Moody, J. Scott (ed.) (2001), *Facts and Figures on Government Finance,* Washington, DC: Tax Foundation.
US Department of Commerce, Bureau of the Census, (various years), *Census of Governments, Compendium of Government Finances,* Washington, DC.
US Department of Commerce (various issues), *Survey of Current Business,* Washington, DC.
US Department of Health and Human Services, Centers for Medicare and Medicaid Services (2001), *CMS Data and Statistics*, Washington, DC.
US Department of Health and Human Services (2001), *Indicators of Welfare Dependence*, Annual Report to Congress, March, Washington, DC.
US Department of Health and Human Services, Social Security Administration (2000), *Social Security Bulletin, Annual Statistical Supplement*, Washington, DC.
US Department of Justice, Bureau of Justice Statistics (2000), *Corrections Statistics*, Washington, DC.
US Department of Justice, Bureau of Justice Statistics (various years), *Prison Statistics,* Washington, DC.

3. Changing times: Demographic and economic changes and state and local government finances

Sally Wallace

INTRODUCTION

The US population is rapidly changing its demographic profile. In 1994, one out of every eight Americans was elderly. By 2030, the overall rate of population growth in the US will have decreased relative to levels of the 1990s, but one out of every five people will be elderly and children under the age of 18 will become a smaller percentage of the population.[1] Immigrants have played a large role in US population growth in the most recent decade, and will continue to influence the profile of laborers and consumers in the future. Over the next several decades, families are less likely to have young children in the household.

In addition to these demographic changes, the economic profile of the US economy has also changed. In 1990, manufacturing output accounted for 17.9 per cent of total gross domestic product (GDP); finance, insurance and real estate accounted for 17.4 per cent of total GDP; and services accounted for 18.4 per cent of GDP. By 2000, these percentages had changed to 15.8, 19.6 and 21.9 per cent respectively. Commensurate with these output changes, the distribution of employment has changed as well. In 1990, 20 per cent of the workforce were employed in the goods producing sector and 67.4 per cent of the employed workforce were in the services sector. In 2000, those percentages changed to 16.1 and 74.7 respectively.[2] In general, income continues to grow, with real per capita income increasing nearly 21 per cent from 1990 to 2000.[3] The composition of income has changed slightly with wages and salaries accounting for about 57 per cent of personal income, transfer payments about 13.5 per cent and capital income (rent, dividends and interest) making up approximately 19 per cent of personal income.

The impact of these economic and demographic changes on public finances could be very dramatic.[4] As people age, they spend down their savings, earn relatively little labor income, and purchase different types of goods.

Each of these changes can affect revenues as well as expenditures. As the economic structure of an economy changes, there are demands for different types of infrastructure and changes to property and income tax bases. Some of the impacts of economic and demographic changes are more predictable than others. For example, the issue of the impact of the growth of retirees on social security payments can be estimated with some degree of accuracy. On the other hand, the impact of globalization on tax bases is perhaps more difficult to estimate. From a policy perspective, we should ask: how big are these economic and demographic changes and how important are they to the stability of state and local finances? This chapter analyses the impact of a set of economic and demographic changes on public finances for state and local levels.[5]

The next section presents a basic analysis of how these changes affect state and local finances. The third section provide information on trends in economic and demographic change in the US. The fourth section analyses how these changes affect the fiscal structure of state and local governments, with an emphasis on the revenue side. The final section presents an outlook for state and local government revenues, given the major trends discussed. The emphasis in this chapter is on some of the most important economic and demographic changes, including the following: on changes in the growth and age distribution of the population, the level and composition of income and consumption, and the major sector shifts in production and employment.

HOW ECONOMIC AND DEMOGRAPHIC CHANGES AFFECT STATE AND LOCAL FINANCES

Individuals earn and spend money and in doing so, pay state and local taxes and fees. Individuals and firms demand public services from the government and thereby affect the expenditures of state and local budgets. As the individuals change from young to old, and production switches from manufacturing to service-oriented, we should expect different demands for public services, and different income and spending patterns. State and local governments do not have revenue systems that are perfectly adaptable to these types of changes but can look for ways to mitigate the stress put on finances due to demographic and economic changes.

While we have witnessed an overwhelming number of demographic and economic changes over the past two decades and the same overwhelming number of budgetary consequences, in this chapter we will concentrate on the largest and most significant changes and outline the likely responses to them. The economic behavior (such as consumption, savings, labor supply) of individuals and families with respect to changes in their circumstances is complicated and even though we have been studying such behavior for many decades, there is still much uncertainty regarding exactly why individuals behave as they do. This chapter will therefore analyse how some of the economic and demographic changes can impact state and local budgets, but it does not discuss all changes nor present with certainty all of the impacts. The remainder of this section presents the 'theoretical' discussion of the impacts of economic and demographic changes on state and local budgets by discussing the potential revenue and expenditure impacts separately.

Expenditure Impacts

Since public expenditures (Exp) are driven by the needs of the population or clients,[6] a very basic relationship between public expenditures and demographic factors is as follows:

$$\text{Exp}_i = Q_g \times C_g \tag{1}$$

$$d\text{Exp}_i = dQ_g \times C_g + Q_g \times dC_g \tag{2}$$

$$Q_g = f \text{ (client population)} \tag{3}$$

where Q_g is the output of the public good and C_g is the cost per unit.

In equation (2), the left hand side is the change in expenditure for a particular spending category, Exp_i, and the right hand side of the equation contains the components of the change in expenditures. These are changes in the client population (elderly for retirement programs, school aged children for school expenditures, telecommunications businesses for utilities and infrastructure, and so on) and changes in the costs of production associated with the cost of inputs (wages, materials, and so forth). Demographic changes can influence both components of the expenditure calculation. For example, consider a change in the age distribution of the population. If a population is becoming increasingly elderly, this will increase the need for expenditures for retirement and health-based expenditures. However, such a trend will also influence the direct cost of providing those services as labor shortages may also ensue.

Revenues

A simplified expression for the relationship between public revenues of type i, Rev_i and demographic and economic factors may also be expressed as follows (assuming no changes in enforcement nor compliance behavior):

$$Rev_i = (taxbase_i \times taxrate_i) \times pop_i \tag{4}$$

$$dRev_i = dtaxbase_i \times taxrate_i \times pop_i + taxbase_i \times dtaxrate_i \times pop_i$$
$$+ taxbase_i \times taxrate_i \times dpop_i \tag{5}$$

On the revenue side, 'taxbase' is determined by the laws and economic activity of a particular revenue source and 'taxrate' is determined by the relevant legislature and executive bodies. Pop_i is the taxpaying population for a given revenue source. For personal or individual income taxes, the tax base would be some measure of taxable income, and the population would be individuals with wage and salary and capital income. For consumption taxes, the base would be a measure of consumption, and the population would be individuals and businesses making taxable purchases. Economic and demographic changes will directly influence these tax bases as well as the relevant population. In the case of a consumption-based revenue source for example, the level of population will affect the total potentially taxable consumption and the age distribution of the population will affect the type of consumption made. The breadth of the tax base of each state and local government will determine how much revenues will fluctuate as a result of these demographic changes – if a state or local government taxes individual income broadly, they will be less subject to changes in the composition of income, for example.

The tax rate, while exogenous to these demographic and economic changes, is a policy variable that can be used to compensate for changes in the tax base. For example, if we analyse the elasticity of personal income taxes (PIT) with respect to income, we can decompose the change as follows (holding population constant, this is a measure of the elasticity of the individual income tax with respect to income):[7]

$$\%\Delta PIT/\%\Delta income = (\%\Delta PIT/\%\Delta taxable\ income) \times$$
$$(\%\Delta taxable\ income/\%\Delta income) \tag{6}$$

On the right hand side of this expression, the first term is referred to as the 'rate elasticity' and measures how tax revenues change as taxable income changes. The second term is the 'base elasticity' and measures how the amount of taxable income changes as overall income in the economy changes. This expression demonstrates that public finances are a function of both economic and demographic changes (since they directly affect taxable income in this example), and institutional factors (since they affect the divergence between economic activity measured as 'income' and taxable activity measured here as 'taxable income'). If demographic patterns were such that the tax base for the individual income tax is shrinking (if there are proportionately less working age individuals in the population), we would project a decline in revenues from the individual income tax. To maintain constant revenues in light of these demographic changes, the tax rate itself could be increased to make up for the reduced tax base. Such a policy change is not without cost, but this example simply shows the trade-offs available to policy makers.

These simple relationships between expenditures and revenues and their component parts demonstrate that economic and demographic trends will affect state and local public finances through various means. Expenditures will be directly affected by the demands for different types of public goods and services as the population and industry base changes.[8] At the same time, the costs of public goods and services are affected by similar economic and demographic changes. On the revenue side of the equation, tax bases are directly influenced by population and income shifts as individuals and businesses change how they earn income and how they consume. The basic number of taxpayers is also directly affected by demographic changes.

The next section provides an analysis of the major changes in demographic and economic variables that we expect will significantly affect state and local finances in this century. The remainder of this chapter concentrates on the revenue side of the story, although the expenditure side is also critically important.

TRENDS

State and local finances during most of the 1990s were strong. From 1992–1999, state and local tax revenues grew by over 46 per cent in nominal terms or approximately 23 per cent in real terms. Most states shared in this revenue growth, and the natural growth of the economy encouraged states to reduce taxes in a variety of ways. Rafool (2002) reported that state governments enacted tax cuts amounting to $9.9 billion in fiscal year (FY) 2001.

Beginning in mid to late 2001, the revenue story changed quite dramatically. State tax revenue collections for July–December FY2002 compared to the same period for FY2001 were down 2.7 per cent for the US as a whole. States of the Great Lakes region posted a model increase of 1.3 per cent for the period, while states of the Far West region saw a 9.9 per cent decrease in revenue over the same period (Jenny, 2002). These revenue difficulties were largely the result of the general state of the US economy, which experienced a recession in 2001–02. The future of the underlying economy is still a little murky and some forecasters predict a strong recovery while others are less optimistic. It is important to consider the general state of the economy as we analyse the impact of economic and demographic changes on state and local governments as the macroeconomic situation provides a general indication of changes in income, prices, and employment. These changes may affect the magnitude of the impact of demographic changes on state and local finances.

The federal government, via the Congressional Budget Office (CBO), and the Executive Office of the President both make forecasts of the state of the economy. The data in Table 3.1 show that both branches of government expect the economy to pick up significantly in 2003 with growth in GDP of 3.8 per cent and 4.1 per cent for the Administration and CBO, respectively. There are some significant differences in the forecasts for unemployment and the financial markets. CBO's unemployment rate is higher than that of the Administration for the entire forecast period, which reflects CBO's slightly more pessimistic view of the coming years. The differences between CBO and the Administration on the three-month Treasury Bill and on the ten-year Treasury Note are relatively large. The impact in terms of federal budgeting is that the Administration's forecasts of various expenditures that are influenced by these finance costs are lower than those expenditure items under the CBO scenarios. In CBO's March Update the strength of the economy led CBO to revise their GDP figures for 2002. These are not updated in Table 3.1 so that comparisons are more easily made with the Administration's figures.

These general forecasts of the economy, which suggest a smooth pattern of growth and a stable recovery, should not be taken as an indication that state and local finances could be expected to grow smoothly. There are structural changes in the economies of states across the country that will impact states differently. The remainder of this section highlights the trends expected in income, age distribution, employment, and consumption of the US population and regions and pays particular attention to the underlying changes in the composition of these variables so that we can analyse their impacts on state and local finances.

Income

Income is one of the primary indicators of the fiscal health of a country, region, or state. As discussed earlier, income is the driver for many of the tax bases, and it also influences the demand for public services. While there are various measures of income, personal income is one that is widely used in tracking the growth of an economy, and it is used here. The US Department of Commerce, Bureau of Economic Analysis (BEA) defines personal income as the sum of wages and salaries, dividends, rents, interest, transfer payments, other labor income, and income of proprietors. The information in Table 3.2 provides this decomposition for personal income for 2001. As seen there, wage and salary income is the largest component of personal income, but transfer payments and capital income are both significant sources of personal income as well.

Table 3.1   Calendar year administration and Congressional Budget Office (CBO) forecasts of key economic indicators 2001–2007

Measure	Estimated 2001	Forecast 2002	Forecast 2003	2004	Projected 2005	Projected 2006	Projected 2007
Administration							
Real GDP (billions)	9313	9382	9739	10 101	10 462	10 802	11 136
Per cent change in real GDP (year over year)	1.0	0.7	3.8	3.7	3.6	3.2	3.1
Per cent change in CPI-U	2.0	2.4	2.2	2.3	2.4	2.4	2.4
Unemployment rate (annual average)	4.8	5.9	5.5	5.2	5.0	4.9	4.9
91-day treasury bill (per cent)	3.4	2.2	3.5	4.0	4.3	4.3	4.3
Ten-year treasury note (per cent)	5.0	5.1	5.1	5.1	5.1	5.2	5.2
CBO							
Real GDP (billions)	9320	9398	9783	10 145	10 470	10 805	11 151
Per cent change in real GDP (year over year)	1.0	0.8	4.1	3.7	3.2	3.2	3.2
Per cent change in CPI-U	2.9	1.8	2.5	2.5	2.5	2.5	2.5
Unemployment rate (annual average)	4.8	6.1	5.9	5.4	5.2	5.2	5.2
Three-month treasury bill (per cent)	3.4	2.2	4.5	4.9	4.9	4.9	4.9
Ten-year treasury note (per cent)	5.0	5.0	5.5	5.8	5.8	5.8	5.8

Sources: Executive Office of the President (2002) and Congressional Budget Office (2002a, 2002b).

Table 3.2   Composition of BEA personal income (2001, billions of dollars)

Sum of:	
Dividends, interest, and rent	1552.5
Transfer payments	1148.8
Wages and salaries	5098.2
Other labor income	553.8
Proprietor's income	743.5
Less:	
Personal contributions for social insurance	373.3
Equals:	
Total personal income	8723.5

Source: US Department of Commerce, Bureau of Economic Analysis (2002b).

Real per capita personal income has grown in the last two decades, although somewhat more slowly than in the previous decades. From 1970 to 1980, the average annual growth in real per capita income was 3.04 per cent nationwide. The 1980–90 decade saw growth slow to 1.8 per cent annually. The estimated average annual growth in real per capita income for 1990–2000 is 0.7 per cent, with a decline coming in the early 1990s and rapid growth in the latter 1990s (Table 3.3).

Not surprisingly, the growth in real per capita personal income among the regions is quite different than the national average. As seen in Table 3.3, the

Table 3.3   Actual average annual growth in real per capita personal income (in per cent) 1970–1980 to 1995–2000

Area	1970–1980	1980–1990	1990–1995	1995–2000
United States	3.04	1.80	−1.12	2.43
New England	2.74	3.04	−1.28	3.42
Mideast	2.31	2.68	−1.48	2.51
Great Lakes	2.78	1.44	−0.52	1.93
Plains	2.99	1.76	−0.74	2.56
Southeast	3.92	2.20	−0.74	1.92
Southwest	4.50	0.65	−0.91	2.75
Rocky Mountains	3.80	0.93	−0.57	2.94
Far West	3.23	1.12	−2.10	3.03

Source: US Department of Commerce, Bureau of Economic Analysis (2002a; June 1995). A description of the states in each region is available in Appendix A to this chapter.

BEA data show that the states of the New England and Mideast regions had strong income growth in the 1980–1990 period. More recently, however, the states of the Rocky Mountains, Southwest and Far West regions posted the relatively high growth in real per capita income, along with those states of the New England region. All else held constant, we would expect that the states located in these regions would have an easier time meeting their expenditure demands due to their relatively strong recent performance in the growth of real per capita income.

Unfortunately, BEA no longer provides forecasts of regional income.[9] If we look simply at the growth in real per capita income from 2000–01, while the real per capita income in the US remained relatively flat, the Mideast, Plains and Southeast states were estimated to have had greater than average growth in real per capita income. Given the recent recession and other global issues, we can not easily project regional income growth from these most recent figures. However, over the last decade, the relatively strong growth in real per capita income for the Mideast, Plains, Southeast and Southwest states may be an indication of stronger future growth in those states.

From the viewpoint of state and local finances, a forecasted positive growth in personal income may be viewed as a sound indicator of future fiscal health if the growth in personal income yields a similar growth in the tax base (be this base income or consumption). To better understand how tax bases are affected, Figure 3.1 presents the changing composition of personal income nationwide.[10] As seen there, wages and salaries, the largest share of personal income, declined in importance through 2000, while transfer payments and capital income as a share of personal income have generally grown since 1970. If this increase in transfer payments comes at the expense of wage and salary income growth, it creates a tension for state and local finances since transfer payments are largely untaxed while wages comprise over 70 per cent of state and local income tax bases.[11] Therefore, if wage and salary income grows more slowly and nontaxed sources such as transfer payment grow more quickly, the income tax base grows more slowly; and revenues from income taxes grow more slowly.

Transfer payments include transfers made by government, business, and payments to nonprofit institutions.[12] The fastest growing transfer sector has been transfer payments made by government. These include federal, state and local government payments for: retirement and disability insurance, medical, income maintenance benefits, unemployment insurance benefits, veterans benefits and others. Among these types of payments, the fastest growing individual payments have been medical payments – largely those under the Medicaid and Medicare programs, and income maintenance benefits (AFDC, food stamps, and others). The category of old-age, survivors, disability, and health insurance benefits increased by over 75 per cent form 1990–2000 (in

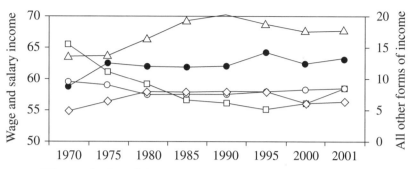

-□- Wage and salary disbursements
-◇- Other labor income
-○- Proprietors' income with inventory valuation and capital consumption
    adjustments
-△- Dividends, interest, rent
-●- Transfer payments to persons

Source: US Department of Commerce, Bureau of Economic Analysis (2002b).

*Figure 3.1   Changing composition of income (as a percentage of personal
            income), 1970–2001*

nominal terms). In FY2001, the social security benefits paid were equivalent
to approximately 25 per cent of the total federal budget expenditure (CBO,
2001). Projections of expenditures on social security and Medicare by both
CBO and the Administration underscore the impacts of the aging population
on the composition of income. CBO projects annual average increases in
federal expenditures for social security, Medicare and Medicaid of 5.5 per
cent, 7.2 per cent and 8.5 per cent, respectively, through 2012; the Administration projects average annual increases of 4.7 per cent, 4.3 per cent, and
10.0 per cent, respectively, through 2007.

Employer contributions to private pension and welfare funds, employer
payments for workers' compensation, and employer payments for private
health insurance are included in other labor income (OLI). Other labor income has increased from about four per cent of personal income in 1970 to
about 6.2 per cent in 2000. While it is still a relatively small share of personal
income, this is another largely nontaxable income source and as such it adds
to the story of a potentially slower growing tax base for state and local
governments.

The shift in income toward transfer payments affects both the revenue and
expenditure side of state and local government budgets.[13] Since Medicaid
payments are funded by federal as well as state and local governments, these
mandated income transfers are directly affecting nondiscretionary expendi-

tures of state and local governments. In addition, of the 41 states and District of Columbia that impose a broad-based income tax, virtually all have some exemptions for general retirement and/or social security income. Most states have practically eliminated the tax on social security income (Edwards and Wallace, 2002). Many states allow retirees to exempt some part of private pension income as well. In addition, some states offer other forms of elderly credits. Local governments that impose income taxes use a variety of income definitions, but few include any type of retirement or pension income in their tax base. Most other forms of transfer payments (such as Medicaid and Medicare) are not taxable.

The tax expenditure associated with the tax treatment of transfer payments such as social security is large. As an example of the magnitude of the revenue loss from the exclusion of social security income, we can make a rough estimate of the state income tax revenue loss associated with the taxation of social security income. The IRS *Statistics of Income Bulletin* reports that $163 billion of social security income was included in federal adjusted gross income in 1999. If all states imposed an average tax rate of three per cent on this income, taxation of this income could increase state tax revenues by as much as $5 billion, or almost three per cent of total state income tax revenue collected in 1999. If we compare the same calculation based on 1995 data, we find that the revenue loss increased by 40 per cent from 1995 to 1999 due to the growth in social security income. As more types of excluded income are accounted for, this revenue cost would grow proportionately.

The net effect of this compositional change in personal income for state and local tax bases is that a smaller share of personal income will be subject to tax, if transfer payments and nontaxable other labor income grow as a percentage of total personal income. Most states project personal income for their own use. An unscientific sample of ten state websites reveals that local forecasters predict that wage and salary income will grow somewhat more slowly than overall state personal income. Since taxable and nontaxable income are both included as 'nonwage income' these projections do not reveal a definitive answer regarding the growth of nontaxable sources of income relative to taxable sources.

The CBO does report its forecast of taxable personal income. Recall that the federal government's definition of taxable personal income generally includes more pension and social security income than do those of most states. CBO forecasts a decrease in taxable income as a share of GDP from 72.7 per cent in 2002 to 69.5 per cent in 2010 (CBO, 2002a). This means that, in nominal terms, the growth in federal taxable income will be less than the growth in overall income (measured by GDP) as nontaxable sources rise faster than taxable sources of income. State and local governments could expect to see the growth in their income tax revenues slow down due to this change in the composition of income toward more nontaxable sources of income. Continued state and local government decisions to exempt the growing forms of income (retirement income in particular) from their tax bases may make this problem worse over time. Additionally, heavy reliance on income taxes may place state and local governments in more stressful positions in the future as they are forced to deal with slower growing revenue.

The overall distribution of income is also an important factor in terms of affecting state and local government finances. Over the past decade, there has been an increase in the percentage of income held by the highest percentiles of the population (distributed by income). In 1978, the Gini coefficient of household income was 0.403; in 1992 it was 0.413 and by 1998 it had jumped to 0.50 and among regions, the distribution of income has become more similar over time (Alm, Lee, and Wallace, 2002). There is likely to be an impact of the distribution of income on state and local finances separate from the impact of general increases in income. Many states impose progressive marginal income tax structures on taxpayers. As top income earners hold a larger share of income, all other things constant, we would expect to see increased growth in state personal income taxes. Similar to the notion of the tax base eroding as retirement income is exempted, more income showing up in the top income tax brackets could buoy state income tax revenue collections.[14]

The polarization of income could also increase the demand for a number of services, especially social services. Medicaid recipients would be expected to increase, thus increasing demands on state and local governments. The impact of the income distribution thus affects both the revenue and the expenditure side of the budget for state and local governments, and possibly in opposite directions as revenue growth could increase and expenditure demands could increase thereby pressuring the gains in revenue.

AGE DISTRIBUTION AND COMPOSITION

Since 1973, the US population has grown close to one per cent per year (Table 3.4). The Census Bureau's projections of population growth show a slight decrease in the overall growth rate of the population through 2010 (approximately 0.8 per cent per year from 2000–10). Regionally, Census projects that the West and South regions will see the largest overall increases in population for the next two decades (Table 3.5). However, the US population is growing old. By 2050, the population aged 65 or older will constitute 20 per cent of the US population. During the same time period, the economically important age groups 25–44 and 45–65 will become a smaller part of the US population.

Table 3.4   Growth in total US population, 1979–1999

Year	Population	Average annual per cent growth
1979	225 055	1.03
1983	233 791	0.97
1995	262 803	1.03
1996	265 228	0.92
1997	267 783	0.96
1998	270 248	0.92
1999	272 690	0.90

Source: US Department of Commerce, Bureau of the Census (2000).

Table 3.5   Population projections by region (in thousands), 1995–2020

Region	1995	2000	2010	2020
US	262 755	274 634	297 716	322 742
Northeast	51 466	52 107	53 692	56 103
Midwest	61 804	63 502	65 915	68 114
South	91 880	97 613	107 597	117 060
West	57 596	61 413	70 512	81 465

Source: US Department of Commerce, Bureau of the Census (1997).

A general growth in population is not necessarily associated with any particular fiscal stresses for state and local governments. Both revenues and expenditures could be expected to expand as population increases. What we are more concerned with is the underlying composition of the population in that changes in the age distribution may create some areas of fiscal stress. The data in Table 3.6 show the age distribution for the US population as a whole. What is immediately obvious is the growing polarization of the population according to age. From 2000–05, those over the age of 75 are expected to be the fastest increasing age group in the US. From 2005–20, the population over 65 is expected to grow faster than the school age population and the working age population.

The strongest growth in school-aged children is expected to come in the next five years, and then again at the end of the forecast period, 2015–20. At the same time, the working age population is expected to increase slowly throughout the forecasted period. The US Bureau of the Census produces an

Table 3.6   Age distribution of US population (in thousands), 2000–2020

Year	5–19 years	25–54 years	65–74 years	75 and over
2000	59 586	119 501	179 087	16 667
2005	60 746	121 540	182 286	17 911
2010	61 014	122 455	183 469	18 561
2015	61 442	122 023	183 465	19 652
2020	63 773	122 343	186 116	22 271
Average annual growth				
2000–2005	0.39%	0.34%	0.30%	1.49%
2005–2010	0.09%	0.15%	2.92%	0.73%
2010–2015	0.14%	−0.07%	4.87%	1.18%
2015–2020	0.76%	0.05%	3.92%	2.67%

Source: US Department of Commerce, Bureau of the Census (2000).

interesting set of charts that plot the relative age distribution of the US population (as well as other countries, see http://www.census.gov/ipc/www/idbpyr.html). These data show how the working age population changes relative to the school age population, elderly, and so on. They also show that the US pyramid is losing its triangular shape, and becoming more rectangular (Figures 3.2 and 3.3). This means that there are less young and working age relative to the older population groups. The term 'dependency ratio' is taken as the number of retirees divided by the working population. As the number of retirees grows, if the working population grows more slowly, the dependency ratio rises. Funding for public pensions at any level of government would be at risk as the dependency ratio grows. This ratio has been growing in the US.

These forecasted compositional changes in the age distribution of the population may have a number of serious repercussions for state and local budgets. First, the changing age distribution signals a potential change in popular demand for certain public services and financing mechanisms. Simple majority voting mechanics mean that the elderly population will become increasingly influential at the voting booth and can therefore influence decisions about revenues and expenditures. We should expect that state and local governments will see an increased demand for spending on services preferred by the elderly including health, hospital, and medical services, social security, transportation services, and some types of recreational services. We have also witnessed demands for tax relief for the elderly, particularly for property taxes at the local level.

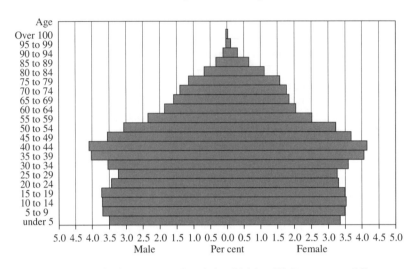

Source: National Projections Program Population Division US Department of Commerce, Bureau of the Census (2002).

Figure 3.2   Projected resident population of the United States as of July 1, 2000, middle series

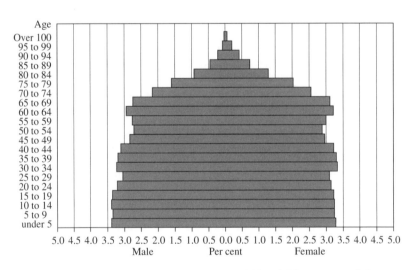

Source: National Projections Program Population Division US Department of Commerce, Bureau of the Census (2002).

Figure 3.3   Projected resident population of the United States as of July 1, 2025, middle series

Second, a growing elderly population is associated with changes in consumption patterns, which will in turn affect the revenues raised by state and local governments. Details on consumption pattern changes will be discussed below. To some extent, this change in consumption pattern is associated with the graying of America. Many of the goods demanded by older citizens are not included in state and local government sales tax bases. Thus, as the country ages and naturally shifts its consumption focus away from taxable goods toward nontaxables, the growth of the sales tax base is decreased, again reducing the monies available for public expenditures.

Many local governments grant property tax credits and exemptions to elderly homeowners, reducing the revenue raised by the property tax and as the population continues to age, this revenue cost grows. These preferences range from credits equal to a certain percentage of property taxes owed to full scale property tax exemptions for the elderly (Mackey and Carter, 1995). Local governments in the vast majority of states now offer some form of property tax relief for the elderly.

Increased age by itself may translate into a lower demand for housing, in addition to a number of other factors (Mankiw and Weil, 1989 and Goodman, 1990).[15] This decreased demand for housing occurs due to changes in income as individuals age, changes in the family structure of elderly households, and the movement of the elderly from their owner occupied homes to other types of institutions. As more and more elderly move to smaller houses or retirement homes, the housing stock available to those looking to buy homes increases without increases in the amount of property subject to local property taxes. As noted earlier, a policy response may be to adjust millage rates. The housing stock made available by the elderly moving to smaller homes is more likely to accommodate the relatively slow growing home ownership age group – those between 30 and 55. Absent property tax rate increases or repeal of exemptions, without additional building, the property tax base simply does not grow as fast as if the demand for housing were not dampened by this demographic impact.

The continued aging of the population therefore has significant potential to affect state and local governments budgets through potentially reduced growth in property, income, and sales tax bases. While all regions of the country can expect these pressures, the Census projections suggest that the South will see the largest increases in their elderly populations (see the regional differences in the data in Table 3.7).

Another significant population-related trend is the change in the race or ethnicity of the population. In 1990, the US population was over 75 per cent white, in 2000 it was 71.4 per cent and in 2010, Census predicts that the population will be 67.3 per cent white. The Hispanic population is expected to grow from nine per cent of the population in 1990 to 14.6 per cent in 2010

Table 3.7   Average annual growth in age distribution of the population by region, 1995–2010 to 2010–2025

Region	1995–2010	2010–2025
Under 20 years		
Northeast	–0.05%	–0.03%
Midwest	–0.14%	–0.05%
South	–0.15%	–0.09%
West	–0.04%	0.01%
20 to 64 years		
Northeast	0.08%	–0.27%
Midwest	0.11%	–0.31%
South	0.07%	–0.33%
West	0.01%	–0.30%
65 years and over		
Northeast	–0.03%	0.30%
Midwest	0.03%	0.37%
South	0.07%	0.41%
West	0.03%	0.29%

Source: US Department of Commerce, Bureau of the Census (2000).

and the black population is expected to grow from 11.8 per cent to 12.5 per cent from 1990 to 2010 (US Department of Commerce, Bureau of Census, 2002). These trends reflect the growing diversity of the US population and pose some challenges for state and local financing.

The changes in racial composition of the US are due to migration as well as the natural growth of populations within the US. As noted by Little and Triest (2002), the migration component of this demographic shift may help reduce the dependency ratio due to increased labor force participation (versus the ratio without migration). At the same time, there is pressure on the education systems and other support programs to assist new migrants. These pressures will be felt very strongly by local governments via the demands for services in elementary and secondary schools. State and local governments may witness an increased demand for support services such as translation in provision of other public goods as well. These pressures are not spread evenly among the states. California, Texas, Arizona, and New Mexico have the highest levels of Hispanic population relative to total population.

Trends in Employment

Changes in the level and composition of employment are a function of many factors. These include the demographic changes we have already discussed as well as other factors such as global trade, productivity, and economic development policies of the federal, state and local governments. We will not attempt to disentangle these relationships, but we analyse the trends in the composition of employment in terms of the effects of changes in the composition on tax bases.

The Bureau of Labor Statistics (BLS, 2001a) projects that total employment growth will remain positive through 2010, although the growth will decline throughout the forecast period. From 1990–2000, the US experienced average annual employment growth of 1.6 per cent, and from 2000–10, BLS projects an average annual rate of growth of 1.4 per cent. While the overall level of employment sustains state and local income and consumption tax revenues, the composition of income is likely to have more subtle effects on state and local finances. Table 3.8 provides detailed information regarding the change in composition of employment in the US.

Table 3.8   *Composition of US employment (per cent of total employment), 1970–2000*

Area of employment	1970	1980	1990	2000
Agriculture, forestry, and fishing	1.8	1.8	1.5	1.7
Mining	0.9	1.2	0.7	0.4
Construction	4.9	4.9	4.8	5.4
Manufacturing	26.5	22.7	17.8	14.5
Transportation and public utilities	6.1	5.6	5.2	5.3
Wholesale trade	5.4	5.9	5.7	5.5
Retail trade	13.1	14.2	15.8	16.2
Finance, insurance, and real estate	4.9	5.8	6.2	5.7
Services	15.8	19.3	24.9	30.4
Government	20.6	18.7	17.5	15.3

Source: US Department of Commerce, Bureau of Economic Analysis (2000).

The most dramatic changes in employment are found in the switch from manufacturing to services. While other changes exist, manufacturing moved from representing over a quarter of all employment in 1970 to less than 15 per cent by 2000, while services moved in the complete opposite direction. Services now represent over 30 per cent of the employment in the US. BLS projects that manufacturing will continue to decline in importance and services will continue to rise in importance through 2010 (US Department of Labor, BLS, 2001b). Output has followed similar trends. In the past decade, manufacturing output as a share of total GDP has decreased from 17.9 per cent in 1990 to 15.9 per cent in 2000. The service industry output increased from 18.5 per cent to 22 per cent as a share of total GDP over the same period.

These trends in employment (and output) of the service sector relative to the manufacturing sector may have a significant impact on property taxes. The service sector is less heavily invested in tangible property and capital than the manufacturing sector causing a potential reduction in the amount of equipment and machinery subject to the property tax (Snell, 1993 and Fox, 1996).

In fact, if we compare the real value of net capital stock (equipment and structures) per employee in the manufacturing and service sectors from 1987 through 1997, we see that capital per employee was about three times larger in the manufacturing versus the service sector in 1987 and has grown to almost four times larger by 1997.[16] This ratio has been increasing in both sectors, but has increased more dramatically for the manufacturing sector. If the manufacturing sector continues to decline in importance, then the big boosts to equipment and structures from this industry can be expect to decline over time. This could impact that portion of property taxes that is based on equipment and structures. Additionally, revenues from state and/or local property taxes based on inventories of companies will decline as an economy moves toward the service sector.

Overall, the forecasted growth in employment is expected to slow down slightly for the forecast years of 2000–10, from an average annual rate of growth of 1.6 for 1990–2000 to 1.4 per cent per year for 2000–10. The BLS projects the service industry to continue to lead the way in the growth of employment. The continued change in the composition of employment away from manufacturing toward services may influence state and local government finances through lower property tax revenue growth in the future as noted above.

Changes in Consumption

Due to state and local governments' heavy reliance on the sales tax, consumption is a main driver for many state and local finance systems. For years, the National Income and Product Accounts (NIPA) and BLS' Consumer Expenditure Survey have reported increased consumption of largely nontaxed goods and services by US households. NIPA reports that nonhousing service expenditures rose from 39.9 per cent of total personal consumption expenditures in 1990 to 44 per cent in 2000 (US Department of Commerce, BEA, 2002b). Medical care rose from 14 per cent to 15 per cent of expenditures – the single largest expenditure category reported by NIPA. From 1984 to 1998, BLS reports that food fell from 17.5 per cent of family expenditures to 16 per cent; housing increased from 32.3 per cent of family expenditures to 35.3 per cent, health care rose from 3.5 to 4.8 per cent, and entertainment increased from 5 to 6 per cent (Johnson, Rogers and Tan, 2001).

The threat to state and local budgets of the change in consumption toward nontaxable goods and services is obvious. Housing and other services are largely nontaxable and growing consumption of these items will erode the growth in sales taxes for state and local governments. Governments in most states are susceptible to this type of erosion due to the limited amount of taxation of services in the US. The Federation of Tax Administrators (FTA, 1996) conducted an update of a survey of the tax treatment of over 164 services across the country.[17] The results of the survey show that most states tax less than half of the services included in the survey. The broadest service sector tax states are Hawaii and New Mexico followed by South Dakota, West Virginia, and Iowa. FTA (2001) also reports that all states exempt prescription drugs.[18]

The changes in consumption away from traditionally taxable items will continue to cost the state and local governments significant amounts of revenue in the future. Some states have calculated the tax expenditures associated with their sales tax exemptions of various items. In Georgia, it is estimated that exemptions to the sales tax base cost the state at least $7.6 billion in 1997 (Walker, 1998). Estimates of the revenue cost associated with tax exemptions in Texas exceed $18 billion in 2001 (Rylander, 2001). The revenue costs associated with these exemptions have increased as the consumption of nontaxed items has increased.

A comprehensive way to look at the effect of the changing composition of consumption on sales tax revenue is as follows. If we take an average statutory state sales tax rate used nationwide, we can calculate the average revenue associated with each percentage point of the state general sales tax nationwide and compare this with total consumption expenditures. For example, in 1970, on average, each percentage point of state general sales tax produced about $4 billion in sales tax revenue nationwide, or approximately 0.62 per cent of total personal consumption expenditures. In 1998, each percentage point of the tax generated about $30 billion in sales tax revenue, but this was only 0.51 per cent of total consumption expenditures. Therefore, a given sales tax rate structure is capturing less of total expenditures in tax because a smaller share of consumption expenditures are part of the tax base.[19]

The net effect of the increase in the consumption share of nontaxable items is obvious – less growth in sales tax revenue over time. Not only do most

Table 3.9   Summary of economic and demographic impacts on state and local budgets

Economic/ demographic variable	Trend	Forecast	Anticipated impact on state and local government budgets
Personal income	Relatively stable growth in overall personal income. The composition has changed and shows an increase in nonwage and salary components including transfer payments. Higher income families hold an increasing share of total US income.	Stable growth in overall income at a rate approximately equal to that of the past decade.	Reduced taxable income base, most directly affecting state and local individual income taxes through tax elasticities. Relative increases in income for high income families could increase income tax revenues for states with progressive marginal tax rate structures.
Population	Increased proportion of the elderly in the population and increased growth in school aged children in the short run. Population growth in general has stabilized. The population has also undergone a significant change in race, with the Hispanic population growing most rapidly.	Slower growth in the overall population, large increases in the population 65 and older. The South and Midwest regions are expected to see the largest increase in elderly population growth.	*Age:* Property tax exemptions for the elderly could expand. Changes in consumption patterns may reduce the growth of taxable sales. Housing turnover could affect the value of housing stock and therefore property tax bases. Income tax exemptions for retirement income could further reduce income tax bases. *Ethnicity:* Consumption patterns and housing tenure may impact sales and property tax bases (see text).

Employment/ Production concentration	Continued shift from manufacturing employment and output to service employment and output. E-commerce as an increasing way to do business.	Steady growth in overall employment at an average annual rate of 1.4 per cent. Service employment and output will continue to increase relative to manufacturing.	Potential decrease in the rate of capital investment thus affecting property and sales tax bases. E-commerce will affect sales tax revenues directly.
Consumption	Increase in consumption of services throughout last decade.	Continued growth in service consumption, increased importance of consumption of non-white families.	Increased consumption of largely nontaxed goods will lower the growth in sales tax revenue over time.

states fail to tax the growing consumption groups, they do not tax some of the largest components of consumption – food and housing. In the long run, these consumption trends will reduce the natural growth of the sales tax revenues for both state and local governments.

NET IMPACT OF ECONOMIC AND DEMOGRAPHIC CHANGES ON STATE AND LOCAL BUDGETS

It is difficult to summarize the vast implications of the economic and demographic changes on state and local finances. The information in Table 3.9 presents a summary of the trends and their potential impacts on state and local budgets. The changes that we have experienced in income, age, consumption and composition of employment will impact state and local government finances over the long run. In most cases, the trends in these variables and the forecasted trends suggest that the elasticities of major revenue sources will be reduced over a number of years, unless changes are made to state and local tax bases.[20] If demands for public goods and services grow proportionately with personal income, the reduced elasticity of revenue sources is important since it suggests that revenue growth will not keep pace with expenditure demand growth.[21]

Individual Income Tax

The fundamental changes in the composition of income from wage and salary income to retirement income and other transfer payments will influence state and local income tax bases. As noted earlier, CBO projects that taxable income will decrease as a share of GDP by 3.2 percentage points from 2002 to 2010. This means that as overall income grows, taxable income will grow less and tax revenues will grow more slowly than the general economy.[22] Since most states exempt more retirement income than does the federal government, state and local governments should expect to see taxable income as a share of overall income decline even more than that of the federal government. Edwards and Wallace (2002) find that the state income treatment of the elderly has significantly reduced effective income tax rates for the elderly versus the nonelderly in most states. They found that the revenue consequences of this treatment were relatively small but significant for a sample of ten states (for example, Georgia would expect income tax revenues that are three per cent lower per year through 2005 due to the tax treatment of the elderly in the state).[23]

Sales Taxes

As noted above, a number of factors will influence both the elasticity of the sales tax as well as the absolute growth rate in sales tax revenue. The changing composition of consumption toward services has reduced the natural growth of sales taxes in most states. There is evidence that the elderly consume more services, so this trend could be expected to continue, based on the aging of the population alone (Mullins and Wallace, 1996).

Paulin (1998) analysed the consumption patters of Hispanic consumers relative to other groups in the US population. He concludes that there are some similarities in consumption among groups, but that Hispanic consumers have a significantly larger marginal propensity to consume transportation, shelter and utilities, and recreation. Note that many of these consumption items are not taxable in most states. Therefore, we might expect that regions with dynamic Hispanic population growth could see a reduced sales tax revenue growth, all else held constant. Since the differences in consumption patterns are relatively small, the impacts on the sales tax growth relative to the general income growth would also be small. However, we have only just begun to investigate the role that ethnicity within the US population plays on consumption.

Gregory (1990) suggests that sales tax purchases are more likely to come from wage and salary income than from other forms of income.[24] This is related to the idea that there is a different marginal propensity to consume out of different types of income. There is some intuitive appeal to this notion if we think of retirement income and income from maintenance programs as less liquid, or less fungible (interchangeable). If this is true, then the growth in transfer payments that is expected to continue from the year 2000 would also reduce both the elasticity and the absolute growth of sales tax revenues. Also, as noted many times, the use of e-commerce for transactions has direct implications for sales taxes (see Chapter Seven).

Property Taxes

Both the demographic trends and the economic trends could influence the property tax base, but the impacts are less clear than for some of the other taxes. The exercise presented above shows some evidence that the manufacturing/service sector shift may reduce the elasticity of the property tax due to the reduction in the growth of the equipment portion of real capital assets. The aging of the US population may also yield an increase in the availability of existing residential properties. If this impact were large enough to influence the price of residential housing (depressing the price), property tax bases could see reduced growth in the future.

There is also some evidence that certain types of migrants have a relatively high upward mobility in terms of attainment of home ownership. Myers (1999) and Myers, Megbolugbe, and Lee (1998) report steep 'upward trajectories' in home ownership status for Latinos and Asians in many metropolitan areas.

Other state and local government revenue sources would also be affected by the economic and demographic trends discussed in this report. User fees for recreation may be negatively affected by the aging of the population, but fees for utilities may increase. In some states, gross receipts taxes are specific to certain industries and would therefore be affected by changes in the economic bases of their localities. These types of impacts have not been discussed, but are obviously important. The expenditure side of the story, also not discussed in this chapter, is critical to the fiscal health of state and local governments in future years. More research should be devoted on the expenditure side in the future.

The final section of this chapter analyses options available to state and local government to deal with potential reductions in tax bases caused by the economic and demographic changes.

OPTIONS FOR STATE AND LOCAL GOVERNMENTS

This chapter has analysed many of the economic and demographic changes that we expect to affect state and local finances over the next decades. The analysis has not included every change, and has not attempted to develop a true 'model' of demographics, economics, and state and local finances. Most of the variables discussed have effects on other variables and on the economy as a whole. The focus of the chapter has been a practical analysis of the more important trends and their likely impacts on state and local fiscal health via the revenue side of the budget.

Every politician knows that it is very difficult to adjust taxes. Once exemptions are given to individuals or corporations, it is very difficult to take those away. However, from the viewpoint of long-term fiscal stability, it may be in the best interest of all to slow or stop the trend of tax base erosion through state and local revenue-source 'give-aways' that occur via sales tax exemptions, income tax exemptions, and economic development tools. This advice is not for the purpose of increasing taxes, but rather to help put revenue growth on a higher growth path. Demographic changes suggest that the cost of some of these exemptions will just continue to increase over time.

In tax policy there is no 'one size fits all' solution to structural problems. Here we suggest some options for state and local tax systems that apply to some but not all state and local governments in the US. These options are put forth as examples of issues that governments may want to explore in light of the trends discussed in this chapter:

- Aging of the population:
  Reduce the retirement income exclusion, or stop the growth of the expansion of retirement income exclusions.
  Analyse the long-term impact of property tax exemptions and credits; redesign such exemptions to consider the equity of exemptions.
- Changing structure of the economy and consumption:
  Eliminate the preferential property tax treatment for manufacturing inventories and equipment.
  Expand the sales tax base of state and local governments to include more services and possibly food if it is not currently taxed.
  Expand the use of user fees and charges to capitalize on personal income growth.
- Income composition and distribution:
  Analyse the long-term costs of retirement income exemptions; means test exemptions.
  Broaden the use of other tax instruments to reduce reliance on the income tax.
  Remain aware of the distribution of income and the impacts of a progressive marginal rate structure.

The main idea in these example options is that state and local tax structures should look at the benefits and costs of expanding or broadening their tax bases – which itself is an old story. A broader base will help protect against the general ups and downs of the economy, but will specifically help smooth the revenue path in light of the demographic changes of the US.

NOTES

1. http://www.census.gov/population/www/pop-profile/elderpop.html
2. http://www.bls.gov/news.release/ecopro.t01.html
3. http://www.census.gov/prod/2002pubs/01statab/income.pdf
4. The literature on demographic changes and their economic effects is growing, but there is still relatively little research that examines direct effects on state and local budgets. For an earlier review, see Wallace (1995).
5. The specific issue of globalization and its impact on state and local finances is analysed in Chapter Seven of this volume.
6. In this context, the clients include private individuals as well as representatives of businesses.
7. A similar decomposition could be done for other revenue sources as well. In each case, the second term on the right hand side is based on the difference between the taxable base

and the overall level of economic activity. In general, the larger the difference between these, the less impact a general change in economic activity will have on the tax base.

8. Expenditures would also be affected by federal mandates as well. These are not discussed in this chapter. However, various formulae exist for determining certain types of expenditures, especially education and welfare programs. The impact of demographic changes on these types of expenditures is even more transparent.

9. The last forecasts were produced in 1995. At that time, the following regions were forecasted to have higher than average growth in real per capita income from 2005–25: Plains, Southeast, Southwest, Rocky Mountains and Far West (Wallace, 1995). BLS does produce forecasts of total personal income. The current BLS forecast for personal income is an average annual growth rate of 5.5 per cent from 2000–10, compared to a 7.8 per cent and 5.4 per cent average annual growth rate in total personal income for 1980–90 and 1990–2000 respectively (Su, 2001).

10. In Figure 3.1, the left hand vertical axis applies to wage and salary income only, the right hand vertical axis applies to all other forms of income.

11. This trend has been noted in a number of studies including, Snell (1993), and Mullins and Wallace (1992).

12. Payments to nonprofit institutions include payments by the federal, state, and local governments, as well as by businesses.

13. The federal government budget is also affected but this analysis is focused on state and local governments and as such, the impacts on the federal budget will not be analysed.

14. There is some evidence, however, that higher income earners are more affected by marginal tax rates and respond by sheltering income from taxation at a higher rate than lower income individuals (Alm and Wallace, 2000).

15. McFadden (1994) concludes that the net interaction between changes in housing demand and the housing stock due to the aging of the US population will be to lower the growth in the real value of the housing stock. This will decrease the growth in property tax revenue accordingly.

16. This analysis was done using data on fixed reproducible tangible wealth from (US Department of Commerce, BEA, 1998).

17. The broad categories of these services (and the types of each service) include: utilities (16), personal services (20), business services (34), computer services (6), administrative/ amusement services (14), professional services (8), fabrication, repair and installation services (19), and other services (47). For more information regarding the detail of these services, see Federation of Tax Administrators (1996).

18. Illinois is the single exception but the state sales tax rate for prescription drugs is only one per cent versus the state rate of 6.25 per cent.

19. Since this exercise does not hold sales tax bases constant, the change in the effective tax rate on personal consumption expenditures could come from the growth in consumption of nontaxable goods and services and/or from more state imposed exclusions. Information presented in Fox (1992) suggested that the latter case is less likely to be true across the country.

20. There have been few national studies of the impact of changing demographics on fiscal health of state and local governments. Hondroyiannis and Papapetrou (2000) did study the impact of demographic changes (namely age) on public finances in Greece and found that an aging population in Greece has had a negative impact on public finances.

21. This impact has been discussed in the literature, see Bergstrom and Goodman (1973), Gramlich and Galper (1973), and Snell (1993).

22. This is the issue of the tax base elasticity that was presented in equation (6).

23. Another example is for the income tax in the state of Ohio. Edwards and Wallace (1994) estimated that the rate elasticity of Ohio's state income tax is relatively high (1.5) but its base elasticity has fallen from 1.2 to .85 over the past two decades (Edwards and Wallace, 1994) due to the erosion in tax base from the changing composition of income.

24. See also Hurd (1993).

APPENDIX A   BEA CLASSIFICATION OF STATES

New England:
  Connecticut
  Maine
  Massachusetts
  New Hampshire
  Rhode Island
  Vermont

Mideast:
  Delaware
  District of Columbia
  Maryland
  New Jersey
  New York
  Pennsylvania

Great Lakes:
  Illinois
  Indiana
  Michigan
  Ohio
  Wisconsin

Plains:
  Iowa
  Kansas
  Minnesota
  Missouri
  Nebraska
  North Dakota
  South Dakota

Southeast:
  Alabama
  Arkansas
  Florida
  Georgia
  Kentucky
  Louisiana
  Mississippi
  North Carolina
  South Carolina
  Tennessee
  Virginia
  West Virginia

Southwest:
  Arizona
  New Mexico
  Oklahoma
  Texas

Rocky Mountains:
  Colorado
  Idaho
  Montana
  Utah
  Wyoming

Far West:
  California
  Nevada
  Oregon
  Washington

REFERENCES

Alm, James, Fitzroy Lee and Sally Wallace (2002), 'How fair: Changes in federal income taxation 1978–1998', Working paper, Atlanta, GA: Andrew Young School of Policy Studies, Georgia State University.

Alm, James and Sally Wallace (2000), 'Are the rich different?', in Joel Slemrod (ed.), *Does Atlas Shrug?*, New York, and Cambridge, UK: Russell Sage Foundation.

Bergstrom, Theodore C. and Robert P. Goodman (1973), 'Private demand for public goods', *American Economic Review*, 63: 280–96.

Congressional Budget Office (2001), 'Social Security: A primer', Washington, DC: Congressional Budget Office, September.

Congressional Budget Office (2002a), 'The economic and budget outlook: Fiscal years 2003–2012', Washington, DC: Congressional Budget Office, January.

Congressional Budget Office (2002b), 'An analysis of the President's budgetary proposals for fiscal year 2003', Washington, DC: Congressional Budget Office, March.

Edwards, Barbara and Sally Wallace (1994), 'Ohio's state and local income taxes: Analysis and options', Commission to Study the Ohio Economy and Tax Structure, Policy Research Center, Georgia State University, November.

Edwards, Barbara and Sally Wallace (2002), 'How much preference: Effective personal income tax rates for the elderly', Fiscal Research Program Working Paper No. 70, April.

Executive Office of the President, Office of Management and Budget (2002), *Analytical Perspectives Budget of the United States Government Fiscal Year 2003*, Washington, DC: US Government Printing Office.

Federation of Tax Administrators (FTA) (1996), *Sales Taxation of Services: An Update*, Washington, DC: Federation of Tax Administrators.

Federation of Tax Administrators (FTA) (2001), *State Sales Taxes, Food and Drug Exemption*, from website: http://www.taxadmin.org/fta/rate/tax_stru.html

Fox, William (1992), 'Sales taxation of services: Has its time come?', in William Fox (ed.), *Sales Taxation: Critical Issues in Policy and Administration*, Westport, CT: Praeger.

Fox, William (1996), 'Sales tax: Current condition and policy options', in Roy Bahl (ed.), *Taxation and Economic Development: A Blueprint for Tax Reform in Ohio*, Columbus, OH: Battelle Press.

Goodman, Allen C. (1990), 'Demographics of individual housing demand', *Regional Science and Urban Economics*, 20: 83–102.

Gramlich, Edward M. and Harvey Galper (1973), 'State and local fiscal behavior and federal grant policy', *Brookings Papers on Economic Activities*, 15–58.

Gregory, Warren C. (1990), 'Solving Michigan's budget deficit: Opportunity from crisis', Lansing, MI: Michigan State House of Representatives Fiscal Agency.

Hondroyiannis, George and Evangelia Papapetrou (2000), 'Do demographic changes affect fiscal developments?', *Public Finance Review*, 28(5): 468–88.

Hurd, Michael D. (1993), 'The effect of demographic trends on consumption, saving, and government expenditures in the US', *National Bureau of Economic Research Working Paper* No. 4601, Cambridge, MA: NBER, December.

Internal Revenue Service (2000), *Statistics of Income Bulletin*, Spring.

Jenny, Nicholas W. (2002), 'State revenue report: A second quarter of decline in state tax revenue', Fiscal Studies Program, The Nelson A. Rockefeller Institute of Government, No. 47.

Johnson, David S., John M. Rogers and Lucilla Tan (2001), 'A century of family budgets in the United States', *Monthly Labor Review*, Washington, DC: US Government Printing Office, May.

Little, Jane Sneddon and Robert K. Triest (2002), 'The impact of demographic change on US labor markets', *New England Economic Review*, First quarter: 47–68.

Mackey, Scott and Karen Carter (1995), 'State tax policy and senior citizens: Property, sales, and death taxes', *State Tax Notes*, 3 April: 1405–25.

Mankiw, N. Gregory and David N. Weil (1989), 'The baby boom, the baby bust, and the housing market', *Regional Science and Urban Economics*, 19: 235–58.

McFadden, Daniel (1994), 'Demographics, the housing market, and the welfare of the elderly', in David Wise (ed.), *Studies of the Economics of Aging*, Chicago, IL: University of Chicago Press, pp. 225–90.

Mullins, Daniel R. and Sally Wallace (1992), 'Demographics and state fiscal pressure: Escalation or relaxation?', Paper presented at the Southern Economic Association Meetings.

Mullins, Daniel R. and Sally Wallace (1996), 'Changing demographics and state fiscal outlook: The case of sales taxes', *Public Finance Quarterly*, 24(2): 237–62.

Myers, Dowell (1999), 'Demographic dynamism and metropolitan change: Comparing Los Angeles, New York, Chicago, and Washington, DC', *Housing Policy Debate*, 10(4): 919–54.

Myers, Dowell, Isaac Megbolugbe and Seong Woo Lee (1998), 'Cohort estimation of homeownership attainment among native-born and immigrant populations', *Journal of Housing Research*, 9(2): 237–69.

Paulin, Geoffrey D. (1998), 'A growing market: Expenditures by Hispanic consumers', *Monthly Labor Review*, Washington, DC: US Government Printing Office, March.

Rafool, Many (2002), 'State tax actions 2001', *State Tax Notes*, 6 May: 523–48.

Rylander, Carole Keeton (2001), *Window on State Government: Tax Exemptions and Tax Incidence*, Texas Comptroller of Public Accounts, from website: http://www.window.state.tx.us/taxinfo/incidence/letter.html

Snell, Ronald (ed.) (1993), *Financing State Government in the 1990s*, Denver, CO and Washington, DC: National Conference of State Legislators, National Governors' Association.

Su, Betty W. (2001), 'The US economy to 2010', *Monthly Labor Review*, Washington, DC: US Government Printing Office, November.

US Department of Commerce, Bureau of the Census (1997), *Population Projections*, from website www.census.gov/population/www/projections/popproj/htm

US Department of Commerce, Bureau of the Census (2002), *2001 Statistical Abstract of the United States*, Washington, DC: US Government Printing Office.

US Department of Commerce, Bureau of Economic Analysis (BEA) (1998), *Survey of Current Business*, Washington, DC: US Government Printing Office, September.

US Department of Commerce, Bureau of Economic Analysis (BEA) (2002a), *Survey of Current Business*, Washington, DC: US Government Printing Office, May.

US Department of Commerce, Bureau of Economic Analysis (BEA) (2002b), *National Income and Product Accounts Tables*, from website: http://www.bea.doc.gov/bea/dn/nipaweb/index.asp

US Department of Labor, Bureau of Labor Statistics (BLS) (various years), *Consumer Expenditures*, Washington, DC: US Government Printing Office, various years.

US Department of Labor, Bureau of Labor Statistics (BLS) (2001a), *Economic and Employment Projections*, from website: http://www.bls.gov/news.release/ecopro.toc.htm

US Department of Labor, Bureau of Labor Statistics (BLS) (2001b), *Employees on Non-Farm Payrolls by Major Industries, 1950 to date*, from website: ftp://ftp.bls.gov/pub/suppl/empsit.ceseeb1.txt

Walker, Mary Beth (1998), 'Revenue losses from exemptions of goods from the Georgia sales tax', Fiscal Research Program Policy Reports No. 24, Atlanta, GA: Andrew Young School of Policy Studies, Georgia State University, November.

Wallace, Sally (1995), 'The effects of economic and demographic change on state budgets', The Finance Project Working Paper, Washington, DC, December.

4. Politics, the courts, and the economy: Implications for the future of school financing

Ross Rubenstein and Lawrence O. Picus

INTRODUCTION

Primary and secondary education, the largest area of state and local government expenditure, is in a time of transition. Parents and teachers are increasingly calling for greater school site autonomy. Policy makers in states around the country are developing accountability mechanisms providing rewards to high performing and improving schools, and sanctions for low performing schools that do not improve. At the same time, competition from 'market-based' alternatives such as vouchers, public school choice and charter schools is changing the landscape of public school finance in the 21st century.

One outcome of all of these initiatives has been greater focus on the school site rather than the district. There have been increased efforts to direct more decision making responsibility to the school site through site-based management. New accountability measures are generally focused on schools and not school districts. Additionally, most of the new market-based alternatives focus on individual schools. A number of states have begun major efforts to collect school level fiscal data, and others are considering various approaches to developing a better understanding of how educational resources are used at the school level. All of this has caused some in the school finance community to call for more direct funding of schools (see for example, Odden and Busch, 1998; Odden and Picus, 2000).

In this chapter, we focus on these key factors shaping school finance policy and research at the start of the 21st century and we consider the implications for the finance and taxation systems currently in place for public schools. The chapter has five sections following this introduction. In the second section of the chapter, we consider the current state of school finance equity, discussing changes in the distribution of education resources since California's landmark Supreme Court decision in *Serrano* v. *Priest*,[1] and review the current issues surrounding the definition of adequacy in school finance. The third section looks at the increased role of state funding in education in recent years and the implications of this increased state role, both for levels of educational funding and the effect it might have on school systems. In the fourth section, we consider the market-based alternatives that have garnered attention in recent years including private management of public schools, educational vouchers and charter schools. All of these changes have led to calls for school-based funding, which will be considered in the fifth section. We conclude by presenting our observations of the challenges facing school finance policy during the early years of the 21st century.

ADEQUACY AND EQUITY OF SCHOOL FINANCE SYSTEMS

The 1990s saw a resurgence in school finance litigation. Since 1989, a total of 21 cases have found their way to the highest court in their respective state. In 13 of those, the court decided in favor of the plaintiffs. Beginning with the 1989 landmark decision in Kentucky,[2] courts have been more willing to overthrow the existing funding system, define remedies and establish concrete requirements for constitutional remedy. In many instances, these decisions have focused on an alternative concept in school finance–adequacy.

In the past, school finance cases were brought on the more narrow grounds of funding equity for students, or taxpayer equity through remedies such as fiscal neutrality.[3] Adequacy cases argue that it is the responsibility of the state to provide an 'adequate' level of resources to ensure each child receives a satisfactory education. As envisioned by William Clune (1994), adequacy shifts the focus of school finance reform from inputs to an emphasis on high minimum outcomes.

Although this may sound simple on the surface, it represents a major change in the way states – and consequently school districts – will think about school funding issues in the future.

Defining Adequacy

Equity generally focuses on relative levels or distributions of funds across districts or schools. Adequacy differs in that the focus is on provision of sufficient and absolute levels of funding. Adequacy is not necessarily a new concept. In fact, one of the basic building blocks of any school finance system, the foundation program, is one way states have attempted to ensure adequate funds are available for education. A foundation program ensures that a base level of funding is available for each child at a fixed tax rate; with the amount of state aid a district receives inversely related to its property wealth per pupil (Odden and Picus, 2000). Early proponents of this funding model treated adequacy as an assumed condition in determining the foundation level (for example, see Cubberley, 1919; Mort, Reusser and Polley, 1960; Johns, Morphet and Alexander, 1983).

The problem with this approach has been that adequacy has often been defined on the basis of the revenue available to the state. This is, in essence, a political decision rather than a decision based on student needs. Driving this change in how adequacy is defined is the establishment, for the first time, of ambitious national education goals aimed at raising outcomes for all students (Verstegen, 1998).

Adequacy has been at the core of many recent court decisions across the nation. Verstegen (1998) suggests that in states where adequacy is thought of as providing a *minimum* standard, courts have upheld the existing school finance system. For example, the Texas Supreme Court in upholding the new school finance plan enacted by the state legislature, held in Edgewood IV[4] that the lower court had defined spending of $3500 per pupil to be adequate. How that figure was derived is not clear in either ruling, but to date the declaration has held sway in Texas. Other states where the highest court has upheld the existing funding system by arguing, in part, that the plaintiffs either did not mount an adequacy challenge or conceded that the system was adequate, include Virginia, Minnesota, Wisconsin, Maine, Rhode Island and Alaska.[5]

In states where the school finance system has been declared unconstitutional, courts have taken a different approach, arguing that a minimum or basic education is insufficient. In New Jersey's *Abbott* v. *Burke*,[6] the court argued that students in the 28 poorest (and lowest spending) districts were entitled to the same educational opportunities as students in the wealthiest (and highest spending) districts in the state. The Wyoming court in Campbell[7] argued that the state was required to define a 'proper' education and then establish a system to fund that education for all children.

These court decisions are important in that they appear to be the first of many requiring states to define more specifically what constitutes an adequate education. The next section considers the various approaches to defining adequacy being considered today.

Defining Adequacy in the States

Finding a definition of adequacy that is acceptable to the courts, to policy makers and to educators has not been easy, nor has there been agreement over what an adequate education really is. Perhaps the first judicial attempt to define an adequate education was in West Virginia's *Pauley* v. *Kelley* in

1979.[8] In that ruling the court stated that an adequate education includes the following:

- Literacy
- Ability to add, subtract, multiply and divide numbers
- Knowledge of government to the extent that the child will be equipped as a citizen to make informed choices among persons and issues that affect his own governance
- Self-knowledge and knowledge of his or her total environment to allow the child to intelligently choose life work – to know his or her options
- Work training and advanced academic training as the child may intelligently choose
- Recreational pursuits
- Interests in all creative arts, such as music, theater, literature, and the visual arts
- Social ethics, both behavioral and abstract, to facilitate compatibility with others in this society.

Clearly, operationalization of this definition is difficult if one only thinks of fiscal issues. Yet, states are faced with finding ways to, at a minimum, determine what it would cost to be sure each child meets these standards.

How have state policy makers and researchers attempted to determine the cost of an adequate program? To date, four methods have evolved. The first relies on the use of complex statistical analysis to ascertain the mix of inputs needed to reach a given level of student outcomes. This approach, known as a cost function, is gaining favor among economists. The second is similar except that it replaces the statistical analysis with observation of individual school districts that meet the previously identified outcome levels and then measures the expenditures in those districts. The advantage of this approach is that it is easier to explain to policy makers who are not well versed in econometric theory. The third relies on professional judgement to create an instructional resource model that can then be 'costed out'. The main advantage of this approach, often referred to as the Resource Cost Model, is that spending levels for adequacy can be estimated in the absence of a sophisticated student assessment system. The fourth estimates the costs of existing models of school reform if implemented in an individual state. Each is described in more detail below.

Cost functions

In recent years, there has been considerable debate over whether or not additional spending will lead to improvements in student outcomes. While educators nationwide agree that more money is better, researchers have had a difficult time finding a conclusive link between money and student achievement (for a discussion of this issue, see Picus 1997a). The approach to adequacy taken by some economists has been to turn the equation around. Rather than attempt to estimate student outcomes as a function of spending and other district and student characteristics – the traditional production function – cost functions estimate per-pupil expenditures as a function of school inputs (see for example, Duncombe, Ruggerio and Yinger, 1996; Reschovsky and Imazeki, 1998; Duncombe and Yinger, 1999). These inputs include measures of student achievement.

In short, once these cost functions have been estimated, student outcome levels can be set to a higher level, and the cost of reaching those goals estimated for each district in the state. The approach can include controls for district and student characteristics including price differences across a state. In reality, the computations for this are very complex and hard to describe to policy makers and state education leaders. Moreover, the few estimates that have been developed to date result in dramatic differences in the levels of spending needed across school districts. Reschovsky and Imazeki (1998) estimate that in Wisconsin, Milwaukee would require more than double the amount of money it currently receives through the state aid formula. Duncombe, Ruggerio and Yinger (1996) show similar large disparities for New York City schools in their model.

The difficulty with these models is that, despite the apparent precision they offer in estimating what an adequate education would cost, they rely on data that do not always accurately measure the variables in question. These limits to educational data sets are well established and in some instances hard to eliminate (for an excellent discussion of the limitations of education finance data collections see the *Journal of Education Finance*, Volume 22, Number 3, Winter 1997 and Volume 23, Number 4, Spring 1998).

Finally, as described above, cost function approaches require access to reliable student assessment data as well as agreement among policy makers and educators that the assessment system measures the desired outcome for students. As the assessment debates in this country make clear, we are far from reaching agreement on these issues. Thus, although cost functions show a great deal of promise, their complexity, and reliance on data that do not always provide accurate measures of inputs and outputs, make this approach problematic at the present time.

Observational methods

The observational approach determines a level of student performance that is acceptable or adequate, searches for districts that attain this level of performance and then defines the spending level of those districts to be adequate. Once determined, this adequate level of funding can be adjusted by differences in student characteristics and needs, district characteristics and price differences across districts. The underlying theory is that if some districts can achieve high performance at the identified spending level, others should be able to do so as well (Augenblick, 1997). This approach was used in Ohio as the state struggled to respond to the Ohio Supreme Court's ruling in *DeRolph* v. *Ohio*[9] that the state's school finance system is unconstitutional.

In 1995, Augenblick, Alexander and Guthrie (1995) first estimated the costs of adequacy in Ohio in response to a lower court ruling that held the system unconstitutional. They began with all districts in the state. After eliminating outliers in terms of high and low property wealth and spending levels, Augenblick, Alexander and Guthrie identified those districts that ranked above the 70th percentile on a number of measures of student performance. For this sub-set of districts, they examined organizational and instructional methods in an effort to identify 'exemplary' practices. They then determined the mix of inputs, such as teacher/pupil ratios, school sizes, administrative ratios and ratios of teachers to other professional staff, needed to support these practices. The costs associated with these inputs were estimated and used as the estimate of adequate spending.

This approach received some criticism because the input mixes identified and funded might not reflect what all successful districts do. Funding based on these input combinations might be restrictive to otherwise high performing districts. Thus, in his 1997 revision of this methodology, Augenblick (1997) estimated the average cost of providing education in the 102 out of 607 districts in Ohio identified as meeting the minimum performance requirements. The process led to a definition of adequacy at $3930 per pupil for 1996 spending in Ohio. The process also calls for making adjustments to this figure based on specific student needs and characteristics. Comparable studies have been conducted in Illinois and Mississippi using similar methodologies.

Difficulties with this approach include the general concerns about the quality of student assessment and our ability to measure the student outcomes we truly value, as well as concerns over the quality of the expenditure data generally. Moreover, adjustments for special needs programs must still be made, and methods for determining the costs of these programs are subject to debate. Finally, determination of the specifications for district inclusion in the list of high performers will have a major impact on the districts selected and the estimate of costs thus derived.

On the other hand, the procedures are much easier to explain to policy makers and educational leaders. Greater understandability on the part of these individuals is likely to improve the acceptance of this approach compared to the cost function methodology described above.

Professional judgement

Both the observational method and the cost function approach require access to high quality data on student outcomes and educational inputs. An alternative is to establish a system that relies on professional judgement to construct an ideal delivery system and then estimate the costs of that system. The genesis of this process is the Resource Cost Model (RCM) developed by Chambers and Parrish (see for example, Chambers and Parrish, 1994). The RCM model relies on professional judgement to identify the components needed to provide an appropriate education. Once identified and agreed to, costs can be assigned to each component and the cost of an appropriate, or adequate, education can be estimated. The model as espoused by Chambers and Parrish relies on a range of regression analyses to ascertain the final cost estimates.

This process was used in Wyoming in response to *Campbell* (Guthrie et al., 1997). The major variation used by Guthrie's team was to combine national research with the judgement of Wyoming practitioners to derive an estimate of the components of a proper education.[10] In addition, the economic approach to estimating the costs of each component was simplified to make explanations to policy makers more straightforward.

This approach has the benefit of being easier to understand, and it also includes many, if not all, of the constituent groups involved in education in the process of defining adequacy. The approach does not have the apparent statistical precision of the other two methods, but Guthrie et al. (1997) argue that the level of precision depends on the quality of the data available, making it less clear that more sophisticated analyses techniques lead to more accurate estimates of costs.

On the other hand, this approach relies heavily on the status quo to identify what needs to be done to educate children. If substantial changes are in reality necessary, they may not be identified through this approach. Moreover, despite the apparent simplicity of this approach compared to others, the need to consider price differentials, and the market price of unique inputs (like teachers) leads to enhanced complexity and some room to disagree with the final result.

At the present time, this approach seems to have gained the most favor among the states. Wyoming's school finance system was developed using the professional judgement model. In addition, the Oregon Quality Education Model, which will be used to estimate the fiscal needs of school districts across the state relies on the same professional judgement approach. Finally, Maine is attempting to implement a funding system based on an adequacy standard established through a similar process.

Cost of effective schoolwide strategies

The fourth approach takes research findings as embodied in a high performance, or a comprehensive school design, identifies all the ingredients needed for all elements of the design's educational strategies, determines a cost for each of those ingredients, and then uses that figure to determine an adequate spending base for each school. This system was developed in part because it identifies a set of specific educational programs and strategies that represent state-of-the-art knowledge about education effectiveness and puts a dollar figure on their costs. It combines several of the advantages of some of the preceding methods; because each comprehensive school design draws upon research that links strategy to student performance, this method has a direct performance link, and by drawing upon the compilation of strategies incorporated into several comprehensive school designs, it draws upon the craft wisdom of some of the best educators in the country who have combined research on individual programs into comprehensive schoolwide strategies. When used, moreover, it provides schools with a funding level that allows them to deploy any of a large number of schoolwide educational strategies, each of which represents the best of what both research and the top practitioners claim are the most effective educational strategies and that represent current state-of-the-art professional knowledge in education.

Odden (1997) identified the costs of seven schoolwide designs that were created by the New American Schools, and in subsequent analyses, showed how, via resource reallocation, they were affordable at schools spending at the average or median level of expenditure per pupil in the country (Odden and Busch, 1998; Odden and Picus, 2000). His analysis, however, did not include adequate planning and preparation time for teachers and did not standardize costs across various designs, so his cost figures are probably somewhat underestimated.

Implications of the Adequacy Standard for Schools and Districts

The discussion above shows that a definition of adequacy is hard to establish. Four very different approaches to measuring adequacy have been proposed, each with its own strengths and weaknesses, and none has been fully implemented to date in one or more of the 50 states. As adequacy grows increasingly important in school finance, what are the implications for school district spending?

School districts generally distribute resources to school sites through algorithms designed with equity in mind (see for example Hentschke, 1988). As Picus (1997b, 1998) has pointed out, school districts often go to great lengths to assign equal levels of resources to school sites, even when alternatives that could lead to improved student performance and better management of instructional resources exist. Shifting the focus of resource distribution to adequacy will result in even greater need to be attentive to individual student needs, often at the expense of providing every school site with identical sets of resources.

Perhaps the simplest version of this is Underwood's (1995) suggestion that adequacy is really a form of vertical equity. Districts are accustomed to providing different levels of inputs to meet the individual needs of specific students on the basis of disabling conditions, poverty and other factors. However, this is still an input-based approach to the distribution of resources and does not address the adequacy concern over outcomes. What adequacy seems to call for is providing the resources needed over the time frame required to allow a student to reach a certain level of achievement in a subject. Thus while it will probably take the average child one year to complete the third grade, or one year to learn Algebra I, some will require more time and others less. Systems that allow schools to organize in ways that facilitate differential time to completion will need to be developed in school districts.

Distributing resources in ways to support achievement of outcomes rather than providing inputs will mean school districts will need to develop better information systems. They will need more accurate information on the costs of individual instructional and support components, more accurate information on the time it takes children to complete different courses of study and more information on the teaching resources needed to meet the varying needs of students.

Schools will also have to consider alternative organizational structures to meet these student needs. Such changes could be as simple as keeping groups of elementary students with one teacher or group of teachers for multiple years, or as complex as providing revolving start dates for sequential classes so that students who complete a course in Biology in one and a half years can start Chemistry immediately (or in a relatively short period of time) rather than waiting until the beginning of the next school year. Odden and Busch (1998) show the expected costs of using one of the research-based school designs supported by the New American Schools, all of which appear to show positive gains in student achievement.

All of this provides educators with a major challenge to the way they currently approach their job. If they think of the school district office as providing service to schools to support the instructional program needed for each child, the transition will be complex but achievable. If they try to ignore these potential changes, it will greatly complicate the goal of providing every child with an adequate education.

THE CHANGING ROLES OF THE STATE AND LOCAL DISTRICTS

One impact of the school finance litigation of the past quarter century is that many states have made substantial progress in improving school finance equity. However, as the discussion of adequacy above suggests, it may be time to look at other ways to distribute funds to schools if we are going to shift our thinking away from the distribution of dollars and give greater weight to improving student achievement at all levels.

Defining Equity

Three concepts are traditionally used to define equity in school finance – horizontal equity, fiscal neutrality and vertical equity.

Horizontal equity refers to equal per-pupil spending across school districts. This approach requires that differences in per-pupil spending be largely eliminated, and in many states funding formulas have been designed to limit the ability of school districts to spend beyond the means of the more average districts in the state. The problem with the principle of horizontal equity is that it does not allow district residents to elect to spend more on the education of their children if they so desire. Many state courts have held that per-pupil spending does not have to be equal, but that all districts must have equal access to revenues. In many states, there is still a strong relationship between per-pupil property wealth and per-pupil revenues.

Fiscal neutrality requires that regardless of a district's per-pupil property wealth, it is able to raise the same level of per-pupil funding at a given tax rate as any other district in the state levying the same tax rate. Under a fiscally neutral system, the state provides aid to districts in inverse relationship to their per-pupil property wealth. The amount of the grant is typically also dependent upon each district's tax effort.

Vertical equity refers to the importance of providing different levels of resources to children with differing needs. For example, children with disabilities often require special education programs that cost more than the regular education program. In addition, many states, as well as the Federal government, provide compensatory funding to school districts to provide educational services to children from low income families. The principle of vertical equity is achieved when all children receive a level of resources appropriate to their needs.

Historical Trends

One cannot consider the implications of equity without looking closely at the history of school finance litigation in the last 30 years. The primary trend one sees in court rulings has been an effort to improve the equity or equality of spending per pupil across school districts within individual states. The first state Supreme Court decision in this set of cases was *Serrano* v. *Priest*.[11] In that case, the California Supreme Court held that the school finance system in the Golden State allowed some districts to spend substantially more than other districts, often with considerably lower property tax rates. Holding that this violated the equal protection clauses of both the state and federal constitutions, the Court called for substantial equalization of spending across districts.

Since that time, many other state courts have made similar rulings, and many states have acted to equalize spending across districts ahead of court rulings to avoid unfavorable court actions. Federal action was precluded in 1973, when the US Supreme Court, in a 5–4 ruling in *San Antonio Independent School District* v. *Rodriguez*[12] held that, important as education was for the US citizens and for discharging citizen responsibilities, it was not mentioned in the US Constitution. Further, all public school students in Texas (where the case was filed) were provided some type of education program. Thus, the Court was unwilling, on its own, to recognize education as a fundamental right. This ruling effectively foreclosed further school finance litigation focused on equity at the federal level.

However, there was a great deal of action in the states in the late 1970s and early 1980s, with court rulings in New Jersey and Minnesota, among others, forcing states to make substantial changes to their school finance formulas. In all, some 23 states were involved in school finance litigation during the 1970s and early 1980s, with approximately half of the state courts ruling for the state and half for the plaintiffs (see for example, Odden and Picus, 2000, Chapter Two).

Although school finance activity declined in the early 1980s, there was a resurgence in the latter part of the decade. This increased judicial activity continued in the 1990s, with some new twists to the old issues. The primary addition to many suits today is adequacy. Plaintiffs argue that spending is so low in some districts in their state that children living in those districts do not have access to an adequate educational opportunity. While this argument has seen some success, notably in Kentucky, judges have been reluctant to prescribe what constitutes an adequate level of funding. The courts in Florida rejected an adequacy suit[13] and in a recent 380-page opinion in South Dakota, the circuit court upheld that state's school funding system, including the adequacy of funding levels.[14]

Three rulings, all in favor of the plaintiffs, in Vermont (*Brigham* v. *State*) Ohio (*DeRolph* v. *Ohio*), and New York (*CEF* v. *State of New York*) – since overturned – may be signals of the future. In all three rulings, the court ruled that the existing state funding formula was unconstitutional and the court indicated that conditions in the lowest spending districts were unacceptable and improvements were needed. The courts in Vermont and Ohio also indicated that low wealth districts were entitled to greater access to the total wealth of the state. However, none of the rulings specified a minimum level of funding as adequate, and in Vermont and Ohio, the Court went to lengths to state that nothing in their rulings should be construed as meaning that the wealthiest districts should be restricted in what they could spend on their children's education. In all of these court cases, there seems to be a sense on the part of the justices that more money leads to better schools. The courts were also willing to let some districts spend more, provided the poorest districts had access to more resources.

One of the results of school finance litigation over time has been dramatically increased state appropriations for education, largely to provide for greater equalization. While many claim that states have been forced to equalize everyone down, the reality is that over time, substantial amounts of new money have flowed to school districts as a result of school finance reforms (see for example, Picus, 1994c; Evans, Murray and Schwab, 1999). While a few of the wealthiest districts in each state do suffer, many poor districts reap windfalls in revenue in the early years of school finance reform. In fact, in recent years, a new phenomenon has developed. Even with access to substantially higher revenues through equalization formulas, many low wealth, low spending districts elect to remain low spending and choose to lower taxes as well (Odden and Picus, 2000). The implications of these decisions in terms of the debate over whether or not money matters are critical; it appears that taxpayers in many districts may already feel that their schools have enough money to do the job they want to do, a far cry from the usual expectation that schools should have as much as possible.

Re-thinking Equity

Despite the tremendous efforts that have been made in improving school finance equity, if we are to truly manage to find ways to help all students to perform at high levels – a somewhat different, but arguably more important equity goal – then it is essential that we begin looking at alternative ways to think about our school finance systems.

Hanushek (1994, 1997) argues that the proper incentives for better performance and efficient use of educational resources are not in place, and that a system that holds schools accountable for student performance is essential

to the successful use of existing and new money. Improving student performance, with or without new funds requires four ingredients:

- Reallocation of existing resources (Efficiency)
- Incentives for improved performance (Effectiveness)
- A more market-based budgeting approach (Efficiency and Effective-
  ness)
- Developing the concept of 'venture capital' for schools and school
  systems (Equity)

Each is described in more detail below.

Reallocation of existing resources (Efficiency)

Regardless of what impact additional funds might have, it is important that
existing resources be used as efficiently as possible. Miles (1995) found that if
all individuals classified as teachers were to teach equal sized classes, the
average class in the district could be reduced from 22 to 13 students. While this
would place all children with disabilities in regular programs, Miles also provides estimates of what the average class size would be if some of the most
severely disabled children continued to receive services under current programs. Dramatic class size reductions would still be possible. Miles' work
highlights the fact that in many districts it may be possible to further reduce
class sizes through different assignments of teachers throughout the district. To
the extent that smaller class size improves student performance, these changes
would offer an improvement in student performance at little or no cost.

Odden (1997), and Odden and Busch (1998), in their analyses of the costs
of the New American Schools, argue that schools can find the additional
funds (ranging from $50 000 to $250 000 per school per year) to finance the
various school designs through a combination of creative use of categorical
funds, elimination of classroom aides, and reallocation of resources (such as
elimination of one or two teaching positions). While some of these options
may result in larger classes, or fewer teachers, the more intensive use of staff
and greater professional development activities available seem to result in
improved student performance in many of the schools that have adopted these
designs.

In sum, before seeking additional funds, there may be ways to restructure
what is done with current funds first. Levin's Accelerated Schools Program,
the New American Schools program designs, and hard analyses of current
staffing patterns could all yield improved student performance.

The role of teachers   Approximately half of any school district's employees
are teachers. Total compensation for teachers (salary and benefits) typically

represents something on the order of 60 per cent of a school district's budget. Moreover, it is teachers who have daily contact with students. Thus, real gains in productivity are most likely to be found in the way teachers use their time, the way they are trained and how they are compensated.

Perhaps the first question to ask is: do we have enough teachers? Or, should a greater proportion of district budgets be devoted to teachers? Moreover, if a greater share of the budget should be used to purchase the services of teachers, what other functions should be reduced? Answering these questions is not straightforward. First, it is necessary to consider how teachers are currently utilized, and then to make decisions about whether more teachers are needed.

There is virtually universal agreement that smaller classes lead to improved student achievement. On the surface, that implies hiring more teachers, something that has been happening in California to meet incentives for reduced class size in grades K–3. Pupil/teacher ratios have consistently declined since the mid-1950s, but despite this dramatic reduction, teachers continue to be concerned with large class size. Picus (1994a) analysed data from the Schools and Staffing Survey and found that while the average pupil–teacher ratio across the schools in the sample was approximately 16:1, self reported class size for nonspecial education teachers averaged 24:1, a difference of 50 per cent.

How are these other teacher resources being used? Not all of it is in smaller special education classes. Many schools use teachers for specialist functions, and in some cases, as quasi-administrators. Miles's (1995) analysis of the Boston School District (described above) shows how teachers can be used differently to lower class size and discusses the trade-offs in doing so. Anecdotal evidence from the Southern California area shows that most schools offer some of their teachers release time to do administrative tasks, leading to larger class sizes for those who continue in the classroom. Clearly, schools are deciding that these quasi-administrative functions are important, but we must consider whether using teachers who would otherwise be in the classroom is the most productive way to meet these administrative requirements.

Other staff   To the extent that other staff positions can be eliminated, more teachers can be hired and class size reduced. Although the 40 per cent of district expenditures not focused directly on the classroom are an attractive target for generating more teachers and instructional materials, these funds purchase important services including pupil transportation, maintenance and operations, and administrative support. For example, reduction of administrative positions (a common approach) could put further administrative burdens on schools or individual teachers, limiting the time they have available for direct instruction. Such actions could end up being counterproductive. Similarly, clerical, custodial and other classified staff provide important services to schools. If some of these positions are eliminated, the impact could be a degradation in the appearance and structure of school facilities. Many school officials argue that well maintained facilities are important to student learning, and districts have often used new funds for repair, renovation and school construction (see for example, Adams, 1994; Firestone et al. 1994; Picus, 1994c).

Incentives for improved performance (Effectiveness)
The use of incentives to improve school performance is not a new idea (see for example, Picus, 1992). Unfortunately, the incentives that may have the most success are sanctions. Schools faced with threats of intervention often act quickly to improve performance rather than risk the stigma of a sanction. Many positive incentives have been less successful. For example, high performing schools are often granted waivers from state regulations in exchange for success. But, why reward districts that have succeeded within the regulatory system with relief they may not need? Perhaps the more appropriate incentive would be to provide such waivers to underperforming schools with the hope that increased flexibility would lead to improvements.

Hanushek (1997) argues that the incentives currently in place do not encourage teachers to work to improve student performance and that those incentives need to be changed. He suggests that we do not really know enough about what kinds of performance incentives will work, and that more experimentation and research are needed.

Market-based approaches (Efficiency and Effectiveness)
Many of today's reformers call for market-based changes in the organization of schools. They propose choice programs, vouchers, and other models that ostensibly force out poor performers and allow high performing schools to grow and multiply. It seems unlikely though, particularly in large, overcrowded urban districts, that poor performing schools will actually close as a result of these programs. More likely, students whose families have the necessary resources, time or acumen will get into the better schools, while others will continue to suffer.

Picus (1994b) suggests that market type mechanisms within school systems are needed. He argues that for markets to succeed, failure is an essential ingredient. Since it is unlikely schools will close (or fail), a proxy for that failure is needed. He suggests that schools be given more authority over the use of their resources, particularly professional development funds, and that they be held accountable for student outcomes. Schools implementing successful programs will meet their goals, those selecting inappropriate programs most likely will fall short of those goals. Providers of unsuccessful programs will go out of business – creating the failure that is part of a market – and providers of successful programs will thrive, be they school districts, consortia of school personnel or private companies. Picus goes on to suggest that the market for teachers within a district be made less restrictive, with principals seeking teachers who share their management style and programmatic vision.

Market mechanisms are a powerful tool for improving the performance of an organization, but current proposals for market structures in public education (discussed more fully below) have met with tremendous resistance.

Developing the concept of 'venture capital' (Equity)

In a study of the costs of implementing California's 'Caught in the Middle' reforms – that state's attempt to reform middle school education through a program of smaller school communities within a school, organization for success for all students, and enhanced authority for teachers and principals in educating the children – Marsh and Sevilla (1992) found that the annual costs of restructuring schools to meet the requirements of this program were between three and six per cent higher than current average expenditures per pupil in California schools. However, they also concluded that the first year 'start-up' costs amounted to approximately 25 per cent of annual costs. The problem schools face is finding those start-up funds. For example, in a large district with ten middle schools, each with a budget of $10 million, the initial start-up costs would be $25 million, a figure that would be hard to find in a district budget. However, if the program were started in two schools a year, the annual cost would be only $5 million. Since the money would be for start-up purposes only, the $5 million could be transferred to two different schools each year until all ten schools had implemented the program. After all start-up costs had been met, the district would have $5 million in its budget available for other uses.

Related to the concept of venture capital are revolving funds. This seems to be a concept that offers a way for school districts to deal with large purchases that occur on a regular, but nonannual basis. Computers represent an excellent example. The average computer purchased for use in a school probably has a useful life of three to five years. Many schools are unable to replace computers after that period of time, though. As a result, many schools continue to use old Apple IIe and similar vintage computers.

Budget procedures in school districts typically do not reward schools for saving resources in one year to make large purchases the next year. A school that receives a sum of discretionary money in one year is likely to lose any of the funds it has not expended by the end of the fiscal year. As a result, schools are often unable to make a large coordinated purchase of computers and associated equipment at one time. Moreover, they are prevented from saving money to make such a purchase to replace a computer lab once it has become old or obsolete.

A district revolving fund to pay for such purchases provides one possible solution. Take, for example a district with eight elementary schools hoping to support a computer lab of 25 stations in each school. The district estimates that each lab's computers need to be replaced once every four years, and in today's dollars, the cost of replacing the entire lab is approximately $70 000. Assuming the district found one-time funds to establish the labs, it would probably try to provide each school with equal annual funding for replacement of computers. The cost would be $140 000 (0.25 × $70 000 × 8). If this funding were enough to replace one quarter of the computers each year (a four year replacement cycle), schools would find themselves with four different computer versions in each lab all the time. This solution is generally used in districts in an attempt to provide equitable funding to each school.

An alternative would be to establish a revolving fund of $140 000 a year. This fund could be used to completely replace the labs in two schools each year, thus establishing a four-year replacement cycle and ensuring that each school's computing facility is filled with similar computers. It is likely that under these circumstances, the labs would function more smoothly with fewer problems related to the difficulties of networking different computers with different capabilities. Schools would know exactly when the computers in their lab were to be replaced. Although capital spending across the eight schools would not be equitable on a year-to-year basis, equity over the lifetime of the computers in the labs would be maintained. The revolving fund approach could also be applied to the provision of professional development services, and other school reform efforts that require one-time or nonannual expenditures.

Finding a way to use the money in a revolving fashion would facilitate continued improvements in educational programs, but a major problem is determining who gets the venture capital funds first and who has to wait. In many large districts, superintendents publish lists of the best and worst performing schools, and such lists could be used to prioritize the allocation of these funds. Another issue is the equity of the distribution. While some schools will get more one year than others, over the established time period all schools will receive the funds, so one simply has to accept the idea that equity is measured over some time frame, and not on an annual basis.

Implications of the Changing Role of States and Districts

The extensive school finance litigation of the past 30 years has produced momentous changes in education funding systems within states and in the relative roles of state and local governments. State share of funding has largely increased since the early 1970s, and court-ordered reforms have, in many cases improved the equity of funding within states (Evans, Murray and Schwab, 1997). Funding increases are inevitably limited, though. Increasingly, educators are being asked to do more with lower or flat funding levels. The accountability and standards movement, emphasizing measurable improvements in student performance, has put more pressure on school and district administrators to creatively use existing resources to improve their schools.

As the preceding discussion of adequacy highlights, the traditional focus on inputs to schooling has largely shifted to encompass student outputs and outcomes. While research has yet to fully specify the relationship between educational inputs and outputs, a number of resource reallocation models hold considerable promise for improving school effectiveness and efficiency at little or no increase in cost. Many of these models are premised, though, on a more decentralized decision making and resource allocation structure among states, districts and schools. The use of incentives, market-based reforms and venture capital approaches all put increased control over success – and failure – into the hands of local educators.

MARKET-BASED FUNDING ALTERNATIVES

A growing number of reform proposals call for a fundamental restructuring of government's role in primary and secondary education. School voucher proponents seek to enhance families' choices of educational providers by having governments primarily subsidize, rather than directly provide, education. Proponents believe that increasing competition by expanding the choices available to families will improve the efficiency and quality of educational service delivery. Charter school proposals attempt to accomplish similar goals by freeing individual public schools from many of the constraints typically found in public school systems and by providing families an alternative to zoned neighborhood schools. Under a third broad category of 'privatization' reforms, school districts contract with private firms to provide some, or all, educational programs.

Though different, each of these reforms is premised on the belief that, through increased competition, market forces will lead to significant improvements in the education students receive. However, they differ in the extent to which educational services are actually privatized. While voucher and privatization programs rely, at least partially, on private organizations to educate children, charter proposals more typically seek to bring characteristics of private educational enterprises and increased competition into the public sector.

Market-based solutions to the perceived failures of public school systems date to the 1700s but have been more widely discussed since Friedman's (1962) influential voucher proposals over 40 years ago. In recent years, states and school districts have increasingly debated and implemented plans to provide vouchers to offset the cost of private school tuition and to contract with private educational management organizations (EMOs). For example, the state of Wisconsin has been providing vouchers to low income students in Milwaukee since the early 1990s, and at least five other privately and publicly funded voucher programs started between 1991 and 1997 (Peterson, 1998). In the first statewide foray into vouchers, Florida passed legislation to provide vouchers for students in the state's lowest performing schools, though ballot initiatives to introduce vouchers in Michigan and California failed in the 2000 election (Ziebarth, 2000). Public school districts in Minneapolis and Hartford, and individual schools around the country have entered into contracts with EMOs to manage their educational enterprises. And, as of 1999, 36 states and the District of Columbia had passed legislation to permit state-funded charter schools and over 1400 charter schools had opened around the country (Nelson et al., 2000).

Strictly speaking, these proposals focus on the mechanisms used to *provide*, rather than *fund*, education. However, the implications of these proposals for school finance systems are immense. While the budget impact of small scale programs, such as publicly funded efforts in Milwaukee and Cleveland, may be relatively easy for policy makers to manage, the fiscal implications of more extensive programs serving a larger proportion of students must be evaluated. While the effects are likely to vary substantially according to the specifics of the plan and its implementation, these programs promise to greatly affect state and local expenditures and revenues as the initiatives expand. Although proponents often see such plans as budget-neutral (or as cost saving measures), evidence from current programs suggests that the expenditure impact is far from clear. Moreover, such plans potentially weaken the district's role as the focus of state funding and equalization mechanisms, suggesting that school-based financing (in the case of charter schools) or student-based financing (in the case of vouchers) may be more appropriate.

Funding Voucher Plans

Plans to provide students with publicly funded vouchers to pay all or a part of the tuition at private schools have been among the most controversial issues in education policy and research. In recent years, evidence on the effects of the Milwaukee and Cleveland programs has begun to accumulate. In addition, privately funded scholarships for students in New York and elsewhere are providing additional data to analyse differences in the performance of low income students attending public and private schools. The data from the Milwaukee and Cleveland experiments have been analysed and reanalysed (Witte et al., 1995; Greene et al., 1997; Rouse, 1997; Goldhaber et al., 1999) but little consensus has emerged regarding the programs' effects on student achievement. Regardless of the educational impact of vouchers, they are likely to remain a popular policy proposal and, as such, the fiscal consequences for state and local governments bear examination.

Two fundamental financial questions face state and local governments seeking to implement voucher plans:

- What is the total cost of such a program?
- How will the financial resources be raised and distributed?

Cost of a voucher plan

An undeniable aspect of voucher proposals' appeal lies in their promise of increasing efficiency in education. By using the power of the market, advocates hope to provide superior education for students at a lower total cost per student. Pointing to the lower average per-pupil costs typically found in private schools, proponents argue that if private schools can deliver an education of even comparable quality to that in public schools, society will benefit through an increase in efficiency.

At its most basic, the cost of a voucher system will simply be the product of the number of students served and the amount of the voucher.[15] In the existing programs, the number of students served has typically been limited by factors such as family income, current choice of educational sector, quality of a child's public school and total funding available for the program. For example, in both the Milwaukee and Cleveland programs, only a limited number of scholarships have been offered and vouchers have been awarded only to children from low income families (Greene, Howell and Peterson, 1998; Greene, Peterson and Du, 1998).

In many of the existing voucher programs, the voucher amount covers only a portion of private school tuition (Peterson, 1998). For example, in the Milwaukee program the voucher amount has been set equal to per-pupil state aid, with no local contribution required from the Milwaukee Public Schools (Witte et al., 1995). While the Milwaukee schools do lose state funding for each student switching to private schools, they retain their locally raised revenues while serving fewer students. This type of voucher arrangement – akin to a flat per-pupil grant to school districts – appears to have little relationship to notions of adequacy or equity, however. If state aid per pupil is lower than the tuition charged by most private schools, students from the poorest families will receive limited benefits from a voucher tied to state aid levels.

If voucher programs continue to grow in size (more total students served) and scope (a higher proportion of districts' students), determination of the voucher amount will inevitably need to be tied to reasonable cost estimates and recognition of variations in student needs and circumstances. Current programs typically enroll a relatively homogeneous student population. For example, all students in the Milwaukee program must come from families with income below 175 per cent of the poverty level (Witte et al., 1995), and in Cleveland, children from low income families are given priority and, therefore, comprise nearly all of the program participants (Anderson et al., 1997). In Milwaukee, 95 per cent of participating children were African-American or Hispanic, as were two-thirds of recipients in Cleveland (Witte et al., 1995; Greene, Howell and Peterson, 1998).

If the pool of participating students becomes more diverse, policy makers will confront the same equity- and adequacy-related issues described above. For example, what provisions should be made for students with disabilities or those with limited proficiency in English? Clearly, in a pure market-based system, a school will have no incentive to enroll students with special needs if they face higher costs but receive no additional funding. Alternatively, schools may enroll these students but supply additional programs or services only up to the amount of the voucher. For example, if a student with learning disabilities receives a voucher for $5000, a school's incentive is to provide less than $5000 in services, or to not enroll that student. Current state finance systems typically account for students' different needs through foundation programs with weights that increase base funding according to student needs and through categorical grant programs. Similar approaches would be needed to enhance equity even in a system relying primarily on private provision.

Just as provisions would have to be made to ensure the equity of large scale voucher programs, voucher levels would also need to have some relationship to notions of adequacy. As described, the concept has been exceedingly difficult to measure in public education, and the use of a student-based funding system in which students are educated in public, for-profit and not-for-profit schools would introduce additional difficulties. Private school tuition is, on average, substantially lower than per-pupil spending in public schools, but may not reflect the true cost of educating students. Nationally, private school tuition averaged $3116 in 1993–94 as compared to average public school expenditures of $6492 per pupil in the same school year (US Department of Education, 2001). Average tuition at religious schools (Catholic and non-Catholic) was below $3000 (US Department of Education, 2001). Parochial and other private schools are, of course, able to leverage substantial in-kind resources from religious organizations and parents that lower average per-pupil costs. Whether and how to factor these and other in-kind resources into the estimation of an adequate funding level presents another challenge yet to be faced.

Clearly, determination of the value of the voucher is not straightforward. Neither, though, is determination of the number of eligible pupils. As described, current programs focus on providing public school students access to private schools, and often no provision is made for students already in private schools. If voucher programs grow large enough, it is unlikely that private school students could continue to be excluded. Inclusion of private school students would immediately increase the number of students receiving public funding by an average of 11 per cent,[16] with large variations across states and districts. Therefore, average per-pupil expenditure levels would have to decrease by 11 per cent if the program is to be budget-neutral. Levin (1998) estimates that if all private school students nationwide were funded publicly at average per-pupil public school expenditure levels, the cost would be approximately $33 billion.

Expenditures are not the same as costs, however. Therefore, using current per-pupil expenditures makes sense only as a rough estimate of an appropriate voucher level. A host of implementation issues would need to be addressed before more reasonable cost estimates can be delivered.[17] Moreover, the focus on average costs obscures the fact that the marginal cost of serving an additional student may be far less than the average cost. Therefore, private schools may experience a windfall if voucher levels are based on average public school per-pupil costs. At the same time, lost revenue to existing public schools would exceed the savings realized in the short run by serving fewer students.

Distributing vouchers

Assuming we can derive reasonable estimates of total program costs, and assuming, for the moment, that these costs are comparable to those in the current system, myriad funding questions remain unresolved. As described earlier, overcoming the educational inequities caused by reliance on local property taxes has been a dominant theme of school finance research, policy making and litigation for over 30 years. Current voucher programs have been limited to individual districts and have not faced problems arising from interdistrict disparities in wealth, educational costs and per-pupil funding levels. A system that essentially mirrors current funding structures – with a voucher in the amount of average district per-pupil expenditures following students to a school of choice within the district – would not alleviate existing interdistrict inequities. In large districts with many schools, persistent intradistrict inequities may decline to some degree since families would be able to choose the best and most appropriate schools for their children from among all public and private schools in the district, rather than attending a neighborhood school that does not meet their child's needs.[18] If the system ignores district boundaries, allowing students to enroll in any school regardless of district (or possibly, state), student-based financing – rather than district-based – becomes more essential.

The simplest approach to funding voucher initiatives may be to have funding follow the student. Each student carries his or her voucher to any school, with the amount set by his or her district of residence. To the extent that voucher levels differ across districts just as per-pupil expenditure levels currently differ, students in higher spending districts (and students from higher income families) will presumably be able to purchase a higher quality education. If students increasingly move across district boundaries to attend school, the link between local property taxes and benefits received becomes more tenuous.[19] If students from low spending (and presumably, lower quality) districts are able to enroll in higher quality schools in higher spending districts, the benefits of higher educational spending will spill over into neighboring districts. Taxpayers in receiving districts may increasingly resist efforts to raise local taxes, or may move to different districts, if a substantial portion of the benefits accrues outside their district (Odden and Picus, 2000). Moreover, if larger proportions of families send their children to private schools, willingness to pay taxes perceived as supporting public education could decline, resulting in lower per-pupil expenditures on average (Goldhaber, 2001). Case studies of states with current interdistrict choice programs have found that 'sending' districts have suffered relatively small financial losses (Armor and Peiser, 1998; Doering, 1998), suggesting that such taxpayer revolts may be unlikely to occur, particularly if movement across districts is limited. If schools in high spending districts set tuition at a level that prevents most students from poorer districts from enrolling, the inequities found in the present system will persist.

Other voucher models would more fundamentally alter school financing and have greater implications for revenue systems. For example, Coons, Clune and Sugarman (1970) propose a 'Family Power Equalizing' approach that is similar in concept to a 'District Power Equalizing' or Guaranteed Tax Base intergovernmental grant. Under this model, a child's family would choose the level of tax effort they wish to make for education, with tax effort linked to predetermined voucher amounts. Each family's voucher amount would be based on its chosen tax effort.

Such a student-based plan has the potential to significantly improve both freedom and equity beyond what can be achieved in a district-based system. Since educational spending would be linked to a tax effort chosen by individual families (rather than school district voters), and would equalize *family* rather than *district* wealth or income, the plan would more closely align tax payments to benefits received. Presumably, either property or income taxes could be used as the tax base, although the revenue source would need to be accessible to the state.

Funding Charters and EMOs

While we have, thus far, focused on vouchers, similar issues arise in both privatization and charter school proposals. As in voucher plans, determination of the appropriate payment to the private organization is difficult to determine when a district contracts with an EMO to run some or all schools in the district. In practice, it is typically linked to average district spending per pupil, with some percentage deducted to account for the cost of district overhead (Engle and Scafidi, 1999). Since the rate is typically set through contract negotiations between the local government and contractor, costs may be more predictable than under a large scale voucher program. In times of budget shortfalls, however, multi-year contracts offer little opportunity for cost cutting. Refusal to renegotiate contracts during economic downturns may have been partially responsible for the Baltimore and Hartford school districts canceling contracts with Education Alternatives Inc. in the 1990s (Ascher et al., 1996; Engle and Scafidi, 1999).

In the case of charter schools, the administering organization may be public, for-profit or not-for-profit, but by virtue of the school's autonomy, many of the same issues discussed in relation to voucher funding arise. State provisions related to funding, governance and oversight of charter schools vary greatly. Charters may be granted by either state or local boards of education, or by institutions of higher education. Funding may come directly from the state, or may flow through the school district. Funding levels or minimums may be specified in legislation or left to negotiation between the school and district. Funding provisions also may vary within individual states depending upon the sponsoring entity (for instance, state, local, university) (see Jennings et al., 1999 for an overview of charter school provisions across the nation).

Several states fund charter schools at the full state foundation level, in effect treating schools as school districts with no property wealth (Odden and Busch, 1998). Additional resources for students with special needs are provided through funding weights built into the foundation or through categorical grants. In some states, charter schools receive no local funding, but the majority of states rely on the existing state–local funding partnership to provide charter schools with all or some portion of the local funds that other schools in the district receive. Using existing finance structures to fund charter schools does little to alter state and local revenue or expenditure patterns, and, consequently, does little to address equity or adequacy issues that may be present in the absence of charter initiatives.

While voucher and privatization programs typically deliver services through existing public or private schools, charter schools may be entirely new entities. Start-up and capital costs are, therefore, often a major obstacle to charter school creation (Bierlein and Fulton, 1996). While public school districts can issue bonds for construction backed by the property tax base within the district, charter schools have little independent revenue raising capability and, therefore, limited access to capital markets. Moreover, state restrictions often limit a school's ability to use operating funds for capital expenditures. Charter schools have thus far relied heavily on leased facilities, but as the number of charters expands, a more cost-effective approach to capital funding will be needed. Likewise, if states enact large scale choice programs, demand would likely outstrip supply in the short-run, raising questions about the appropriate public sector response to increase supply.

Implications of Market-Based Reforms

The national popularity of market-based responses to problems of public school systems shows no sign of abating. As the preceding discussion suggests, the implications for state and local government finance will depend largely on the specifics of such programs and could range from radical restructuring of revenue and expenditure patterns to marginal changes in tax policy and funding formulas. But if market-based reforms expand beyond isolated efforts, they will undoubtedly force major changes in traditional school finance structures. Much like the equity-based reforms of earlier decades, research and litigation could prove to be critical factors in the continuation and expansion of these approaches. Until fundamental legal issues are essentially resolved, it is unlikely that voucher programs will expand on a wide scale (though the charter school movement may be largely unaffected by these challenges). And despite the high political and ideological stakes, research could potentially play a critical role in the expansion and design of market-based reforms policies. As evidence continues to accumulate on whether, how, and for whom such programs do or do not work to improve student achievement, these reform efforts could become firmly entrenched, or could simply be dismissed as another ineffective education reform 'fad'.

SCHOOL-BASED FINANCING

The history of American school finance in the 20th century centered on state-to-district funding structures (Odden and Picus, 2000). With increased interest in charter schools and other school choice efforts, though, the traditional structure of district-based funding and budgeting has come under increasing scrutiny and criticism. Schools are the primary units of education 'production' and are the focus of many recent accountability efforts. Yet most states continue to fund school districts, paying little attention to the distribution or use of resources at the school or classroom level. A growing chorus of researchers and policy makers is calling for schools – rather than districts – to be the primary funding unit, with the vast majority of resources flowing directly from the state to the school site (Guthrie, 1997; Odden and Clune, 1998; Odden and Busch, 1998; Odden and Picus, 2000). While such a change could potentially improve efficiency and lower overall spending, states and school districts would face a dramatic restructuring of traditional state-district-school fiscal relationships.

American education has a long tradition of local control exerted through the power of school districts. School boards have been the primary policy setting bodies, with implementation, rather than decision making, carried out by schools. Independent school districts' taxing authority presumably gives local taxpayers more direct control over tax and expenditure levels than they might have under a purely state-financed system (Tiebout, 1956). While the number of school districts has drastically declined, from over 100 000 earlier in the century to fewer than 15 000 currently (US Department of Education, 2001), districts remain the dominant method of exerting local control in 49 states.[20]

Interest in school-based approaches to financing education grows out of a number of recent trends in education. One of these – the charter school movement – we discuss above. A second trend has been the increasing focus on the performance of individual schools for accountability purposes. A third trend, closely related to the first two, has been the increasing prevalence across the country of school-based management and budgeting. Along with the shrinking role of districts in raising education revenues, the past 20 years have seen a shift in the locus of control over educational management and resource allocation decisions, with many districts providing individual schools with greater decision making discretion and responsibility. Most decentralization efforts in the United States began no earlier than the 1980s, but several other countries (for example, Australia and Canada) have much longer experiences with school-based control (Clune and White, 1988; Hill, 1997).

Shifting the locus of control over resource allocation decisions does not, on its own, have fiscal implications for state and local governments. Overall spending levels need not change, but decentralized management may offer opportunities for enhanced efficiency and, therefore, lower per-pupil spending. At least a portion of any savings should be retained at the school to provide an incentive for improved efficiency, however (Wohlstetter and Mohrman, 1996).

Intradistrict allocation formulas could conflict with efforts to enhance school-level discretion, though. Formulas vary, but most large districts allocate the majority of resources to individual schools based on positions rather than dollars per pupil (Guthrie, 1997). For example, a school might receive one teacher position for every 20 students in first through third grades, with additional per-pupil allocations for books and other direct costs. Under this type of system, the school is essentially charged for an average teacher's salary, and there is no financial impact to the school for hiring a higher or lower paid teacher. The school's principal (or other school-based committee) could select specific teachers to fill positions, but the district pays the teachers' salaries and benefits.

This type of allocation formula has several shortcomings for a decentralized system. First, funding based primarily on positions leaves schools little discretion to choose their mix of staff. For example, most schools would not have the authority to trade a teacher for several aides, or to trade half time art and music positions for a maths teacher. Second, schools must work within the districts' class size guidelines unless enough categorical or discretionary funding is available to hire additional teachers. Substantially decreasing or increasing class size by redirecting other resources is unlikely to be an option. Third, since salaries and benefits account for the majority of spending in a typical school, position-based allocations can leave little funding for discretionary resource allocation decisions.

Position-based allocations also raise related concerns regarding funding equity across schools within districts. All else being equal, demand is likely to be highest for more experienced, more educated teachers. To the extent that these teachers, who command higher salaries, choose to work in schools with more advantaged students, those schools will have higher per-pupil spending when teacher salaries are converted to dollars (Berne and Stiefel, 1994; Rubenstein, 1998).

The obvious alternative is to allocate dollars rather than positions, or some combination of positions and dollars, to schools. Schools in England, for example, are charged for actual rather than average teacher salaries. To prevent drastic changes in schools' staffing patterns, the transition to this system took seven years (Odden and Picus, 2000). The Chicago Public Schools District provides most General Fund allocations to schools as positions, but also provides schools access to large amounts of discretionary state money that flows to schools as dollars and can be used to hire staff or for other purposes (Hess, 1995; Rubenstein, 1998). The Los Angeles Unified School District entered into a consent decree that requires the district to allocate dollars rather than positions to schools. The consent decree arose from a lawsuit challenging intradistrict inequities that arose from position-based allocations (*Rodriguez* v. *LAUSD*).

School-based financing proposals draw on the experiences of other nations, particularly England and Australia (Odden and Busch, 1998; Odden and Clune, 1998). Both countries allocate over 85 per cent of educational dollars directly to schools, with allocations in England flowing through Local Education Authorities (LEAs). England's experiences may be particularly instructive for the United States because the system includes LEAs, which are similar to American school districts.

Odden and Busch (1998) offer a detailed proposal for a school-based financing system in the United States. Under their plan, school districts would retain certain 'core functions', such as developing curriculum and performance standards, providing budgeting guidelines for schools, implementing a school-based information system and controlling capital financing and outlay. The district could optionally perform a variety of other functions, with decisions about the distribution of functions left to each district. Funding for all other functions would flow as a lump sum allocation from the district to the school.

Under the Odden and Busch proposal, districts would have the discretion to develop their own intradistrict allocation formulas. In practice, district formulas could easily be mandated or constrained by the state in order to maintain intradistrict equity. It is worth noting that intradistrict formulas would not be complex in most districts since almost 75 per cent contain fewer than five schools. However, the largest 5.5 per cent of districts enroll over 50 per cent of total public school students (US Department of Education, 2001), therefore intradistrict allocation formulas would still affect a large number of pupils.

A school-based financing system in which each school receives a lump sum allocation would presumably raise awareness among educators and parents about intra- and interdistrict disparities across schools, and about the relationship of funding to notions of adequacy (Odden and Busch, 1998). As described above, school-level financial data have often been difficult to obtain and use, making it unlikely that the public – or even policy makers – would have access to information about funding levels across schools (see Picus and Fazal, 1996; Berne, Stiefel and Moser, 1997; Stiefel, Rubenstein and Berne, 1998). School-based financing could make disparities both within and across districts more transparent to families and to taxpayers.

By moving a step closer to the individual student, school-based financing could improve the likelihood that students receive the appropriate level of services to which they are entitled. For example, assume that a state funds school districts through a foundation formula program with weights for students at various grade levels and for those with special needs. Further assume that a student with learning disabilities has a weight of 2.3 and therefore generates 230 per cent of the base per-pupil allocation for his or her district.

Under district-based financing, the additional funds for that student may not find their way to his or her school, let alone to their classroom. School-based financing could help to improve both equity and adequacy by ensuring that schools have access to adequate and equitable levels of resources for the students they actually serve.

A school-based approach to funding might also call for a reduction in districts' revenue raising function and greater centralization of funding at the state level. This centralization could take a number of forms. The relative mix of funding sources could remain the same, but the state could tax some or all property centrally. Such a change could be relatively moderate – for example a statewide tax on nonresidential property, with the revenues distributed using state funding formulas (Ladd and Harris, 1995). Alternatively, the state could impose more drastic changes, such as eliminating local property taxes in favor of state property and sales taxes (as Michigan has done), or state income taxes (Wassmer and Fisher, 1996; Courant and Loeb, 1997). School-based financing can be accomplished without greater centralization of revenue responsibility, but reduction of districts' role in raising revenue may be a natural result of the reforms.

Implications of School-Based Financing

School-based financing presents state and local governments with an opportunity to rethink state formula and revenue structures. As charter schools, school-based management, choice and enhanced accountability efforts expand and continue, movement toward school-based financing may be inevitable. Whether revenue reforms accompany these funding changes also remains to be seen. But the shift away from districts as the primary locus of educational funding and policy making is well underway around the country.

CONCLUSION

This chapter presents a number of alternative approaches to thinking about the future of school finance in the United States. These proposals deal not only with equity as it is traditionally defined, but with a broader definition of what school finance should help to achieve, including efficiency and effectiveness. In short, school finance should increasingly play a more direct role in improving the productivity of our educational systems. Alternatives for improving educational productivity may focus on measuring and providing adequate levels of funding, developing systems of incentives and sanctions, privatizing services (both support services and educational program services), and implementing public school choice through mechanisms such as tax credits for private school tuition and vouchers. While these approaches differ from each other in method and theoretical underpinnings, all seek to improve productivity by utilizing resources more effectively and by enhancing competition, either within schools, across schools or districts, or between the public and private educational sectors.

Proposals aimed at improving educational equity, productivity and efficiency call into question not only traditional notions about the use of educational resources, but also dominant state and local revenue structures and relations. As research and policy in school finance increasingly focus on student outputs and outcomes rather than district inputs, it may be inevitable that district-based revenue and grant structures will lose much of their relevance. If so, a widespread shift to school-based or student-based financing could result. Still, the strong possibility exists that current revenue and intergovernmental grant structures will largely continue for the foreseeable future, with only incremental adjustments. Such marginal changes may present obstacles to reformers as they seek to improve educational productivity.

The best ways to improve educational productivity are to focus resources into educational programs and reforms that research has shown to be effective, and to continue rigorous research into the efficacy of new alternatives. Options for reallocating resources do exist and a number of them have been identified in this chapter. Others will require hard work on the part of educational policy makers and all those charged with the responsibility for ensuring that our educational funds are used in the most efficient and equitable manner possible.

NOTES

1. 5 Cal 3d 584, 96 Cal. Rptr. 601, 487 p.2d 1241 [Calif. 1971].
2. *Rose* v. *Council for Better Education*, 790 S.W.2d 186 (1989).
3. The fiscal neutrality principle states that the quality of a child's education should not be a function of the wealth or fiscal capacity of the child's school district (Berne and Stiefel, 1994).
4. *Edgewood Independent School District* v. *Meno*, 893 S.W.2d 450 1995.
5. Alaska – *Matanuska-Susitna Borough School District* v. *Alaska*, 931 P.2d 391 (1997); Maine – *School Admin. District No. 1 et al* v. *Commissioner*, 659 A.2d 854 (1994); Minnesota – *Skeen* v. *State*, 505 N.W. 2d 299 (1993); Rhode Island – *Pawtucket* v. *Sundlan*, 662 A.2d 40 (1995); Virginia – *Scott* v. *Commonwealth of Virginia*, 443 S.E.2d 138 (1994); Wisconsin – *Kukor* v. *Grover*, 436 N.W.2d 568 (1989).
6. *Abbott* v. *Burke*, 575 A.2d 359 (1985).
7. *Campbell County School District* v. *Wyoming*, 907 P.2d 1238 (1995).
8. *Pauley* v. *Kelley*, 255 S.E.2d 859 (1979).
9. *DeRolph* v. *Ohio*, 677 N.E. 733 (1997).
10. 'Proper' is the term used by the Court in *Campbell*.
11. 5 Cal 3d 584, 96 Cal.Rptr. 601, 487 p.2nd 1241 [Calif. 1971].
12. 411 US 1, 93 S.Ct. 1278, 1973.

13. *Coalition for Adequacy and Fairness in School Funding, Inc.* v. *Chiles.*
14. *Bezdichek* v. *State*; Civ. No. 91-209, 6th Judicial Circuit Court.
15. This rough estimate ignores the administrative overhead associated with such programs, such as creating an office to coordinate the program and disseminate information on schools (see Chubb and Moe, 1990).
16. Based on the number of students nationally enrolled in private schools (US Department of Education, 2001).
17. For example, should estimates assume that schools are subject to collective bargaining agreements and salary schedules that fix the cost of public school teachers over the short run?
18. Intradistrict open enrollment or 'public school choice' programs, such as those made famous in New York City's Community School District 4, seek to provide such benefits from competition solely within the public sector.
19. Students' ability to move across district boundaries depends upon a number of factors, such as the number of and size of school districts in a region, and transportation constraints. See Hoxby (1998) for a discussion of competition among public school districts.
20. Hawaii, with no local districts, is the lone exception.

REFERENCES

Adams, J.E. (1994), 'Spending school reform dollars in Kentucky: Familiar patterns and new programs, but is this reform?', *Educational Evaluation and Policy Analysis*, 16(4): 375–90.
Anderson, R., L. Boster, M. Dangaran and S.V. Roth (1997), *School Choice*, (Legislative Service Commission *Members Only* Brief), Columbus, OH: Ohio General Assembly.
Armor, D.L. and B.M. Peiser (1998), 'Interdistrict choice in Massachusetts', in P.E Peterson and B.C. Hasell (eds), *Learning From School Choice*, Washington, DC: Brooking Institution Press, pp. 157–86.
Ascher, C., N. Fruchter and R. Berne (1996), *Hard Lessons: Public Schools and Privatization*, New York: Twentieth Century Fund Press.
Augenblick, J. (1997), *Recommendations for a Base Figure and Pupil-Weighted Adjustments to the Base Figure for Use in a New School Finance System in Ohio*, Columbus, OH: School Funding Task Force, Ohio Department of Education, 17 July.
Augenblick, J., K. Alexander and J.W. Guthrie (1995), *Report of the Panel of Experts: Proposals for the Elimination of Wealth Based Disparities in Education*, submitted by Ohio Chief State School Officer Theodore Sanders to the Ohio State Legislature, June.
Berne, R. and L. Stiefel (1994), 'Measuring equity at the school level: The finance perspective', *Education Evaluation and Policy Analysis*, 16: 405–21.
Berne, R., L. Stiefel and M. Moser (1997), 'The coming of age of school-level finance', *Journal of Education Finance*, 22: 246–54.
Bierlein, L.A. and M.F. Fulton (1996), *Emerging Issues In Charter School Financing: Policy Brief*, Denver, CO: Education Commission of the States.
Chambers, J. and T. Parrish (1994), 'State level education finance', in W.S. Barnett (ed.), *Cost Analysis for Education Decisions: Methods and Examples: Advances in Educational Productivity*, Volume 4. Greenwich, CT: JAI Press Inc., pp. 45–74.
Chubb, J.E. and T.M. Moe (1990), *Politics, Markets and America's Schools*, Washington, DC: Brookings Institution.

Clune, W.H. (1994), 'The shift from equity to adequacy in school finance', *Educational Policy*, 8(4): 376–95.

Clune, W.H. and P. White (1988), *School-Based Management: Institutional Variation, Implementation and Issues for Further Research*, New Brunswick, NJ: Rutgers University, Center for Policy Research in Education.

Coons, J., W. Clune and S. Sugarman (1970), *Private Wealth and Public Education*, Cambridge, MA: Belknap Press of Harvard University Press.

Courant, P. and S. Loeb (1997), 'Centralization of school finance in Michigan', *Journal of Policy Analysis and Management*, 16: 114–36.

Cubberley, E.P. (1919), *Public Education in the United States: A Study and Interpretation of American Educational History: An Introductory Textbook Dealing with the Larger Problems of Present-Day Education in the Light of Their Historical Development*, New York, NY: Houghton Mifflin Co.

Doering, D.R. (1998), *Interdistrict School Choice in Georgia: Issues of Equity*, FRP Report 6, Atlanta, GA: Fiscal Research Program, Georgia State University.

Duncombe, W.D., J. Ruggiero and J.M. Yinger (1996), 'Alternative approaches to measuring the cost of education', in H.F. Ladd (ed.), *Holding Schools Accountable*, Washington, DC: The Brookings Institution, pp. 327–56.

Duncombe, W.D. and J.M. Yinger (1999), 'Performance standards and educational cost indexes: You can't have one without the other', in H.F. Ladd, R. Chalk and J.S. Hansen (eds), *Equity and Adequacy in Education Finance: Issues and Perspectives*, Washington, DC: National Academy Press, pp. 260–97.

Engle, S. and B. Scafidi (1999), *Is It Better for Michael and Maya? Contracting for the Management of Public Schools*, Atlanta, GA: Research Atlanta.

Evans, W.N., S. Murray and R.M. Schwab (1997), 'Schoolhouses, courthouses, and statehouses after Serrano', *Journal of Policy Analysis and Management*, 16(1): 10–31.

Evans, W.N., S. Murray and R.M. Schwab (1999), 'The impact of court mandated school finance reform', in H.F. Ladd, R. Chalk and J.S. Hansen (eds), *Equity and Adequacy in Education Finance*, Washington, DC: National Academy Press, pp. 72–98.

Firestone, W.A., M.E. Goertz, B. Nagle and M.F. Smelkinson (1994), 'Where did the $800 million go? The first years of New Jersey's Quality Education Act', *Educational Evaluation and Policy Analysis*, 16(4): 359–74.

Friedman, M. (1962), *Capitalism and Freedom*, Chicago, IL: University of Chicago Press.

Goldhaber, D.D. (2001), 'The interface between public and private schooling: marker pressure and the impact on student performance', in D.H. Monk, H.J. Walberg and M.C. Wang (eds), *Improving Educational Productivity*, Greenwich, CN: Information Age Publishing, pp. 47–76.

Goldhaber, D.D., D.J. Brewer, E.R. Eide and D.I. Rees (1999), 'Testing for sample selection in the Milwaukee school choice experiment', *Economics of Education Review*, 18: 259–67.

Greene, J.P., W.G. Howell and P.E. Peterson (1997), *An Evaluation of the Cleveland Scholarship Program*, Cambridge, MA: Harvard Program on Educational Policy and Governance.

Greene, J.P., W.G. Howell and P.E. Peterson (1998), 'Lessons from the Cleveland scholarship program', in P.E Peterson and B.C. Hasell (eds), *Learning From School Choice*, Washington, DC: Brooking Institution Press, pp. 357–94.

Greene, J.P., P.E. Peterson and J. Du (1998), 'School choice in Milwaukee: A randomized experiment', in P.E Peterson and B.C. Hasell (eds), *Learning From School Choice*, Washington, DC: Brooking Institution Press, pp. 335–56.

Guthrie, J.W. (1997), 'Reinventing education finance: Alternatives for allocating resources to individual schools', in W.J. Fowler (ed.), *Selected Papers in School Finance, 1996*, Washington, DC: US Department of Education, National Center for Education Statistics, pp. 89–107.

Guthrie, J.W., G.C. Hayward, J.R. Smith, R. Rothstein, R.W. Bennett, J.E. Koppich, E. Bowman, L. DeLapp, B. Brandes and S. Clark (1997), *A Proposed Cost-Based Block Grant Model for Wyoming School Finance*, Sacramento, CA: Management Analysis and Planning Associates.

Hanushek, E.A. (1994), *Making Schools Work: Improving Performance and Controlling Costs*, Washington, DC: The Brookings Institution.

Hanushek, E.A. (1997), 'Assessing the effects of school resources on student performance: An update', *Educational Evaluation and Policy Analysis*, 19(2): 141–64.

Hentschke, G.C. (1988), 'Budgetary theory and reality: a microview', in D.H. Monk and J. Underwood (eds), *Microlevel School Finance: Issues and Implications for Policy*, New York, NY: Ballinger, pp. 311–36.

Hess, G.A., Jr. (1995), *Restructuring Urban Schools: A Chicago Perspective*, New York, NY: Teachers College Press.

Hill, P.W. (1997), 'Building equity and effectiveness into school-based funding models: An Australian case study', in W.J. Fowler (ed.), *Developments in School Finance, 1996*, Washington, DC: US Department of Education, National Center for Education Statistics, pp. 139–57.

Hoxby, C.M. (1998), 'Analyzing school choice reforms that use America's traditional forms of parental choice', in P.E Peterson and B.C. Hasell (eds), *Learning From School Choice*, Washington, DC: Brooking Institution Press, pp. 133–56.

Jennings, W., E. Premack, A. Adelmann and D. Solomon (1999), *A Comparison of Charter School Legislation*, Report prepared for the US Department of Education by RPP International.

Johns, R.L., E.L. Morphet and K. Alexander (1983), *The Economics and Financing of Education*, Englewood Cliffs, NJ: Prentice Hall.

Ladd, H.F. and E. Harris (1995), 'Statewide taxation of nonresidential property for education', *Journal of Education Finance*, Summer: 103–22.

Levin, H.M. (1998), 'Educational vouchers: effectiveness, choice and costs', *Journal of Policy Analysis and Management*, 17: 373–92.

Marsh, D. and J. Sevilla (1992), 'Financing Middle School Reform: Linking Costs and Education Goals', in A.R. Odden (ed.), *Rethinking School Finance: An Agenda for the 1990s*, San Francisco, CA: Josey Bass Inc., pp. 97–127.

Miles, K.H. (1995), 'Freeing resources for improving schools: A case study of teacher allocation in Boston public schools', *Educational Evaluation and Policy Analysis*, 17(4): 476–93.

Mort, P.R., W.C. Reusser and J.W. Polley (1960), *Public School Finance: Its Background, Structure and Operation*, New York, NY: McGraw-Hill.

Nelson, B.R., P. Berman, J. Ericson, N. Kamprath, R. Perry, D. Silverman and D. Solomon (2000), *The State of Charter Schools 2000: Fourth Year Report*, Washington, DC: US Department of Education.

Odden, A. (1997), *The Finance Side of Implementing New American Schools*, Paper prepared for the New American Schools, Alexandria, VA.

Odden, A., and C. Busch (1998), *Financing School for High Performance*, San Francisco, CA: Josey Bass Inc.

Odden, A. and W.H. Clune (1998), 'School finance systems: Aging structures in need of renovation', *Educational Evaluation and Policy Analysis*, 20: 157–78.

Odden, A.R., and L.O. Picus (2000), *School Finance: A Policy Perspective*, 2nd edn, New York, NY: McGraw-Hill.

Peterson, P.E. (1998), 'School choice: A report card', in P.E Peterson and B.C. Hasell (eds), *Learning From School Choice*, Washington, DC: Brooking Institution Press, pp. 3–32.

Picus, L.O. (1992), 'Using Incentives to Promote School Improvement', in A.R. Odden (ed.), *Rethinking School Finance: An Agenda for the 1990s*, San Francisco, CA: Josey Bass Inc., pp. 166–200.

Picus, L.O. (1994a), 'Estimating the determinants of pupil/teacher ratios: Evidence from the schools and staffing survey', *Educational Considerations*, 21(2): 44–52.

Picus, L.O. (1994b), 'Achieving program equity: Are markets the answer?', *Educational Policy*, 8(4): 568–81.

Picus, L.O. (1994c), 'The local impact of school finance reform in four Texas school districts', *Educational Evaluation and Policy Analysis*, 16(4): 391–404.

Picus, L.O. (1997a), 'Does money matter in education? A policymaker's guide', in W. Fowler (ed.), *Selected Papers in School Finance, 1995*, Washington, DC: National Center for Education Statistics, pp. 15–36.

Picus, L.O. (1997b), 'Assigning responsibilities: Where do the dollars go?', *School Business Affairs*, 63(11): 8–15.

Picus, L.O. (1998), 'Rethinking equity: There are alternatives', *School Business Affairs*, 64(4): 3–8.

Picus, L.O. and M. Fazal (1996), 'Why do we need to know what money buys? Research on resource allocation patterns in elementary and secondary schools', in *Where Does the Money Go?: Resource Allocation in Elementary and Secondary Schools* (1995 Yearbook of the American Education Finance Association), Newbury Park, CA: Corwin Press, pp. 1–19.

Reschovsky, A. and J. Imazeki (1998), 'The development of school finance formulas to guarantee the provision of adequate education to low-income students', in W.J. Fowler (ed.), *Developments in School Finance 1997*, Washington, DC: National Center for Education Statistics, pp. 98–212.

Rouse, C.E. (1997), 'Lessons from the Milwaukee parental choice program', *Policy Options*, 18: 43–6.

Rubenstein, R. (1998), 'Resource equity in the Chicago public schools: A school-level approach', *Journal of Education Finance*, 23: 468–89.

Stiefel, L., R. Rubenstein and R. Berne (1998), 'Intra-district equity in four large cities: Methods, data and results', *Journal of Education Finance*, 23: 447–67.

Tiebout, C.M. (1956), 'A pure theory of local expenditures', *Journal of Political Economy*, 54: 416–24.

Underwood, J. (1995), 'School finance adequacy as vertical equity', *University of Michigan Journal of Law Reform*, 28(3): 493–519.

US Department of Education, National Center for Education Statistics (2001), *Digest of Education Statistics, 2001*, NCES 1999-036, Washington, DC: Government Printing Office.

Verstegen, D.A. (1998), 'Judicial analysis during the new wave of school finance litigation: The new adequacy in education', *Journal of Education Finance*, 24(1): 51–68.

Wassmer, R.W. and R.C. Fisher (1996), 'An evaluation of the recent move to centralize the finance of public schools in Michigan', *Public Budgeting and Finance*,16: 90–112.

Witte, J.F., T.D. Sterr and C.A. Thorn (1995), *Fifth Year Report: Milwaukee Parental Choice Program*, Madison, WI: La Follette Institute of Public Affairs.

Wohlstetter, P. and S.A. Mohrman (1996), *Assessment of School-Based Management*, Washington, DC: Office of Educational Research and Improvement, US Department of Education.

Ziebarth, T. (2000), '2000 voucher ballot initiatives,' *ECS State Notes*, Denver, CO: Education Commission of the States.

5. Popular processes and the transformation of state and local government finance*

Daniel R. Mullins

INTRODUCTION

The final decades of the 20th century witnessed a significant fiscal reshaping of the state and local public sectors across the United States. Not since the structural and political adjustment in cities in the mid 19th century and the transformation of public responsibilities at the turn of the past century has so much fiscal restructuring taken place in so short a period. This change has, however, been more subtle. It is less visible than the growth of service responsibility and formal restructuring of political/representational systems or the emergence of home rule. This subtly belies its importance in shaping the ability of the sector to respond to and meet the varied needs of local populations. It may also reflect the most significant erosion of local autonomy since the establishment of home rule.

Changes over the past three decades have emerged from a varied set of pressures, but have largely been driven by external forces and a heightened perception of spatial competition. Much of the pressure reshaping the local public fisc has been related to the perceived need to respond to a new level of mobility of both residents and business investment. States and cities have increasingly attempted to alter their revenue systems, expenditure mixes and service delivery vehicles in a manner intended to soften the potential impact on asset rich mobile populations and economic bases. They have also been subject to the imposition of constraints on revenues and expenditures via both local political processes and through statewide initiatives and referenda.

While the need for responsiveness to mobile populations and investment is heavily influenced by the structure of local governance within urban areas, much of this pressure is a function of implications of broader scale economic change for spatial competition. Constraints imposed by the initiatives and referenda process, on the other hand, represent deliberate action taken to restrain the ability of both state and local governments. This chapter focuses on constraints, wrought through political/institutional mechanisms more than economic processes, which have and will serve to reshape state and local fiscal structures.

These mechanisms have been summarized as elements of a modern period 'tax and expenditure limitations movement' directed at limiting the ability of state and local governments to generate revenue or make expenditures. While often considered a rather recent phenomenon, in many cases the existence of these local limitations can be traced back to the 19th century and earlier. The more recent 'taxpayer's revolt' has as often as not reflected a reinforcement of existing limitations rather than the addition of new limitations. The most recent focus of this 'movement' has been state government, with 31 states functioning under measures to limit state taxes and/or expenditures. The most common of these are limitations on total legislative appropriations, with limitations on total or tax revenue not far behind.

State limitations are important to the degree to which they actually are binding upon state governments. This is influenced by the level at which they are set and the difficulty of suspending them. These state limitations often tie the growth in state revenues and appropriations to a rate less than or equal to the growth in state personal income, with a variety of override provisions. While initially perceived to be relatively nonconstraining, the severity of state limitations more recently imposed has increased.

At the local level, the bulk of the limitations initiatives were initially directed at the property tax; however their scope has substantially widened over the past decade. Some form of general local revenue or expenditure limitations exists in 46 states; however, their nature and the degree of actual constraint imposed on the ability of local governments to raise revenue and make expenditures is broad and varied. Previous research has shown that these limitations have substantially altered the structure of local finance, and have created shifts in the distribution of service responsibilities between units of government and are associated with poorer educational service outcomes.

Limitations on local property taxes and general expenditures have brought a shift toward nontax sources of revenues (fees and charges, state transfers and debt) for financing local public services; have created a vertical shift of power and responsibility to the state (through, in addition to an increased reliance on state revenue sources, a state assumption of service responsibilities); have produced horizontal shifts of responsibility for local government functions (through the increased role of special service and finance districts); are associated with reduced educational inputs and teacher qualifications and poorer educational performance; and result in poorer quality municipal services (Mullins and Joyce, 1996; Danziger, 1980; Joyce and Mullins, 1991; Doyle, 1994; Downes et al., 1998; Downes and Figlio, 1999; Figlio and Reuben, 2001).[1] Most recent evidence also suggests local limitations have had differential effects across governments within states, with the most significant implications for central cities and less prosperous communities. The overall effect may be to significantly alter the relationship between local governments and local populations and significantly affect the capacity to provide for public needs and wants. The effects vary by type of government and service subgroups, and by the demographics of resident populations (Mullins, 2001).

Expenditure and revenue authority/responsibility has shifted away from local governments in general (and local general purpose governments in particular), altering access and voice within a framework of constraint. The result may entail serious implications for local autonomy and the ability of communities to match their service/tax packages to the preferences of their residents, seriously reducing the efficiency of resource allocation within the sector.

THE LOCAL AUTONOMY MASQUERADE

Proposals to limit the revenue or expenditure authority of 'local' government have often masqueraded within the costume of 'grass roots initiative' and 'public choice'. However, the impetus for these initiatives appears neither local nor grass roots. They are championed at the state level (by state level constituencies and often the result of the initiative of a small group of 'reformers'), resulting in statutory or constitutional provisions of broad scope and wide applicability across virtually all local jurisdictions or classes of jurisdictions within a state.[2] By definition, they tend to provide for little in the way of local discretion in the application of their provisions to individual jurisdictions, and thus seriously limit local choice.[3] Such a result is diametrically opposed to local autonomy, as the universal and arbitrary imposition of constraints across local jurisdictions limits the ability of local populations to realize local community and public service goals.

In spite of their broad bush nature, the effects of these limitations across jurisdiction are nonuniform. They impose differential welfare losses across classes of communities depending on how binding a particular provision is in an individual setting. It is precisely the fact that the effects of limitations are likely to be differentially felt by governments in different phases of growth and maturity (and with populations with different preferences and capacities for the outputs from the public sector) that makes these effects simultaneously so potentially arbitrary and biased. Further, the imposition of fiscal uniformity across areas with diverse preference and population bases is a prescription for inefficiency and dissatisfaction.[4] Because of desires to avoid these outcomes, the introduction of a policy wedge between public service

demand and resource access is also a prescription for adaptation and muta-
tion by/of the state and local public sector to avoid the welfare losses implied
by the existence of arbitrary constraints. These adaptations provide only
second best solutions and create their own set of distortions. The likely
results are: (1) a Darwinian survival of the fittest at the local level, where
localities possessing the greatest resource slack and resource options prove
the most adaptable; (2) the emergence of ever greater layers of complexity
between citizens of states and localities and the governance structures intended to service their needs and preferences (see Sheffrin, 1998); and (3) a
new set of barriers to the maintenance of adequate public service levels in
areas of greatest need.

TAKING STOCK OF THE LOCAL LIMITATIONS INVENTORY

The only comprehensive inventory of the provisions of statewide limitations
on local fiscal autonomy identifies their existence in one form or another in
46 states (see Table 5.1 at the end of the chapter). Only Connecticut, Maine,
New Hampshire and Vermont have none;[5] five additional states have adopted
only limited full disclosure requirements since 1970 (see Mullins and Cox,
1995). To be sure, several of these limitations have existed for as long as a
century; however, most emerged as a function of the more modern period of
'tax revolt' beginning during the 1970s. Half of all local limitations (48 per
cent) were initially adopted after 1977 and more than a quarter (27 per cent)
since 1990. While often associated with California's Proposition 13 in 1978,
17 states adopted some form of local limitation between 1970 and 1976. A
more accurate beginning point would be the 1970 imposition of a statutory
property tax revenue limit (exceedable through local referenda) on counties
and municipalities in Kansas, or Alabama's 1972 adoption of a constitutional
amendment limiting overall property tax rates.

Limitations take seven basic forms: (1) overall property tax rate limits
applying to all local governments; (2) specific property tax rate limits applying to specific types of local government (municipalities, counties, school
districts and special districts) or specific functions; (3) property tax levy
(revenue) limits; (4) general revenue or (5) general expenditure increase
limits; (6) limits on assessment (base) increases; and (7) full disclosure (truth
in taxation) requirements. Box 5.1 describes each of these forms of limitation. Limitations enacted across states vary dramatically in the severity of the
constraint imposed. Within a given state, limitations may prove to be seriously binding constraints on some local governments but not others.

BOX 5.1   TYPES AND CLASSIFICATION OF TAX
AND EXPENDITURE LIMITATIONS

Overall property tax rate limitations: Limits on property tax rates are the most common form of TEL. If the limit is on overall property tax rates, a rate ceiling is set that cannot be exceeded without a vote of the electorate, and applies to the aggregate tax rate of all local government.

> **Nonbinding:** easily circumvented through alterations in assessment practices.
> **Potentially binding:** if coupled with a limit on assessment increases.

Specific property tax rate limit: Same as for overall property tax rate limits except it applies to specific types of local jurisdictions (for example, school districts or counties) or narrowly defined service areas.

> **Nonbinding:** can be circumvented through alterations in assessment practices or, in the case of specific services, through inter-fund transfers (fungibility).
> **Potentially binding:** if coupled with a limit on assessment increases.

Property tax levy limit: This type of limitation constrains the total amount of revenue that can be raised from the property tax, independent of the property tax rate. It is often enacted as an allowable annual percentage increase in the levy.

> **Potentially binding:** the fixed nature of the revenue ceiling makes this, ceteris paribus, a more formidable constraint, however, it can be limited through a diversification of revenue sources (which is its underlying intent).

General revenue or general expenditure Increases: In the case of revenue limits, these cap the amount of revenue that can be collected, while expenditure limits attempt to constrain spending during the fiscal year. These are often indexed to the rate of inflation.

Potentially binding: the fixed nature of the revenue or expenditure ceiling makes this, ceteris paribus, a more formidable constraint.

Limits on assessment increases: Since the property tax collected is a function of the assessed valuation of the property, and the tax rate, this type of limitation controls the ability of local governments to raise revenue by reassessment of property or through natural or administrative escalation of property values.

Nonbinding: the constraint is easily avoided through an increase in property tax rate.
Potentially binding: if coupled with an overall or specific property tax rate limit.

Full disclosure – Truth in taxation: These types of limitations generally require some type of public discussion and specific legislative vote prior to the enactment of tax rate or levy increases.

Nonbinding: requires only a formal vote (generally a simple majority) of the local legislative body to increase the tax rate or levy.

Source: Joyce and Mullins (1991).

Twelve states impose overall property tax rate limits; 33 states limit specific local governments (28 limit counties, 31 municipalities, 26 school districts, and 23 limit all three types of local governments); 26 states currently limit local tax levies[6] (23 limit counties, 23 limit municipalities, 14 limit school districts and 14 limit all three); ten states currently limit the growth in assessments;[7] two states limit general revenue increases;[8] eight limit expenditure growth, and a least 22 have some form of full disclosure requirement. Table 5.2 provides a summary of all existing local limitations.[9] Some 37 states have a combination of limitations. Of these Arizona, California, Colorado, New Mexico, Oregon and Washington have among the most restrictive.[10]

The initiatives and referenda have continued as the dominant vehicle for establishing local tax and expenditure limitations. More than 150 measures were brought to vote during the 1990s alone (Brunori, 1999). Since 1995, new and strengthened limitations have been enacted in several states. For example, in:

California, Article XIII of the state constitution was amended via Proposition 218: 'Right to Vote on Taxes Act'. Effective 1 July 1997, Proposition 218 requires majority voter approval for general taxes and a super majority (2/3) for special taxes, and prohibits the use of fee and charge revenue for general services. All property-related fee and charge increases are subject to majority approval of property owners or two-thirds voter approval (Doerr, 1996).

Oklahoma, new assessment limits took effect 1 January 1997, limiting residential assessment increases to five per cent per year, until the property is sold, changed or improved. This was coupled with a freeze on the valuation of homesteads belonging to people over the age of 65 with household income of $25 000 or less (Hamilton, 1996).

Oregon, a property tax revenue limit (Measure 47) approved by referendum in November of 1996 was superseded through referendum (Measure 50) in March of 1997. It provides for a revised property tax assessment limit coupled with a levy-based rate freeze. Measure 50 rolled back assessments to 1996 levels less ten per cent and capped annual growth to three per cent. It also established rates at a level producing a 17 per cent reduction over that which would have occurred under Measure 47. New or additional taxes are to be approved at election with a minimum of 50 per cent turnout and new fees also require voter approval (Mayer, 1997).

New Mexico, legislation was enacted (during February 2000) to stiffen the state's limit on assessment increases beginning in 2001. Yearly residential assessment increases are limited to three per cent, with increases of five per cent in counties with existing assessment sales rations of less than 85 per cent (Massey, 2000).

Washington, Initiative 695 requiring voter approval of any increase in taxes, or licenses by state or local governments was adopted in 1999 (Burrows, 2000c). Before it could be implemented, the requirement for voter approval was ruled unconstitutional by the Washington Superior Court, 14 March 2000 (Alsdorj, 2000), a verdict ultimately concurred with by the State Supreme Court 26 October (Burrows, 2000b). A substitute provision, Initiative 722, was subsequently approved by voters in November 2000. It voids all taxes enacted without voter approval between certification of I-695 (2 July 1999) and its intended effective date (1 January, 2000). It also limits property tax revenue increases to two per cent per year or the rate of inflation, which ever is less with similar limits on assessment increases (Brunori, 2000). In December, implementation of 772 was also blocked by the Washington Superior Court (Burrows, 2000a). In early June, the Washington Supreme Court heard arguments to restore implementation (Burrows, 2001a). A new fall back petition (Initiative 747) to limit annual property tax revenue increases was approved for

Table 5.2   Summary of state imposed limitations on local governments – number of states by characteristic

Type of limitation	Occurrence	Scope/classification	Growth provisions	Exclusions	Override provisions
Overall property tax rate limits	Prior to 1978: 8 1978 or after: 4 (Adopted or mod. 1990+: 1)	Multiple classifications: 11 Residential only: 1	Not applicable	Debt service: 9 Special/excess levies: 6 Home rule: 2 Special dst: 1	Referenda: Simple majority: 5 Super majority: 1 Legislative: 1 Temporary: 2
Specific property tax rate limits	Prior to 1978: 28 1978 or after: 5 (Adopted or mod. 1990+: 8)	Counties: 28 Municipalities: 31 School dst.: 26 All: 23	Not applicable	Debt service: 23 Special levies: 19 Home rule: 3	Referenda: Simple majority: 20 Super majority: 3 Legislative: 1
Property tax levy limits	Prior to 1978: 11 1978 or after: 17 (Adopted or mod. 1990+: 6)	Counties: 23 Municipalities: 23 School dst.: 14 All: 14	Fixed percent: 15 Base growth: 3 Inflation: 4 Fixed $ amount: 2 Limited to assessment rollback: 7	Debt service: 12 Annex., improvements, construction: 9 Capital improvements: 2 Contracts: 2 Emergencies: 2 Mandates: 1 Home rule: 1	Referenda: Simple majority: 12 Super majority: 2 State board: 1 Court appeal: 1
General revenue limits	Prior to 1978: 1 1978 or after: 3 (Adopted or mod. 1990+: 2)	Counties: 3 Municipalities: 3 School dst.: 2 All: 1	Fixed percent/$: 2 Base growth: 1 Inflation/CPI: 2 No new tax or rate increase: 1	Debt service: 1 Special assessments: 1 Court judgments: 1	Referenda: Simple majority: 2

General expenditure limits	Prior to 1978: 6 1978 or after: 2 (Adopted or mod. 1990+: 3)	Counties: 4 Municipalities: 5 School dst.: 8 All: 4	Fixed per cent: 3 Inflation/CPI: 3 Base growth: 2 Income: 2 Pupils: 3	Debt service: 2 Mandates: 2 Emergencies: 2 Special dst.: 2 Special education: 2 Contracts: 2	Referenda: Simple majority: 6 Legislative: Simple majority: 1 Super majority: 1 State board: 1
Property assessment limits	Prior to 1978: 1 1978 or after: 11 (Adopted or mod. 1990+: 7)	Base: Individual parcel: 9 Aggregate: 2 Residential only: 3	Fixed per cent: 9 (% range: 2–10, ave. 4.9) Fixed per cent or CPI: 1	Reassessment on sale: 4 Improvements/new construction: 9	Referenda: Simple majority: 1
Full disclosure limits	Prior to 1978: 7 1978 or after: 15 (Adopted or mod. 1990+: 5)	Counties: 21 Municipalities: 19 School dst.: 14 All: 14 Limited to reassessment: 2	Not applicable	Debt service: 2 New construction/additions: 2 Annexation: 1 Within specified per cent: 4	Not applicable

Source: Based on and updated from Mullins and Cox (1995).

103

Table 5.3   Regional distribution of local government tax and expenditure limitations (number/per cent of states with limitation)

Type of limitation	Northeast		Midwest		South		West		Total	
	#	%	#	%	#	%	#	%	#	%
Overall property tax rate limit	0	0	2	17	3	19	7	54	12	24
Specific property tax rate limit	3	33	10	83	9	56	11	85	33	66
Property tax revenue limit	4	44	8	67	6	38	10	77	28	56
Assessment increase limit	1	11	2	17	4	25	5	38	12	24
General revenue limit	0	0	2	17	0	0	2	15	4	8
General expenditure limit	1	11	4	33	0	0	3	23	8	16
Full disclosure	1	11	5	42	10	63	6	46	22	44
Total/average per state	10	1.11	33	2.75	32	2	44	3.38	119	2.38
Total w/o full disclosure/average state	9	1	28	2.33	22	1.38	38	2.92	97	1.94

Source: Author's update and compilation based on Mullins and Cox (1995).

signature gathering in February (Burrows, 2001b, 2001c) and adopted at the polls during November 2001. It limits property tax revenue growth to one per cent per year unless approved by voters.

Local limitations have been widely adopted. In total, at least one of the seven categories of limitations has been imposed on local governments 119 times across the 50 states, with each state employing on average more than two categories of limitations. Some 57 of these have been adopted since 1978. Limitations are least prevalent in the Northeast, where they average approximately one per state. Western states have been most active in imposing local tax and expenditure limitations, accounting for nearly 40 per cent of the total and averaging more than three different types of limitations per state (see Table 5.3). States in the Midwestern region are second most active.

Limitations in Western states also tend to be of more recent origin and more stringent in their effects on local government's ability to exercise revenue and expenditure autonomy. This additional stringency occurs through broader application to local government forms (that is, counties, municipalities and school districts), more restrictive ceilings and override provisions on individual limitations and due to the simultaneous imposition of multiple forms of limitations. Some 85 per cent of Western states have specific property tax rate limits, 77 per cent have property tax revenue limits, 54 per cent have overall property tax rate limits, and 38 per cent have assessment increase limits. Percentages for the Midwest are 83 per cent, 67 per cent, 17 per cent and 17 per cent, respectively. Further, Western states account for two of the four local general revenue limits (with the Midwest accounting for the remainder) and three of the eight general expenditure limits (with the Midwest accounting for four).

TAKING STOCK OF THE STATE LIMITATIONS INVENTORY

The newest entrants into the limitation 'movement' have been focused on the state level. These state limitations limit revenues or expenditures and range from rather comprehensive limitations on revenue or expenditure growth to inconsequential anti-deficiency requirements or prohibitions on 'excess' revenue.[11] Some 53 limitations (27 revenue limits and 26 expenditure limits) have been adopted in 31 states, with 25 states providing for legislative override most often with a minimum of a three-fifths majority vote (see Table 5.4 at the end of the chapter). Approximately one half (26) of these limitations have been enacted in 20 different states since 1990, including 59 per cent of revenue limits and 39 per cent of expenditure limits. Some 17 of the revenue limitations and 13 of the expenditure limitations were adopted after 1985. Only two states had such limitations prior to 1970 and 20 enacted their first or a new form of limit since 1985, with nine since 1995. Some 24 states have adopted limits on expenditures and 18 have limited revenues, with 16 states having two or more and 11 limiting both revenues and expenditures. Some 22 of the 27 limits on revenue directly limit total taxes or income taxes, with 18 requiring (or allowing) a super majority legislative vote to override the limitation. Some 22 of the expenditure limitations limit general fund expenditures or appropriations, with at least 16 providing for some form of legislative override. Revenue and expenditure limits are often tied (in at least 26 cases) to growth in population, income, prices, economy or wages.

State limitations are of substantial local significance. Increased state aid to localities, while possibly undermining local autonomy, has provided an important offset to some of the local fiscal pressure created by local limitations. Increasing stringency of state limitations will likely constrain the availability of this revenue option. While previous research has shown state limitations to be rather inconsequential in their effect (Mullins and Joyce, 1996) more recent assessments have indicated that the effect of their constraint is growing and is related to the mechanism of adoption. Constitutional amendments enacted through citizen initiative appear to be the most constraining and least likely to provide escape clauses (New, 2001).

Two thirds (36) of all state limitations adopted in 24 different states are in the form of constitutional amendments. The method of adoption varies, however, the citizen initiative processes is the most common (20), followed by legislative adoption (15) and referendum (15). In 13 states, more than one method of adoption has been used. Adoption methods used by individual states are quite evenly distributed (at 16 using legislative, 15 initiative and 13 referenda); however, the initiative is frequently used repetitively. In the 13 states that have used more than one adoption method, the most recent adoption method employed has been the initiative 76 per cent of the time. Since 1990, the initiative has accounted for half of all limitations adopted and more than 60 per cent excluding legislative modifications to preexisting limits. This is particularly significant given that the initiative process is available in only 26 states and consequential given the tendency of initiative-based constraints to be more formidable.[12] Initiatives have tended to follow legislatively proposed and enacted limitations, due to a popular dissatisfaction with their lack of stringency.

Geographically, state limitations are least prevalent in the Northeast and Midwest census regions, where approximately 43 per cent of the states in each of these regions have adopted limitations (Table 5.5). Between these two regions, five states limit revenues (24 per cent) and five limit expenditures. Only Delaware has both types. Limitations are much more prevalent in

Table 5.5   Distribution of state revenue and expenditure limitations across regions

Northeast states	Midwest states
w/state limitation: 4 (44%)	*w/state limitation: 5 (42%)*
w/revenue limit: 2 (22%)	w/revenue limit: 3 (25%)
w/expenditure limit: 3 (33%)	w/expenditure limit: 2 (17%)
(States w/both: DE)	(States w/both: none)
Southern states	Western states
w/state limitation: 11 (69%)	*w/state limitation: 10 (77%)*
w/revenue limit: 6 (38%)	w/revenue limit: 7 (54%)
w/expenditure limit: 8 (52%)	w/expenditure limit: 10 (77%)
(States w/both: LA, MS, OK)	(States w/both: AZ, CA, CO, MT, NV, OR, WA)

Source: Author's compilation.

the South and West. Some 69 per cent of Southern states have enacted state limitations as have 77 per cent of Western states. Six southern states have revenue limitations (38 per cent) and eight limit state expenditures (50 per cent). Louisiana, Missouri and Oklahoma have imposed both types. Of the ten Western states with limitations, all have adopted them for expenditures (77 per cent of all Western states) and seven (54 per cent) have revenue limits. This obviously translates into seven Western states that have imposed both forms of limitations: these are Arizona, California, Colorado, Montana, Nevada, Oregon and Washington. They include the states adopting the most constraining forms of limitations, with revenue limits having been adopted much more recently, and include those also enacting the most onerous local limitations. Several states (Michigan, California, Missouri, Colorado and Oregon) require a refund of taxes collected above limitations.

POLITICAL SUPPORT

Two 'policy environments' have existed for the adoption of limitations: (1) those resulting from the 'presumably more deliberative actions of governors and legislatures' and (2) those 'sparked by the rhetoric of populist leaders and organizations' (Sokolow, 2000: 94). Limitations in states such as California, Michigan, Massachusetts, Colorado, Oregon and Missouri have been associated predominantly with single individuals or groups. The severest of limitations have been adopted via the initiative process, available in 26 states, often after the perception of inaction at the state legislative level. Between 1978 and 1990, 58 such tax and expenditure limitations were voted on and more than 40 per cent passed (Alm and Skidmore, 1999). Limitations are most severe in the Western states, where 11 of 13 states have the initiative and 12 have adopted some form of limitation since 1970 (Sokolow, 2000). In the ten Western states with both the initiative and tax and expenditure limitations, between 1970 and 1996, a total of 467 initiatives were voted on (36 dealing with property taxes and 104 with other state and local revenue restrictions). This does not mean that the initiative is directly responsible, however, as in 40 per cent of these states, the limitations were legislatively adopted. The simple existence of the initiative may create substantial motivation for legislative action, if for no other reason than to avoid the imposition of more severe initiative derived limitations. Initiative limitations have often come as the result of several failed attempts. Oregon's Measure 5 was adopted after ten failures, three failed attempts led to Proposition 13, and Proposition 2½ was adopted after 15 failed attempts at legislative local tax and spending limitations (Sokolow, 2000; Wallin, 2001).

Numerous less than satisfying explanations have been offered for the popularity of tax and expenditure limitations. Several suggest that government has reached a size inconsistent with the preferences of the voters, and that the intended effect was an adjustment downward in scale.[13] One view suggests that government has grown in large part because of the activity of self-interested bureaucrats, who use an asymmetrical information advantage to gain support from their legislative sponsors, who are either acquiescent or in collusion with them (Niskanen, 1971; Brennan and Buchanan, 1979). Regardless of the specific reasons for the growth of government, limitation movements have been linked to efforts to constrain it. However, support for limitations occurs relatively independently of any public desire for government services. In fact, numerous surveys in states where tax and expenditure limitations have been passed suggest that citizens were satisfied with the level of public services and often desired more, but they simply wanted to avoid the unpleasantness of paying for them (Brazer, 1981).

Why Voters Support the Adoption of Limitations

Most significant limitations have been adopted statewide, rather than by the residents of individual local governments. Assessments of general voter support for these limitations suggests a desire for lower taxes and more efficiency in government, rather than any desire for reduced public services. Voters were, in essence, attempting to lower the price of the existing service package. Others have found that voters support tax and expenditure limitations because of self-interest, with those whose tax burdens would be most clearly affected being most supportive (Ladd and Wilson, 1981, 1982, 1983; Stein et al., 1983; Courant et al., 1985; Temple, 1996; Cutler et al., 1997; Bradbury et al., 1998; Alm and Skidmore, 1999).[14] The more recent research in this area finds that the passage of limitations is more related to economic growth. Growth in property taxes and local government's share of the state and local public sector were found to be more important than demographic or political factors (Alm and Skidmore, 1999). Still no general desire to limit or alter public services appears active.

Support for limiting local governments has often been couched in terms of excessive and costly local expenditure packages. However, at the time of adoption, growth at the local level was significantly below that of the national and state governments. The 1978 two to one adoption of California's Proposition 13 was linked to growth in the assessed value of property (Danziger, 1980); an increase in the relative residential portion of the tax burden (Oates, 1981; Chernick and Reschovsky, 1982) and to the accountability problems created by the complexity and fragmentation of government (Danziger, 1980). Assessments of voter perceptions revealed a belief that government was inefficient and that limitations could be adopted to force greater efficiency without affecting service levels. Some 38 per cent of California voters felt that state and local governments could absorb a 40 per cent budget reduction without affecting services (Citrin, 1979). Further, California voters tended to favor higher service levels.

Property taxes have been motivating factors for a number of states. Support for limitations in general have been linked to an overall displeasure with taxes,[15] general frustration and objections to particular types of spending (Danziger and Ring, 1982). Voters seem to believe that their own taxes would be reduced without affecting services received (Sears and Citrin, 1982; Courant et al., 1985). In Michigan, voters surveyed after narrow passage (with 52 per cent of the vote) of the Headlee Amendment in 1978 voiced a general satisfaction with service levels, with the exception of welfare spending, and a desire for service increases (Courant et al., 1985). Massachusetts voter surveys regarding the 1980 adoption of Proposition 2½ revealed similar desires for greater efficiency and a belief that limitations, while potentially reducing local services, would have little effect on basic services. Supporters expected reductions in only welfare services, after school programs, adult education and local transportation. They expected cuts in service not directly affecting them and greater state aid to offset losses (Ladd and Wilson, 1981).

Later passages of tax and expenditure limitations reveal similar public perspectives. In 1992, Colorado voters approved (53.6 to 46.4) one of the severest restriction on state and local fiscal autonomy. With already among the lowest aggregate state[16] and local tax liabilities in the nation and no evidence of a desire for reduced service levels, the 'Taxpayer Bill of Rights'

(TABOR) was adopted. It incorporated into the state constitution an annual cap on the growth of state and individual local government total revenue (and by implication, spending) to the rate of inflation plus a growth factor.[17] 'Excess revenue' can only be retained and spent if approved by a majority vote of the electorate. Tax rate increases, new taxes and reinstatement of expiring taxes (and any change in tax policy producing a revenue increase) must also be approved by voters. Increases in fees and charges are allowable, but are credited against the overall growth limit (James, 2001). TABOR was largely the initiative of a transplanted participant in the California campaign (Douglas Bruce) and passed after three failed attempts. While state and local jurisdictions have frequently been able to 'de-Bruce' through electoral over-rides, TABOR remains quite popular; though a proposal (TABOR 205) reducing state and local taxes was defeated in 2000.

Based on the result of public opinion polls, dissatisfaction with the 'size and scope' of the state and local public sector has not been a primary motivation for the adoption of limitations. Much of the early support across several states was based on a desire to restructure the revenue system to reduce the role of property taxes along with perceptions of government waste (Oates, 1981). These desires may have been motivated by a combination of wishful thinking and a self-interested attempt to shift the burden of government finance (Citrin, 1979). It should also be noted that, during 1980, limitations modeled after Proposition 13 were defeated in five states: Arizona, Nevada, Oregon, South Dakota and Utah (Oates, 1981).

Local Political Economy, Principal-Agent Relationships and Limitation Passage

The probability of a limitations passage appears to be entirely unrelated to its specific features as a constraint. Likewise, political and demographic characteristics appear to have little effect (Alm and Skidmore, 1999). If voters (a) appear to be unaffected by the potential severity of the limitation in their calculus for adoption, are (b) not interested in seeing service reductions, and (c) are (in many cases) satisfied with existing services, what has accounted for their popularity? The median voter model suggests that passage of a statewide limitation applied uniformly to local governments would be ir-rational.[18] Even for limitations providing local voter approval for overrides or exceptions, the median voter for the TEL provisions would be the same as for other revenue and expenditure issues and would therefore be redundant.

Two sets of factors are often suggested as explanations for voter motivations, categorized as supply side and demand side issues (Temple, 1996; Alm and Skidmore, 1999). Demand factors include: (i) fiscal illusion on the part of voters (or Citrin's characterization of voters' 'something for nothing' desires); and (ii) intracommunity heterogeneity, asymmetric preference distributions and systematic differences in preference intensities. The former is a 'free lunch' motivation, the later is based on risk aversion created by the possibility of increased 'external costs' in local collective decisions leading to a desire to limit local choice. Supply side factors include: (i) the existence of public official monopoly power, agenda manipulation and log-rolling; (ii) similar principal-agent difficulties, information asymmetry and difficulties of observing actual service quality; (iii) excess interest group influence; and (iv) the absence of mechanisms to reveal and incorporate preference intensity. These could be expected to result in service levels in excess of the true preferences of the median voter. Demand side indicators that would be expected to affect the outcome would include income, population demographic characteristics, service cost, tax mix and resulting tax price, and altruism. Supply side indicators would include the level of redistributional expenditures, political leadership, and evidence of monopoly power (expenditure growth). The median voter's position should be based on 'net fiscal residual' and a limitation would only be approved if it is expected to result in an increase in this residual. Alm and Skidmore (1999) find that few of these indicators affect probability of a limitation's passage.

Figlio and O'Sullivan (2001), in their review of local public officials' response to the imposition of limitations, suggest that supply side factors may be at play, but that they may be checked by interjurisdictional competition. They find that local officials attempt to reduce direct service staffing levels (for police, fire and education) subsequent to the adoption of a limitation in order to foster support for overrides. The effect is greater in cities organized under the council-manager plan and is lessened by the existence of greater spatial competition for residency location. This, however, does not imply that they do so in a limitation's absence and the fact that such a relationship is found to exist suggests that they in fact do not maximize this opportunity under 'unlimited' circumstances.

Actual outcomes of local voter override referenda provide an opportunity to assess voter satisfaction with limitations and explicit local support for the constraints they imply. Massachusetts, where Proposition 2½ resulted in an average 25 per cent reduction of property taxes in 42 per cent of the state's communities (Cutler et al., 1999), has been the focus of several assessments. The Massachusetts state legislature has acted on several occasions to amend Proposition 2½ to provide for simple majority voting for overrides, rather than the super majority contained in the initially adopted constraint (Wallin, 2001). It also altered the classification structure and shifted property tax burdens away from residential property in 1989. After removal of the super majority requirement, override election success moved from 40 per cent in 1986 to 69 per cent in 1989 to 60 per cent in 1990 (Wallin, 2001). By 1990,

83 per cent of 245 towns (or 58 per cent of all towns in Massachusetts) holding override elections did so successfully on at least one occasion.

Cutler et al. (1999) have proposed four theories of voter sentiment as explanations of support for limitations and have tested these based on Massachusetts override votes. *Agency loss theory* suggests that, without limitations, local governments would undertake spending projects which are not valued by voters. Constraints limit this wasteful spending. *Regret theory* accepts the assumption of agency loss theory, but voters ultimately regret the severity of the constraint as it bites into desired spending. Summarized as 'mission accomplished theory', excessive waste is presumed to have been eliminated. *Personal finance theory* implies that government efficiency is assessed by individual voters based on the size of their tax burden. When that burden is judged to be too high, government is assumed to be inefficient. A limitation which reduces specific tax burdens is sought. *Demographic difference theory* suggests that voters perceive government waste to be spending on groups demographically different from themselves. Limitations are presumed to limit spending only to that preferred by the majority of voters.

Cutler, Elmendorf and Zeckhauser appear to find results supporting the agency loss, regret and personal finance theories. The fact that communities have spent up to the limit is assumed to be support for agency loss. Regret theory is supported by findings of a correlation between the level of support for passage of Proposition 2½ and the scale of the initial tax reductions required, followed by subsequently more successful override and exclusion elections. The personal finance theory is also supported by findings that communities with higher individual tax burdens voted more heavily in favor of the proposition and had fewer successful overrides and exclusions. However, use of property taxes up to the limit may only imply that property taxes are the first resort for (or preferred mechanism of) local finance. In and of itself, it indicates nothing about the actual desirability of spending projects to voters. Opinion polls have failed to demonstrate dissatisfaction.

Illinois has provided an additional opportunity to directly observe local populations' response to tax limitations. Cities below 25 000 population can vote to eliminate property tax restrictions by adopting home rule status. The choice to do so appears to be associated with the level of community heterogeneity. Heterogeneity implies differential demands for public spending within the resident population and greater variation from the position of the median voter. This variation suggests the potential risk that home rule might allow the capture of the local agenda by groups disposed to higher levels of spending. Coalitions between different groups (such as higher income and lower income or age cohorts in the distribution) might be able to defeat more moderate positions. To guard against higher risks in more heterogeneous communities, those communities with more heterogeneous populations would be expected to be less likely to adopt home rule. The results of Illinois home rule elections tend to confirm these expectations, as communities with greater age heterogeneity and lower income levels were found significantly less likely to convert to home rule (Temple, 1996). A key element of the preference for limitations may be to limit the range and form of local service benefits, particularly limiting the degree of redistributive spending that is possible. This suggests that motivation may come as much from self-interest on the spending side as on the revenue side.

Tiebout/Hamilton Efficiency Distortions and Local Limitations

Looking at housing prices and school enrollment changes, it appears that Massachusetts' Proposition 2½ property tax limitations have had a significant effect on location decisions (and Tiebout/Hamilton efficiency). After the initial cuts required in the years after Proposition 2½'s adoption, state aid, the real estate boom and declining school enrollments limited its effects between 1985 and 1990 (Bradbury et al., 1998). By the end of the 80s, however, these trends had reversed. Less able to provide for the spending preferences of their residents, constrained communities (due to a relative reduction in demand for residence in such localities) saw housing price declines or slower growth than unconstrained places between 1990 through 1994 (Bradbury et al., 1997). The effect may have been greatest for an inability to meet education preferences. Families with children selected residency based on the severity of a community's limit. Based on education enrollment changes, less constrained cities and towns became relatively more attractive as constrained cities saw enrollment declines and unconstrained ones saw enrollment increases. This 'significantly shifted the pattern of enrollment ... with students moving, on net, to districts ... less constrained' (Bradbury et al., 1998: 17). This effect is particularly troubling due to its interference with efficient sorting as 'families with children appear to be "voting with their feet" ... chasing communities that have excess capacity to support schools because they are below their mandated tax limit'. The limitation artificially impaired communities' access to resources needed for quality education. It is likely to most significantly impair education levels for the least affluent, as they are least able to achieve desired education (and general public) services through mobility.

William Fischel (1989, 2001) suggests a possible reason for the appeal of Proposition 13 in California and why it wasn't directly transferable to other states. In his view, Proposition 13 reflected less a revolt against the property tax than a revolt against a newly instituted education finance system and the resulting inability of the property tax to serve as a benefit-based financing instrument. The California Supreme Court's 1976 ruling in *Serrano* v. *Priest* (1976) required state redistribution of property taxes from wealthier to poorer jurisdictions to fund local education. This necessitated increasing property taxes in wealthier jurisdictions to maintain net local spending after transfers, such that these increases were divorced from increases in local education quality. In effect, the median voter lost power over local schools. What would have been an irrational move for wealthier communities in the absence of the court's ruling, created an environment conducive to using the limitation to restrict the level of transfer.

The property tax system had benefited communities, particularly wealthier communities, in the past by allowing spending responsive to local desires. Under the reformed system, this relationship would have been severed. Serrano's elimination of the local fiscal advantage via property tax financing of local services replaced an efficient benefit-based local revenue structure with one posing a deadweight loss to wealthier communities, resulting in support for the property tax limitation. Fischel suggests that under the transfer system, property values in wealthier communities would have been suppressed due to the transfer explicitly introduced into the post-Serrano property tax regime and points to the rapid rate of increase of property values in wealthier communities post-Proposition 13 as support for the existence of this deadweight loss and its subsequent elimination. He also points to the fact that past attempts to reform property taxes had failed. The difference between those and the success of Proposition 13 was Serrano. Under these conditions, support for the limitation becomes a rational response to a court-required constraint.

'PROPERTY TAXES', THE RALLYING CRY

While not uniformly the case, it cannot be denied that the focus of much of the local portion of the 'tax revolt' has been the property tax, either in general or for education purposes.[19] Continued erosion, however, may be less sustainable. As constraints on revenues and expenditures (particularly property taxes) become more binding their distortionary effects on the local public sector will dramatically increase. The subtle effects of 'creative' financing and service delivery will likely give way to quite blatant evidence of serious revenue constraints and serious efficiency and equity problems in these transformed revenue structures. Successful adaptability to date has led to a perception of an absence of cost; the next several years will likely dramatically expose the true cost of the imposition of artificial constraints on the abilities of state and local governments to meet the desires of their populations.

What explains this outcome? On all economic counts, this tax has rather positive attributes as a local revenue generator. Public opinion polls, however, consistently rate the property tax as among the 'worst' or 'least fair' taxes.

The first position alters between it and the federal income tax. A 1999 national survey revealed that 29 per cent of respondents viewed the property tax as the worst/least fair tax, second only to the income tax (at 36 per cent) (Cole and Kincaid, 2000). While this is an improvement over an anomalously high ranking in 1972, it reflects a level similar to that of the late 1970s and early 1980s, suggesting that limitations and 'reforms' have not altered the view of the public.

What is surprising is that at the same time the public decries its most important revenue source, it consistently shows equal or more trust and confidence in local government compared to national and state governments and favors local governments in value received per dollar in taxes. What is even more surprising is that the Western states, those recently imposing the most serious limitations, are among the least likely to view the property tax as the worst tax, equally as likely to have trust and confidence in local government, and feel as though they are receiving value for their tax dollars (Cole and Kincaid, 2000).

How is it that the primary revenue source for the level of government for which the public has most confidence and perceives the greatest value is held in such disrepute? While usage of income and sales taxes at the local level has been increasing, the property tax is still the primary vehicle for local discretion to meet citizens' preferences. Is this voter irrationality and a search for a 'free lunch' as suggested by Citrin (1979) or is the tax critically flawed? David Lowery (1985) argues that the property tax is caught between the citizen/voter's inconsistent desires for reduced taxes and higher service levels and tax certainty. Faced with these irrational inconsistencies, local officials are forced (through tax manipulation) to construct a corresponding 'fiscal illusion' of taxes lower than they actually are. This violates the tenets of certainty (equity, simplicity and controllability), resulting in public outrage and the introduction of tax limitations. The result is an unworkable situation for local officials and the political demise of property taxation. Further tax manipulation implemented in response to limitations and to voter inconsistencies reinforces a cycle of decline. However, trends suggest that there has been some stabilization in the relative role of the property tax.

There have certainly been legitimate concerns raised regarding the property tax over time (see Fisher, 1996), but these do not supersede its basic appeal as a local revenue source. The marginal adjustments in the general implementation of the property tax over the last several decades, to the degree to which they have created departures from the theoretical property tax in its administration, tend to benefit the resident citizen voter (Gold, 1979) and more specifically those with the longest tenure.

Property Tax 'Relief': Classification, Valuation, Exemptions and Burden Shifting

Classification systems which value property for tax purposes at different percentages of its base or apply different rates to residential, commercial, industrial and agricultural properties are used in approximately two-fifths of the states. Classification tends to significantly benefit homeowners and farmers by reducing relative effective tax rates for these forms of property compared to commercial and industrial. Additionally, valuation methods provide additional relief. In 42 states, agricultural land is valued at its current use rather than its highest and best economic use (O'Sullivan et al., 1995, p. 29), clearly benefiting agricultural properties. While the comparative sales approach to valuation used in 40 states tends to track residential property tax quite accurately (if frequently updated), departures introduced (many with limitations) limiting assessment increases have tended to reduce relative residential property tax burdens. Flat deductions from the assessed value for homesteads in 47 states further reduce the relative burden of property taxes on resident homeowners. Deductions do so in a somewhat progressive manner due to the effect of a flat exemption in providing greater relative base relief to lower valued properties. Means-tested property tax relief is generally available to elderly and low income renters and homeowners in 35 states in the form of 'circuit breakers', which activate when property taxes become too burdensome relative to income. Even the application of selective reassessment schedules can benefit particular property classes. While the tax base is still composed largely of residential property, these administrative adjustments would presumably increase the tax's viability with local constituencies.

The existence and effect of these adjustments are shown in Table 5.6 at the end of the chapter. It displays the results of state classification systems, effective tax rates for the largest cities in each state, homestead exemptions and circuit breakers. While the data displayed for property tax classification are incomplete, they quite dramatically demonstrate its effect. Column One shows the ratio between the single family residential assessment ratio (or rate) and that of commercial and industrial property and the resulting implicit residential tax burden as a per cent of the commercial/industrial.[20] The low ranges from 33.4 per cent in Colorado to a high of 96.8 per cent in New York. These ratios tend to hover around 50 per cent, implying that effective tax rates for owner-occupied residential property in classification states is approximately one half of that of commercial/industrial property. Classification is only one element in determining relative effective tax rates. Differences in valuation methods, assessment cycles, composition of the base (such as differences in treatment of personal verses real property) and exemptions can also dramatically affect relative tax burdens. Significant differences can (and do) exist across properties with uniform classification systems. Columns Two, Three and Four show estimated effective tax rates in the largest cities in each state for the three classes of property. Columns Five and Six show, respectively, the ratio of the commercial tax rate to residential tax rate and the industrial tax rate to residential. States using classified systems tend to have significantly higher relative commercial/industrial tax burdens. Several other states also have widely divergent relative burdens favoring homeowners effected through valuation mechanisms and administrative systems.

Overall, effective commercial tax rates are on average 42 per cent higher than residential and industrial are 11 per cent greater. The commercial highs are in New York City, Chicago, Minneapolis, Jacksonville and Denver. In New York this class is taxed at four times the rate of residential, 3.4 times in Chicago, 3.3 times in Minneapolis, 2.6 times in Jacksonville and 2.4 times in Denver. Lows are in New Hampshire and Connecticut (states with among the most traditional property tax systems) where commercial property is taxed at only 81 per cent of residential. Likely due to valuation methods (the income approach verses cost/replacement) and treatment of personal property, industrial variations are lower. These range from 2.4 times residential in New York, and twice that of residential in Minneapolis and Jacksonville to only approximately 60 per cent or less of residential tax rates in Milwaukee, Manchester, Sioux Falls, Fargo, Delaware, Bridgeport and Baltimore. The calculation of these relative burdens are done without considering that the tax base for most states includes business personal property (machinery, equipment and inventories), but excludes this for households. Residential effective tax rates are also calculated prior to the application of selective exemptions and circuit breakers. The true effect is even more favorable to residential property than that shown.

Additional relief from residential tax burdens is provided through homestead exemptions and circuit breakers. Homestead exemptions range from quite limited reductions in assessed value or tax credit available to all homeowners to a total property tax exemption for disabled homeowners. As of 1994, of the 47 states with homestead exemptions, 17 provided exemptions to all homeowners.[21] These include a $50 000 (or up to 50 per cent) reduction in assessed value in Idaho, a 20 per cent average assessed value reduction in Massachusetts, a minimum $5000 exemption coupled with an optional local deduction of up to 20 per cent of assessed value in Texas, a $30 000 deduction in the District of Columbia, a $25 000 deduction in Florida and a $20 000 deduction in Hawaii. Additional reductions in assessed value are commonly available for elderly, veterans, disabled and disabled veterans. At least 24 states provide specific exemptions for elderly homeowners. These include a $150 000 assessed value reduction in Alaska, means tested deductions of up to approximately $35 000 in Nebraska and Washington, $15 000 in North

Carolina, and a 20–100 per cent deduction in North Dakota, and a flat $20 000 deduction for all elderly in South Carolina and West Virginia.

Further means-tested reductions in property tax burdens existed for home-owners (and for the implicit tax burdens for renters) in 35 states by 1992. These programs are quite new, with all of them having been adopted since 1964. The first was in Wisconsin, followed by Minnesota and California in 1967. By 1980, they existed in 32 states. Most have been very frequently amended to keep threshold and relief levels current with income. Between the early 1970s and 1992, Colorado's and Tennessee's was amended ten times, Illinois' 11, and Nebraska's nine. These are available to all homeown-ers in nine states and all renters in 11 states. Circuit breakers specifically for elderly homeowners exist in 26 additional states and 20 states have programs for elderly renters. Two states (Hawaii and Oregon) have circuit breakers only for renters. Average benefit levels in 1992 ranged from nearly $600 in Maryland and over $500 in Michigan, Oregon, Vermont and Wyoming to less than $100 in Arkansas, Hawaii, New York and Tennessee.[22]

The Restructured Tax: Efficient/Equitable?

If the tax revolt were about 'improving' local revenue systems, the post-reform tax would be expected to more closely match its potential ideals along efficiency and equity dimensions. However, the restructured tax emerging out of the more extreme (and not uncommon) instances of the 'tax revolt' can hardly be seen as improving equity or efficiency performance. Arbitrary caps on assessment increases and movement to assessment on sale processes have created serious equity and efficiency problems. Prospects of increased prop-erty tax liabilities triggered by residence or business location changes likely constrain mobility and filtering in the housing and property markets. Differ-ent classes of property will have different effective tax rates based on frequency of sale and tremendous disparities in effective tax rates will emerge within a class.

As the most extreme example of these effects, California's Proposition 13 established an acquisition value property tax system. It set property values (residential, commercial and industrial) for tax purposes at their 1975–76 market values and allowed only a two per cent annual increase until the time of sale or significant modification.[23] Proposition 13 also limited tax rates to one per cent.[24] Due to the 1975–76 base freeze, by 1991 effective tax rates across all property classes in nine California counties ranged from 0.51 per cent in Los Angeles to 0.74 per cent in the faster growing counties of San Bernardino and Kern (O'Sullivan et al., 1995, Chapter Four). Because of tax incentives to retain valuable property and modify it rather than sell, effective tax rates on modified properties were lower than for nonmodified. In Los

Angeles County, 1991 effective tax rates for nonmodified owner-occupied homes were 0.483 per cent versus 0.431 per cent for modified homes. Nonmodified commercial and industrial property had an effective tax rate of 0.52 per cent compared to 0.43 for modified. Across the nine counties, 1991 effective tax rates for owner-occupied homes were 0.51 per cent compared to 0.56 per cent for commercial and industrial. Nonowner-occupied single family homes and multifamily residential structures tended to have effective tax rates higher than the average across property classes in these counties.

Substantial variation appears to exist across California counties in relative burdens within classes. Differences in effective tax rates emerge from differences between the ratio of market values to assessed values, driven by the most recent selling date of properties and market increases in property value. Considering the differences between properties assessed at their 1975–76 values and their 1991 market values, within the owner-occupied (nonmodified) property classification, tax burden disparities range from 5.19 times in Los Angeles County to 3.03 in Butte. This implies that owner-occupied housing in Los Angeles for which assessments had remained unadjusted since 1975 had an average effective tax rate of only 19.3 per cent of housing sold in 1991 or, conversely, that newly purchased property paid taxes 5.19 times greater. Effective tax rates for these properties were less than 25 per cent of that on recently sold property in five of the nine counties, with tax payments more than four times that of nonreassessed properties. In Los Angeles County, 43 per cent of all owner-occupied property was still assessed at the 1975–76 base year. In five of the nine counties, 30 per cent or more of their property was in this assessment category. The result is that the population affected by these disparities was and is substantial. A similar situation exists for commercial and industrial property. For these nonmodified properties, the disparity ratio is 5.66 in Los Angeles County and 3.7 in Alameda County, with 36 and 26 per cent of nonmodified commercial property falling into the 1975 base year.

The equity problems implied from the above are problems that the Supreme Court has determined are ineligible for court remedy. In *Nordlinger* v. *Hahn* (1992), the US Supreme Court denied the petitioner relief from her claims of an inequitable tax structure. Nordlinger showed that the tax burden on her property was five times greater than that of the nearly identical property of her neighbors and that the acquisition value assessment system favored property of higher income classes. These properties saw the greatest relative increases in market values and thus the lowest effective tax rates. Nordlinger argued that this system was not likely to be changed through means other than court intervention because it favored longer term (and therefore more politically active) resident segments of the population. The Court determined that the state had overriding 'legitimate' interests that could be reasonably pursued via the acquisition assessment system. These interests included (1) neighborhood preservation, continuity and stability, and (2) protecting the reliance interest of the property owner against an escalating absolute tax burden due to inflation-induced increases in the market value of their unrealized investment in property. The fact that the tax did not discriminate regarding the tax rate applied, even though real base variation might be substantial, appeared important to the Court.[25]

While the situation in California is most extreme, assessment limitations (targeted predominantly at homesteads) have been adopted in several states which are likely to have similar effects over time.[26] States with assessment limits include Arizona (1980), Arkansas (2000), Florida (1995), Iowa (1978), Michigan (1994), New Mexico (1979), New York (1981), Oklahoma (1996), Oregon (1997) and Washington (2000). Some of these are of rather limited effect because the growth rate is set rather high (Arizona), because they only apply to general reassessment (Arkansas), apply to a limited set of jurisdictions (New York), or because they have been overturned by the courts (Washington). Others such as Florida, Iowa, Michigan, New Mexico, Oklahoma and Oregon may have more substantial equity and efficiency ramifications. Tax reforms have institutionalized most serious departures from what would generally be regarded as tenets of tax equity and efficiency. The scale of these departures may, in fact, justify the relegation of this tax to a significantly lessened role in local finance. This role is not an inherent function of the tax itself, but of the damage done to it in the name of 'reform'. Still, however, the tax survives, sometimes in a significantly disfigured form, and sometimes with rather little relevance as a vehicle for local choice in a significantly restructured state/local fiscal system.

THE ALTERED STATE AND LOCAL FISCAL STRUCTURE IN PERSPECTIVE

Limitations are aimed at controlling the size of government or the level of reliance on property taxes. Thus, in this section we discuss changes in the state and local financial structure, expanding on some of the analysis presented by Fisher (Chapter Two of this volume).

Shifting Responsibilities and Centralization

The imposition of constraints has not scaled back the size of the state and local public sector in the United States, but it has changed its composition. As Fisher shows in Chapter Two, state and local expenditures relative to state personal income increased between 1965 and 1999. This upward trend reveals clear centralizing tendencies. The greatest growth has occurred in the 'state' portion of the state and local public sector. The scope of the local component of the sector (as measured by general revenue relative to personal income) has remained relatively flat, growing by 12.5 per cent (from 8.7 to 9.8); with the state component growing by nearly three times this rate (at 33.8 per cent).[27, 28]

Within the local sector, there has also been a shift in the relative level of revenue control exercised by type of government. Between 1968 and 1997, the revenue responsibilities of municipalities and school districts declined by approximately 11 per cent (Figure 5.1).[29] The role of cities peaked during the 1970s and bottomed during the 1990s. School districts reached their relative revenue low during the early 1980s and have since somewhat rebounded. County and special district responsibilities have increased. Counties gained 21 per cent in revenue responsibility and the fiscal role of special districts more than doubled.

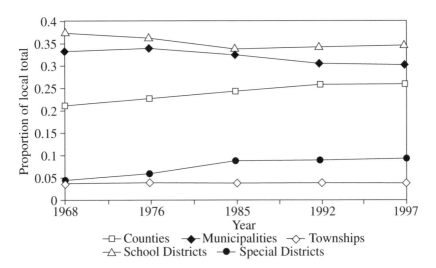

Source: US Department of Commerce (various years), *State and Local Government Finances*, Series, Washington, DC: Bureau of the Census.

Figure 5.1   Total local general revenue by type of government, 1968–1997

Shifting Revenue Reliance

The combined state and local sector

The state and local sector as a whole is relying less on broad based revenue sources. General revenue composition has moved away from taxes, and particularly property taxes, toward charges and miscellaneous sources (Figure

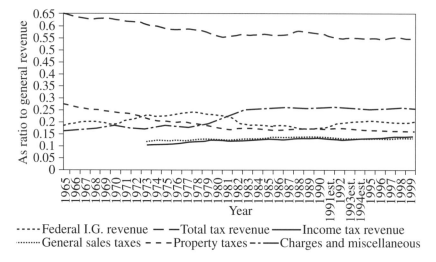

----- Federal I.G. revenue — —Total tax revenue ——Income tax revenue
········· General sales taxes - - -Property taxes --—Charges and miscellaneous

Source: US Department of Commerce (various years), *State and Local Government Finances*, Series, Washington, DC: Bureau of the Census.

Figure 5.2   Components of total state and local general revenue, 1965–1999

5.2). The cross state average for all taxes has declined by 16 per cent (from 64.6 to 54.4 per cent of general revenue) and property taxes have declined by 42 per cent (from 27.3 to 16 per cent). Offsetting these declines have been increases in charges and miscellaneous revenues of 56 per cent.

The steep decline in property taxes occurred between 1965 and 1980.[30] The 1980 through 1999 period shows a relatively consistent share of state and local general revenue from property taxes, with slight declines again occurring during the late 1990s.

The aggregate local sector

Trends in local components of general revenue are a magnified mirror image of that of the state and local sector as a whole. Since 1965, own-source local revenue has declined only modestly from 67.4 per cent of total general revenue to 61.6 (Figure 5.3). This overall decline masks significant fluctuations which correspond to the peak in direct federal transfers to local governments during the 1977–79 period.[31] State transfers to local governments demonstrate a remarkably consistent level over the 35 year period, increasing from 29.4 per cent of general revenue in 1965 to 34.8 per cent in 1999. Their focus has become more concentrated on school districts. The variation across states in state transfers as a portion of total local general revenue declined by 33 per cent between 1965 and 1999.

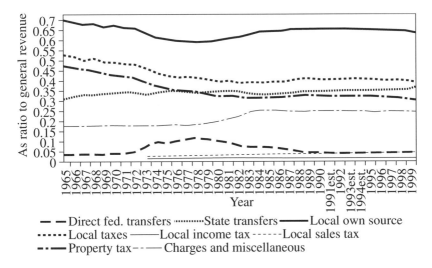

Source: US Department of Commerce (various years), *State and Local Government Finances*, Series, Washington, DC: Bureau of the Census.

Figure 5.3   Total local general revenue components, 1965–1999

The downward trend in local taxes is more pronounced. In 1965, one half (50.6 per cent) of local general revenue came from taxes. By 1999, that figure had declined by 25 per cent to 37.6. The entirety of this decline occurred gradually through 1982, reaching 36.9 per cent of general revenue. The role of taxes then increased slightly and again declined in the later years of the 1990s. This pattern is amplified for property taxes (Figure 5.3). In 1965, property taxes represented 91 per cent of total local tax revenue. By 1997, local tax diversification and property tax constraints reduced the relative role of property taxes to 77 per cent (not shown). The property tax portion of total local general revenue declined substantially more, by 37 per cent between 1965 and 1999 from 46.2 to 29.1 per cent of general revenue (Figure 5.3). This decline occurred predominantly between 1965 and 1982, when property taxes reached 30.4 per cent of local general revenue. The relative role of property taxes increased ever so slightly by 1990 before it declined to 1999 levels. While the cross state variation in the contribution of local taxes to general revenues has remained reasonably stable within this declining trend, the same is not so for property taxes. The relative variations in cross state reliance on property taxes has increased by approximately 25 per cent (from 30.66 to 40.45), suggesting an increasing lack of uniformity across states.[32]

Revenue reliance by local government type

Municipalities and school districts collect nearly an equal share of total local tax revenue. While taking slightly different routes,[33] cities and school districts begin and end the 1968 through 1997 period in nearly equal positions, with 1997 totals approximately nine per cent below 1968 levels (not shown). However, municipalities are somewhat more dependent on taxes as a share of total general revenues (at 43 to 37 per cent respectively). The importance of taxes in general revenue for each has experienced a similar decline since 1968 (down 21 and 24 per cent respectively). The trend for municipalities bottomed during the 1980s and the pattern for school districts shows evidence of slightly more continuous decline. A similar pattern of decline in taxes as a proportion of general revenue is present for counties and special districts, even though county share of total tax revenue has increased slightly and special district's rather limited share has nearly doubled (to 3.7 per cent). Townships are most dependent on taxes, accounting for more than 60 per cent of general revenue.

Patterns for the share of total local property taxes collected by type of government diverge somewhat from that of total tax revenue. School districts are by far the largest recipients of local property tax revenue. The distribution remained relatively stable between 1968 and 1997, with a 1968 low of 42.4 per cent of total collections going to school districts and a 1997 high of 44.5 per cent (not shown). Still, given the growing importance of state intergovernmental transfers for education, school district dependence on the property tax has declined markedly (by 25 per cent), from 48 per cent of district general revenue in 1968 to 36 per cent by 1997 (Figure 5.4).

Municipalities and counties received virtually equal portions of total local property taxes in 1997, at 22.0 and 22.6 per cent respectively (not shown). This equality was achieved through decidedly different paths over the past three decades. The city share of property taxes declined by 24 per cent over the period and the county share increased slightly (by 7 per cent). Still, property tax reliance as a portion of city and county general revenue has declined sharply for each through the early to mid 1980s, after which temporarily rebounding for municipalities and leveling and again declining for counties (Figure 5.4). By 1997, the total decline was 44 per cent for cities and 42 per cent for counties. The share of total property taxes going to special districts and townships has increased significantly, but together both types of government accounted for only 10.9 per cent of the total by 1997 (not shown). However, property taxes as a per cent of total general revenue of special districts declined by 47 per cent (Figure 5.4). Property tax revenue of townships initially also declined as a share of total township general revenue, but has rebounded somewhat in the last decade.

Charges and miscellaneous revenue are dominated by municipalities, at 37 per cent of total local collections, although the municipal share of the total

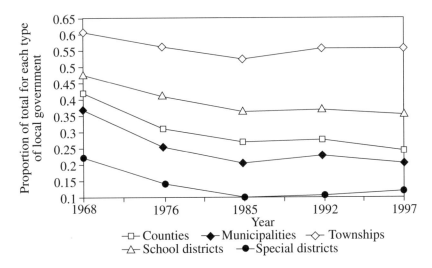

Source: US Department of Commerce (various years), *State and Local Government Finances*, Series, Washington, DC: Bureau of the Census.

Figure 5.4   Local property tax revenue as a proportion of general revenue, 1968–1997

has declined over the period as other local governments (counties and special districts) increased their reliance on these sources (not shown). The greatest growth in the share of these revenue sources is at the county level (with a 48 per cent increase to 29.4 per cent of the total between 1967 and 1997) and the greatest decline is in school districts (at 42 per cent). School districts are least reliant on charges and miscellaneous revenues as a component of general revenues (at less than eight per cent) and special districts are most reliant at over 50 per cent (52.1 per cent), with the proportion growing (Figure 5.5). For 1997, cities received 30 per cent of their total general revenue from these sources, while counties and townships received 27 per cent and 16 per cent, respectively. Reliance on these sources by these units has been steadily growing since the mid 1980s.

Local shares of intergovernmental revenue have also shifted. School districts now receive 50 per cent of all state and federal intergovernmental transfers to the local level. This is up from a low of 42 per cent in the later half of the 1970s (not shown). Correspondingly, city shares have declined by one third (from a 1970s peak of approximately 32 per cent to a 1997 low of 22 per cent). The relative share of transfers to special districts has more than tripled (to eight per cent). The dominance of school districts as recipients of state intergovernmental transfers is even greater. By 1997, school districts received 53 per cent of the

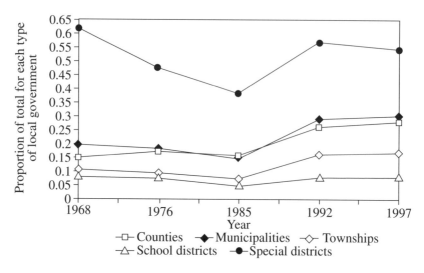

Source: US Department of Commerce (various years), *State and Local Government Finances*, Series, Washington, DC: Bureau of the Census.

Figure 5.5   Charges and miscellaneous revenue as a proportion of general revenue, 1968–1997

total (not shown). As with total transfers, the share of the state component going to municipalities declined by nearly one-third to 18 per cent by 1997. For all types of local governments (municipalities, counties, townships and special districts), except school districts, intergovernmental revenue as a portion of total general revenue has declined since the mid 1970s (not shown). The decline for municipalities has been the most dramatic at 30 per cent. Counties also experienced a 17 per cent decline. As a result of this shift, school districts have become more dependent on intergovernmental transfers, which now account for more than 55 per cent of district general revenue.

SHIFTING PROPERTY TAXES

There has been considerable variability in the relative role of the local property tax over time and between states. Table 5.7 at the end of the chapter displays for 1972 and 1999 local property taxes as a ratio to state personal income, general revenue, charges and miscellaneous revenues, and intergovernmental revenue from the state. It also provides ratios of own-source local revenue to own-source state revenue and to intergovernmental revenue received from the state.

Property Tax Burden

Overall local property tax burden, measured as a proportion of state personal income, has declined by one quarter (to a cross state average of 2.9 per cent), due to a downward leveling in the higher revenue states. This lower yield shows greater consistency, as the coefficient of variation between states has also declined. A considerable amount of reshuffling has taken place in the position of states ranked on this measure. Only five of ten states with the greatest yield from property taxes in 1972 remain in the top ten for 1999. States occupying the first four positions drop completely from the top ten. Three of these are states which adopted rather severe limitations over the period (California, Massachusetts and Montana).[34] States remaining in the top ten and moving toward the highest ranks include three of the four states with no limitations (New Hampshire at rank one,[35] Maine at rank three, and Connecticut at position six). Additional states entering or remaining in the top ten include New York (rank five) and Illinois (rank eight), which have limitations with limited application.[36] Wisconsin, adopting limitations on counties and school districts in 1994, remains at rank eight. Texas, which has a 'revenue limit' which is more accurately classified as full disclosure roll back is new to the top ten for 1999.

There is less variability in the ranking of states with the lowest property tax burden. These ranks are heavily populated by southern states. Only three states appear in the bottom ten for 1999 that were not there in 1972. Two of these, Washington and Oklahoma, adopted a range of limitations during the period. South Carolina, adopting only full disclosure in 1975, moved in the other direction from 43 to 28.

Property Taxes as a Proportion of Total General Revenue

The pattern of local property taxes to total local general revenue is similar to that for personal income. Accounting for an average of 40.3 per cent of local general revenue in 1972, the property tax share fell by 28 per cent to 29.1. The nonlimited states (New Hampshire, Connecticut, Vermont and Maine) occupied four of the five top positions in 1972 and three continue in the top six for 1999.[37] Montana and Indiana, limitation adopting states, drop slightly from the top ten by 1999. Illinois and Texas again move into the ninth and tenth positions on this measure for 1999. Hawaii is also high, but this is due to its rather highly state-centered fiscal system.

Still dominated by the South, states with local governments relying least on property taxes (rank 41–50) show a 40 per cent shift. The pattern is somewhat similar as that for personal income. New entrants into the ranks of least reliant on property taxes include Washington, Nevada, Oklahoma and

California (moving from position 20 to 45). All four of these states have adopted more severe limitations.

Ratio of Property Taxes to Current Charges and Miscellaneous Revenue

Compared to property taxes, fee and miscellaneous charge revenue has increased dramatically. In 1972, only three states (Mississippi, Alaska and Alabama) generated more local revenue from fees, charges and miscellaneous sources than from property taxes; by 1999, 23 states did. The 1999 variation across states is substantial. The highest fee, charge and miscellaneous contribution (Alabama) is three times that of property taxes. In the state with the lowest (Rhode Island), property taxes are five and a half times greater. In 1999, property taxes averaged one and a half times the revenue of fee, charge and miscellaneous sources. This is, however, only half of the 1972 average of 2.9. Compared to property taxes, the relative role of this source of revenue has doubled since 1972. Heavy relative property tax contributions and low fee and charge reliance are typical of New England states. For 1972, each of the top six positions on this ratio were occupied by the six states from this census division. The situation was nearly identical for 1999, where six of the top seven were New England states. Outside New England, the drop is rather dramatic. The difference between rank seven (Vermont) and rank eight (Illinois) is 0.5, or 25 per cent. Southern states are again highly represented as those with greater relative fee and charge reliance. They held seven of the ten lowest positions in 1972 and six in 1999. California also moved into position 43 from position 13.

Ratio of Property Taxes to State Intergovernmental Transfers

State intergovernmental transfers have also increased substantially relative to property taxes. The relative role of the property tax declined by one third over the period. In 1972, property taxes on average contributed 48 per cent more in local government revenue than did state transfers. By 1999, transfers had reached almost exact parity. The role of state transfers in financing local government is nearly identical (on average) to that of property taxes. However, with a coefficient of variation of 88, there is more cross state variation on this measure than for any other. State transfers range from five times that of property tax revenue in New Mexico, to less than 20 per cent of property taxes in New Hampshire. States with the lowest relative transfer reliance compared to property taxes (those ranking in the top ten in the property tax to intergovernmental revenue ratio) included all six New England states in 1975 and four of the six in 1999. Both Massachusetts and Vermont dropped from the top ten. The ten states with the least property tax revenue compared to state transfers were in 1972, with the exception of Alaska and New Mexico, all Southern. By 1999, six of the bottom ten were located in the South. What is more interesting are the additions to this group. Three of the non-Southern states include Vermont, Michigan and California. Vermont moved from a position of eighth least reliant on state aide relative to property taxes to tenth most reliant (rank 41). Michigan moved from 24 to 42 and California moved from 23 to 48.

Ratio of Local Own-Source Revenue to State Intergovernmental Revenue

More directly considering overall reliance on state transfers for local finance, the last two columns of Table 5.7 compare total own source local revenue to state transfers. This demonstrates the relative role of local resources overall in contributing to local services. This measure shows more instability across time in the top and bottom rankings than have others. Augmented by revenue sources other than property taxes, the relative own-source share of local resources has not declined as much as the property tax share. Still, own-source revenue has dropped on average by 23 points (or more than ten per cent). The range across states is considerable. For 1999, Vermont's own-source revenue was equal to only 71 per cent of state transfers while Hawaii's was 767 per cent. Notable shifts have occurred in the group of states least reliant on own-source revenue (ranks 41 through 50). Vermont moved from a 1972 position of 11th most reliant on local sources to least reliant (rank 50) by 1999. California and Michigan also occupied the 46th and 48th positions, moving from positions 30 and 29, respectively.

Ratio of Local Own-Source Revenue to State Own-Source Revenue

The ratio of local own-source revenue to state own-source revenue also provides an alternative measure of state and local sector dominance or decen-tralization/centralization. It fulfills the adage 'He who pays the piper calls the tune.' On average, the state/local sector is somewhat fiscally centralized. This centralization has increased by 12 per cent from 1972 to 1999. During 1972, 18 states had local revenue structures with yields approximate equal to or greater than their states. By 1999, that number had been cut in half. In only four states was local own-source revenue greater than state, compared to 13 previously. Differences across states are again dramatic. 1999 shows a clearly state-dominated structure in New Mexico, Alaska, Vermont, Hawaii and Dela-ware, and a more locally centered system in New York and New Hampshire. California and Massachusetts (ranked three and nine in 1972) dropped to 20 and 42. Michigan dropped from 22 to 40. The relative role of local government in California declined by 38 per cent, New Jersey's by 40 per cent, Michigan's by 36 per cent, Massachusetts' by 55 per cent, and Vermont's by 47 per cent.

RAMIFICATIONS AND OUTLOOK

The fiscal limitations wave, while certainly not the only factor, has contributed substantially to a significantly changed state and local sector. Average total state and local general revenue relative to state personal income has increased over the past decades and has done so with a centralizing effect. The state component of the sector has increased at nearly three times the rate of the local. For the state and local sector as a whole, components of general revenue have moved away from taxes, and particularly property taxes, toward charges and miscellaneous sources.

The relative role of the property tax in local general revenue has declined by 37 per cent. This 'demise' is not terminal. Over the past decade the property tax has stabilized at approximately 30 per cent of revenue. However, the remaining tax is often at considerable variance with tenets of equity and efficiency. It has been pulled and twisted by pressures to shift the relative burden away from owner-occupied residential property and limit its role in education finance (see Chapter Four). While still the dominant local revenue source, in some cases (such as California) where limitations on its use are so severe and constrained, it takes on the characteristics of a state tax from which revenue has simply been assigned to local jurisdictions. In such situations it provides little local fiscal autonomy. In other states (such as New Hampshire, Maine and Connecticut) it is still largely the foundation of the local fisc. With no viable replacement, the property tax will continue to play a significant role in local public finance.[38] However, it will also continue to be the focus of tinkering and 'reform'. The property tax that remains will likely distribute its burden less equitably and less efficiently within and between property classifications. The tax we love to hate will endure. It is, after all, the oldest tax in recorded history.[39]

The local revenue system of which the property tax is a part will likely fund a local public sector which is less redistributive in its effects. It will be augmented by a continued expansion in current charges and miscellaneous revenues.[40] Fee-based service delivery, while potentially improving efficiency (if not used to finance public goods and services with significant externalities), will likely challenge equity in the sector. With the most obvious candidates for fee-based financing long since brought into the local revenue fold, it is likely that future augmentations will strain the dimensions of economic appropriateness. The search for service 'efficiency' in the face of revenue constraints will also likely lead to increased pressures to use privatization and service contracts. These also may engender additional distributional limitations and sacrifices in control and accountability.

The possible negative equity implications of the trends toward greater current charges and miscellaneous sources could be offset by greater intergovernmental transfers emanating from more progressive state revenue systems. However, for all levels of local governments except school districts, the general trend has been a decline in the relative role of these revenues in local finance. It is unlikely that pressures for state financing of social assistance, medical care and 'reformed' education finance systems will allow significant augmentation of local general purpose government functions through these sources. The increased state role that has emerged has not been one sympathetic to local autonomy, suggesting that further back stepping in this area may be expected.

While the subject of Chapter Four in this volume, two reforms of education finance during the previous decade may shed light on future expectations. Michigan's 1994 education finance reform combined a strict limit on the use of local property taxes for local education with a two percentage point increase in the state general retail sales tax devoted to education. In order to promote 'equity' (defined as reducing the variation in per-student education spending) lower spending districts were leveled up to a per-student spending floor and higher spending districts were to be gradually leveled down. Strict caps were erected to limit spending in jurisdictions desiring greater education services, even if willing to pay for it through taxes (Knittel and Haas, 1998). Vermont's 1997 Act 60 education reform was also motivated by equity, in response to a State Supreme Court ruling. While not strictly a property tax limitation, it combines a flat per-pupil grant funded by a uniform state property tax levy with a guaranteed tax base system. Property taxes generated from a local jurisdiction above a specified threshold are partially credited to a state pool for distribution across school systems. Some jurisdictions' contribution is as much 70 cents per dollar. Local jurisdictions are free to raise taxes to fund education, but reap only part of the benefit of the revenue generated (Brunori, 1999b; Swaine and Browne, 1999).

In both cases, the state government was attempting to limit its outlays to reach its education objectives. In Michigan, it did so by attempting to limit the range of variation it would presumably need to offset via sales taxes. In Vermont, it did so by pooling what had previously been local resources for state purposes. In both cases, the response of local populations is instructive as to the implications of such attempts to constrict local spending. In Michigan, off-budget foundations have been established by residents in many of the state's high education service districts to allow continued spending above the caps (Hornbeck, 2001). In Vermont, local community pressure was brought to bear on resident and particularly business taxpayers to make voluntary contributions to fund education in lieu of a tax increase (Associated Press, 1999, 2001). In essence, taxpayers were given the choice of appearing non-community-oriented and risking higher 'official' tax increases (due to high proportionate diversions to the state pool) or paying the informal assessment.[41] In both cases, a rather complicated structure (with relatively high coordinating and high transaction costs) was established to circumvent restrictions on the use of local resources imposed from above.

One of the lasting legacies of the limitations movement has been local adaptation to avoid constraints judged to be undesirable at the local level. While these have the desired result of circumventing a constraint, they also entail a most undesirable outcome resulting in the degradation of accountability. These necessary adaptations to allow local government to continue to be 'responsive' to an undiminished demand for local public services, leave open the question of 'responsive and accountable to whom and what institutions'? The cases of Michigan and Vermont demonstrate but one example, however, the most elaborate might again be found in the state of California.

In order to overcome the obstacles to local finance created by Proposition 13 and its progeny (most notably Proposition 218) in California, local finance has metamorphosed into an overlapping patchwork of disjointed revenue jurisdictions (Sheffrin, 1998; Youngman, 1998). These include benefit assessment districts, special assessment districts, community facilities districts, and business improvement districts, levying developer fees and exactions, special assessments, parcel taxes and property transfer fees. Many of these have been stimulated simply to avoid the majority and super majority approval requirements of general and special taxes, and/or meet the requirements to levy assessments or fees (under Proposition 218). All of these have differing popular approval requirements ranging from a two-thirds vote of the electorate for special taxes to a majority of property owners within a district containing fewer than a dozen voters for the assessment of flat parcel charges or fees. The result is what Sheffrin refers to as the 'particularization' of local taxation, as general taxation gives way to levies specifically dedicated to particular purposes and narrowly constrained geographic areas. To this extent, even 'taxes' represent direct service charges with limited ability to finance general benefit services. For voter-approved taxes, assessments and fees in a jurisdiction, it is possible for different electoral groupings to be voting on each question. While Proposition 218 provisions provide for various forms of direct democracy applicable to an array of instruments, they do so in a quite disjointed fashion. California voters are left with discretion over everything except what might matter most, ad valorem property taxes and education spending (Sheffrin, 1998, p. 139). Similar patterns may also be emerging in Colorado.

The resulting structure is an extremely complicated and almost indecipherable labyrinth to the individual citizen/voter. Local adaptations necessary to continue to provide for the needs and desires of populations within the restrictions of artificial revenue constraints have engendered this complexity and, as a result, have created a loss of transparency, responsiveness and accountability at the local level. According to Sheffrin and similar to that suggested by Lowery (1985), the cycle of fiscal innovation leading to a loss in transparency is at least partially responsible for demands for more direct citizen control in California. As this cycle works its way through a variety of states, the likely result is that this will foster additional needs for fiscal innovation, additional losses in transparency and additional initiatives for 'reform'.

More macro elements of this effect can be seen in the overall structure of local government. There has been a shift in the relative level of revenue control across types of local jurisdictions. Between 1968 and 1997 the relative revenue responsibilities of general purpose governments have declined while the role of limited purpose jurisdictions has increased. In sheer magnitude, the number of special districts in the United States increased by 45 per cent between 1972 and 1997. Recent time series research into the effects of local tax and expenditure limitations within 787 metropolitan counties finds that these constraints have potentially important substantive effects on the structure of local government in urban areas, the package of services provided, and long term mechanisms of finance (Mullins, 2001).[42] It has identified significant increases in the relative revenue and expenditure authority of limited purpose governments and away from general purpose governments in counties located in states adopting limitations. Reductions in the role of general purpose governments suggest the possibility of service coordination problems, more limited abilities to meet distributive service needs of varied populations, and difficulties in efficient budgetary trade-offs at the local level. While there are multiple explanations for changes in broad fiscal structural characteristics over several decades, the evidence suggests that a significant element in shaping this evolving structure is the imposition of fiscal constraints. Further, evidence suggests that within these broader trends there are more significant effects across different communities and types of governments.

Different types of limitations have different overall effects, which vary with the spatial/structural position of the jurisdiction (urban core or suburban fringe) and with the relative prosperity of the community. Communities located in the older urban core and those with less prosperous populations are most constrained. The result is lessened capacity to provide services for populations in greatest need, increasing service disparities. Effects are not confined to directly limited jurisdictions. Limitations on general purpose or school district governments may provide increased revenue or expenditure flexibility for nonlimited forms of government by decreasing competition for shared tax bases. Limitations have been found to increase the variation in per capita revenue collections and expenditures across general purpose governments and school districts, through asymmetrically constraining those units under greater fiscal stress, producing increased fiscal disparity, and to increase reliance on nonguaranteed debt finance.

State and local fiscal limitations have the potential to substantially alter the relationship between governments and local populations and significantly affect the capacity to provide for public needs and wants. These effects are reshaping the state and local public sector in often unintended ways. Effects vary by type of government and service subgroup, and by the demographics of resident populations. The implications of such effects are not benign and are likely to increase over time, particularly in an environment of economic contraction. The local public sector will continue to struggle to make do within the confines of these constraints. The adaptations will continue to distort the fiscal and service delivery structures and make for a more fragmented, complex, and particularized, and a less transparent, equitable, efficient, responsive and accountable state and local public sector.

Table 5.1 Tax and expenditure limitations currently imposed statewide on local governments (original year of imposition/amendment)

State	Overall property tax rate limit	Specific property tax rate limit	Property tax revenue limit	Assessment increase limit	General revenue limit	General expenditure limit	Full disclosure
ALABAMA							
County	1972/78	1875					
Municipality	1972/78	1875					
School district	1972/78	1916					
ALASKA							
County							
Municipality		1972	1972				
School district							
ARIZONA							
County	1980		1913/80	1980		1921/80	
Municipality	1980		1913/80	1980		1921/80	
School district	1980			1980		1974/81	
ARKANSAS							
County		1883	1981	2000			
Municipality		1883	1981	2000			
School district			1981	2000			

Table 5.1 *(continued)*

State	Overall property tax rate limit	Specific property tax rate limit	Property tax revenue limit	Assessment increase limit	General revenue limit	General expenditure limit	Full disclosure
CALIFORNIA							
County	1978/86	1997		1978		1979/90	
Municipality	1978/86	1997		1978		1979/90	
School district	1978/86	1997		1978	1972	1979/90	
COLORADO							
County		1992	1913		1992	1992	1983
Municipality		1992	1913		1992	1992	1983
School district		1992	1992		1992	1973	1992
CONNECTICUT: NONE							
DELAWARE							
County			1972				1976
Municipality							
School district							

FLORIDA					
County		1968		1995	1974/80
Municipality		1968		1995	1974/80
School district		1855/68/73		1995	1974/80
GEORGIA					
County		c.1890/81(r)			1991
Municipality					1991
School district		1945			1991
HAWAII					
County					1977
Municipality					
School district					
IDAHO					
County	1978	1913	1979/92(r)		1991
Municipality	1978	1967	1979/92(r)		1991
School district	1978	1963	1979/92(r)		1991
ILLINOIS					
County		1939	1991*		1981
Municipality		1961	1991		1981
School district		1961	1991		1981

Table 5.1 (continued)

State	Overall property tax rate limit	Specific property tax rate limit	Property tax revenue limit	Assessment increase limit	General revenue limit	General expenditure limit	Full disclosure
INDIANA							
County			1973/77/80				
Municipality			1973/77/80				
School district			1973/77/80				
IOWA							
County		n.a./83		1978/80			1983
Municipality		1972/92		1978/80			
School district		1989		1978/80		1971	
KANSAS							
County		1933/89(s)	1970/89(s)				
Municipality		1933/89(s)	1970/89(s)				
School district		1933/89(s)				1973	
KENTUCKY							
County		1908	1979				1979
Municipality		1908/85	1979				1979
School district		1946	1979				1979

138

LOUISIANA							
County		1974	1978				
Municipality		1974	1978				
School district		1974	1978				
MAINE: NONE							
MARYLAND							
County				1957/91			1977
Municipality				1957/91			1977
School district				1957/91			
MASSACHUSETTS							
County		1980/91	1980/83				
Municipality							
School district							
MICHIGAN							
County	1933		1978	1994			1982
Municipality		1949	1978	1994			1982
School district	1933	1994	1978	1994			1982
MINNESOTA							
County		1993(r)			1971/93(r)		1988
Municipality					1971/93(r)		1988
School district						1971	1988

Table 5.1 (continued)

State	Overall property tax rate limit	Specific property tax rate limit	Property tax revenue limit	Assessment increase limit	General revenue limit	General expenditure limit	Full disclosure
MISSISSIPPI							
County			1980				
Municipality			1980				
School district			1983/90				
MISSOURI							
County		1875	1980				
Municipality		1875	1980				
School district		1987	1980				
MONTANA							
County		1931/87	1987				1974
Municipality		n.a/65	1987				1974
School district		1971					1974
NEBRASKA							
County		1903	1990			1996	1990
Municipality		1957	1990			1996	1990
School district		1921/99				1991/96	

140

State / Government							
NEVADA							
County	1936		1983				1985
Municipality	1936	1929	1983/87		1984/89(r)	1976/91	1985
School district	1936	1956			1984/89(r)	1976/90	1985
NEW HAMPSHIRE: NONE							
NEW JERSEY							
County							
Municipality			1980				
School district							
NEW MEXICO							
County	1914	1973/87	1979	1979/00			
Municipality	1914	1973/87	1979	1979/00			
School district	1914	1973/87	1979	1979/00			
NEW YORK							
County		1894		1981**			
Municipality		1894		1986***			
School district		1894					
NORTH CAROLINA							
County		1973					
Municipality		1973					
School district							

Table 5.1 (continued)

State	Overall property tax rate limit	Specific property tax rate limit	Property tax revenue limit	Assessment increase limit	General revenue limit	General expenditure limit	Full disclosure
NORTH DAKOTA							
County		1929	1981				
Municipality		1929	1981				
School district		1929					
OHIO							
County	1929/34/53		1976				
Municipality	1929/34/53		1976				
School district	1929/34/53		1976				
OKLAHOMA							
County	1933			1996			
Municipality	1933			1996			
School district	1933			1996			
OREGON							
County	1991	1997	1916/97	1997			
Municipality	1991	1997	1916/97	1997			
School district	1991	1991/97	1916/97	1997			

PENNSYLVANIA			
County	1959		
Municipality	1959		
School district	1959	c.1940	
RHODE ISLAND			
County			
Municipality		1985	1979
School district			
SOUTH CAROLINA			
County			1975
Municipality			1975
School district			1975
SOUTH DAKOTA			
County	1915		
Municipality	1915		
School district	1915		
TENNESSEE			
County			1979
Municipality			1979
School district			

Table 5.1 *(continued)*

State	Overall property tax rate limit	Specific property tax rate limit	Property tax revenue limit	Assessment increase limit	General revenue limit	General expenditure limit	Full disclosure
TEXAS							
County		1876	1982				1982
Municipality		1876	1982				1982
School district		1883	1982				1982
UTAH							
County		1898/61	1969/86(r)				1986
Municipality		1929	1969/86(r)				1986
School district		1929/88	1969/86(r)				1986
VERMONT: NONE							
VIRGINIA							
County							1976
Municipality							1976
School district							

144

WASHINGTON					
County	1944/73	1973	1971/79/01	2000****	1990
Municipality	1944/73	1973	1971/79/01	2000****	1990
School district	1944/73		1979/01	2000****	1990
WEST VIRGINIA					
County	1939	1939	1990		
Municipality	1939	1939	1990		
School district	1939	1939	1990		
WISCONSIN					
County		1994			
Municipality					
School district				1994	
WYOMING					
County	1980				
Municipality	1890				
School district	1911				

Notes:

*   Applies to non-home rule taxing units located in counties contiguous to Cook County.

**   Nassau County only.

****   New York City only.

****   Ruled unconstitutional by Washington State Supreme Court, 2001.

(r)   Repealed effective year specified.

(s)   Suspended effective year specified.

Source: Updated from Mullins and Cox (1995).

Table 5.4 State level tax, revenue and expenditure limitations

State	Adoption method	Statutory/ constitutional	Revenue limit	Expenditure limit	Growth restriction	Override provision	Exemptions
Alaska	R	Con		1982 (A)	POP/CPI	3/4 L	C
Arizona	R	Con	1979 (T)	1978 (AT)	INC	2/3 L	
	R	Con	1992 (T)		T	2/3 L	
	I	Con			T	2/3 L	
Arkansas	L	Con	1934 (T)		T	3/4 L	
California	I	Con	1978 (T)		T	2/3 L	
	I	Con		1979 (AT)	INC	EM	
Colorado	L	Stat		1991 (GF)	INC or 6%	EM – 2/3 L	
	I	Con	1992 (T)		T, Refund	EM – 2/3 L V	
	I	Con		1992 (E)	POP/CPI	EM – 2/3 L V	
Connecticut	R	Con		1992 (A)	INC/CPI	EM – 3/5 L	D,G,M,BR
Delaware	R	Con		1978 (GF)	PCT	EM – 3/5 L	
	I	Con	1980/81 (T)		T	3/5 L	
Florida	R	Con	1971 (CIT)		T	3/5 L	
	R	Con	1994 (R)		INC	2/3 L	
	I	Con	1996 (T)		T	2/3 V	

146

State	CC	Type	Year	Year	Base	Limit	Notes
Hawaii		Con		1978 (GF)	ECN	2/3 L	
Idaho	L	Stat		1980/94 (GF)	INC		N-R
Iowa	L	Stat		1992 (GF)	PCT		
Louisiana	L	Stat	1979 (T)	1993 (GF)	INC	L	
	R	Con	1996 (T)		INC	2/3 L	
	I	Con			T	2/3 L	
Maryland	L	Stat		1979 (E)	ECN	L	Advisory
Massachusetts	I	Stat	1986 (T)		WAGES	L	Amendable
	I	Con	2000 (IT)				
Michigan	I	Con	1978		INC	2/3 L-EM	
Mississippi	R	Con	1970 (T)	1992 (A)	3/5 L	3/5 L	
	L	Stat			PCT		
Missouri	I	Con	1980 (GF, T)		INC, Refund	2/3 L-EM, V	
	L	Con	1996 (T)		V	L-EM, 1 year	
Montana	L	Stat		1981 (A)	INC	2/3 L-EM	Invalidated
	I	Con	1998 (T)		V	3/4 L	
Nevada	L	Stat		1979 (PE)	POP/CPI	Discretionary	
	I	Con	1996 (T)		2/3 L	2/3 L	

Table 5.4 (continued)

State	Adoption method	Statutory/ constitutional	Revenue limit	Expenditure limit	Growth restriction	Override provision	Exemptions
New Jersey	L	Stat		1990 (GF)	INC		D,C,G
North Carolina	L	Stat		1991 (GF)	INC		
Oklahoma	R	Con			PCT, CPI		
	I	Con	1992 (T)	1985 (A)	3/4 L	3/4 L	
Oregon	L	Stat		1979 (A)	INC		
	R	Con	1996 (T)		3/5 L	3/5 L	
	I	Con	2000		Refund		
Rhode Island	L	Stat		1935/1994 (A)	FIXED		
	R	Con		1992 (GF)	PCT		
South Carolina	R	Con		1980/1984 (A)	INC, EMP	2/3 L-EM 1 yr.	
South Dakota	I	Con	1978 (T)		2/3 L, V		
	R	Con	1996 (T)		2/3 L, V	2/3 L	
Tennessee	CC	Con		1978 (AT)	INC	L	
Texas	R	Con		1978 (AT)	INC/ECN	L-EM	

Utah	L	Stat		1988 (A)	INC/POP	2/3 L-EM, V
Virginia	L	Con	1992		EXP	
Washington	I	Stat	1993 (T)	1993 (E)	POP/CPI	2/3 L-EM
	I	Stat	1999 (T)		OEL, V	
	I	Stat			V	V

Key to abbreviations

INC	= Per capita income or personal income		CIT	= Corporate income tax
POP	= Population		R	= Revenue
CPI	= Inflation or consumer price index		ECN	= Growth in state economy
C	= Capital projects		N-R	= Nonrecurring general fund appropriations exempt
L	= Legislature		WAGES	= Growth limited to growth in wages and salaries
Con	= Constitutional		IT	= Alters personal income tax rate structure
Stat	= Statutory		FIXED	= Fixed percentage allowable growth
R	= Referenda		EMP	= Limits employment growth
I	= Initiative		EXP	= Revenue limited to expenditures
A	= Appropriation increase		OEL	= Limit tax changes to amounts below the expenditure limit w 2/3 L, amounts over
E	= Expenditure increase			expenditure limit requires V
T	= New or increased taxes and/or fees		G	= Grants
EM	= Emergency		M	= Court mandates
V	= Voter approval		BR	= Budget reserves
GF	= General fund		PE	= Proposed expenditures
PCT	= Percent of revenue, creates a reserve		CC	= Constitutional convention
D	= Debt payment		At	= Appropriation of tax revenue

Sources: Compiled from Rafool (1996, 1998), James and Rudiuk (2001) and Rudiuk (2001).

Table 5.6 Property tax classification, effective tax rates, residential exemptions and circuit breakers

State	Classification/rate favoring owner-occupied housing (OO% of C/I)[1]	1996 Residential effective tax rates, largest city in state	1998 Commercial effective tax rate, largest urban area	1998 Industrial effective tax rate, largest urban area	Ratio commercial effective tax rate to residential	Ratio industrial effective tax rate to residential	Homestead exemption (1994) Eligibility	Homestead exemption (1994) Amount	Year of adoption/amendments	Circuit breaker (1992) Eligibility	Circuit breaker (1992) Amount
Alaska	–	1.54	1.774	1.811	1.152	1.176	EHR,DV,S	$150 000(AV)	–	–	–
Alabama	50.00%	0.70	1.166	0.977	1.666	1.396	AE,EH,B,D	$6000 Total	–	–	–
Arizona	40.00%	1.83	3.194	2.741	1.745	1.498	S,D,V	$2300	1973(4)	EH,AR	$266
Arkansas	–	1.25	1.120	1.183	0.896	0.946	DV,S,M	Total	1973(5)	EH,S	$118
California	–	0.74	1.053	0.842	1.423	1.138	AH, DV,S	7000–100 000	1967(7)	EHR,D	$80
Colorado	72%/33.4%[2]	0.84	2.024	1.647	2.410	1.961	E,D	Variable	1971(10)	EHR,D	$336
Connecticut	–	3.96	3.235	2.422	0.817	0.612	D,V,DV	1000–30 000	1974(5)	EHR,D	$450
Delaware	–	1.13	0.945	0.657	0.836	0.581	EH,LID	$5000(AV)	–	–	–
District of Columbia	60.00%	0.95	2.254	2.033	2.373	2.140	AH	$30 000	1974(1)	AHR,DHR,EHR	$292–377
Florida	–	1.11	2.845	2.262	2.563	2.038	AH	$25 000(AV)	–	–	–
Georgia	–	2.04	1.883	1.906	0.923	0.934	AH,E,B,D,DV	$2000–35 000(AV)	–	–	–
Hawaii	79.00%	0.33	0.678	0.407	2.055	1.233	AH,E,B,DV	$20 000+	1977(4)	AR	$49
Idaho	–	1.83	1.723	1.396	0.942	0.763	AH	$50 000/50%	1974(6)	EH,S,D	$284
Illinois	44%[3]	1.79	6.018	3.420	3.362	1.911	AH,EH,DV	3500+	1972(11)	EHR,D	$272
Indiana	–	1.93	2.284	2.741	1.183	1.420	AH,E,B,D,V	4%–4000(AV)	1985(–)	EH,AR	$251
Iowa	22.54%	2.95	3.704	2.556	1.256	0.866	AH,DV	$4850(AV)	1973(8)	EHR,D	$196
Kansas	40.00%	1.38	2.528	2.054	1.832	1.488	AH,DV		1970(8)	EHR,D,B	
Kentucky	–	1.38	1.241	0.978	0.899	0.709	EH,D	$6500(AV)	–	–	–
Louisiana	40.00%	1.61	2.179	2.313	1.353	1.437	AH	$7500(AV)	–	–	–
Maine	–	2.46	2.423	1.945	0.985	0.791	EV,D,B	$7000+	1971(8)	EHR,DS	$369
Maryland	–	2.42	3.030	1.515	1.252	0.626	B,DV	$6000 Total	1973(6)	AH,ER	$594
Massachusetts	–	1.37	3.201	1.921	2.336	1.402	AH,EH,V,S,B	20% Total(AV)	–	–	–
Michigan	–	2.76	3.453	3.027	1.251	1.097	DV	Total	1973(2)	AHR	$504
Minnesota	65.00%	1.34	4.471	2.682	3.337	2.001	AH	State Credit	1967(P)	AHR	$290
Mississippi	–	0.95	2.131	1.765	2.243	1.858	AH,D,EH	$5850(AV)+	–	–	–
Missouri	59.00%	1.20	2.615	2.032	2.179	1.693			1973(6)	EH R	$262
Montana	–	1.48	1.650	1.608	1.115	1.086	LI,DV	$80 000 Total	1981(3)	EH R	$237
Nebraska	–	2.43	2.263	1.838	0.931	0.756	EH,D,V,DV	$35 000(AV)	–	–	–
Nevada	–	1.00	1.018	0.821	1.018	0.821	W,O,V,DV	$1000–$10 000	1973(9)	EH R	$210
New Hampshire	–	3.48	2.830	1.698	0.813	0.488	EH,B,DV	$5000(AV) Total	–	–	–

State	Assessment ratio						Classification	Amount	Year	Classification	Amount
New Jersey	–	4.02	4.971	2.983	1.237	0.742	EH.D.S.V.DV	$250(tax) Total	1990(0)	AHR	–
New Mexico	96.±0%	1.38	1.209	0.997	0.876	0.722	AH.V	2000(AV)	1977(2)	EH R	$142
New York		0.86	3.443	2.066	4.003	2.402	EH.V.DV	Local	1978(3)	AHR	$93
North Carolina	90.(0%	1.12	1.255	1.004	1.121	0.896	EH.D.V	$15 000–38 000(AV)	–	–	–
North Dakota	90.(0%	1.97	1.829	1.098	0.928	0.557	EH.D.V	20–100%	1969(9)	EH R	$317
Ohio		1.82	1.638	1.794	0.900	0.986	LIED	$1000–$5000	1971(7)	EH.D.S	$199
Oklahoma		1.10	1.195	1.315	1.086	1.195	AH.LIHH	$1000(AV)+	1974(4)	EH.D	$118
Oregon		1.55	1.454	1.265	0.938	0.816	DV.W	$7500(AV)–10 000	1971(6)	ER	$560
Pennsylvania		2.64	3.401	2.041	1.288	0.773	B.D.DV	Total	1971(5)	EH R.D.S	$257
Rhode Island		3.04	3.938	2.574	1.295	0.847	B.V.DV.POW	$1000–15 000(AV)	1977(1)	EH R.D	$170
South Carolina	66.65%	1.42	1.637	2.196	1.153	1.546	EH.B.D.DV	$20 000 Total	–	–	–
South Dakota	66.65%	2.23	1.975	1.185	0.886	0.531	DV	Total	1976(3)	EH R.D	$146
Tennessee		1.53	2.214	1.709	1.447	1.117		Total	1973(10)	EH.D.V.S	$90
Texas	62.5%	2.61	2.743	2.764	1.051	1.059	AH.E.D.DV	$5000+20%(AV) +	1977(4)	EHR.W	
Utah		1.55	1.396	1.130	0.901	0.729	EH.DV.B.S	$475(C)–30 000(AV)	1969(5)	AHR	$518
Vermont	75.00%	1.98	2.422	1.939	1.223	0.979	V.DV	$10 000–20 000		AHR	
Virginia		1.12	1.624	1.019	1.450	0.910	EH.D	Local		EH.D	
Washington		1.14	1.119	0.914	0.982	0.802	LIED	Up to Total	1972(–)	EH.D	–
West Virginia		1.84	1.711	1.771	0.930	0.963	EH.D	$20 000(AV)	1964(9)	EH R	
Wisconsin	50.00%	3.32	2.756	1.511	0.830	0.455	AH	$9150(AV)	1975(7)	AHR	$425
Wyoming		0.77	0.753	0.729	0.978	0.947	AH.V.DV	$590(C) Total		AHR.D	$521
Average		1.75	2.27	1.75	1.42	1.11					

Notes:

1 The assessment ratio (or rate) for owner occupied housing is divided by that for commercial/industrial property and then multiplied by 100 to produce this column.

2 In 1991 Colorado's relative assessment ration for owner occupied housing was 72 per cent of commercial/industrial. By 1997 it was 33.4 per cent.

3 Classification applies only in Cook County.

A – all	C – tax credit	HH – head of household	M – minor	R – renter:
AV – assessed value	D – disabled	H – homeowner	P – periodically	S – surviving spouse
B – blind	E – elderly	LI – low income	POW – prisoner of war	W – widow

Sources: Advisory Commission on Intergovernmental Relations. *Significant Features of Fiscal Federalism, Volume 1* (Washington, DC: US Government Printing Office, 1990, 1992, 1994). 1996 residential effective tax rates, 1998 commercial and industrial tax rates, International Association of Assessing Officers, online library excerpts from Edward W Wyatt, *Tax Rates and Tax Burdens in the District of Columbia: A Nationwide Comparison 1996* (Washington, DC: Office of Tax and Revenue, Government of the District of Columbia, 1997); and Minnesota Taxpayers Association, *50 State Property Tax Comparison Study 1998* (St. Paul, MN: Minnesota Taxpayers Association, 1998).

Table 5.7   Relative reliance on property taxes by states, 1972 and 1999

Rank	Ratio of Local Property Tax to State Personal Income				Ratio of Total Local Property Taxes to Local General Revenue				Ratio of Total Local Own-Source Revenue to Total State Own Source Revenue			
	1972		1999		1972		1999		1972		1999	
1	Massachusetts	0.063	New Hampshire	0.054	New Hampshire	0.681	New Hampshire	0.695	New Jersey	1.401	New York	1.238
2	South Dakota	0.063	New Jersey	0.050	Massachusetts	0.664	Rhode Island	0.575	Nebraska	1.262	New Hampshire	1.224
3	Montana	0.058	Maine	0.049	Connecticut	0.662	California	0.551	California	1.210	Florida	1.056
4	California	0.058	Rhode Island	0.044	Vermont	0.647	New Jersey	0.516	Ohio	1.182	Colorado	1.027
5	New Jersey	0.055	New York	0.040	Maine	0.646	Maine	0.502	New Hampshire	1.168	Texas	1.005
6	Connecticut	0.055	Connecticut	0.040	South Dakota	0.601	Massachusetts	0.420	New York	1.152	Georgia	0.953
7	New Hampshire	0.054	Alaska	0.039	Rhode Island	0.591	Hawaii	0.417	South Dakota	1.091	Wyoming	0.933
8	Wisconsin	0.054	Wisconsin	0.038	Montana	0.586	South Dakota	0.382	Missouri	1.085	Tennessee	0.925
9	Iowa	0.053	Illinois	0.037	New Jersey	0.553	Illinois	0.379	Massachusetts	1.066	Illinois	0.909
10	New York	0.052	Texas	0.035	Indiana	0.519	Nevada	0.354	Nevada	1.065	Nevada	0.881
11	Vermont	0.052	Iowa	0.035	Nebraska	0.514	Texas	0.344	Kansas	1.049	Ohio	0.874
12	Minnesota	0.051	Nebraska	0.035	Oregon	0.500	Montana	0.331	Oregon	1.021	New Jersey	0.843
13	Nebraska	0.051	Montana	0.034	Iowa	0.495	Indiana	0.328	Indiana	1.015	Nebraska	0.842
14	Maine	0.051	South Dakota	0.034	Kansas	0.486	Virginia	0.323	Montana	1.002	Kansas	0.816
15	Indiana	0.049	Massachusetts	0.034	Illinois	0.485	Wisconsin	0.322	Illinois	0.991	Arizona	0.806
36	Virginia	0.026	Missouri	0.023	Virginia	0.312	Utah	0.226	Oklahoma	0.586	Maine	0.591
37	Oklahoma	0.025	California	0.022	Maryland	0.309	Delaware	0.220	Arkansas	0.574	Wisconsin	0.589
38	Tennessee	0.025	North Carolina	0.022	West Virginia	0.302	Wyoming	0.216	Alabama	0.573	Rhode Island	0.570
39	Mississippi	0.024	West Virginia	0.022	Nevada	0.297	Mississippi	0.216	Utah	0.572	North Dakota	0.550
40	North Carolina	0.023	Nevada	0.021	South Carolina	0.285	Tennessee	0.212	Vermont	0.547	Michigan	0.536
41	West Virginia	0.022	Washington	0.021	Arkansas	0.284	North Carolina	0.208	Mississippi	0.542	Connecticut	0.533
42	Hawaii	0.022	Tennessee	0.019	Tennessee	0.280	Washington	0.201	Louisiana	0.487	Massachusetts	0.484
43	South Carolina	0.022	Hawaii	0.018	North Carolina	0.271	Nevada	0.194	Kentucky	0.473	Arkansas	0.469
44	Arkansas	0.022	Arkansas	0.017	Kentucky	0.250	Arkansas	0.190	South Carolina	0.464	Kentucky	0.460
45	Louisiana	0.019	Louisiana	0.016	Mississippi	0.241	California	0.172	North Carolina	0.447	West Virginia	0.426
46	New Mexico	0.019	Oklahoma	0.016	Delaware	0.226	Kentucky	0.167	West Virginia	0.427	New Mexico	0.388
47	Alaska	0.019	Delaware	0.015	Louisiana	0.189	Oklahoma	0.166	Alaska	0.384	Alaska	0.321
48	Delaware	0.018	New Mexico	0.015	New Mexico	0.179	Louisiana	0.147	Delaware	0.351	Vermont	0.291
49	Kentucky	0.018	Kentucky	0.014	Alaska	0.179	New Mexico	0.123	New Mexico	0.346	Hawaii	0.263
50	Alabama	0.010	Alabama	0.010	Alabama	0.123	Alabama	0.103	Hawaii	0.314	Delaware	0.24
Cross 50 State Average:		0.038		0.029		0.403		0.291		0.793		0.698
Coefficient of Variation:		37.11		33.2		34.74		40.05		33.94		31.73

Rat-o of Local Property Taxes to Local Current Charges and Miscellaneous Revenues

Rank	State (1972)	1972	State (1999)	1999
1	Vermont	8.675	Rhode Island	5.553
2	Connecticut	8.497	Connecticut	5.095
3	Rhode Island	8.489	New Hampshire	4.999
4	Maine	7.662	New Jersey	3.272
5	New Hampshire	6.621	Massachusetts	3.240
6	Massachusetts	6.539	Maine	3.154
7	New Jersey	5.482	Vermont	2.426
8	South Dakota	4.420	Illinois	1.936
9	Montana	4.062	South Dakota	1.918
10	Illinois	3.968	Wisconsin	1.787
11	Wisconsin	3.719	Virginia	1.643
12	Virginia	3.461	Maryland	1.537
13	Hawaii	3.274	Hawaii	1.500
14	California	3.186	New York	1.487
15	Indiana	3.032	Texas	1.463
36	Oklahoma	1.482	Florida	0.841
37	Washington	1.410	South Carolina	0.789
38	Florida	1.359	Washington	0.731
39	South Carolina	1.314	Arkansas	0.709
40	Tennessee	1.304	Tennessee	0.700
41	Nevada	1.253	Nevada	0.698
42	Delaware	1.186	North Carolina	0.687
43	Kentucky	1.150	California	0.685
44	Georgia	1.138	Mississippi	0.632
45	Louisiana	1.050	Wyoming	0.629
46	New Mexico	1.031	Kentucky	0.626
47	Arkansas	1.024	Louisiana	0.584
48	Mississippi	0.939	New Mexico	0.573
49	Alaska	0.721	Oklahoma	0.544
50	Alabama	0.431	Alabama	0.329
Cross 50 State Average:		2.915		1.456
Coefficient of Variation:		71.16		79.24

Ratio of Local Property Taxes to Local Intergovernmental Revenues from the State

Rank	State (1972)	1972	State (1999)	1999
1	New Hampshire	4.131	New Hampshire	5.449
2	Massachusetts	3.838	Hawaii	3.991
3	Hawaii	3.575	Rhode Island	2.121
4	South Dakota	3.516	Connecticut	1.843
5	Connecticut	3.034	New Jersey	1.763
6	Maine	2.895	Maine	1.716
7	Montana	2.710	South Dakota	1.421
8	Vermont	2.582	Texas	1.285
9	Nebraska	2.562	Illinois	1.244
10	Rhode Island	2.232	Nebraska	1.197
11	Oregon	2.150	Colorado	1.118
12	New Jersey	2.108	Massachusetts	1.086
13	Indiana	1.838	Montana	1.027
14	Ohio	1.825	Virginia	1.005
15	Illinois	1.764	Maryland	0.963
36	Virginia	0.881	Washington	0.553
37	Minnesota	0.861	Mississippi	0.543
38	Maryland	0.795	North Carolina	0.532
39	New York	0.786	West Virginia	0.521
40	West Virginia	0.748	Nevada	0.511
41	Kentucky	0.703	Michigan	0.488
42	South Carolina	0.671	Oklahoma	0.487
43	Mississippi	0.665	Delaware	0.471
44	North Carolina	0.544	Arkansas	0.469
45	Delaware	0.524	Kentucky	0.461
46	Louisiana	0.478	Louisiana	0.440
47	Alaska	0.446	California	0.427
48	New Mexico	0.373	Alabama	0.383
49	Alabama	0.356	New Mexico	0.278
50		0.338		0.246
Cross 50 State Average:		1.48		0.989
Coefficient of Variation:		64.62		88.22

Ratio of Local Own-Source Revenue to Local Intergovernmental Revenues from the State

Rank	State (1972)	1972	State (1999)	1999
1	Hawaii	5.607	Hawaii	7.675
2	New Hampshire	4.825	New Hampshire	6.608
3	South Dakota	4.549	Colorado	2.956
4	Massachusetts	4.455	South Dakota	2.542
5	Nebraska	3.809	Rhode Island	2.532
6	Montana	3.484	Texas	2.487
7	Connecticut	3.415	Maryland	2.373
8	Maine	3.325	Nebraska	2.365
9	Ohio	3.058	New Jersey	2.341
10	Oregon	2.968	Maine	2.302
11	Vermont	2.927	Florida	2.294
12	Missouri	2.788	Connecticut	2.237
13	New Jersey	2.713	Tennessee	2.170
14	Rhode Island	2.520	Georgia	2.166
15	Illinois	2.483	Illinois	2.144
36	Kentucky	1.541	Kentucky	1.521
37	Alabama	1.536	North Carolina	1.490
38	Utah	1.532	Arizona	1.457
39	Maryland	1.444	Massachusetts	1.457
40	Wisconsin	1.334	Idaho	1.453
41	New York	1.298	Mississippi	1.450
42	West Virginia	1.253	Arkansas	1.365
43	Minnesota	1.247	Minnesota	1.350
44	Louisiana	1.218	West Virginia	1.224
45	South Carolina	1.210	Wisconsin	1.157
46	Mississippi	1.179	California	1.139
47	Alaska	1.023	Delaware	1.066
48	Delaware	0.959	Michigan	1.010
49	North Carolina	0.859	New Mexico	0.885
50	New Mexico	0.754	Vermont	0.711
Cross 50 State Average:		2.222		1.993
Coefficient of Variation:		47.59		57.92

Source: US Department of Commerce, *State and Local Government Finances,* 1972 and 1999.

153

NOTES

1. Studies of the fiscal effect of tax and expenditure limitations on the state and local sector have focused on tax burdens, the impact of limitations on single jurisdictions, and the affects of limitations on the level and mix of government revenues and expenditures in a cross-section of jurisdictions. Most of these have focused on single states, rather than evaluating effects generally (Danziger, 1980; Kemp, 1982; Shapiro and Sonstelle, 1982; Susskind and Horan, 1983; Megdal, 1986; Merriman, 1986; Sherwood-Call, 1987; Reid, 1988; Fisher and Gade, 1991; Cutler et al., 1997; Dye and McGuire, 1997; Bradbury et al., 1998; Sexton et al., 1999). The earlier cross-sectional studies tested only very general effects, with the most prominent focus being the size/scope of government (Kenyon and Benker, 1984; Cebula, 1986; Howard, 1989). Comprehensive analyses of overall effects of these limitations on the composition and structure of the state and local public sector have occurred more recently (Joyce and Mullins, 1991; Preston and Ichniowski, 1991; Elder, 1992; Mullins and Joyce, 1996; Shadbegian, 1996, 1998, 1999; Skidmore, 1999). The findings of these studies include (i) little effect on the overall size of the state and local public sector (some studies find this effect to be larger than others, Shadbegian, 1996); (ii) decreased use of local broad based taxes (specifically property taxes) and shifts to state aid, user charges and miscellaneous revenues; (iii) expanded relative fiscal (revenue and expenditure) role for state governments (Preston and Ichniowski, 1991; Mullins, 1992; Mullins and Joyce, 1996; Shadbegian, 1998, 1999). Some have attempted to also assess the impact of limitation on long term public service performance. Downes and Figlio (1999) provide a summary assessment of limitations effects on school performance based on a review of previous research. The authors conclude that limitations have adversely affected outcomes in public schools. Such conclusions are not universal (see Downes, Dye and McGuire, 1998). Others have more specifically focused on public sector employment and wage effects. One such study assesses the effect of limitations on employment levels, wages and public sector wage premiums, finding that limitations have limited effect on employment levels, while reducing relative wages in the local public sector (Poterba and Rueben, 1995).
2. This modern wave of initiatives to limit local government can be viewed as a continuation of a centuries long struggle for autonomy between cities and their states (see Teaford, 1973).
3. Some point to the existence of local override measures, usually via popular vote (and sometimes requiring super majorities), as mechanisms for maintaining local control. However, the effectiveness of these measures for such is suspect.
4. The result is the opposite of the prescription offered by the leading and most enduring model of local government efficiency articulated by Charles Tiebout (1956) and contrary to median voter prescripts. This assessment, however, is not universal (see McGuire, 1999). Some argue that if the Leviathan model of the budget maximizing bureaucrat is operational at the local level of government (the least likely level of government for it to be) the effect of limitations may be to constrain excessive government and waste. This view seems less than compelling, as it is highly unlikely that such excess would be universally existent in the local sector of a state and that the uniform application of local limitations would be effective in targeting and constraining only local jurisdictions operating in excess. Such broad brush application handed down from the state level is unlikely to enhance local efficiency in the aggregate.
5. While not technically in the category of a limitation, in 1997 the state of Vermont adopted an education finance reform (in response to a State Supreme Court decision) which has substantially altered the level of accessibility of the local property tax base for local education. Above a threshold level, a portion of revenues generated by increased local property tax levies are pooled for distribution across school districts in the state. This has significantly altered the role of the property tax in local finance. New Hampshire has also recently instituted a statewide property tax to fund education in response to an order from

its Supreme Court to restructure education finance. The role of the property tax is undergoing redefinition.

6. As many as 29 states have had such limitations, however, Idaho's 1979 limitation was repealed in 1992 and Utah's 1969 limitation was repealed in 1986.

7. At least 12 states have adopted such limitations, however, Maryland's 1957 assessment increase limitation was repealed in 1991 and Washington's 2000 limitation was ruled unconstitutional in 2001.

8. General revenue limits were repealed in Minnesota and Nevada during 1993 and 1989, respectively.

9. See Mullins and Cox (1995) for a description of all limitations existent through 1995.

10. Arizona combines property tax revenue limits with general expenditure limits (both enacted more than 75 years ago, except for those affecting school districts) with modern period (1980) limits on both overall property tax rates and assessment increases. In addition to a school district general revenue limit enacted in 1972, California established an overall property tax rate limit coupled with an assessment increase limit in 1978 and added a general expenditure limit in 1979 and a comprehensive set of new tax, fee and rate increase limitations in 1997. Colorado's 1913 property tax revenue limits (applying to counties and municipalities) were reinforced in 1992 with a provision applying to school districts. In 1992 Colorado also applied specific property tax rate limits, general revenue limits, and general expenditure limits across all local governments (although school district general expenditure limits had existed since 1973). Colorado also requires full disclosure. New Mexico's limitations include overall property tax rate limits (1914), specific property tax rate limits (1973), property tax revenue limits (1979) and limits on assessment increases (1979). In addition to its 1991 overall property tax rate limits, Oregon adopted a stringent set of specific rate and assessment limits coupled with revenue and fee limitations during 1997. During each of the past three years, Washington has added to its existing set of property tax rate and revenue limitations. Measures adopted during 1999 and 2000 requiring voter approval for all increases in taxes and licenses were struck down by the Court. A new revenue limitation was adopted during 2001 limiting annual property tax revenue growth to one per cent.

11. For example, in 1992 the Virginia legislature adopted a constitutional amendment limiting revenue to expenditures and in the same year Rhode Island adopted (by referenda) a measure limiting expenditures to an amount less that 100 per cent of revenue. Similar anti-deficiency provisions have been enacted in Delaware, Iowa and Mississippi. These generally do not apply to capital expenditures financed by debt. On the other hand Washington, Oregon and Colorado have adopted rather stringent limits on tax revenues and have also limited expenditures or appropriations.

12. For evidence of the greater efficacy of constraints imposed through the initiative process see New (2001).

13. This point of view is represented by the 'public choice' school, and its most extreme embodiment is probably that offered by the 'Leviathan' champions (see Brazer, 1981).

14. Illinois offers a somewhat unique context. Because state-imposed limitations do not affect home rule cities, local populations can effectively choose to opt out of these limitations by adopting a home rule charter. Temple (1996) tests the conditions affecting such local choice and finds that less homogenous communities are less likely to choose to opt out of state limitations. The execution of vote override options provides a similar research opportunity. Studies of Proposition 2½ in Massachusetts have attempted to assess the determinants of support for such overrides and their implications (see Cutler et al., 1997; Bradbury et al , 1998).

15. There was, however, no consensus on displeasure by level of government.

16. Across states, Colorado ranks 44th in the level of state and local taxes per $1000 of personal income.

17. The growth factors are population for the state, pupils for school districts and additions to real property for local jurisdictions. Government enterprise activities receiving less than ten per cent of revenue from tax sources are excluded.

18.   This is the exception of Fischel's arguments for California's Proposition 13 passage, see below.
19.   As such, the elements surrounding it offer a microcosm of the issues dominant across the broader restructuring of the local public sector. It simultaneously reflects the political agenda and strength of residents, businesses, elderly and 'home owners' groups. It captures conflicts between the public and government for higher quality government services at lower cost to particular individuals and groups, and conflict between governments in the use of shared tax bases and the distribution of expenditure responsibilities. The success of the local public sector at adapting and evolving alternative revenue and service delivery structures to compensate for the imposition of constraints has been at least partially responsible for their continued popular support. It has played to a public perception that it is continuously possible to reduce and shift revenue burdens and simultaneously maintain service levels. It has given rise to a popular belief in the proverbial 'free lunch'. This has been furthered by the extraordinary economic prosperity experienced across the nation during the mid 1990s through the turn of the century.
20.   It should be noted that this differential is often considerably higher for telecommunications property.
21.   Table 5.6 shows, for states with a general exemption, the amount of that exemption first in the column, with the high end applying to exemptions for special circumstances.
22.   Renter-oriented programs tend to have significantly lower benefit levels, as the programs assume that renters pay only a fraction of the property taxes on residential structures.
23.   At the time of ownership change, the property is revalued for tax purposes at its selling price. If properties are significantly modified through structural additions, the addition is valued at its market value at the time of alteration and added to the base value of the existing property for tax purposes. In essence, the alteration is treated as a separate parcel for tax purposes aggregated with the original parcel. The California structure also allows for property to be passed between immediate family members (parents to children) without triggering reassessment. Property owners under age 55 can change residences within the same county and retain their existing assessment as long as they purchase a property with a lower market value than the one they are selling.
24.   A study by O'Sullivan et al. (1995, Chapter Four) offers an assessment of these effects. The review that follows relies on their estimates and findings.
25.   For a more detailed discussion of the Court's opinion in this case and how it distinguished it from an earlier West Virginia case in which it reached an opposing conclusion see Mullins (1992).
26.   Unlike California, the overwhelming tendency in these states is to limit the increase in residential assessments only.
27.   These figures are based on average scope of the state and local sector across states, not state and local general revenue divided by national personal income. That is state and local general revenue as a portion of personal income is calculated for each state, and from these figures the cross state mean is calculated. This implicitly uses the state as the unit of analysis and eliminates the influence of differences in population size in generating a national average. All subsequent figures are based on cross state averages rather than aggregate national averages, unless otherwise indicated. Data comes from the US Department of Commerce (various years).
28.   State and local figures cannot be summed to produce state and local sectoral totals due to intergovernmental transfers from states to localities appearing as revenue for both levels.
29.   Figures for comparisons between local governments are based on aggregate levels across the US, not based on the average of individual state ratios. Data comes from the Department of Commerce.
30.   This is the continuation of a trend begun much earlier in the century.
31.   During the 1977–79 period direct federal transfers to the local sector topped ten per cent of general revenue and own-source revenue dipped under 58 per cent.
32.   The overall tax contribution to local general revenue has been slightly buoyed by modest and gradual increases in the use of local sales taxes. By 1999, local general sales taxes still accounted for only 3.9 per cent of local general revenue, with selective sales taxes

adding an additional 1.5 per cent. Income taxes, on average, remain inconsequential at the local level, accounting for 1.3 per cent of general revenue across states.

33. School districts' share of revenue dropped between the mid 1970s and mid 1980s. Municipalities show two different periods of earlier and later decline.
34. California drops from fourth to 37th.
35. The situation for New Hampshire is likely to be altered considerably due to the state's implementation of a property tax-based education finance reform.
36. Illinois' limitation applies to only non-home rule jurisdictions and New York's focus on Nassau County and New York City.
37. Vermont drops due to the state education finance reform.
38. A compelling attribute of the property tax over fees and charges which we have not discussed is the substantially reduced tax price afforded through federal and some state income tax deductibility.
39. The oldest recorded evidence of the property tax can be found in the *Book of the Dead* in 15th century BC Egypt. It also appears in the *Dead Sea Scrolls* in 134 AD. The first recorded discussion of its potential regressivity is found regarding its 284–305 AD application in Rome. The first religious exemption to appear was during 573–594 in France. The *Domesday Book*, during the reign of King William I of England, reflects the first comprehensive recording and inventorying of property for tax roll purposes in 1086. It was deemed the book from which there is no appeal. The first recorded relief due to economic obsolescence was in 1430 England due to the flooding of crop land (Daw, 2001). Medieval tax administration dealt with issues of valuation similar to those of today (Seligman, 1931).
40. Current discussions in the State of Maryland have highlighted the potential of slot machines as a state and local revenue generator.
41. In protest of the new education finance system, numerous communities across the state withheld their payments to the 'shark pool'. Some also withheld their payment of the state property tax levy.
42. This research uses time series data on all units of government in 787 metropolitan counties in the United States to begin to assess the more micro effects of state-imposed tax and expenditure limitations on the fiscal structure of local government in states enacting these limits. The time frame of the study extends from 1972 through 1997 and draws on observation from six successive censuses of governments and a variety of geographically specific demographic and economic data to estimate the effects of these limitations, controlling for the demographic and economic characteristics of each unit of local government. Units studied include over 30 000 counties, cities, towns, school districts, and special districts in the 48 contiguous states for 1972, 1977, 1982, 1987, 1992 and 1997. The resulting data set includes over 190 000 observations and approximately 500 measures for each jurisdiction.

REFERENCES

Alm, James and Mark Skidmore (1999), 'Why do tax and expenditure limitations pass in state elections?', *Public Finance Review*, 27(5): 481–510.

Alsdorj, Robert H. (2000), 'Initiative 695 unconstitutional, says superior court', *State Tax Notes*, 20 March 2000: 895.

Associated Press (1999), 'Manchester raises enough money to avoid Act 60 sharing pool for two years', Manchester, VT, 5 May.

Associated Press (2001), 'School fund nears goal', Dorset, VT, 27 April.

Bradbury, Katherine, Karl E. Case and Christopher J. Mayer (1997), 'Property tax limits and local fiscal behavior: Did Massachusetts' cities and towns spend too little on town services under Proposition 2½?', Federal Reserve Bank of Boston Working Paper 97–2, Boston, MA, July.

Bradbury, Katherine, Karl E. Case and Christopher J. Mayer (1998), 'School quality and Massachusetts enrollment shifts in the context of tax limitations', *New England Economic Review*, July/August: 3–18.
Brazer, H.E. (1981), 'On tax limitations', in Norman Walzer and David Chicoine (eds), *Financing State and Local Government in the 1980s*, Cambridge, MA: Oelgeschlager, Gunn and Hain, pp. 19–34.
Brennan, Geoffrey and James Buchanan (1979), 'The logic of tax limits: Alternative constitutional constraints of the power to tax', *National Tax Journal*, 32(2): 11–22.
Brunori, David (1999), 'The politics of state taxation', *State Tax Notes*, 27 September: 841.
Brunori, David (2000), 'Politics of state taxation: The citizens set policy in the 2000 elections', *State Tax Notes*, 20 November: 1379.
Burrows, Don (2000a), 'Judge's injunction blocks property tax limit', *State Tax Notes*, 11 December: 1564–65.
Burrows, Don (2000b), 'State high court rejects measure to require vote on tax, fee increase', *State Tax Notes*, 6 November: 1213.
Burrows, Don (2000c), '1999: The year of the citizen tax revolt', *State Tax Notes*, 10 January: 96.
Burrows, Don (2001a), 'High court hears arguments to restore rollback-limit measure', *State Tax Notes*, 18 June: 2123.
Burrows, Don (2001b), 'Activist sees property tax limit petition approved', *State Tax Notes*, 12 February: 507.
Burrows, Don (2001c), 'Activist files new local tax limit initiative', *State Tax Notes*, 15 January: 175.
Cebula, Richard J. (1986), 'Tax-expenditure limitation in the US: Two alternative evaluations', *Economic Notes*: 140–51.
Chernick, Howard and Andrew Reschovsky (1982), 'The distributional impact of Proposition 13: A microsimulation approach', *National Tax Journal*, 35(2): 149–70.
Citrin, Jack (1979), 'Do people want something for nothing? Public opinion on taxes and government spending', *National Tax Journal*, 32(2), 113–29.
Cole, Richard L. and John Kincaid (2000), 'Public opinion and American federalism: Perspectives on taxes, spending, and trust: an ACIR update', *Publius*, 30(1–2): 189–201.
Courant, Paul, Edward Gramlich and Daniel Rubinfeld (1985), 'Why voters support tax limitations: The Michigan case', *National Tax Journal*, 38(1): 1–20.
Cutler, David M., Douglas W. Elmendorf and Richard J. Zeckhauser (1997), 'Restraining the Leviathan: property tax limitation in Massachusetts', NBER Working paper No. 6196, Cambridge, MA: National Bureau of Economic Research, September.
Cutler, David M., Douglas W. Elmendorf and Richard J. Zeckhauser (1999), 'Restraining the Leviathan: property tax limitation in Massachusetts', *Journal of Public Economics*, 71: 313–34.
Danziger, James N. (1980), 'California's Proposition 13 and the fiscal limitations movement in the United States', *Political Studies*, 28(4): 599–612.
Danziger, James N. and Peter Smith Ring (1982), 'Fiscal limitations: A selective review of recent research', *Public Administration Review* 42 (January/February): 47–55.
Daw, C.A. (2001), 'Revolts, exemptions, and regressivity: Ruminations on the past', *Assessment Journal*, March/April: 45–50.

Doerr, David (1996), 'Voters approve right to vote on taxes', *State Tax Notes*, 11 November: 1334.

Downes, Thomas A. and David N. Figlio (1999), 'Do tax and expenditure limits provide a free lunch? Evidence on the link between limits and public sector service quality', *National Tax Journal*, 52(1): 113–28.

Downes, Thomas A., Richard F. Dye and Therese J. McGuire (1998), 'Do limits matter? Evidence of the effects of tax limitations on student performance', *Journal of Urban Economics*, 43(3): 401–17.

Doyle, Maura (1994), 'Property tax limitations and the delivery of fire protection services', Working paper, Federal Reserve Bank Board of Governors.

Dye, Richard F. and Therese J. McGuire (1997), 'The effect of property tax limitation measures on local government fiscal behavior', *Journal of Public Economics*, 66(3): 469–87.

Elder, Harold W. (1992), 'Exploring the tax revolt: An analysis of the effects of state tax and expenditure limitation laws', *Public Finance Quarterly*, 20(1): 47–63.

Figlio, David N. and Kim S. Rueben (2001), 'Tax limits and the qualifications of new teachers', *Journal of Public Economics*, 80: 49–71.

Figlio, David N. and Arthur O'Sullivan (2001), 'The local response to tax limitation measures: Do local governments manipulate voters to increase revenues?', *Journal of Law and Economics*, 44 (April): 233–57.

Fischel, William A. (1989), 'Did "Serrano" cause Proposition 13?', *National Tax Journal*, 42(4): 465–73.

Fischel, William A. (2001), 'Homevoters, municipal corporate governance, and the benefit view of the property tax', *National Tax Journal*, 54(1): 157–73.

Fisher, Glenn W. (1996), *The Worst Tax? A History of the Property Tax in America*, Lawrence, KS: University Press of Kansas.

Fisher, Ronald C. and Mary N. Gade (1991), 'Local property tax and expenditure limits', in T.J. McGuire and D. Wolf Naimark (eds), *State and Local Finance for the 1990s: A Case Study of Arizona*, Tempe, AZ: Arizona State University, pp. 449–64.

Gold, Steven David (1979), *Property Tax Relief*, Lexington, MA: Lexington Books.

Hamilton, Amy (1996), 'Voters pass three property tax amendments', *State Tax Notes*, 11 November: 1352.

Hornbeck, Mark (2001), 'Schools build private reserves', *The Detroit News*, 24 December.

Howard, Marcia (1989), 'State tax and expenditure limitations: There is no story', *Public Budgeting and Finance*, 9(2): 83–90.

James, Franklin (2001), 'Tax and spending limits in Colorado', Working paper, Lincoln Land Institute, Conference on Tax and Expenditure Limitations, Graduate School of Public Affairs, University of Colorado, Denver, CO, July.

James, Franklin J. and Oksana Rudiuk (2001), 'Inventory: Tax and spending limits in the United States', Working paper, Graduate School of Public Affairs, University of Colorado at Denver, CO, July.

Joyce, Philip G. and Daniel R. Mullins (1991), 'The changing fiscal structure of the state and local public sector: The impact of tax and expenditure limitations', *Public Administration Review*, 51(3): 240–53.

Kemp, Roger (1982), 'California's Proposition 13: A one-year assessment', *State and Local Government Review*, 14, January: 44–7.

Kenyon, Daphne and Karen Benker (1984), 'Fiscal discipline: Lessons from the state experience', *National Tax Journal*, 37: 437–46.

Knittel, Matthew J. and Mark P. Haas (1998), 'Michigan's proposal A: A retrospective', *State Tax Notes*, 26 October: 1061.

Ladd, Helen and Julie Boatright Wilson (1981), *Proposition 2½: Explaining the Vote*, Cambridge, MA: John F. Kennedy School of Government.

Ladd, Helen and Julie Boatright Wilson (1982), 'Why voters support tax limitations: Evidence from Massachusetts' Proposition 2½', *National Tax Journal* 35(2): 121–47.

Ladd, Helen and Julie Boatright Wilson (1983), 'Who supports tax limitations: Evidence from Massachusetts' Proposition 2½', *Journal of Policy Analysis and Management*, 2(2): 256–79.

Lowery, David (1985), 'Public opinion, fiscal illusion, and tax revolution: The political demise of the property tax', *Public Budgeting & Finance*, 5(3): 76–88.

Massey, Barry (2000), 'Governor signs property tax limit', *State Tax Notes*, 28 February: 648.

Mayer, James (1997), 'Lawmakers put rewrite of property tax limit on May ballot', *State Tax Notes*, 7 April: 1059.

McGuire, Therese J. (1999), 'Proposition 13 and its offspring: For good or for evil?', *National Tax Journal*, 52(1): 129–38.

Megdal, Sharon Bernstein (1986), 'Estimating a public school expenditure model under binding spending limitations', *Journal of Urban Economics*, 19: 277–95.

Merriman, David (1986), 'The distributional effects of New Jersey's tax and expenditure limitations', *Land Economics*, 62(4): 354–61.

Mullins, Daniel R. (1992), '"Welcome stranger" assessment prevails', Association for Budgeting and Financial Management, SBFM Newsletter, *News & Views*, Winter.

Mullins, Daniel R. (2001), *The Effects of Tax and Expenditure Limitations on the Fiscal Structure of Local Government*, Lincoln Land Institute, Conference of Tax and Expenditure Limitations, Denver, CO, July.

Mullins, Daniel R. and Kimberly A. Cox (1995), *Tax and Expenditure Limits on Local Governments*, M-194, Washington, DC: Advisory Commission on Inter-Governmental Relations.

Mullins, Daniel R. and Philip G. Joyce (1996), 'Tax and expenditure limitations and state and local fiscal structure: An empirical assessment', *Public Budgeting & Finance*, 16(1): 75–101.

New, Michael (2001), 'Tax and expenditure limitations and budgetary outcomes', Conference on Tax and Expenditure Limitations, University of Colorado at Denver, Graduate School of Public Affairs, Denver, CO, July.

Niskanen, William A. (1971), *Bureaucracy and Representative Government*, Chicago, IL: Aldine-Atherton Press.

Nordlinger v. *Hahn* (1992), US Law Week, 60 LW 4563–4574.

Oates, Wallace E. (1981), 'Fiscal limitations: An assessment of the US experience', *Sloan Working Paper*, 5–81.

O'Sullivan, Arthur, Terri A. Sexton and Steven M. Sheffrin (1995), *Property Taxes and Tax Revolts: The Legacy of Proposition 13*, New York, NY: Cambridge University Press.

Poterba, James and Kim S. Rueben (1995), 'The effect of property-tax limits on wages and employment in the public sector', *American Economic Review* 84(2): 384–9.

Preston, Anne E. and Casey Ichniowski (1991), 'A national perspective on the nature and effects of the local property tax revolt: 1976–1987', *National Tax Journal*, 44(2), 123–45.

Rafool, Mandy (1996), 'State tax and expenditure limitations', *The Fiscal Perspective*, (NCSL), 18(5).

Rafool, Mandy (1998), 'State tax and expenditure limits: Appendix C', *Fiscal Affairs*, National Conference of State Legislatures, electronic publications, March.

Reid, Gary J. (1988), 'How cities in California have responded to fiscal pressures since Proposition 13', *Public Budgeting and Finance*, 8(1), 20–37.

Rudiuk, Oksana (2001), 'The new wave of tax revolt: How it is different from the first one?', Working paper, Graduate School of Public Affairs, University of Colorado at Denver, CO, 1 June.

Sears, David O. and Jack Citrin (1982), *Tax Revolt: Something for Nothing in California*, Cambridge, MA: Harvard University Press.

Seligman, Edwin R.A. (1931), 'A mediaeval tax problem', *The American Economic Review*, 21(4): 672–81.

Serrano v. *Priest* (1976), 135 California Reporter 345, 30 December.

Sexton, Terri A., Steven M. Sheffrin and Arthur O'Sullivan (1999), 'Proposition 13: Unintended effects and feasible reforms', *National Tax Journal*, 52(1): 99–111.

Shadbegian, Ronald J. (1996), 'Do tax and expenditure limitations affect the size and growth of state government?', *Contemporary Economic Policy*, 14 (January): 22–35.

Shadbegian, Ronald J. (1998), 'Do tax and expenditure limitations affect local government budgets? Evidence from panel data', *Public Finance Review*, 26(2): 118–36.

Shadbegian, Ronald J. (1999), 'The effect of tax and expenditure limitations on the revenue structure of local government, 1962–87', *National Tax Journal*, 52(2): 221–37.

Shapiro, Perry and Jon Sonstelle (1982), 'Did Proposition 13 slay Leviathan?', *AEA Papers and Proceedings*, 72(2): 184–90.

Sheffrin, Steven M. (1998), 'The future of the property tax: A political economy perspective', in David Brunori (ed.), *The Future of State Taxation,* Washington, DC: The Urban Institute Press, pp. 129–45.

Sherwood-Call, Carolyn (1987), 'Tax revolt or tax reform: The effect of local government limitation measures in California', *Economic Notes*, San Francisco: Federal Reserve Bank: 57–67.

Skidmore, Mark (1999), 'Tax and expenditure limitations and the fiscal relationship between state and local governments', *Public Choice*, 99(1): 77–102.

Sokolow, Alvin D. (2000), 'The changing property tax in the West: State centralization of local finances', *Public Budgeting & Finance*, 20(1): 85–104.

Stein, Robert M., Keith E. Hamm and Patricia K. Freeman (1983), 'An analysis of support for tax limitation referenda', *Public Choice*, 40(2): 187–94.

Susskind, Lawrence and Cynthia Horan (1983), 'Proposition 2½ : The Response to tax restrictions in Massachusetts', in L.E. Susskind (ed.), *Proposition 2½*, Cambridge, MA: Massachusetts Institute of Technology, pp. 159–71.

Swaine, Daniel G. and Lynn E. Browne (1999), 'Can guaranteed tax base formulas achieve either wealth neutrality of spending equality, Part 2', *New England Fiscal Facts*, Spring/Summer (21): www.bos.frb.org/economic.htm

Teaford, Jon (1973), 'City versus state: The struggle for legal ascendancy', *The American Journal of Legal History*, 17: 51–65.

Temple, Judy A. (1996), 'Community composition and voter support for tax limitations: Evidence from home rule elections', *Southern Economic Journal*, 62(4): 1002–16.

Tiebout, Charles M. (1956), 'A pure theory of local expenditures', *Journal of Political Economy*, 63(3): 416–24.

US Department of Commerce (various years), *State and Local Government Finances*, series, Washington, DC: Bureau of the Census.

Wallin, Bruce A. (2001), 'The tax revolt in Massachusetts', Working paper, Lincoln Land Institute, Conference on Tax and Expenditure Limitations, Graduate School of Public Affairs, University of Colorado, Denver, CO, July.

Youngman, Joan M. (1998), 'Property, taxes, and the future of property taxes', in David Brunori (ed.), *The Future of State Taxation*, Washington, DC: The Urban Institute Press, pp. 111–28.

6. The federal government's impact on state and local government finances

Daphne A. Kenyon[1]

INTRODUCTION

The federal impact on state and local finances changed, as did much else in the United States, on 11 September, 2001. To begin with, the role of the federal government changed, which has important consequences for the responsibilities and finances of state and local governments. Equally important in the short run, the terrorist attacks of 11 September pushed the nation into a recession and recessions themselves have important effects on state and local finances.

This chapter is structured as follows. First there will be a general discussion of the ways in which the federal government affects state and local finances. Then there will be a discussion of recent changes in federal-state-local fiscal relationships: as a result of 11 September, and as a result of other factors. The last section of the chapter will focus on critical longer term issues regarding the federal government's impact on state–local finances. This final section will include recommendations.

THROUGH WHAT MEANS DOES THE FEDERAL GOVERNMENT AFFECT STATE AND LOCAL FINANCES?

Grants-in-Aid

The federal government affects state and local finances through many avenues. Perhaps the first avenue that comes to mind is the grants-in-aid provided by the federal government to state and local governments. This encompasses many aid programs from the food stamp program (administered by the US Department of Agriculture), special education grants (Department of Education), community development block grants (Department of Housing and Urban Development), Temporary Assistance to Needy Families (Department of Health and Human Services), and the highway trust fund (Department of Transportation).

From 1970 to 1999, federal grants equaled between 25 and 40 per cent of total state–local expenditures from own sources. Federal grants peaked in importance in 1980 (at 40 per cent of total state–local expenditures from own sources) and bottomed out in 1990 (at 25 per cent). From 1992 through 1999, the importance of federal aid remained very close to 30 per cent (US Bureau of Census, 2000, p. 304).

Recent years have seen important changes in the composition of federal grants-in-aid to state and local governments. The proportion of grants to individuals (rather than grants to places, such as grants for state and local capital investment) has increased from 36 per cent in 1970 to 63 per cent in 1999. Over that same time period, Medicaid has become the single largest grant to state and local governments. In 1970, Medicaid accounted for 11 per cent of total grants; by 2000, Medicaid accounted for 41 per cent (US Bureau of Census, 2000, p. 304) (see Fisher, Chapter Two of this volume).

A critical issue in the coming years will be the temptation for the federal government to react to its declining budget surpluses by cutting grants-in-aid to state and local governments.

Indirect Forms of Aid

The federal government also provides indirect aid to state and local governments through the federal tax code. Two federal income tax provisions of interest are the federal deductibility of state and local taxes and the exemption of interest on state and local bonds from taxation.

Presently individuals can deduct individual income, real estate, and personal property taxes if they itemize deductions on their federal income tax returns. The benefit from tax deductibility increases with the individual's marginal tax bracket. Someone in the 15 per cent tax bracket can receive $150 in federal tax savings for every extra $1000 in state and local taxes deducted ($1000 × 0.15); an individual in the 31 per cent tax bracket receives $310 for every extra $1000. This aid costs the federal government money in the sense that, without the allowed deduction, the existing tax code would bring in more revenue. This foregone revenue is called a 'tax expenditure'.

Tax deductibility is also considered a form of implicit aid to state and local governments. Table 6.1, which presents the costs of the major forms of federal aid to state and local governments, shows that federal revenue foregone in 2000 because of federal deductibility of state and local taxes is estimated at $64.8 billion. Thus federal tax deductibility is second in importance in terms of cost as a form of aid to state and local governments, after grants-in-aid.

Table 6.1   Cost of major forms of aid to state and local governments, 2000

Type of aid	Dollars (billions)	Per cent of total
Grants	284.1	72.2
Tax deductibility	64.8	16.5
Exclusion of interest on debt	38.4	9.8
Credit for state death tax	6.4	1.6
Total	393.7	100.0

Source: Data on grants from *US Statistical Abstract*; tax expenditure estimates from US Government Budget, FY2002.

Benefits to state and local governments are indirect: tax deductibility may make it easier for state and local governments to raise taxes or increase spending; it may also make it possible for these governments to adopt more progressive fiscal policies than they would otherwise be able to. There should be no presumption that the benefits to state and local governments from tax deductibility equal the costs to the federal government. One research study found that benefits to state and local governments may be as little as one fourth of federal costs (Kenyon, 1995, p. 38).

Benefits derived from the exemption from federal taxation of interest on state and local debt are a second form of implicit aid to state and local governments. The governments can issue debt at lower interest rates than otherwise necessary because potential investors equate the return of tax-exempt bonds to the after-tax return of taxable bonds.

For example, consider a ten year Treasury issue having an average yield of 4.25 per cent compared to 3.75 per cent for ten year municipal bonds. An individual investor in the 31 per cent marginal federal tax bracket would have received greater net benefits from the average tax-exempt bonds because the 3.75 per cent return exceeds the *net* return of 2.93 per cent from the taxable bond ($[1 - 0.31] \times 4.25$). Alternatively, all else equal, state and local governments should have been able to entice investors in the 31 per cent marginal federal tax bracket and above to buy their debt by offering a return only slightly above 2.93 per cent.

The cost to the federal government of exempting interest on municipal debt was estimated at $38.4 billion in 2000. This makes this form of implicit aid the third most costly form of federal aid to state and local governments.

A final form of implicit federal aid, that is quite small, but which has been in the news recently, is the federal credit for state death taxes. This cost the federal government $6.4 billion in 2000. It works as follows:

> Most states tie their estate tax to the federal estate tax, with taxpayers receiving a dollar-for-dollar credit against their federal liability. As of January 2001, 35 states had their estate tax structured to exactly equal this 'pickup tax'. In effect, this sends a portion of federal estate tax revenues to the states without increasing the total tax paid. (Katz, 2001: 28)

Most attention has been paid to Congress' repeal of the federal estate tax, which takes effect in 2010. However, from the states' perspectives, the repeal of the state credit in 2005 is more problematic. New England, Vermont, Rhode Island and Connecticut now receive about two per cent of state tax revenue from the 'pickup' tax; New Hampshire derives 4.6 per cent of its revenue from that tax (Katz, 2001, p. 28). Given that the repeal of the estate tax is likely to be revised (because under law, it is reinstated in 2011, the year after it is repealed), perhaps the repeal of the 'pickup' tax that benefits the states can be revisited as well.

State Linkages to Federal Tax Code

State personal income and corporate income taxes are often linked to their federal counterparts (Research Institute of America, 2002, pp. 53–4). This has numerous implications for state finances.

Consider, for example, the basic structure of the federal personal income tax. Computation of tax liability proceeds in steps, from calculation of adjusted gross income (AGI) to taxable income to tax liability. In practice, some states that impose personal income taxes link their taxes to federal AGI, others to federal taxable income or to federal tax liability. Some states have no explicit linkage to the federal personal income tax.[2]

Linkage of the state personal income tax to the federal personal income tax reduces compliance costs for taxpayers and administrative costs for state tax departments. State tax departments have entered into information sharing agreements with the federal government. These agreements save auditing expenses for the states.

A downside to these linkages to the federal code arises when the federal government enacts changes to its taxes. For example, federal individual income tax cuts will have an initial negative impact on states whose personal income taxes are linked to federal individual income tax liability. Of course, state legislatures may react by unlinking their state income taxes from the federal tax, but this action may not be easily accomplished.

The state government discussion following President Bush's signing of the March 2002 economic stimulus package focused on the unintended effects on state corporate income tax revenues. The most important part of the economic stimulus package was an improvement in business depreciation schedules. Forty-six states link their corporate income tax codes to the federal code, and of those states, 25 have corporate income taxes that automatically incorporate federal tax changes. Because of that, it was estimated that state revenues could decline by as much as $14.7 billion over the three years following enactment of the stimulus package (Caffrey, 2002).

From time to time intensive discussion arises regarding the possibility of fundamental tax reform at the federal level. Such discussion often focuses on substituting consumption taxes of some kind for our current income taxes. For example, the federal government might at some point enact a consumption-type value added tax in lieu of its personal and corporate income taxes. This could have a radical impact on state and local tax systems. The indirect forms of federal aid to state and local governments through the tax code discussed in the subsection above could be eliminated, and states would no longer have the option of piggybacking on federal corporate and personal income taxes. In the worst case, fundamental federal tax reform might force state governments to repeal their income taxes (Brunori, 1998). Movement to a consumption base is often supported with the argument that it would raise savings (and lower consumption). Another impact of such fundamental federal tax reform on state and local governments, then, would be to decrease the revenues from state and local retail sales taxes (Holtz-Eakin, 1996).

Mandates

The federal government also imposes costs on state and local governments, typically referred to as 'mandates'. The issue of mandates has become increasingly visible since the 1970s. Although not all concerns regarding mandates are fiscal, fiscal concerns appear to top the list of complaints that state and local officials have about mandates.

There are many different types of mandates, and not all types will be defined in this chapter (but see Posner, 1998, pp. 13–14). Some of the major types of mandates include:

- *Direct orders* to implement some federal standard, such as the requirement by the Americans with Disabilities Act that all public transportation systems be fully accessible to handicapped individuals
- *Cross-cutting requirements* that are attached to certain federally funded programs such as the National Environmental Policy Act's requirement for environmental impact statements
- *Cross-over sanctions* that impose penalties in one area to enforce compliance in another; for example, failure to comply with the 21-year-old drinking age can trigger withholding of some part of a state's highway grant funds.

Despite certain valiant attempts, there have been no credible, comprehensive estimates of the costs that mandates impose on state and local governments. Part of the problem in estimating mandate costs is methodological. Mandate cost estimates are typically predicated on the assumption that a federal mandate does not impose a cost on a state or local government if that government would have undertaken the activity and associated expense in the absence of the mandate. But such counterfactuals are inherently difficult to establish.

Focusing on one salient example can provide helpful insight into the mandate problem. One of the most burdensome federal mandates appears to be the 1975 legislation on special education. In brief, this legislation requires that: (1) each state provide a free and appropriate education to all handicapped children between six and 17 years of age; (2) mainstream handicapped children when appropriate; and (3) prepare individualized education plans for each child (Posner, 1998, pp. 130–1). It is generally acknowledged that under this legislation, the cost of educating a handicapped child is from two to three times the cost of educating a nonhandicapped child. The federal government initially promised to fund a certain fraction of this new mandate, but in the years since 1975 has not come close to providing the funding initially promised. In addition, school districts in financial difficulties have found that they must protect special education because of the federal mandate, and impose all budget cuts on the regular education program. The de facto policy of exempting some part of a school district's education program from budget cuts, no matter how dire the financial emergency, appears suspect.

The cumulative effects of many mandates passed over the last three decades have led some observers of our federal system to conclude that 'The proliferation of federal mandates threatens the institutional capacity of subnational governments to survive as politically viable and independent jurisdictions capable of responding to unique state or local needs' (Posner, 1998, p. 6). Given that federal policy makers can take credit for solving a problem of pressing national interest, but often foist the costs onto state and local governments, the temptation to continue mandating is obvious. Certain procedural reforms have been enacted, but there is no indication that the mandate problem has been solved. At a time when federal budget surpluses have been transformed into deficits, it is realistic to expect that federal mandates on state and local governments will continue to be an issue.

Rules of the Game

Another avenue through which the federal government has an important impact on state and local finances is through the Constitution, court interpretations of the Constitution, and federal law (other than explicit mandates on state and local governments just discussed) that affect the 'rules of the game'. For example, it can be argued that the eroding base of the once very import-ant state sales tax arises in large part because of federal court rulings on the obscure concept of 'nexus' which make it difficult for states to tax sales in a world of interstate and international corporations and electronic commerce.

A consumer contemplating traveling to a low tax state, ordering from a mail order catalog or making a purchase via the internet may be able to obtain a tax advantage relative to another consumer who drives down the street to make the same purchase. Assume that the second consumer pays a sales tax on his or her purchase. The first consumer is then legally liable to pay a companion use tax, but typically never does. States generally are able to collect use taxes only when they can require out-of-state businesses to collect them. However, this collection requirement may be imposed only when the out-of-state business has substantial nexus (measured by physical presence) within the state. This requirement goes back to the *Bellas Hess* Supreme Court case that ruled that a firm could not be required to collect a use tax in a state in which its only contact is through the US Mail or common carrier.[3]

William Fox argues that the current nexus standard results in a number of problems including distortion of economic activity, erosion of the sales tax base, and expensive litigation (Fox, 1998, pp. 41–2). He further argues that nexus should be based on a concept of economic exploitation rather than physical presence. There are at least two possible solutions to this problem, neither highly likely. One is for state governments to achieve greater uni-formity in sales taxation. The second is for Congress to pass a law changing the nexus standard to one that makes more sense in the modern economy. A third, more radical option, would be for the federal government to adopt a sales tax (presumably a VAT), thereby preempting the state sales tax base, but providing compensation by allowing states to levy a piggyback VAT on the federal tax base.

A second state tax that appears to have even greater problems, but is of less quantitative importance for state–local revenue systems, is the corporate in-come tax. Richard Pomp describes a situation of aggressive corporate tax planners, unmatched by understaffed and underfunded state tax administra-tions, who are not aided by state policy makers concerned about the impact of tax policy on economic development (Pomp, 1998). This leads to an eroding corporate tax base. The only feasible solution to this problem appears to be legislation by Congress that limits the states' freedom to use tax incentives or to modify their corporate tax bases.

Macroeconomic Policy

A final means by which the federal government affects state and local governments is through fiscal and monetary policy. This is not typically discussed in the context of various ways in which the federal government aids state and local governments, but arguably may have the greatest impact of all.

It is during a recession that state and local finances are the most strained. This is evidenced by bond rating downgrades, which can be common during a severe recession. During economic downturns, state and local governments experience declines in revenues and greater expenditure burdens, in the face of requirements to balance their budgets. In the face of an economic downturn, state governments turn to short term measures such as hiring freezes (and some budgetary gimmicks), but also enact budget cuts and tax increases. In addition, it is not unusual for states to cut back on local aid. Thus, some of the state fiscal problems are thereby passed on to local governments.

The decade from 1991 to 2001, when the nation experienced an unprecedented period of steady economic growth, was a good one for state and local finances. In the fourth quarter of 2001, in the wake of 11 September, that period of sustained economic growth was declared to be at an end: the National Bureau of Economic Research officially announced that a recession had begun in March 2001. At the time this chapter went to press, however, it looked as though the recession would be a brief and mild one. Yet because personal and corporate income taxes typically lag the economic cycle, it was predicted that state and local finances would be depressed for one to one and one half years after the first signs of economic upturn (NASBO, 2002).

The seriousness of the fiscal problems imposed by recessions depends in part on state actions. For example, has the state set in place a sound revenue forecasting system that includes incentives for politicians to make realistic assessments of technical information? Does the state have a rainy day fund of adequate size? Federal policies obviously impact the seriousness of the recession's impact as well. Fiscal policy actions are often timed poorly and the early returns on the 2001 recession are no exception. At the time the economic stimulus package was enacted in March 2002, there were many signs that the economy was already recovering from the economic downturn.

HOW ARE THE RESPONSIBILITIES OF FEDERAL, STATE AND LOCAL GOVERNMENTS CHANGING AS A RESULT OF 11 SEPTEMBER?

One of the most dramatic changes in the federal government after 11 September is the changed focus from domestic issues to issues of national defense and foreign policy. The reader may recall that during the 2000 presidential election one pundit complained that the candidates sounded more like school board candidates than presidential candidates. *The Economist* described President Bush's old policy agenda as follows:

> His mantra was localism at home and modesty abroad. Compassionate conservatism was all about little local acts of charity...The morning of 11th September found the leader of the free world reading to schoolchildren, trying to push through relatively minor education reforms. (*The Economist*, 3 November, 2001, p. 39)

Devolution Reprised

At first glance, the switch from domestic to foreign issues on the part of the federal government would seem to place more of a burden on state and local governments tackling such important domestic issues as education and health care policy. One could argue that this change in federal agenda might have a salutary effect in more appropriately dividing the responsibilities among federal, state and local governments. Certainly, Alice Rivlin (1992), some years back, argued that, 'Washington not only has too much to do, it has taken on domestic responsibilities that would be better handled by the states' (p. 31). She argued that the federal government should eliminate many of its programs in education, housing, highways, and social services, and focus on such specifically federal issues as national security. With heavier responsibilities for national defense and homeland security, perhaps many traditional domestic functions will eventually be devolved to state and local governments.

New Era of Cooperative, or Perhaps Coercive Federalism

An alternative view is that the terrorist attacks of 11 September and the bioterrorist incidents that followed may force a new degree of cooperation among federal, state, and local governments. This cooperation may take on overtones of coercion on the part of the federal government.

Consider one issue: identity cards. For some time, state drivers' licenses have served as de facto identity cards. One might assume that this results in 50 different identity cards in the US, but in fact states allow different forms of drivers' licenses, so there are really 243 different drivers' licenses. And this does not count the 16 000 different versions of birth certificates used in the country.

A very important further consideration is that the 19 hijackers on 11 September all used some form of identity fraud, and many took advantage of a particularly weak system for issuance of identity cards used in Virginia.

What is the solution? One possible solution is the issuance of a national identity card. Presumably issuance of such cards would become a federal government responsibility, thereby preempting previous roles of state governments. Alternatively, the federal government could regulate state government issuance of drivers' licenses so that there are no more weak links which future terrorists can take advantage of. A third alternative might be to provide better coordination between federal and state governments so that background information available to the federal government could be accessed by state governments when individuals seek to obtain drivers' licenses or other forms of identification.

A second example involves the response to bioterrorist threats like the recent letters filled with anthrax. The response inevitably involves federal, state, and local governments. All look to the federal government for guidelines and information on the latest research. Local governments provide police, firemen, and other emergency personnel who respond at a particular spot where anthrax is alleged to be found. State governments serve as intermediaries, and produce plans for large scale public health threats.

Both the example of identity cards and that of bioterrorist threats point to a new era of necessary cooperation among federal, state, and local governments. But cooperation can easily lead to coercion if the federal government imposes solutions on state and local governments. Further, when imposing solutions the federal government may also be imposing costs. Efforts to deal with homeland security may, in the federalism context, lead to new forms of unfunded mandates.

Whether 'devolution reprised' or 'cooperative/coercive federalism' becomes a more apt description of how federal-state-local relationships are impacted by the events of 11 September may depend in large part on whether the war against terrorism is waged abroad or waged within the borders of the United States. In the first instance, military buildup and foreign diplomacy capture the attention of the federal government, leaving many domestic issues to state and local governments. In the second instance, homeland defense involves a new kind of federal-state-local cooperative effort to monitor transportation and the mail and to respond to public health threats. At this point, it is too soon to tell.

OTHER IMPORTANT DEVELOPMENTS IN FEDERAL–STATE–LOCAL FISCAL RELATIONS

While 11 September can be viewed as a turning point in the respective roles of federal, state and local governments, it has not entirely overshadowed other developments. For example, on 8 January, 2002, President George W. Bush signed into law his No Child Left Behind Act. President Bush's major domestic policy initiative was delayed, but not prevented, by the necessary response to the 11 September terrorist events. This piece of legislation has several interesting intergovernmental dimensions.

No Child Left Behind Act

One overarching consideration in the passage of this act is whether it presages an increased federal role in education in the future. Traditionally, education has been the major service offered by state and local governments, and federal financing of education has been relatively minor. The fact that the President of the US made education his most important domestic policy focus could have important implications for the future roles of federal, state and local governments in education.

The No Child Left Behind Act requires additional testing of elementary school students: all public school students must be tested on an annual basis in reading and mathematics in grades three through eight by 2005–06. Although the federal government did not require uniform tests, but allows states to choose their own tests subject to certain guidelines, the Act also requires participation in the National Assessment of Education Progress tests already available for students in grades Four and Eight, which all states do not yet participate in, in order to verify the results of the state tests. School districts must report scores on the newly mandated tests, and schools that do not make adequately yearly progress relative to the state's standards will be subject to certain consequences. For example, at some point students in schools that are considered failing could have the option of moving to other public schools or receiving tutoring services.

Although most states currently have assessment systems and report testing results, and many have accountability systems, these systems are by no means uniform. It remains to be seen whether the federal funds associated with this act will be sufficient to cover the costs imposed. Will this domestic initiative of President Bush's help improve education outcomes nationwide in a cost-effective manner, or will this legislation ultimately be viewed as an additional onerous federal mandate?

Welfare Reform

Probably the most important federalism initiative during the Clinton administration was the 1996 enactment of welfare reform in the Personal Responsibility
and Work Opportunity Reconciliation Act of 1996 (PRWORA). One part of
that act was the abolition of the decades-old Aid to Families With Dependent
Children (AFDC) and replacement with Temporary Assistance to Needy
Families (TANF). Cash assistance is no longer an entitlement. Time limits for
receipt of TANF were imposed as were work requirements.

There were also some very important federalism aspects of PRWORA.
Open-ended matching grants were replaced by block grants, with funding
largely dependent upon historic spending levels. In some respects states have
been given greater flexibility, in other cases, less. Nathan and Gais describe
the changes as follows:

> The 1996 law is complicated – even, in a sense, schizophrenic. It sets strict federal
> requirements about work, as well as setting limits on how long families can
> receive federally aided welfare benefits ... But it also encourages states to develop
> their own welfare reforms by adopting variants on the work-first approach, em-
> phasizing quick engagement in work-related activities and moving people off
> public assistance (Nathan and Gais, 2001: 26).

Until the onset of the recession that began in March 2001, many analysts
were surprised with how well the new system appeared to work. Certainly,
welfare caseloads declined significantly. A critical question is how the economic downturn and TANF will interact, and whether the burdens will be felt
mostly by state and local governments, or mostly be shifted to the poor.

There are some specific questions about federal-state-local relationships
arising from this new welfare system that should also be addressed before
Congress reauthorizes the program at the end of 2002. Specifically, how has
the flexibility given to states turned out? Analysts note that the diversity in
welfare programs among states has increased. Has this allowed useful experimentation and the ability to craft programs to suit regional differences in
needs and preferences? Or have important inequities resulted whereby welfare grants for individuals differ excessively depending upon state of residence?
(Weil and Finegold, 2002, p. 7). One key question is whether Congress will
maintain the current level of funding or decrease it. Any decrease in funding
the block grants would have a negative impact on state finances. Another
important question is how a program based on fixed federal grants to states
will work over the business cycle, knowing that welfare needs vary tremen-
dously over the cycle. This latter question will not be able to be answered
until the country has experienced the new law in both times of economic
prosperity and recession.

Internet Taxation

According to one student of federalism:

> One of the most contentious issues involving federal, state and local relations today is Internet taxation. Internet taxation is a significant battlefield because it involves issues of great import to federalism, including state and local autonomy and revenue adequacy (Powell, 2000: 39).

In the section above on 'rules of the game', the federal standard for sales tax nexus was described, as well as its implications for the base of state and local sales taxes. The use of the internet for sales, particularly business-to-business internet commerce, makes the current nexus standards of even greater concern to state and local governments. It is estimated that states could lose as much as $10 billion in revenue by 2003 from the inability to tax sales through internet commerce (Powell, 2000: 42).

In 1998, Congress passed the Internet Tax Freedom Act, which prohibited discriminatory taxes on the internet and set up the US Advisory Commission on Electronic Commerce (ACEC) to consider tax issues involving electronic commerce and report its recommendations to Congress.[4] However, the April 2000 report of the US ACEC did not resolve the major issues.

Currently the states are involved in the Streamlined Sales Tax Project. A major hope is that streamlined sales taxes could prompt either Congress or the Supreme Court to modify the requirements for remote vendors to collect sales taxes (McLure, 2002: 4). States are concerned that the federal government support, not preempt, any cooperative decisions made by the states. At this point the ultimate results of these state cooperative efforts are uncertain.

CRITICAL ISSUES

There are two critical longer term issues concerning the federal government's impact on state and local finances. One concerns the growing inadequacy of state revenue systems; the other concerns the longstanding tendency for the federal government to impose mandates or regulations on state and local governments.

Nearly a decade ago, two commentators gave these indictments of state revenue systems:

> State revenue systems are increasingly obsolete and not working the way they should ... (Bucks, 1992: 556).
> Designed primarily during the 1930s for a nation of smokestack industries in deep economic depression, state tax systems fall short in the 1990s when services are

supplanting manufacturing as the economic linchpin, the economy is increasingly global, and new information-based industries appear almost daily (Snell, 1993: p. 1).

Since then, none of the major problems facing state tax systems have been resolved. The result is eroding sales and corporate tax bases, and a turn to some less savory revenue sources such as gaming.

If, as outlined above, state and local governments will face increasing expenditure burdens arising from the war on terrorism and homeland defense (not to mention the demographic burdens of an ageing population and greater health care costs), then state–local revenue systems must be repaired so that states can shoulder this burden. Given that cooperative action among 50 states is a formidable goal, the hope is that state and local pressure groups, national leadership, and realization of the problem will lead to federal action. Although state and local governments have an important responsibility in responding to their long term revenue problems, the federal government should not neglect its role.

The other critical issue concerns the ongoing problem of increasing federal mandates on state and local governments. John Kincaid describes this as the:

> ... continuation of the era of coercive or regulatory federalism, which began in the late 1960s. This era has been marked by, among other things, unprecedented levels of federal preemption of state authority, statutory mandates on state and local governments, conditions attached to federal grants in aid, federal court orders on state and local institutions, nationalization of policies originated by states ... (Kincaid, 2001: 68).

At minimum, continuation of the tendency for such coercive federalism can put additional fiscal pressures on state and local governments. At worst, such federal preemption of state government authority can threaten the basic workings of our governmental system that relies on the healthy functioning of state governments as well as the federal government. As this nation responds to the new world realities post 11 September, it will be important to take care of the basic workings of our governmental system. State and local governments will play an important role in homeland defense and response to public health threats. The federal government should make sure that state and local government involvement takes the form of cooperative, and not coercive, arrangements.

NOTES

1. The views in this chapter are not to be attributed to the Josiah Bartlett Center for Public Policy.

2. For example, Connecticut, Maine and Massachusetts link to the federal personal income tax at AGI, North Carolina links to taxable income, and Rhode Island and Vermont link to federal personal income tax liability. New Jersey, on the other hand, does not link its personal income tax to the federal income tax in any substantial way.
3. *National Bellas Hess, Inc.* v. *Illinois Department of Revenue* 386 US 753 (1967). This decision was reaffirmed in 1992 by *Quill Corp.* v. *North Dakota* 504 US 298 (1992).
4. In late 2001, Congress voted to extend the Internet Tax Freedom Act for two years.

REFERENCES

Brunori, David (1998), 'State personal income taxation in the twenty-first century', in David Brunori (ed.), *The Future of State Taxation*, Washington, DC: The Urban Institute Press, pp. 191–206.

Bucks, Dan R. (1992), 'Why state tax systems are in trouble – and what states can do together to fix the problems', *State Tax Notes*, 2(16): 556–61.

Caffrey, Andrew (2002), 'States flinch at business tax breaks contained in new stimulus measure', *The Wall Street Journal Online*, 18 March.

The Economist, (2001), 'Lexington: The imperial presidency', 3 November: 39.

Fisher, Ronald C. (2002), 'The changing state-local fiscal environment: A 25-year retrospective', Chapter Two in this volume.

Fox, William F. (1998), 'Can the state sales tax survive a future like its past?', in David Brunori (ed.), *The Future of State Taxation*, Washington, DC: The Urban Institute Press, pp. 33–48.

Holtz-Eakin, Douglas (1996), 'Fundamental tax reform and state and local governments', *National Tax Journal*, 49(3): 475–86.

Katz, Jane (2001), 'Til death do U$ part', *Regional Review*, Boston: The Federal Reserve Bank of Boston, 11(2): 27–30.

Kenyon, Daphne A. (1995), *The Decade of Declining Federal Aid*, Washington, DC: Economic Policy Institute.

Kincaid, John (2001), 'The state of US federalism, 2000–2001: Continuity in crisis', *Publius: The Journal of Federalism*, 31(3): 1–69.

McLure, Charles E., Jr. (2002), 'SSTP: Out of the great swamp, but whither? A plea to rationalize the state sales tax', *Multistate Tax Commission Review*, 2002(1), February: 1–13.

Nathan, Richard P. and Thomas L. Gais (2001), 'Federal and state roles in welfare: Is devolution working?', *Brookings Review*, Summer: 25–9.

National Association of State Budget Officers (NASBO) (2002), *Fact Sheet: Quick Rebound? State Fiscal Recovery Could be Gradual, Lag National Economy 12–18 months*, 12 March.

Pomp, Richard D. (1998), 'The future of the state corporate income tax: Reflections (and confessions) of a tax lawyer', in David Brunori (ed.), *The Future of State Taxation*, Washington, DC: The Urban Institute, pp. 49–72.

Posner, Paul I. (1998), *The Politics of Unfunded Mandates: Whither Federalism?*, Washington, DC: Georgetown University Press.

Powell, David C. (2000), 'Internet taxation and US intergovernmental relations: From *Quill* to the Present', *Publius: The Journal of Federalism*, 30(1–2) (Winter/Spring): 39–51.

Research Institute of America (2002), *2002 All States Tax Handbook*, New York, NY: Author.

Rivlin, Alice M. (1992), *Reviving the American Dream: The Economy, States, and the Federal Government*, Washington, DC: The Brookings Institution.

Snell, Ronald (ed.) (1993), *Financing State Government in the 1990s*, Washington, DC: National Conference of State Legislatures and National Governors' Association.

US Bureau of Census (2000), *Statistical Abstract of the United States*, Washington, DC: US Government Printing Office.

Weil, Alan and Kenneth Finegold (2002), 'Introduction', in Alan Weil and Kenneth Finegold (eds), *Welfare Reform: The Next Act*, Washington, DC: The Urban Institute Press, pp. xi–xxxi.

7. Prospects and challenges for state and local government in a digital world*

Kelly D. Edmiston and William F. Fox

INTRODUCTION

In recent years e-commerce and other information technology issues relevant for state and local governments have been widely studied in the economics, business, and public policy literatures (see, for example, Westland and Clark, 1999). This chapter is an effort to synthesize much of the material in hopes of providing for a self-contained, relatively comprehensive look at the issues that mass digitization and technological innovation hold for state and local governments at the dawn of the 21st century. In doing so, we are mindful that the subject matter needs to be viewed in the context of the so-called new economy; that is, forces are not confined to digital commerce and information technology. The chapter is divided into two parts. The first section discusses issues and implications of e-government, where the focus is on the expenditure side of the state and local public sector. The second section then discusses implications on the revenue side, with particular reference to the tax implications of e-commerce.

E-GOVERNMENT

In the simplest of terms, e-government is *electronic* government, or the use of digital technology in the management and delivery of public services, predominantly through the internet. As described in some detail below, e-government has great potential to enhance the efficiency of the public sector and to develop more personal, customized relationships between citizens and their government. E-government also brings increased access to a more democratic government. At the same time, e-government brings its own share of problems, not the least of which are privacy concerns, equitable access, and transition financing.

Why E-Government?

Expectations
One of the key characteristics of the US economy at the dawn of the 21st century is flexibility in production. Companies constantly introduce new or improved products with greater variety, and the costs of tailoring products and services to the needs of the individual consumer have dropped dramatically (Kerwin et al., 2000). With the rapid growth of e-commerce in the last five years and accelerated growth projected for the near future,[1] consumers increasingly are demanding, and getting, customized (personalized) goods and services, at their doorstep, at rapid speed. Research further suggests that customers routinely achieve high levels of satisfaction from e-commerce vendors (American Society for Quality, 2001). Sooner or later, the consumers of public services are going to demand the same level of service from their governments (see Horner, 1999).

Improved access to government services
Urban and suburban dwellers enjoy a level and variety of public services that simply are not feasible in rural areas, owing primarily to the ability of urban governments to exploit scale economies in the delivery of public services. A small constituency provides insufficient demand to cost-effectively provide some public services (Figure 7.1). That is, from a societal perspective, the

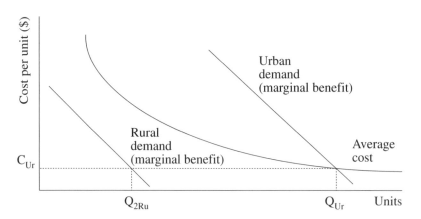

Note: The efficient level of provision for the urban community would be something greater than Q_{Ur}. With decreasing cost, however, provision of the efficient level would require subsidization. Here it is assumed that the government charges (or incurs) average cost.

Figure 7.1   The feasibility of offering public services often depends on the ability to exploit scale economies

cost involved in delivering the service to individuals in small communities outweighs any benefits that might accrue. Moreover, even with sufficiently large constituencies, sparse population densities may make the provision of some public services infeasible as well. The internet and other new digital technologies have great potential to change this, expanding a variety of public services, or public services of better quality, to individuals and businesses that previously were unable to access them. If constituents are able to digitally access public services in urban areas, perhaps via regional or state government provision, rural communities may be able to exploit scale economies by tapping into the urban market, thereby allowing them to provide a near-efficient level of service provision ($Q_{2,Ru}$ in Figure 7.1). Additionally, in consolidating the market for public services in this way, scale economies may be further exploited, pushing per-unit costs for both urban and rural providers below C_{Ur}.[2] The use of new technologies to improve access to public services is especially promising in the health and education sectors, where significant gains already have been made.

Improving access to health   Often in rural communities, diagnosis of critical disease is hampered by a lack of expertise. In the case of acute illness or trauma, rapid diagnoses often may make the difference between full recovery and partial recovery or death. With new digital technologies, teleconferencing in particular,[3] physicians in rural public clinics and hospitals have access to specialized expertise in larger urbanized areas, expertise that often is not available in small communities.

As an example consider the Pediatric Echocardiographic Network, which recently was tested by the National Laboratory for the Study of Rural Telemedicine at the University of Iowa (Kienzle et al., 2000).[4] Although two dimensional echocardiography, which is used to diagnose heart disease, has been available for roughly 20 years, the lack of specific skills in pediatric cardiology has prevented its use to diagnose congenital heart defects in infants and children in many rural communities, even though the equipment generally is available to most of them. The Iowa study linked rural physicians or technicians to pediatric cardiologists in urban areas, who were then able to evaluate the echocardiographs remotely. Over the course of the three and a half year project (spanning inception through preparation of the final report), 633 echocardiographs were transmitted and diagnosed, and the study indicates that 'diagnostic quality was excellent and the speed of diagnosis was enhanced' (p. 1).

Other innovative telemedical applications continue to evolve at a rapid pace. Many of these programs are similar to the Iowa project in that the focus is on digital consultations and they usually involve the evaluation of computer-generated imagery. Others, however, focus on home delivery of medical care for indigent or invalid patients, including MIT's Guardian Angel program (Motluk, 2000),[5] Georgia Tech's Electronic House Call program (Nelson, 1997), and the E-Medicine Project[6] at the University of Washington's Image Computing Systems Laboratory.

Improving access to education   Another promising area for digital service to reach unserved or underserved populations is higher education, in particular, distance education. Distance education can be defined very simply as instruction that does not require student and teacher to be present at the same location at the same time. Although distance education in some form has existed for many decades (for instance, correspondence courses), the internet and other information technologies have greatly intensified its use.

Perhaps the greatest benefit of this type of service is that it has phenomenal potential to provide or expand access to higher education to (1) rural communities where traditional bricks-and-mortar colleges and universities do not exist, and (2) 'nontraditional' (over 26 years of age) students who work full time during the day and generally have restricted course selection, if they have access at all, at traditional institutions (Ludlow, 1994). Although research has failed to provide *conclusive* evidence that distance education improves access and enrollment (Gladieux and Swail, 1999; Lewis et al., 1999), anecdotal evidence of its success abounds. For example, Contact North in Ontario, Canada has developed a distinguished record of reaching remote villages in the northern portion of the province, as has the British Open University in reaching home- and work-bound students (Gladieux and Swail, op. cit). To the extent that virtual education is successful in reaching underrepresented communities and patrons and is deemed to be a socially desirable project, it will likely be government-led in the form of public colleges and universities. The latest available data (1997–98) show that while 72 per cent of public two year colleges and 79 per cent of public four year colleges and universities, respectively, offer distance education courses, only 22 per cent of private colleges and universities do (Lewis et al., 1999).

Of course, the benefits of virtual education are not limited to colleges and universities, as relatively small enrollments or financial resources in many rural and inner city elementary and secondary schools also limit the ability of students to take advanced courses or to expand their horizons in more peripheral disciplines such as foreign languages. Beginning with the Fall semester, 2000, high school students in Michigan were allowed to take such courses over the internet if not offered in their school districts (*Government Technology*, 2000a). The State of Michigan recently has expanded access to virtual education to alternative schools as well (Higgins, 2001).

Efficiency

The real gains from new technology are not from doing high technology things, but rather from doing the everyday things of government better and cheaper. Businesses have already discovered this,[7] and government is beginning to see similar results. A recent survey of chief information officers (CIO) in all 50 states and 38 federal agencies revealed that 86 per cent of CIOs believe that e-government has improved service delivery, 83 per cent believe it has made government more efficient, and 64 per cent believe it has reduced costs (West, 2000). Of course, efficiency is not simply minimizing the government's cost of providing a given level of public services, but rather, efficiency is about minimizing social cost, a large part of which is the cost to constituents in using or receiving public services. The cost savings accruing to individual consumers of public services in the form of time and travel may in some cases be much larger than any pecuniary savings of providers, and often time savings provide the majority of the benefits derived from government projects (Gramlich, 1990).

Remote service delivery In addition to expanding access, many telemedical applications have also resulted in significant cost savings. For example, the use of televised home patient visits in sparsely populated western Kansas and eastern Colorado by the Hays (Kansas) Medical Center reduced the cost of home visits from $135 (for a personal visit by a registered nurse) to only $36 for a televisit (*Economist*, 1997). Of course, savings are likely to accrue not only by reducing costs for public hospitals and clinics, but by cutting costs for private providers as well, potentially leading to a reduction in government-paid health insurance costs. Finally, recent experience suggests that telemedical applications may reduce the cost of providing health care to institutionalized populations (McDonald et al., 1999).

Although there is no conclusive evidence that virtual education is less expensive than traditional education (Gladieux and Swail, 1999), and may be more expensive in the short run,[8] students who enroll online may face lower *net* costs in a virtual university. Even though tuition rates tend to be the same for virtual courses as those for traditional college courses (Lewis et al., 1999), students may face lower net costs due to savings in time and travel expenses (Baer, 1998).

An area in which there appear to be especially large efficiency gains on the consumption side is remote registration. Rather than waiting in what often are extremely long queues for renewing a driver's license, business license, or automobile registration, for example, patrons would simply access their local government website and apply or renew remotely, in seconds, without ever having left their home or office.

Experience with online automobile registrations suggests that transitioning to internet-based license renewals and registrations can lead to considerable savings on both the provider and consumer side. For example, the Alaska Department of Motor Vehicles' per-unit cost for motor vehicle registrations fell from $7.75 to $0.91 after the state implemented online renewals, while waiting time has been reduced from two and one half hours (excluding driving time) to less than three minutes (Johnson, 1999). The State of Arizona has saved an estimated $1.2 million annually since the inception of its electronic vehicle registration renewal system in 1997 (IBM, undated). Because the cost of processing electronic registrations in Arizona is 76 per cent less than processing standard registrations, future savings are likely to be considerably higher. Online registration and licensing appear to be extremely popular as well. In Maryland, which has one of the longest running (1998) online registration and licensing systems in the country, nearly two thirds of business and professional licenses are applied for and paid for over the internet, including over 80 per cent of CPA applications (Newcombe, 2001).

While online options for driver's license renewal only recently have begun to surface,[9] evidence from some of the nation's largest cities suggests that the potential savings in time cost are likely to be substantial. For example, the average driver's license applicant in Daly City, CA (San Francisco metropolitan area) waits 60.4 minutes before being called for service, and an additional 55.3 minutes are then required for the renewal process itself (Cabanatuan, 2001). In metropolitan Atlanta, GA, waits of five hours are 'not uncommon' (*Atlanta Constitution*, 2001: A10), and some patrons must wait up to 'eight hours or longer' (Lewis, 2001: A4).

Of course, consumers of public services often endure substantial time costs not only in utilizing the service, but in simply locating information about the service and determining the necessary steps for taking advantage of the service. Additional savings in time and travel cost are likely to come from the improved organization of information that is made possible by the internet, in particular, the use of a government-wide web portal. Adequately designed, such a portal would provide links to the various electronic applications provided by the government on the internet, organized in a way that makes the site easy to navigate and desired links easy to locate. In the future, the vision is for widespread use of hyperportals based on the one stop shopping concept (similar to Yahoo!), where information and services would be organized around consumer interests such as taxes, employment opportunities, education, or health, or around 'life events' such as moving or giving birth (Newcombe, 2000: 31).[10]

As a final example, electronic submission of tax returns and payment of taxes is very cost-effective and efficiency enhancing, as evidenced by its widespread acceptance by state and local governments. All states now offer electronic filing of taxes, mostly through the joint filing of federal and state taxes via the US Internal Revenue Service, and increasingly states are introducing direct filing over the web, which requires no special software. New Mexico, the first state to offer web filing in 1998, spends an average of $2.17 to process each paper return, but less than $1.00 for similar returns filed online (Young, 2001). Taxpayers appear to be welcoming the convenience as well. An estimated 900 000 of Massachusetts' 3.2 million income tax payers (28 per cent) filed taxes online in 2001 (Young, 2001). New Mexico enjoyed even greater acceptance, with an estimated 235 000 (of 609 000, or 38.6 per cent) of its returns filed online in 2001. Several large counties and municipalities offer online payment of property taxes.

Remote procurement If electronic government has taken hold anywhere, it is in the area of government procurement, or electronic purchasing. Historically government procurement has maintained a reputation for inefficiency. Anecdotal stories abound, for example, of $600 hammers and $3000 toilet seats. Much of the waste, however, actually is on the administrative side. The National Association of Purchasing Management estimates that the administrative cost of handling a single paper-based purchase order averages $120–$150, while 80 per cent of all purchases are for less than $500 (Robb, 2000). Online procurement, by streamlining and automating order processing and facilitating comparison shopping and the proposal process, has demonstrated remarkable potential for reducing cost and enhancing efficiency.

The use of online procurement by Victoria, Australia's state government, has improved the 'purchasing efficiency' of its Department of Natural Resources and environment by 70 per cent, and also has resulted in more effective enforcement of 'business rules' and enhanced transparency and accountability (*The Economist*, 2000). Shopping for loan rates and lease programs over the internet has saved the State of California over $20 million in interest on $300 million in financial transactions since 1996, and reduced the staff time required to obtain the financing by 65 to 80 per cent. Finally, the Massachusetts Emall (http://www.emall.isa.us), a multistate electronic procurement center, has saved 60–80 per cent in labor costs since its inception in 1998 (Robb, 2000).

A related development is the use of internet technology to facilitate governments sales, including US Treasury Securities and surplus property and supplies. The US government sold $3.6 billion in products over the internet in 2000, significantly more than the nation's largest online retailer (Amazon.com), which had $2.8 billion in net sales during the same period (Hasson and Browning, 2001).[11] Resulting reductions in overhead cost are reported to have yielded substantial savings for taxpayers.

Reduction of fraud Reducing fraud is a final way electronic government can be efficiency enhancing. In particular, the use of Electronic Benefits Transfer

(EBT), and eventually smart card technology, has shown great promise in reducing fraud in public assistance programs, among other savings.[12] The outgoing Food Stamps system uses paper coupons to distribute benefits, which are easily lost, sold, or stolen. By allowing the government to electronically track all transactions, food stamp trafficking is more easily identified and documented (Cason, 1998). Just weeks after the State of Texas implemented its Lone Star EBT system, Houston police busted a $1 million illegal food stamp ring that had been in operation for over a year (Rylander, 2001). Lone Star also provided the state with information necessary to remove 1 187 410 dormant food stamps cases ($34.8 million) and 300 450 dormant TANF cases ($6.9 million).

Enhanced democracy

Improved access to government officials   One of the primary benefits of a decentralized government, such as the federal system in the United States, is a government that is more responsive to the needs and desires of local communities. Because local officials are closer to a more narrow constituency, they can better gauge their needs (Inman and Rubinfeld, 1997). Of course, this interaction requires communication from constituent to government, which is dramatically facilitated by electronic communication (Leahy and Goodlatte, 2000). Today virtually all US senators and representatives maintain websites that allow their constituents to e-mail them with their concerns about the issues.[13] Nevertheless, about one half of all county governments have no employees with e-mail access (PTI/ICMA, 2001). Potentially, the internet offers citizens the capacity to truly engage elected officials, whether that be by e-mail, or more advanced and interactive platforms like message boards and real time chat.

Digital democracy   Increased scrutiny is being placed on voting systems, especially older systems, in the wake of events surrounding the 2000 presidential election in the State of Florida. Chief among the alternative systems being considered is internet voting (Internet Policy Institute, 2001). Recent experience with internet voting suggests it to be a positive alternative, and to have great potential for increasing voter turnout. The 2000 Democratic primary in the State of Arizona, which saw more than half of over 80 000 voters participating online, was a particularly successful experiment with internet voting (O'Looney, 2000). The 80 000+ voters, representing about ten per cent of registered Democrats in Arizona, resulted in a 'large gain in the number and proportion of citizens voting in comparison to the previous presidential primary' (O'Looney, 2000: 86).[14] Several potential problems will need to be addressed before internet voting becomes common practice, however. Chief among these are the disparity in internet access across racial, income, and education groups, which is discussed in more detail below; the potential for large scale proxy voting and coercion, and aggravation of an ongoing[15] eradication of American civic life (Phillips, 1999).

The State of E-Governance: Where Do We Stand?

The transition to e-government follows a more or less predictable development process, which is outlined by Accenture's (2001b) definitions of service maturity (Box 7.1).[16] The first step in the process tends to be publishing, and most state and local government websites today remain in this stage. Currently information tends to be quite substantial, but the ability to interact with government online, which is the next step, is much more limited, especially at the local level.

BOX 7.1   ACCENTURE, INC.–E-GOVERNMENT SERVICE MATURITY DEFINITIONS

Publish (passive/passive) – no electronic communication between user and agency other than what is published on the internet, for example, publishing online legislation.

Interact (active/passive) – user may communicate with agency online, but the agency does not communicate electronically (or directly respond) with the user, for example, online application for services.

Transact (active/active) – bi-directional electronic communication between user and agency, for example, user applies for a service online and the agency confirms *via* email.

Source: Accenture (2001b).

State of the states
A recent study of the states by West (2000) indicates that while many states offer access to telephone numbers (91 per cent of websites surveyed) and an e-mail platform (68 per cent), only a few have begun to take full advantage of the citizen outreach made possible by website interactivity, which includes message boards for comments (15 per cent of government websites) and even real time chat rooms (one per cent). A similar study focusing exclusively on

Table 7.1 Where we stand: State DMV use of the internet/e-government, 1999–2000

Customer service	Number of states 1999	Number of states 2000	Share of states 1999 (%)	Share of states 2000 (%)
General information	47	50	92	98
Request/download forms	39	42	76	82
Online registration renewal	9	22	18	43
Online license plates	7	10	14	20
Online citation payment	1	1	2	2
Online inquiry	1	3	2	6
Online driver's license	2	5	4	10
General information or forms service only	35	20	69	39
At least one online service	13	30	25	59
Two or more online services	4	15	8	29

Source: Accenture (2001a).

state departments of motor vehicles (DMV) (Accenture, 2001a) shows similar internet development patterns, and suggests that e-government is fairly rapidly progressing to the second and third stages of development: interact and transact (Table 7.1). While only 25 per cent of state DMVs offered at least one online service in 1999, only one year later the share of states offering services online jumped to 59 per cent.

Of course, the disparity across states in the transition to e-government begs the question, why? West (2000) performed a simple regression of his own state e-government rankings on potential explanatory factors (population size, political complexion, overall state spending, and demographics) and found the only statistically relevant factors to be total population, which showed a positive correlation,[17] and percentage of the population self-classified as liberals, which was negatively correlated with the states' e-government rankings. Large and relatively conservative states, like Texas, for example, seem to have taken the most advantage of the information technology revolution.

State of local e-government

In an effort to appraise the degree to which local governments have made the transition to electronic government, we make use of two surveys, for which selected results are presented in Table 7.2. The first, 'Electronic Government Survey 2000', conducted by Public Technology, Inc. (PTI) and the International City/County Management Association (ICMA) (2001; see also Norris et al., 2001), includes responses from 1881 (50.2 per cent) municipal and county governments. The National Association of Counties (NACo) (2000), also in association with Public Technology, Inc., produced the '2000 E-Government Survey' which focused exclusively on county level governments, from which 714 responses (23.6 per cent) were included in the analysis.

Results from these two surveys suggest that while the majority of local governments maintain internet sites (83.3 per cent and 60.8 per cent in the ICMA and NACo studies, respectively), few have made substantial progress in *integrating* e-government into their daily affairs. Less than 1.5 per cent of local governments allow for online payment of tickets and fines and only 1.5–2.2 per cent of local governments allow for online payments of taxes, despite the fact that, as discussed above, these two online services have shown significant benefits in communities that have utilized them. While almost half of the communities surveyed by ICMA/PTI utilize online services for procuring bids and proposals, only 4.2 per cent of NACo-surveyed county governments do. Comparing the ICMA and NACo studies more generally, municipal governments appear to be significantly more inclined overall to implement electronic and digital technologies than county governments. Surprisingly, more than half of the counties surveyed have no employees with

Table 7.2   Where we stand: Internet usage by local governments in the US, responses from two surveys

Inquiry	Percentage of respondents answering:	PTI/ICMA /a/	NACo /b/
Official website for jurisdiction	Yes	83.3	60.8
E-mail availability for employees	No employees	1.1	50.3
	Some departments	19.2	0.0
	Every department	42.9	32.2
	Every employee	25.8	14.8
	No response	11.0	2.7
Internet availability for employees	No employees	0.6	53.8
	Some departments	24.3	0.0
	Every department	46.7	32.1
	Every employee	16.8	10.8
	No response	11.7	3.3

	Now	In future	Neither/no response	Now	In future	Neither/no response
Payment of tickets/fines	1.4	29.7	68.9	1.3	12.7	86.0
Payment of taxes	2.2	21.5	76.3	1.5	27.7	70.7
Payment of utility bills	1.9	30.8	67.3	0.7	10.5	88.8
Access government	1.7	10.3	88.0	3.2	23.0	73.8
Voter registration	9.4	27.6	63.0	7.8	38.5	53.6
Mapping/GIS	25.3	34.8	39.9	6.7	33.8	59.4
Bids and proposals	48.6	13.5	37.9	4.2	23.1	72.7
Procurement						

Online services /c/

Notes:

/a/ Public Technology, Inc. and International City/County Management Association, 'Electronic Government Survey 2000', February, 2001. Results include responses from 1881 (50.2 per cent) municipal and county governments surveyed by PTI/ICMA.

/b/ National Association of Counties, in association with Public Technology, Inc., '2000 E-government Survey', April, 2000. Results include responses from 714 (23.6 per cent) county governments surveyed by NACo/PTI.

/c/ Not all answers are included in the table.

e-mail availability, compared to just over one per cent of local governments in large municipalities and counties.

Obstacles to Successful Transition: Making E-Government Work

Having briefly summarized the state of e-governance at the state and local level, we end this part of the report by briefly discussing the major issues that have surfaced to undermine the digital/electronic revolution in government. Table 7.3 reports additional results from the ICMA/PTI and NACo/PTI surveys of local governments, which highlight perceived obstacles in implementing e-government. The main barriers can be roughly organized into three groupings: marketing/personnel, privacy concerns, and financing. These issues, along with the pressing equity issue of the 'digital divide', are discussed in detail in this subsection.

Table 7.3   *Where we stand: Barriers to e-government for local communities in the US, responses from two surveys*

Inquiry	Percentage of respondents answering:	PTI/ICMA /a/	NACo /b/
	Staffing issues	66.6	45.8
	Infrastructure	33.9	26.8
Barriers to	Privacy issues	27.7	24.4
e-government /c/	Security issues	42.1	43.4
	Funding	54.3	70.2
	Lack of support from elected officials	12.4	

Notes:
/a/ Public Technology, Inc. and International City/County Management Association, 'Electronic Government Survey 2000', February, 2001. Results include responses from 1881 (50.2 per cent) municipal and county governments surveyed by PTI/ICMA.
/b/ National Association of Counties, in association with Public Technology, Inc., '2000 E-Government Survey', April, 2000. Results include responses from 714 (23.6 per cent) county governments surveyed by NACo/PTI.
/c/ Not all answers are included in the table.

Marketing e-government

Marketing e-government to constituents   For e-government to become a successful reality, state and local administrators will be required not only to build and maintain useful internet sites and portals, but also to educate their constituents about the availability of online public services and the benefits of using digital government resources. Further, the entire constituency must eventually be brought under the internet umbrella, which along with equity concerns, necessitates expanded access to the internet.

Despite the public sector's recent progress in its digital evolution, constituents have been slow to respond. In a nationwide survey conducted in May–June, 2000, only 50.5 per cent of approximately 106 million internet users in the United States stated that they had ever visited a federal, state, or local government website, and only 5.7 per cent had done so on the day they were surveyed.[18] Combined with an overall online population rate of 47.2 per cent, only 23.8 per cent of the total US adult population has ever visited a government site, and only one in 42 will on any given day. A study conducted by Hart-Teeter Research for the Council for Excellence in Government suggests that these web users are more likely to have visited websites of federal agencies (54 per cent of internet users) than to have visited the websites of their state (45 per cent) or local (36 per cent) governments.[19] Consistent with internet usage trends in general, wealthier, more highly educated males were more likely to visit a government website than poorer, less educated females. This result held even when restricting consideration to internet users, however. Among internet users, Democrats were slightly more likely to have visited a government website, but because their online population is larger, any given consumer of digital government resources is more likely to be Republican.

Marketing e-government to public servants   Perhaps more important, and difficult, than marketing e-government to constituents is marketing e-government to public employees. In his well-known treatise, *The Prince* (1532), Niccoló Machiavelli stated: '[t]here is nothing more difficult to take in hand, more perilous to conduct, or more uncertain in its success, than to take the lead in the introduction of a new order of things.'[20] E-government has the potential to radically change the way state and local governments operate, and as a general rule, people are uncomfortable with radical changes. Public employees themselves admit a resistance to change (Perlman, 2000a, 2000b), and research suggests that this reluctance and similar personal issues such as turf battles are more consequential than technical barriers in implementing new technologies in state and local governments (Greeves, 1998).

As a prime example of the reluctance of some public employees to implement new technologies, consider recent comments from James Natoli, head of the Office for Technology in the State of New York (Newcombe, 2000). In a speech to state employees in June, 2000, he recalled that only six years previously, one state agency was still using oversized leather-bound ledgers to record financial transactions, despite the fact that the use of electronic record keeping was so ingrained in the United States that these ledgers were no longer produced domestically. Rather than update its accounting system, the agency found an overseas supplier of the ledgers.

Given a reluctance to change (which is not confined to public sector enterprises of course), the transition to e-governance requires strong leadership – a champion for the cause who has the power and charisma required to get the implementation process started and to keep it going. Although such champions continue to emerge at the state level to pioneer the e-government transition in innovative ways – Utah, Washington, Kansas, and Maine, in particular (*Government Technology*, 2000b) – local governments, especially counties,[21] often lack the 'vigorous leadership needed to be e-governance pioneers' (Streib and Willoughby, 2001, 9).

Privacy issues
Perhaps the most enlightening result from the Pew survey is that of all internet users, only 44.5 per cent of distrustful internet users had ever visited a government website, versus 60.1 per cent of trusting users.[22] This result reinforces the notion of widespread concern about internet privacy in general, and on government websites specifically. Gallup pollsters appearing before a May, 2001 US House Energy and Commerce Subcommittee hearing noted that while only 16 per cent of web users stated that they 'pay attention' to privacy issues on the internet, roughly 63 per cent were 'very concerned' about internet privacy issues involving government websites.[23] In an earlier (April, 2000) EzGov privacy survey, fully two thirds of respondents expressed concern about driving records being made available on the internet, and over half of respondents expressed similar concerns about the online availability of property and deed records.[24] Finally, 90 per cent of Americans are opposed to making arrest and conviction records available on the internet, even if the information is on the public record (Gest, 2001).

Unfortunately, these concerns are not unfounded: especially at the federal level, the government has given web users plenty of reason for concern. Perhaps chief among these is the development of the Federal Bureau of Investigation's (FBI) Carnivore system, which allows the agency to intercept internet content such as e-mail, much like a telephone wire-tap.[25] Other examples abound,[26] including a security leak on a US Department of Commerce privacy website (Safe Harbor), which allowed anyone accessing the site to receive proprietary information on US companies doing business in Europe (McCullagh, 2001).

Internet security breeches are becoming increasingly common at the state and local level as well, as their use of digital information technologies expands. A particularly distressing example recently occurred in the State of Georgia, when online computers for the state's HOPE scholarship program[27] exposed passwords that allow access to computers at the Georgia Student

Finance Commission (Judd and Brister, 2001a, 2001b). Hackers potentially could have altered the value of scholarships, deleted records or used the system as a backdoor to access confidential tax and medical records.

Clearly privacy concerns must be addressed as a first step if constituents are to be enticed to participate in digital government. A 2000 *Business Week/ Harris* poll revealed that roughly two thirds of nonusers of the internet would use the internet if their privacy concerns were alleviated.[28] Alleviating these fears is likely to be an uphill battle, however. First, US social trends suggest that people have become considerably more distrustful over time (Putnam, 2000), which accentuates the privacy problem raised in the April 2000 EzGov survey; that is, that distrustful people are less likely to visit government websites. Secondly, a necessary precondition for use of government websites is that the consumer access the internet, but the web tends not to be a 'haven for caring people looking to bond with like-minded folk' (Uslaner, 2001, p. 18).[29]

The digital divide
One of the more pressing issues in the evolution of the digital economy is that of a 'digital divide', or a gap in computer and internet access across economic, demographic, or social lines. The digital divide is a serious issue generally, as large portions of society are 'left out' of the digital revolution in business, and they have potential to eventually lose touch with government as the e-government transition takes shape, while other, more computer- and internet-savvy citizens become better served by government.

At first, due in large part to a timely report out of Vanderbilt University's *Project 2000* (Hoffman and Novak, 1998), the focus of the digital divide was on racial disparities. Since then, a number of reports (see, for example, National Telecommunications and Information Administration (NTIA), 1995, 1998, 1999, 2000) have noted several digital divides across not only racial lines, but also by income class, educational attainment, and location. Table 7.4 provides statistics on computer and internet access for households by major demographic group for August, 2000.

Whites are much more likely to have a computer (53.5 per cent) and internet access (43.0 per cent) than are nonwhites (39.4 per cent and 29.1 per cent, respectively), and urban dwellers are much more likely to have access to a computer and the internet than are their rural counterparts. Substantial differences in internet access appear across income and education lines as well (77.7 per cent for the over $75K income class vs. 12.7 per cent for the under $15K class, and 64.0 per cent for college-educated vs. 11.7 per cent for those without a high school diploma).

Figure 7.2 shows internet use by household group (from an alternative data source) across several income classes, exhibiting a strong positive associ-

Table 7.4   Per cent of US households with a computer and internet access, 2000

Household group	Computer	Internet
Overall	51.0	41.5
Race:		
White	53.5	43.0
Nonwhite	39.4	29.1
Income:		
< $15K earnings	19.2	12.7
> $75K earnings	86.3	77.7
Education:		
No high school diploma	18.2	11.7
College graduate	74.0	64.0
Location:		
Metropolitan	53.4	43.0
Nonmetropolitan	41.8	30.9

Source: Leigh and Atkinson (2001).

Data source: NTIA (2000).

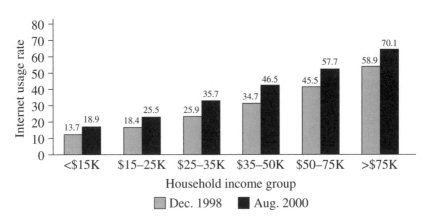

Sources: NTIA and ESA, US Dept. of Commerce (2000).

Figure 7.2   Internet use by household income group, 1998 and 2000

ation. One of the major issues confronting researchers interested in analysing the digital divide is the relative influences of income vs. other demographics such as education, race, and geography in determining internet usage rates. That is, racial differences may simply reflect differences in average income or educational attainment across racial lines, and so on. In an effort to differentiate the relative influences, Leigh and Atkinson (2001) performed a multiple regression of internet usage rates of households on income (in $10 000 increments), years of education, race (white vs. nonwhite), and geography (metro vs. nonmetro). They found that all of these factors are statistically significant at the 99 per cent confidence level, and thus the digital divide appears to exist across several demographic attributes. Table 7.5 presents the Leigh and Atkinson results for household internet access using data from the 2000 Current Population Survey (Computer Ownership Supplement, US Census Bureau).

Table 7.5   Leigh and Atkinson (2001) multiple regression results: household internet access, 2000

Variable	Value	Variable	Value
Overall proportion of households	40.66		
Income (in $10K increments)	3.30	Race (if white, add)	10.76
Education (in years)	4.67	Locality (if metro, add)	6.26
No. of households	47 504	R^2	0.1952

Source: Leigh and Atkinson (2001).

After controlling for other demographic factors, whites are still more likely, about 10.8 per cent more likely, to have internet access than are nonwhites, and metropolitan area residents are approximately 6.3 per cent more likely to have internet access than are nonmetro residents. Education appears to have a substantial impact on the likelihood of having internet access. In fact, and somewhat surprisingly perhaps, one additional year of education improves the likelihood of having internet access (4.7 per cent) more than an additional $10 000 in income (3.3 per cent). These results suggest that successful efforts to bridge the digital divide must necessarily attack the issue on several demographic fronts.

Of course, there is also a geographical digital divide across the states as well. As shown in Figure 7.3 (see also Appendix A), states vary radically in the share of households with internet access. Mississippi has the fewest proportion of households with internet access at 26.3 per cent, while in the

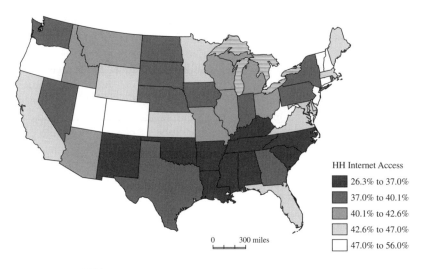

Source: NTIA (2000)

Figure 7.3   Household internet access by state, 2000

State of New Hampshire roughly 56.0 per cent of households have internet access.

The lack of household computers and internet access translates to a lower likelihood of having access to government information and services that increasingly are going online. Consider, for example, the racial divide. As reported in Table 7.4, 43.0 per cent of white households have internet access, compared to only 29.1 per cent of nonwhite households. Not surprisingly, recent data show that whites are more likely to have participated in digital government (24.9 per cent) than nonwhites (18.9 per cent for Hispanics and 17.0 per cent for blacks).[30]

Evidence that minorities, low income people, the less educated, and rural dwellers have less access to the internet, and hence electronic government, is problematic for the public sector, which by its nature must give adequate consideration to equity concerns in its decision calculus. While similar technology gaps have surfaced on numerous occasions over the course of history, including the development of radio, telephony, and television, among others, with widely varying rates of diffusion (Table 7.6), never has a technology surfaced that will alter the operation and administration of government in such a fundamental way. And because internet technology (as well as other electronic and digital technologies) will change the way government interacts with *all* of its constituents, a relatively complete diffusion of digital technology and infrastructure is a necessary requirement for a successful transition

Table 7.6   Penetration rates of new technologies

Technology (year)	Years to 50 per cent penetration	Years to 90 per cent penetration
Telephone (1900)	48	55
Radio (1923)	8	23
Television (1948)	5	15
VCR (1980)	9	28 (est.)
PC (1981)	19	24 (est.)

Source: Leigh and Atkinson (2001), Table 3.

to electronic government. That being said, literacy is perhaps more crucial than the penetration of digital technology, and there is a long way to go before American adult society is fully literate. The transition to electronic government cannot wait out the lag in technology diffusion, rather, efforts to bridge the digital divide must proceed in concert with rather than in lieu of the transition. Fortunately, the diffusion of internet technology is expected to proceed more at the pace of television than of the telephone.[31]

Financing e-government
Results from local government surveys demonstrate that funding issues are viewed as a significant obstacle in the transition to electronic government. In fact, 70.2 per cent of respondents in the NACo survey asserted that 'funding' is a substantial barrier to e-government, which was the modal response to that question (Table 7.3). More than half of the respondents in the ICMA survey (54.3 per cent) noted financial barriers as well. While funding issues are endemic to state and local government, the financing of electronic government presents somewhat unique problems: the necessity of duplicating services during the transition and large costs on the front end and savings on the back end.

Duplicate service provision   As noted in Table 7.4, in August, 2000 only 41.5 per cent of US households had regular access to the internet, and the pervasiveness of the technology varies widely across states (Figure 7.3), and demographic groups (Table 7.4, Figure 7.2). If state and local governments intend to serve their entire constituencies, they may be required initially to duplicate online services. That is, to provide these services both electronically and by traditional means. Thus, initially at least, few of the cost savings from transitioning to electronic government are likely to be realized in the budget, and in fact, the budget may be additionally burdened. One cost-effective way to get around this problem may be to provide public internet kiosks and e-mail outlets for those who do not have private access, perhaps in public libraries, employment centers, transportation terminals, and social service centers. Although many people without private internet access do not take advantage of these resources (NTIA, 1999),[32] research has shown that one important reason for the digital divide is the lack of content in which low income and 'underserved' people would be interested (Lazarus and Mora, 2000). Because internet access is widely available at public libraries (79 per cent in 2000; Library Research Center, 2000) and schools (98 per cent in 2000; Cattagni and Westat, 2001; see also Goolsbee, 2001), perhaps the most important step state and local government can take to bring underserved populations into the electronic government fold is to encourage and provide relevant content.

Front end costs and back end savings   Perhaps the greatest financial problem associated with a transition to electronic government is the characteristic short-sightedness of the public sector brought about by short election cycles. A transition of this magnitude requires immediate expenditure for very large fixed costs, while the savings generally accrue very gradually through reductions in operating costs. In other words, the pain is immediate while the gain is distant. Effective transitions to e-government thus require a large investment in and commitment to the future. Unfortunately, reluctance on the part of some public officials and administrators to implement e-government at such a high cost is completely rational. Only 30 per cent of internet users in the September, 2000 Hart-Teeter survey rated e-government as a 'high priority' or 'very high priority' for government use of their tax dollars. Presumably, those who do not use the internet would feel considerably less favorable.

In some ways the e-government transition can be self-financing. The State of Minnesota recently used savings from the outsourcing of its automobile registration renewal form mailing ($220 000/year) to help finance technology designed to speed up the renewal process on the back end (Swope, 2001).[33] Nevertheless, the same state also recently cancelled a $200 million fiber optic cable project, which would have provided 2200 miles of broadband capacity along Minnesota freeway rights-of-way, because of '[p]rivate sector opposition and lack of funding' (Quay, 2001: 15).

Another option is public-private partnerships. Business, as a substantial consumer of government services and payer of taxes, has a significant financial interest in seeing e-government develop, so getting them to foot part of the bill is in many ways a marketing problem. Public-private partnerships are an important component of e-government transition financing in many of the state and local governments that have successfully launched major e-government initiatives. For example, IBM completely developed Arizona's vehicle registration program and operates the program on its own servers for $1 per transaction and two per cent of revenues (Snell and Moore, 1999). As noted above, this program has resulted in significant cost savings for the State of Arizona. Similarly designed public-private partnerships have been touted as 'the only real solution for e-government. The new model is that we develop the necessary software, run it on our own servers, and take care of all the maintenance and software hassles, all at no charge to the agency. Our compensation is entirely transaction-based.'[34] Nonprofit groups and government-oriented organizations also are making efforts to link state and local governments with potential private partners. Recently, for example, the ICMA's Corporate Partnership Program joined the Minnesota League of Cities with private sector partners Avenet and Microsoft to produce *GovOffice WebCreator*, which allows local communities to offer online government services 'without technical training or specialized staff' (ICMA, 2001, p. 1).

Of course, cost savings are not the only goal of electronic government, nor may they be the primary goal, as an expansion of public service provision to previously underserved populations potentially would yield great benefits. As noted by Willis (2000) in the context of financing virtual education: 'Perhaps the question institutions must answer is whether it is part of their mission as educators to offer programs to those who might not be reached without distance education. The primary benefit to educational institutions through distance education may be the increased number of non-traditional students they are able to attract and serve'.

TAX IMPLICATIONS

Many of the efficiency enhancing aspects of e-government that were discussed above offer the potential to improve tax compliance and administration. The result can be lower cost tax collection and possibly greater revenues in areas where fraud can be reduced. At the same time, technology changes can significantly lower state and local tax bases as they are currently defined. This section addresses effects of new technology on tax bases.

Changes in business processes, because of the development of new technologies, have dramatically complicated state and local governments' ability to raise tax revenues. The full implications for raising revenues are yet to be felt, as new technologies are continuously emerging and business structures are still responding. Nonetheless, some key areas with important implications for revenues can be identified, including development of a new set of products, rapid expansion of remote sales, shifts in the capital intensity of some businesses, development of competition for industries that have traditionally been regulated monopolists, and digitization of certain goods and services.

New Range of Products

The internet and advancements in computers and telecommunications are allowing development of a wide range of new and formerly unanticipated services. These include financial services over ATMs, e-mail, games, enhanced telephone services and a host of services offered over the internet such as weather reports, medical databases, and computer bulletin boards. The sale of newly developed goods would normally be taxable under state tax statutes, but the sale of services often is not. The key reason is that most state sales tax laws require that services be enumerated to be taxable. Many states tax relatively few services and essentially all states are slow to revise their tax laws to incorporate new services. Thus, these services will often lie outside the sales tax base.

Many of the developing services are substitutes (though potentially improved versions) for goods and services already being consumed. Internet telephony is such an example. In many cases the existing good or service is taxed while the new service is not. The non-neutrality subsidizes development of the new technologies, distorts consumer behavior and leads to both horizontal and vertical[35] inequities. Further, the varied treatment of computer-based services within states leads to considerable administration and compliance costs. Frieden (2000) argues that states that broadly tax computer services, such as Hawaii, Texas and South Dakota, and states that lightly tax computer services, such as California, Maryland, and Virginia, will have little additional difficulty. However, states lying on the spectrum between these extremes will find many decisions are necessary on what is and is not taxable.

The technology is also blurring the lines between industries. For example, many of the same services may be offered via the internet and cable television. This increases the likelihood of differential taxation of very similar services, since cable services are more likely to be taxed than internet-based services.

Remote Sales

The implications of remote sales for state and local tax structures are not a new issue. Catalogue sales, drop shipments, cross-border shopping, and remote provision of services have been the focus of considerable discussion for many years. What is new is that technological advances are taking the potential for remote delivery to a whole new level. The rapid development of e-commerce offers the potential for some of the most profound effects on revenues,[36] particularly for the sales and corporate income taxes. For example, Forrester Research, Inc. has estimated that e-commerce sales will be $2.8 trillion by 2004, with nearly 94 per cent being business-to-business transactions.

Differential taxation (or more frequently differential ability to collect taxes) of remote sales portends numerous implications for the US economy (see Fox and Luna, 2000). Perhaps the most important are the economic distortions that will result from business efforts to engage in tax avoidance. As described further below, firms can be expected to change where they operate, where they warehouse, how they set up call centers, their return policies, and so forth, all in an effort to reduce collection responsibilities or tax liabilities. Also, the sales tax, which is regressive against current income and proportional against lifetime income, is likely to become more regressive given the digital divide. Access to computers and the internet is highly correlated with income, suggesting that the ability to evade taxes by purchasing through e-commerce is positively related with income. For state and local governments, the potential for revenue losses is a key issue, and will be the focus of much of this section.

For the sales and use tax, whether a sale is remote normally does not alter its taxability, only the method of compliance. If a transaction is taxable under the sales tax when purchased locally, the use tax is normally due if the same commodity is purchased through remote means (see Due and Mikesell, 1995).[37] The problem can be an inability to collect taxes on remote sales in an effective manner. Vendors are only required to collect use tax on behalf of states where they have nexus. In *Quill* v. *North Dakota*, 112 US 298 (1992) the Supreme Court intended to establish a bright line for determination of nexus – physical presence in a state. The decision left open determination of what degree of physical presence constitutes nexus, thereby creating considerable uncertainty, but gives multi-state businesses an incentive to limit the number of states where they have sufficient physical presence for nexus. Thus, many e-merchants may be advantaged relative to main street retailers, because the former will not be required to collect sales or use tax in many of the states where they exploit the economy. Many multi-state traditional firms, such as Walmart, Borders, and Barnes and Noble, are responding by establishing their e-commerce activities through a separate corporation in hopes that they will only have nexus in a limited number of states. Even if the e-commerce subsidiary corporation does not have nexus, it is possible that the e-tailer has nexus through its affiliation with a firm that has nexus. The California legislature recently passed a law asserting nexus through the affiliated companies, though the legislation was vetoed by the governor. Nonetheless, the California Franchise Tax Board concluded that Borders.com had nexus via its relationship with Borders, Inc. Arkansas passed legislation in the spring of 2001 that was similar to that vetoed in California. Ultimately, it remains for the courts to settle whether Walmart.com (for example) has sufficient affiliation with Walmart through related advertising, accepting returns and other means, to establish nexus for the e-commerce firm.

The means of payment can also alter the taxability (or ability to collect the tax) in some circumstances. For example, most states have chosen to tax prepaid telephone cards at the point of sale, rather than the situs of service consumption. The effect is to allow easy collection in cases when prepaid cards are sold through vendors physically located in the state. However, the tax is effectively an origin-based tax on the purchase of minutes. The tax can be evaded by purchasing minutes from a vendor without nexus in the state that is located in another state that with no sales tax on prepaid cards.

In the event that vendors do not have nexus, use tax compliance is dependent on voluntary reporting. Though little direct analysis has been conducted, it appears that use tax compliance is much lower than sales tax compliance. No studies are available on use tax collections from individual consumers, but voluntary compliance by individuals appears to be nearly nonexistent. Some evidence of the weak performance can be seen from the states that provide a line on their individual income tax return to allow for voluntary remittance of use taxes. In a recent unpublished survey, the Federation of Tax Administrators received data from nine states that include the line on the income tax return, and found no state that collected more than $1.5 million. Maine, which required a minimum payment of 0.4 per cent of AGI, received the largest amount.[38] The second highest, Wisconsin, where payment depends entirely on voluntary reporting, collected $1.4 million, with fewer than one per cent of taxpayers indicating a liability. Such small receipts would seem to evidence very weak compliance by individuals.

Use tax compliance by businesses is better than by individuals, but still lags far behind compliance with the sales and other taxes. Washington State used 1991 data to examine compliance by registered business taxpayers. Use tax noncompliance, at 19.9 per cent, was the highest of all taxes. Sales tax noncompliance, on the other hand, was estimated to be 1.5 per cent. The study probably understates the overall extent of business noncompliance for remote use taxes because it only includes registered businesses. Nonregistered businesses are probably less compliant. Also, use tax noncompliance is a combination of noncompliance for tax due on remote purchases and noncompliance for items purchased with a resale certificate, but for which tax is ultimately due. The latter probably has less noncompliance than the former. The low share that use tax revenues play in total sales and use tax receipts is further evidence of weak use tax compliance. For example, use tax collections on remote sales were less than 2.3 per cent of total sales and use tax revenues in Tennessee during 1998.

Bruce and Fox (2000) forecast the revenue loss that state and local governments can expect because of the inability to collect use taxes due on e-commerce transactions. They estimate that state and local governments stand to lose $20.2 billion in 2003 in taxes due on e-commerce sales. Much of this is shifted from other remote sales on which some of the revenue is not currently being collected. Still, they estimate that the additional loss from e-commerce sales will be $10.8 billion, or about four per cent of sales tax receipts in 2003. Bruce and Fox estimate that 70 per cent of the revenue loss is on business-to-business transactions.

Business Location Effects

All taxes, whether imposed on business inputs or outputs, have the potential to affect location, with the incentives varying by tax and by industry. Technological enhancements making remote operation more feasible have raised the role that taxes can play in location decisions. New technologies make taxes more important in many industries as they reduce transportation costs for both inputs and outputs, thereby allowing businesses realistically to choose their location across a wider set of geographic areas. Effectively, firms in many industries are able to select locations based on labor, taxes, and other factors, with the importance of transportation costs substantially lowered.

Effects of taxes on business location are the focus of a very wide literature.[39] A general conclusion from the literature is that tax differentials have a statistically significant effect on the location decision, but the elasticities implied by the point estimates are so small that there is normally little policy importance in how the differentials affect location. However, the literature has focused on corporate income and property taxes, with sales taxes seldom being considered.

Sales taxes are imposed both on many inputs purchased by business and on many outputs. These taxes, imposed at rates ranging from three to ten per cent of input costs or output price, are much larger as a share of business costs than are profits taxes, which are often levied at about six per cent of profits. Firms may be able to avoid collection responsibilities for the sales and use tax, encounter low or zero sales taxes on their inputs, and limit their corporate income tax liability by carefully selecting the state in which to locate. Thus, estimates obtained from the current academic literature probably substantially understate the effects of sales taxes on location of firms operating in an e-commerce environment. Taxes have traditionally had the greatest effect on location along state or local government borders, where firms can obtain the same access to transportation, labor and other inputs, but reduce their tax burdens by locating on one side of a border versus another. Goolsbee (2000) has noted that ' ... the key issue that the Internet poses for tax policy is not so much its potential to create a world *without* borders but rather to create a world of *only* borders – a world in which everyone is as responsive to local taxation as people who live on geographic borders' (p. 562).

Businesses have a strong incentive to locate in states with low market shares to avoid collection responsibility on sales taxes on their output, if the use tax is not effectively collected on remote commerce. Further, depending on the share of their inputs that is sales taxable, businesses have an incentive to locate in low tax rate states to avoid tax on their inputs. The share of inputs in the tax base varies by industry. A general sense of input taxability is given in Table 7.7, where estimates of the taxable share of gross receipts for various industries are reported. Perhaps the best generalization is that there is a propensity to impose taxes on a greater share of inputs in industries where the sales tax is not imposed on the output. The problem is that the tax on inputs is levied on an origination rather than a destination basis, so the tax cannot be simply viewed as an indirect means of taxing the final product. Firms always

Table 7.7   Taxes on intermediate goods as a per cent of gross receipts by industry, 1992

Services	Taxable amount per cent receipts	Trade	Taxable amount per cent receipts	Manufacturing	Taxable amount per cent receipts
Auto repair	35.4	Eating	7.2	Primary metals	8.1
Research	24.1	Fuel	6.6	Stone, clay, glass	7.9
Memberships	18.9	Apparel	6.3	Printing	6.1
Museums	18.1	Furniture	5.8	Paper	6.0
Hotels	17.7	Building		Apparel	5.8
Amusement	17.1	materials	4.7	Chemicals	4.8
Libraries	16.9	Misc. excluding		Textiles	4.6
Social services	16.9	drug & liquor	4.5	Lumber	4.4
Health	16.2	Food	4.3	Rubber	4.2
Business	15.0	Non-store	3.6	Fabricated metals	4.2
Personal	13.5	Drug	3.2	Petroleum	3.8
Motion pictures	13.3	General		Leather	3.2
Management	12.9	merchandise	3.0	Miscellaneous	3.1
Correspondence		Auto and gas	2.5	Industrial	
schools and		Liquor	2.2	machinery	3.0
vocational				Electronic	
schools	12.7			equipment	3.0
Accounting	11.7			Furniture	2.7
Engineering	11.7			Instruments	2.6
Miscellaneous				Transportation	
repair	11.2			equipment	2.3
Legal	9.5			Tobacco	0.9

Source: Authors' calculations based on US Bureau of the Census, 1992 Census of Services, 1992 Census of Retail Trade and 1992 Census of Manufactures.

have an incentive to choose a location to avoid sales taxes on inputs (an origination tax), but have no incentive to choose a location to avoid a destination tax on their output.

Depending on court rulings with regards to issues such as affiliate nexus, firms may be able to avoid collecting taxes in their output market through careful design of the corporate structure. For example, Dell would be able to divide its activities into a production company and a sales company, and reduce the number of states where its sales company has nexus if the courts ruled that the two companies do not have nexus through their affiliation. Thus, the additional location costs imposed by the sales tax may only be the costs of identifying and establishing an appropriate corporate form.

The growing importance of taxes on location will also encourage a change in state capital taxes. The pattern, that is already strongly underway, is to shift corporate income and franchise taxes from origin-based levies to destination-based levies. This is accomplished by increasing the weight on the sales factor in the allocation formula, and by situsing the sales on a destination basis. Notice that the corporate taxes are both being reduced and moved towards a destination basis without cutting tax rates. This avoids the political fallout from cutting tax rates (which are much more visible and understood than formula apportionment and other reductions being granted) and maintains the tax on firms that are fully domiciled in a state. Further, the destination-based corporate tax allows a nontransparent tax source, which is politically popular with many politicians.

Digitization

Digitization of goods and services creates tax collection issues, both because of remote sales and because of the taxability of transactions. The set of goods and services that can be digitized obviously includes software, telecommunications, information services, and so forth, but potentially carries over to a wide range of other items. Books and music are examples that are frequently discussed, but others might include repair services for appliances and televisions. New areas for digitization, many of which may not be easily envisioned today, will continue to develop. A key aspect of digitization is that it broadens out the set of items where costs of transporting final products to market become unimportant, allowing taxes to rise as a consideration in the location decision. The likelihood is high that the digitized transmissions will be remote and will raise the set of taxability/compliance issues addressed above.

Also, under existing state tax structures, there are a number of circumstances where sales and use tax liability depends on the form in which the item is delivered. Most state tax statutes indicate that sales of tangible personal property are taxable unless otherwise exempted, but services are only taxable if specifically enumerated. Thus, it is very possible that essentially the same item is taxable if delivered in tangible form and exempt when delivered in digitized form. Canned software is often an example. All states tax canned software when sold in the form of a diskette, but a number of states have determined that the transactions are taxable because they represent the sale of a piece of tangible personal property (the diskette). Under the state statutes, the sale of the diskette would only be exempt if specifically enumerated, and no exemption has been enacted. Following similar logic, however, the digitized version of the same software is a service and is taxable only if specifically enumerated. Based on these determinations, 16 states exempt downloaded software, generally arguing that electronic delivery of software is not taxable because there is no transfer of tangible personal property. The issue is broader than software and could easily extend to other digitized transactions. For example, Michigan has concluded that downloaded software is taxable, but the electronic transmission of other items, such as music, is exempt because there is no transfer of tangible personal property. Thus, the tax implications of e-commerce and the internet depend on whether states modernize their tax structures to ensure that digitization of goods and services does not affect the taxability of the underlying transactions. States will be unable to alter their tax structures to anticipate all of the transactions that can be digitized, and will find it necessary to write modernized legislation in broadly encompassing terms.

Digitization could also reduce property taxes. Property tax structures are normally comprised of real and tangible personal property, but not of intangibles. The digitization process effectively converts tangible property into intangible property, meaning the base could shrink.

Finally, digitization has implications for corporate income taxes. The property factor in most state apportionment formulas is only composed of tangible property, so software and other digitized property may not be included in the factor. This could alter which states collect revenues from an individual firm. Of course, this issue becomes less important as states move towards single factor sales apportionment formulas. Also, firms may be able to avoid creating nexus for corporate tax purposes by only locating intangible property in some states.

Shifts in the Competitive Position of Certain Industries: Industry Deregulation

A number of industries that have traditionally been regarded as public utilities, notably electric production and telecommunications, have normally been granted monopolies to operate in each geographic market. Because of the market structure, both state and local governments have often differentially imposed heavy origin-based taxes on these industries. The expectation was that the taxes would simply be shifted forward to consumers as prices were set through the regulatory process. The presumption was that the price elasticity of demand was low so the welfare losses and revenue implications for the firms were very low. However, technological advances have created a series of new competitors for these industries, rapidly eroding their monopoly position and likely creating a much larger price elasticity of demand for the public utilities. For example, telecommunications can be provided by cellular, internet, and cable companies, in addition to more traditional service providers.

Public utilities have frequently been subject to the same wide range of taxes as other businesses, including the corporate income and franchise, sales, and property taxes.[40] These broad based taxes have often been levied more heavily on public utilities than on other industries. For example, public utility property is frequently classified at a higher percentage of appraised value than is property used in other industries (in Tennessee, public utility property is assessed at 55 per cent of value and other business real property is assessed at 40 per cent of appraised value). In addition, public utility property is often appraised using a unit value approach while property used in other businesses is appraised piece by piece. The key difference is that intangible values related to the firm as on ongoing business can be included in public utility property. Further, these industries have been subjected to specialized taxes (sometimes in lieu of more traditional taxes) such as gross receipts, franchise fees, and right-of-way taxes, resulting in an even greater tax burden.

Sale for resale exemptions for utility purchases are relatively rare in state sales tax laws, though they are provided for other retailers. This may have been a modest concern during the era of monopoly provision. However, the absence of such exemptions offers the potential to radically alter the structure of the telecommunications industry (and potentially for the electric industry as well) since firms often purchase telecommunication services for resale. Firms can be expected to arrange their corporate affairs so that they only engage in purchase for resale in states where no tax is imposed on bulk purchases of electricity and telecommunications.

State and local governments are under pressure to eliminate the non-neutral tax structures imposed on the telecommunications industry (and increasingly the electric industry). Unless this occurs, the traditional firms (the Bell operating companies, for example) are placed at a significant disadvantage relative to other firms entering the industries. Some changes have already taken place. For example, some states concluded that long distance service is so competitive that the firms should not be defined as public utilities. This freed long distance carriers from utility specific taxes and tax

treatment, but left long distance and local carriers with differential taxes and
other competitors (cable companies, internet service providers, etc.) with
differential taxes from local carriers.

Conceptually, the problem of non-neutral taxes can be eliminated by either
imposing the industry specific taxes on new entrants or by eliminating the
special taxes. State and local governments often prefer imposing the industry
specific taxes on all competitors in the industry in order to maintain the
traditional capacity to collect significant taxes from the industry. However,
the emergence of new competitors has been so rapid, and the range of competitors so diverse that it can be very difficult to define what comprises the
industries. Some states have tried, but have discovered it to be a daunting
task. For example, today's telecommunications industry certainly includes
closely related service deliverers such as local and long distance service,
internet, cable television, and cellular phones. But it may also include businesses providing similar in-house services, and many other types of firms,
potentially extending the industry to a huge range of firms. Thus, trying to
identify a comprehensive set of businesses on which to impose taxes may not
be possible.

The preferred alternative is to eliminate the special taxes on these industries and for each state to impose broad based business and other taxes on
these increasingly competitive (as well as other) industries. This reduces
problems of non-neutral taxes and precludes the need to define the industries.
The obvious difficulty is that state and local tax revenues are reduced as
effective tax rates on these industries are lowered. The problem is magnified
because new technologies have reduced the relative investments necessary to
deliver telecommunications services, further lowering the property tax revenues generated by the industry. The problem is most severe in local
government areas that have housed major electric generating facilities, or
otherwise had large shares of public utility property. Arrangements have
often been developed to maintain the tax revenues in the interim, which
effectively seeks to bridge the two options. For example, Tennessee working
with BellSouth and other firms, legislated an increase in the telecommunications sales tax rate for business calls. The revenue is being used to provide
BellSouth and other local carriers with a property tax rebate that reduces their
effective tax liability to that imposed on other telecommunications firms (to
the extent that there is sufficient revenue from the new tax). Such maneuvers
will forestall but will not eliminate the need for taxation of these industries
that is consistent with that levied on other industries.

The traditional property tax base of state and local governments was developed in an era where real and tangible personal property were the key capital
inputs. Shifts are underway in the capital intensity of businesses that are
eroding this base. A general trend is towards greater intangible capital, in the

form of knowledge, digitized services, and so forth. This has a number of important implications for government revenues. As already noted, the property and sales tax bases are frequently smaller because intangibles are taxed less extensively than the physical capital they replace. Further, intangible property, some of which may be person specific, is likely to be more mobile than physical capital, making it more difficult to tax on an origin basis using corporate income, property or other taxes. Further, some industries, such as telecommunications are increasingly less capital intensive. Technology has allowed some large capital facilities to be replaced with lesser physical investments. The tax implications are similar to those for the movement to intangible property.

Conclusion

The ultimate outcome of technological changes is that increasingly global markets, competitive industries and mobile factors will force state and local governments to identify new ways to tax, and to focus their taxes more carefully. They will be forced to levy taxes on less mobile factors, which probably means land, residential housing and labor. The movement away from business to residential property is already strongly underway.[41] Nonlabor income and highly progressive taxes will be very difficult to levy. Consumption taxes will also be increasingly attractive if collection responsibilities can be established and enforced for remote vendors. Extraction of rents from business by imposing taxes at levels above the benefits received, will be increasingly difficult to do without facing the loss of economic activity.

APPENDIX A   STATE OF THE STATES IN THE DIGITAL ECONOMY

State	2000 Digital state ranking /a/	2000 Share of households w/ computer access /b/	2000 Share of households w/ internet access /b/	State	2000 Digital state ranking /a/	2000 Share of households w/ computer access /b/	2000 Share of households w/ internet access /b/
Alabama	49	44.2	35.5	Montana	34	51.5	40.6
Alaska	3	64.8	55.6	Nebraska	14	48.5	37.0
Arizona	17	53.5	42.5	Nevada	19	48.8	41.0
Arkansas	31	37.3	26.5	New Hampshire	41	54.3	56.0
California	42	56.6	46.7	New Jersey	6	63.7	47.8
Colorado	21	62.6	51.8	New Mexico	48	47.6	35.7
Connecticut	27	60.4	51.2	New York	32	48.7	39.8
Delaware	39	58.6	50.7	North Carolina	35	45.3	35.3
Washington, DC	/c/	48.8	39.6	North Dakota	47	47.5	37.7
Florida	25	50.1	43.2	Ohio	30	49.5	40.7
Georgia	7	47.1	38.3	Oklahoma	44	41.5	34.3
Hawaii	42	52.4	43.0	Oregon	23	61.1	50.8

State			
Idaho	13	54.5	42.3
Illinois	4	50.2	40.1
Indiana	26	48.8	39.4
Iowa	20	53.6	39.0
Kansas	2	55.8	43.9
Kentucky	29	46.2	36.6
Louisiana	18	41.2	30.2
Maine	35	54.7	42.6
Maryland	9	53.7	43.8
Massachusetts	27	53.0	45.5
Michigan	11	51.5	42.1
Minnesota	37	57.0	43.0
Mississippi	37	37.2	26.3
Missouri	22	52.6	42.5
Pennsylvania	12	48.4	40.1
Rhode Island	50	47.9	38.8
South Carolina	32	43.3	32.0
South Dakota	14	50.4	37.9
Tennessee	40	45.7	36.3
Texas	10	47.9	38.3
Utah	5	66.1	48.4
Vermont	46	53.7	46.7
Virginia	16	53.9	44.3
Washington	1	60.7	39.6
West Virginia	24	42.8	49.7
Wisconsin	8	50.9	40.6
Wyoming	45	58.2	44.1

Notes:
/a/ NTIA (2000).
/b/ CDG (2000).
/c/ Not included in rankings.

NOTES

*   The authors would like to thank participants of a session at the Western Economics Association annual conference 2001 and the annual conference of the National Tax Association 2001 for useful comments and suggestions.

1.   Estimates of the size of e-commerce and forecasts for the future vary widely. For example, estimates for 2003 B2B e-commerce range from \$634 billion to \$2.9 trillion, and B2C estimates range from \$7 billion to \$200 billion (see Fraumeni, 2001 and references therein). Each study, however, projects rapid and accelerated growth.

2.   Of course, there is some cost in accessing urban services, such as IT equipment and fiber optic cable, and so on, which are not incorporated into Figure 7.1. Thus, costs to rural communities would include a premium over costs for similar services in urban communities.

3.   Although two way television conferencing had been in use at least as early as the 1960s for psychiatric care (See Wittson et al., 1961; Wittson and Benschoter, 1972), wider scale use of teleconferencing and other forms of remote medical care is a more recent phenomenon, and has been advancing in line with advances in information technology more generally (Scher and Elder, 1999).

4.   The examples provided here are intended to serve as illustrative ones and may be more or less successful than other programs that are not mentioned. A comprehensive discussion of recent innovations in telemedicine is well outside of the scope of this chapter. Interested readers are referred to Insight Research Corporation (2000), which includes a substantial compendium of telemedicine statistics.

5.   MIT's Guardian Angel is an especially ambitious project on the way to what its progenitor, MIT computer scientist Peter Szolovits, hopes will evolve into a 'fully computerized and integrated' system of medical records for the US (Motluk, 2000, p. 28). The system is designed to follow individuals from cradle to grave, providing comprehensive access to medical records anywhere in the world, more or less continuous health monitoring, and immediate access to relevant medical information and health and medical advice.

6.   For additional information, see the ICSL website at http://icsl.ee. washington.edu

7.   Online purchases of airline tickets cost 87 per cent less than traditional ticket purchases. Similar cost reductions have been reported for online banking transactions (89 per cent), bill payments (70 per cent), and the purchase of insurance policies (50 per cent). See Western City (2001).

8.   In an attempt to recoup costs, capital costs in particular, a small minority of colleges and universities charge more tuition for virtual courses than for traditional courses (Lewis et al., 1999).

9.   Virginia became the first state to implement online drivers' license renewal in January, 2000. See Caterinicchia (2000).

10.   For an insightful demonstration of such a hyper-portal, see http://www.govconnect.com/portal.htm.

11.   Of the total amount, Treasury securities accounted for \$3.3 billion in sales.

12.   Section 825 of the Personal Responsibility and Work Opportunity Act of 1996 (P.L. 104–93, 'Welfare Reform' Bill) requires that all states implement EBT systems by 1 October, 2002, unless a state 'faces unusual barriers to implementation' (Cason, 1998, p. 1). The total net (monetary) savings of a nationwide transition to EBT is projected to be positive, in large part from reduced administrative costs (Humphrey, 1996). See also, Stix (1994). Beyond economy, the EBT system is expected to have additional benefits in fostering the 'economic literacy of low-income consumers' and encouraging 'financial inclusion' (Stegman, 1998, p. 1).

13.   Zolt (2000) reported one US senator and five US representatives without web pages. As of July, 2001, all of these congressmen had websites with the exception of Rep. Jesse Jackson, Jr. (D-IL); however, the websites of Reps. Joel Hefley (R-CO), Alan Mollohan (D-WV), and Robert Stump (R-AZ) do not list an e-mail address. Rep. Mollohan's web page states that an e-mail address is not provided because his staff would be inundated with e-mails from outside of his district.

14. As noted by the author, the 2000 Democratic presidential primary was contested, while the 1996 primary was not, making the impact of internet voting on turnout difficult to assess. However, we note that Vice President Gore's primary rival in the contest, Senator Bill Bradley, withdrew from the race on the day before the 11 March Arizona primary. Moreover, the hotly contested 1992 Democratic presidential primary saw participation by only 4.3 per cent of Arizona's registered Democrats (Leahy and Goodlatte, 2000).

15. See Putnam (2000).

16. For an alternative, but similar model of the e-government development process, see Layne and Lee (2001).

17. See also Brudney and Selden (1995), Norris and Demeter (1999), and Streib and Willoughby (2001).

18. Princeton Survey Associates, July, 2000 for the Pew Internet and American Life Project, Pew Research Center (accessible at http://www.pewinternet.org).

19. For an analysis of the complete results of this survey, see Excelgov (2000).

20. As cited in Lindamood (2000).

21. Due in large part to a lack of authority to implement programs in many counties (Duncombe, 1977; Streib and Waugh, 1991; DeSantis and Renner, 1993).

22. Specifically, the survey asked: 'Do you think most people would try to take advantage of you if they got the chance, or would they try to be fair?' Of all internet users responding, 'Would try to be fair', 60.1 per cent had visited a government website.

23. Audio transcript available at http://energycommerce.house.gov/107/ ram/05082001ctcp.ram. See also Sager (2001).

24. EzGov, Inc., 'EzGov Privacy Survey Results', April, 2000 (http://www.ezgov.com). Less than half of survey respondents were aware that driving records are available at their county courthouse, although almost all (93 per cent) were aware of the availability of property records.

25. For details on the Carnivore technology, see http://www.fbi.gov/hq/lab/carnivore/carnivore2.htm. The ingenuity of this application is that it can differentiate content that may be lawfully (by order of a federal district court) intercepted and content which may not be lawfully intercepted. While the use of Carnivore is subjected to the same Department of Justice oversight as other, older forms of electronic surveillance, the American Civil Liberties Union recently has expressed concern that Carnivore does not require the physical placement of a device and therefore could be used ubiquitously (see *USA Today*, 2000). Wire-taps, on the other hand, require placement by the local telephone company. Of course, private companies already are developing software intended to counteract Carnivore (See Stenger, 2000).

26. For a continuously updated list of major privacy breaches by US companies and governments, see *Wired* 'Privacy Matters', which is accessible at http://www.wired.com/news/privacy

27. HOPE provides free tuition for in-state, academically eligible students to attend Georgia institutions of higher education.

28. See *Business Week* (2000).

29. As evidence, Uslaner notes that 43 per cent of internet users with 'online friends' have used a fake ID at some point in their life, and 38 per cent have used a fake e-mail address, compared to 19 per cent and 15 per cent, respectively, of those without online friends.

30. Author's calculations from data provided by Princeton Survey Associates, July, 2000 for the Pew Internet and American Life Project, Pew Research Center (accessible at http://www.pewinternet.org).

31. Leigh and Atkinson (2001) estimate a 50 per cent penetration for the internet in 2001 and a 90 per cent penetration by the year 2003. For examples of recent community efforts to bridge the digital divide, see the April, 2001 edition of *Government Technology* magazine: 'Bridging the divide one neighborhood at a time'.

32. Not surprisingly, demographic groups that are least likely to have internet access at home are considerably more likely to take advantage of public access points (See NTIA, 1999, Chart II-16 and related text).

33. Total time for registration renewal has since been reduced from 50 days to approximately two weeks. The program is not without controversy, however, because part of the state's savings came out of an agreement to insert advertising for the agent in the official government mailing.
34. Kelly Kimball, CEO, SDR Technologies, San Francisco Chronicle, 13 September, 1999. As cited in Snell and Moore (1999).
35. Access both to computers and to the internet are very progressive with respect to income. As a result, higher income households receive much of the benefits from failure to tax services sold using these media. See NTIA (2000).
36. Current thinking is that the pure dot.com companies (both on the B2B and B2C side) will find it difficult to compete because they lack an acceptable business model. However, the expectation is that other forms of e-commerce, such as e-commerce divisions of companies that operate through more traditional distribution modes, will supplant those companies set up only to operate through the e-commerce channel (see Senn, 2000).
37. All states impose use taxes on goods, but only 24 states levy use taxes on services. The effect in states not imposing use taxes on services is to only levy the tax on goods produced in the home state. Of course, in many cases the states may have very limited taxation of services.
38. Maine has eliminated the minimum payment.
39. See Wasylenko (1997) for a review of the effects of taxes on business location and Fisher (1997) for a review of the effects of access to public services on location.
40. See *Telecommunications Tax Policies: Implications for the Digital Age*, National Governors' Association, 2000, for a summary of how states impose taxes on the telecommunications industry.
41. Strauss reports data for 18 states, all of which have had an increase in the residential share of the property tax base. See Strauss (2001).

REFERENCES

Accenture, Inc. (2001a), 2001 State Motor Vehicle Agencies' Internet Utilization, New York; NY: Accenture, Inc.
Accenture, Inc. (2001b), *E-Government Leadership: Rhetoric vs. Reality – Closing the Gap*, New York, NY: Accenture, Inc.
American Society for Quality (2001), *American Customer Satisfaction Index*, First Quarter.
Atlanta Constitution (2001), 'Cut wait for driver's licenses – now', 19 June.
Baer, Walter S. (1998), 'Will the internet transform higher education?', *Annual Review of the Institute for Information Studies*, www.aspeninst.org/dir/polpro/CSP/IIS/98/98.html
Bruce, Donald, and William F. Fox (2000), 'E-commerce in the context of declining state sales tax bases', *National Tax Journal*, 53(4, part 3): 1373–88.
Brudney, Jeffrey L. and Sally C. Selden (1995), 'The adoption of innovation by smaller local governments: The case of computer technology', *American Review of Public Administration*, 25, March, 77–86.
Business Week (2000), 'It's time for rules in Wonderland', 20 March: 82–6.
Cabanatuan, Michael (2001), 'DMV's greatest gridlock: Daly city office ranks no. 1 for longest wait', *San Francisco Chronicle*, 18 June.
Cason, Katherine L. (1998), 'Electronic benefits transfer: New strategies for improving public assistance programs', *Welfare Reform*, 6, December, Mississippi State, MS: Southern Rural Development Center.

Caterinicchia, Dan (2000), 'Virginia DMV first in nation to offer online license renewals', Press release, FCW Government Technology Group, 19 January.

Cattagni, Anne and Elizabeth Farris Westat (2001), 'Internet access in US public schools and classrooms: 1994–2000', *Statistics in Brief*, NCES 2001-071, National Center for Education Statistics, US Department of Education, Washington, DC, May.

DeSantis, Victor S. and Tari Renner (1993), 'Governing the county: Authority, structure, and elections,' in David R. Berman (ed.), *County Governments in an Era of Change*, Westport, CT: Greenwood, pp. 16–25.

Due, John F. and John L. Mikesell (1995), *Sales Taxation: State and Local Structure and Administration*, 2nd edn, Washington, DC: The Urban Institute Press.

Duncombe, Herber S. (1977), *Modern County Government*, Washington, DC: National Association of Counties.

Economist, The (1997), 'Big sister is watching you', 11 January: 27.

Economist, The (2000), 'Quick fixes', 24 June, Special section: 13.

Excelgov (2000), 'E-Government: the next American revolution', Hart-Teeter for the Council for Excellence in Government, September, 2000 (accessible at http://www.excelgov.org/egovpoll/).

Fisher, Ronald C. (1997), 'The effects of state and local public services on economic development', *New England Economic Review: Proceedings of a Symposium on the Effects of State and Local Public Policies on Economic Development*, March/April: 53–67.

Fox, William F. and LeAnn Luna (2000), 'Taxing e-commerce: Neutral taxation is best for industry and the economy', *Quarterly Journal of Electronic Commerce*, 1(2): 139–50.

Fraumeni, Barbara M. (2001), 'E-commerce: Measurement and measurement issues', *American Economic Review*, 91(2): 318–22.

Frieden, Karl (2000), *Cybertaxation: The Taxation of E-Commerce*, Chicago, IL: CCH Incorporated.

Gest, Ted (2001), 'The cyber rap sheet', *Governing*, September: 26–8.

Gladieux, Lawrence E. and Watson S. Swail (1999), 'The virtual university and educational opportunity: Issues of equity and access for the next generation', *Policy Perspectives*, April, Washington, DC: The College Board.

Goolsbee, Austan (2000), 'In a world without borders: The impact of taxes on internet commerce', *Quarterly Journal of Economics*, 115(2): 561–76.

Goolsbee, Austan (2001), 'Education and the Internet,' in Robert Litan and Alice Rivlin (eds), *The Economic Payoff from the Internet Revolution*, Washington, DC: Internet Policy Institute/Brookings Institution Press, pp. 269–84.

Government Technology (2000a), 'The GT national technology snapshot', September: 22.

Government Technology (2000b), 'The GT national technology snapshot', October: 22.

Gramlich, Edward M. (1990), *A Guide to Benefit-Cost Analysis*, 2nd edn, Prospect Heights, IL, Waveland Press.

Greeves, Robert (1998), *The Penultimate Mile: Local and State Governments Collaborating to Serve Citizens Through Information Technology*, Washington, DC: Council for Excellence in Government.

Hasson, Judi and Graeme Browning (2001), 'Dot-gov goes retail,' *Federal Computer Week*, 28 May.

Higgins, Lori (2001), 'Alternative education goes high tech: Sophisticated computer program is being offered', *Detroit Free Press*, 29 August.

Hoffman, Donna L. and Thomas P. Novak (1998), 'Bridging the racial divide on the internet', *Science*, 280, 17 April: 390–1.

Horner, Raymond (1999), 'Meeting demands: Citizens, empowered by technology-driven access to customized services, are now demanding similar service from state and local government', *Minnesota Cities*, 84(4): 5–6.

Humphrey, David B. (1996), 'The economics of electronic benefit transfer payments', *Economic Quarterly*, 82(2): 77–94 (Federal Reserve Bank of Richmond).

IBM (undated), 'IBM moves MVD solutions to the fast lane', accessed 29 August 2001 at http://houns54.clearlake.ibm.com/solutions/government.

Inman, Robert P. and Daniel L. Rubinfeld (1997), 'Rethinking federalism', *The Journal of Economic Perspectives*, 11(4): 43–64.

Insight Research Corporation (2000), *Health Care and Telecommunications 2000–2005*, October, Parsippany, NJ: IRC.

International City/County Management Association (ICMA) (2001), 'Public-private partnership launches e-government initiative for cities/counties', *ICMA Corporate Partner News*, accessed 31 October at http://www.icma.org.

Internet Policy Institute (2001), *Report of the National Workshop on Internet Voting*, Washington, DC, March.

Johnson, Amy Helen (1999), 'A simple plan', *CIO Magazine*, 1 March.

Judd, Alan and Kathy Brister (2001a), 'Barnes: Tell me how HOPE info got out', *Atlanta Journal Constitution*, 25 July.

Judd, Alan and Kathy Brister (2001b), 'HOPE's online breach worse than feared', *Atlanta Journal Constitution*, 31 July.

Kerwin, Kevin, Marcia Stepanek and David Welch (2000), 'At Ford, e-commerce is job 1', *Business Week*, 28 February: 74.

Kienzle, Michael G., Principal Investigator, et al. (2000), *Rural-Academic Integration: Iowa's National Laboratory for the Study of Rural Telemedicine, Final Report*, March.

Layne, Karen and Jungwoo Lee (2001), 'Developing fully functional e-government: A four stage model', *Government Information Quarterly*, 18: 123–36.

Lazarus, Wendy and Francisco Mora (2000), 'Online content for low-income and underserved Americans: The digital divide's new frontier', Santa Monica, CA: The Children's Partnership, March.

Leahy, Sen. Patrick J. and Rep. Robert Goodlatte (2000), 'The internet and the future of democratic governance', *Briefing the President: What the Next President of the United States Needs to Know About the Internet and Its Transformative Impact on Society*, Washington, DC: Internet Policy Institute.

Leigh, Andrew and Robert D. Atkinson (2001), 'Clear thinking on the digital divide', *Policy Report*, Washington, DC: Progressive Policy Institute, June.

Lewis, Laurie, Kyle Snow, Elizabeth Farris, Douglas Levin and Bernie Greene (1999), 'Distance education at postsecondary education institutions: 1997–98', *Statistical Analysis Report NCES 2000-013*, Washington, DC: National Center for Education Statistics.

Lewis, Sonja (2001), 'Want a Georgia driver's license? Not so fast – a 5-hour wait is not uncommon', *Atlanta Journal Constitution*, 19 June.

Library Research Center (2000), 'Survey of internet access management in public libraries: Summary of findings', Graduate School of Library and Information Science, University of Illinois, Urbana-Champaign, IL.

Lindamood, George (2000), 'E-government as a subversive activity', *Government Technology*, 13(12): 78.

Ludlow, Barbara L. (1994), 'A comparison of traditional and distance education models', *Proceedings of the Annual National Conference of the American Council on Rural Special Education*, Austin, TX.

McCullagh, Declan (2001), '"Secure" US site wasn't very,' *Wired*, 6 July: www.wired. com/news/privacy/o,1848,45031,00.html.

McDonald, Douglas C., A. Hassol, K. Carlson, J. McCullough, E. Fournier and J. Yap (1999), 'Telemedicine can reduce correctional health care costs: An evaluation of a prison telemedicine network', *National Institute of Justice Report No. NIJ 175040*, March.

Motluk, Alison (2000), 'Someone to watch over you', *New Scientist*, 30 September: 28–31.

National Association of Counties (NACo), in association with Public Technology, Incorporated (PTI) (2000), '2000 e-government survey', April.

National Telecommunications & Information Administration (NTIA), Economics and Statistics Administration, United States Department of Commerce (1995), 'Falling through the net: a survey of the "have nots" in rural and urban America', Washington, DC.

National Telecommunications & Information Administration (NTIA), Economics and Statistics Administration, United States Department of Commerce (1998), 'Falling through the net II: New data on the digital divide', Washington, DC, July.

National Telecommunications & Information Administration (NTIA), Economics and Statistics Administration, United States Department of Commerce (1999), 'Falling through the net: Defining the digital divide', Washington, DC, November, revised.

National Telecommunications & Information Administration (NTIA), Economics and Statistics Administration, United States Department of Commerce (2000), 'Falling through the net: Toward digital inclusion', Washington, DC, October.

Nelson, Brian (1997), 'Computers, cable make medical house calls routine', *CNN Interactive*, 14 March.

Newcombe, Tod (2000), 'Opening the knowledge portal', *Government Technology*, 13(12): 26–31.

Newcombe, Tod (2001), 'Licensed to succeed', *Government Technology*, 14(12): 54–6.

Norris, Donald F., Patricia D. Fletcher and Stephen H. Holden (2001), 'Is your local government plugged in? Highlights of electronic government survey 2000, conducted by the International City/County Management Association and Public Technology, Inc.', *Public Management*, 83(5): 4–10.

Norris, Donald F. and Lori A. Demeter (1999), 'Information technology and city government', *The Municipal Yearbook*, 66: 10–19.

O'Looney, John (2000), 'The implications of internet voting', *Government Technology*, 13(12), 86–8.

Perlman, Ellen (2000a), '*Governing's* Managing Technology 2000 Conference: Policy, politics, and leadership', Governing.com.

Perlman, Ellen (2000b), 'Local resistance', Governing.com, September.

Phillips, Deborah M. (1999), 'Are we ready for internet voting?', Arlington, VA: Voting Integrity Project, 12 August.

Public Technology, Incorporated and International City/County Management Association (PTI/ICMA) (2001), 'Electronic government survey 2000', February.

Putnam, Robert D. (2000), *Bowling Alone: The Collapse and Revival of American Community*, New York, NY: Simon & Schuster.
Quay, Ray (2001), 'Bridging the digital divide', *Planning*, 67(7): 12–17.
Robb, Drew (2000), 'Plugging into electronic procurement', *Government Technology*, 13(12): 80–4.
Rylander, Carole Keeton (2001), 'Lone Star card facts', Texas Comptroller of the Currency, accessed 3 October at http://www.window.state.tx.us/comptrol/ebt/ebtfacts.htm.
Sager, Ryan (2001), 'Public: Take our privacy, please', *Wired Magazine Online*, 9 May.
Scher, Bob and Crystal Elder (1999), 'Telemedicine: More than a phone call, a new legal world', *Health Law Journal*, 4(2): 3–18.
Senn, James A. (2000), 'Electronic Commerce Beyond the "dot com" Boom', *National Tax Journal*, 53(3), Part 1, 373–83.
Snell, Lisa and Adrian Moore (1999), 'E-government', *Intellectual Ammunition*, Chicago, IL: The Heartland Institute, November/December.
Stegman, Michael A. (1998), 'Electronic benefit's potential to help the poor', *Policy Brief #32*, The Brookings Institution, March.
Stenger, Richard (2000), 'FBI's "Carnivore" spurs new e-mail cloaking programs', CNN.com, 26 September.
Stix, Gary (1994), 'Welfare plastic', *Scientific American*, 271: 84–7.
Strauss, Robert P. (2001), 'Pennsylvania's local property tax', *State Tax Notes*, June: 1963–83.
Streib, Gregory and William L. Waugh, Jr. (1991), 'Administrative capacity and barriers to effective county management', *Public Productivity and Management Review*, 15(Fall): 61–70.
Streib, Gregory D. and Katherine G. Willoughby (2001), 'Local governments as e-governments: Meeting the implementation challenge', Working paper, Department of Public Administration and Urban Studies, Andrew Young School of Policy Studies, Georgia State University, August.
Swope, Christopher (2001), 'Minnesota drivers: You've got mail – and more', *Governing*, 15(1), October, p. 58.
USA Today (2000), 'FBI: "Carnivore" will play nice', 21 July, available on the internet at http://www.usatoday.com/life/cyber/tech/cti263.htm
Uslaner, Eric M. (2001), 'Trust, civic engagement, and the internet', Paper presented at the 2001 European Consortium for Political Research Workshops, Grenoble, France.
Wasylenko, Michael (1997), 'Taxation and economic development: the state of the economic literature', *New England Economic Review: Proceedings of a Symposium on the Effects of State and Local Public Policies on Economic Development*, March/April, pp. 37–52.
West, Darrell M. (2000), 'Assessing e-government: The internet, democracy, and service delivery by state and federal governments', Taubman Center for Public Policy, Brown University, September.
Western City (2001), 'E-government: What local officials need to know', June, adapted from Public Technology, Inc.'s forthcoming strategic planning guidebook.
Westland, J. Christopher and Theodore H.K. Clark (1999), *Global Electronic Commerce: Theory and Case Studies*, Cambridge, MA and London: MIT Press.
Wheeler, Travis (1994), 'In the beginning: Telemedicine and telepsychiatry', *Telemedicine Today*, 2, Summer: pp. 2–4.

Willis, Barry (2000), 'Distance education: Research', *Distance Education at a Glance*, Guide #9, Engineering Outreach, University of Idaho, Moscow, ID: www.vidato.edu/evo/dist9.html

Wittson, C.L., D.C. Affleck and V. Johnson (1961), 'Two-way television in group therapy', *Mental Hospitals*, 12: 22–3.

Wittson, C.L. and R.A. Benschoter (1972), 'Two-way television: Helping medical centers reach-out', *American Journal of Psychiatry*, 129: 624–7.

Young, Donna (2001), 'E-filing saves time, money', *Government Computer News*, 7(4): www.gcn.com/state/vol17_no4/news/1021-1.html.

Zolt, Stacey (2000), 'Some members still stuck in the digital dark age: Rockefellar, Watts among the lawmakers trying to get colleagues up to speed on technology issues', *Roll Call*, 24 January.

8. Deregulation of utilities: A challenge and an opportunity for state and local tax policy

Bruce A. Seaman and W. Bartley Hildreth

INTRODUCTION TO DEREGULATION

Structural and behavioral changes in the provision of electricity, natural gas, and telecommunications services have confronted many states with serious challenges regarding the tax and administrative burdens to be placed on these newly competitive industries. Historically, the three industries faced state regulations for engaging in intrastate commerce – enjoying a monopoly market within the state in return for limitations on consumer prices and rates of return. While adequate for almost an entire century, this simple formulation failed to keep pace with technological change, demand growth, and other developments in the respective industries that led many to consider opening local *retail* markets to additional competition and expanded consumer choice.

Wholesale electricity competition has a longer history as a result of the Public Utility Regulatory Policies Act (1978), the Energy Policy Act (1992), and administrative actions of the Federal Energy Regulatory Commission (FERC). Ongoing developments in the transmission of energy over greater distances, and the creation of alternative technologies for transmitting information, fundamentally challenged the premise that local energy and telecommunication retail services were best provided by a single 'natural monopolist'. While consumer frustration with the perceived limited price benefits of deregulation, the highly publicized energy crisis in California, and dramatic energy and telecommunication company accounting scandals (such as Enron and WorldCom) have slowed and in some cases reversed the momentum favoring utility deregulation, the effect of deregulation on tax policy remains a complex and important subject.

Although deregulation had become common in the provision of airline, interstate shipping and long distance telephone services, the case for considering local energy and telephone retail services to be 'natural monopolies' had traditionally been a more difficult one to dismiss. However, motivated in part by the strong desire by policy makers to ensure that their states remain competitive and capable of sustaining high growth, some states with especially high energy prices initiated legislative changes that were intended to increase competition and reduce rates for those critical services.[1]

The common term for such deregulation is 'retail unbundling', since the regulated system was characterized by the bundling of utility services as they passed through the various 'vertical channels' to the final consumer (residential, commercial or industrial). For example, in order to provide electricity services, a vertically integrated company generated electricity at distant power plants, then transmitted that power over high voltage power lines, and finally distributed electricity over the last mile to the ultimate consumer. In the mid 1990s, the view gained popularity, especially in the high electricity rate states (see endnote 1), that the electricity sector should be restructured into three unbundled businesses: unregulated alternative generation companies; regulated transmission companies (operated similar to a toll road); and regulated distribution companies.[2]

Similar forces favoring deregulation led to related structural changes in other sectors, such as natural gas, with the marketing of the product being deregulated in many states while the final distribution stage(s) remained regulated. Such fundamental changes in industry structure introduce alternative competitive suppliers, and the prospect of significant consumer benefits in the form of lower prices and higher service quality. While residential and small commercial customers generally did not oppose deregulation, it was the large industrial customers who most actively promoted these industry changes.

Facilitating the structural transition in the energy sector was a product that did not substantially change as a result of the technological developments that were in part responsible for the deregulation movement. Hence, with or without deregulation, the 'unit consumed' was still a kilowatt-hour of electricity, or a therm of natural gas. By contrast, the telecommunications industry has been subjected to both structural changes and significant increases in 'product differentiation'. Significant changes in telecommunications preceded those in the energy sector. In 1984, the telecommunications industry was jolted into a new environment with the break-up of AT&T into local and long distance carriers, and a clearer distinction between the provision of equipment and services. Subsequently, wireless technology has emerged as a viable and increasingly popular alternative to the wired, land based system.

The initial structural changes resulting from the 'unbundling' of telecommunications services after the AT&T breakup were profound, with the entry of many alternative service providers and dramatically falling prices. Over time, long distance telecommunications evolved into a seemingly stable structure, characterized by significant industry consolidation and the domination of long distance by a few very large, but brutally competitive multinational companies. Recent accounting scandals, the recognition that the industry had overestimated demand growth (and underestimated the profound effects of e-mail and wireless alternatives), and the growing awareness of the magnitude of the substantial overinvestment in productive capacity, have rocked the deregulated long distance telecommunications sector, and put the future of deregulation into some question (Consumer Reports, 2002).

By contrast, local phone service has hardly changed over the past 20 years. This has been true even following the federal 1996 Telecommunications Act, intended in part to inject effective competition into local 'wired' residential phone service. Such deregulatory efforts in local wired phone service have been largely (but not entirely) unsuccessful, due in large part to ongoing controversies about the pricing of the 'local access' services to be provided to potential local phone service entrants by the incumbent local exchange carriers ('LECs'), that continue to own the complex local network switching equipment. Thus, when compared to the recent fundamental structural changes in the energy service industries in many states, and the post-1984 tumult in the long distance telecommunications sector, the structure of the local telephone industry has been quite stable, despite legislative efforts to facilitate more local competition.

However, states have not been immune to tax policy challenges linked to local telecommunications. Since the telecommunications product itself has morphed into many alternative techniques for providing a 'unit of communication service', past tax policy designed for a primarily 'wired' world is unlikely to still be appropriate, and the increasingly large wireless market often goes relatively untaxed. In fact, such product changes go beyond the transition from wired to wireless versions of 'traditional' non-face-to-face communication, but now include dramatic increases in the use of electronic mailing (e-mail) and instant messaging (IM).

Thus, changes in both long distance and local telecommunications have related not only to the 'simpler' forms of structural change experienced in the energy sector following the entry of new competitors, but even more compellingly are the result of dramatic technological changes that have redefined the very nature of the 'product'.

This *exogenous* combination of fundamental industry structural change (as in the energy sector) along with greatly increased product differentiation (as in the telecommunications sector) suggested to many scholars and policy makers that statewide re-evaluations of tax and public finance issues were necessary (Joskow, 1997). For example, state and local government budgets depend upon economic vitality and revenue stability, so that any threats to the tax base and economic growth would naturally demand the attention of public officials. Rate-regulated industries have long been an inviting vehicle for state law makers to embed high tax rates within the relatively invisible 'base charges', and therefore ensure large and stable revenues. In fact, since consumers generally view utility services as 'essential', adverse public reaction to such taxes are often thought to be relatively limited, even when such taxes are itemized and displayed separately on the customer's bill. These reasons have contributed to the historical reality that the electrical, natural gas and telecommunications services are among the most heavily taxed industries in the United States (Reeb and Howe, 1985; Walters and Cornia, 1997; Telecommunications Tax Task Force, 2002).

Elected officials face considerable complexity as they try to adjust both regulatory and public finance policies to these structural and technological changes. For example, moving toward greater equality in the overall industrial tax burden would require lowering the previously high tax burdens for the newly competitive energy and telecommunications industries. However, without offsetting increases in the overall tax base, or politically unpopular increases in the tax burdens of other sectors, overall state tax revenues will decline. Revenues from the newly deregulated sectors may decline even further to the extent that the promises of deregulation are realized in the form of lower prices (depending on the extent to which gross revenues constitute the tax base and the price elasticity of demand in the 'relevant price range').

Further complications arise since public officials must design legally acceptable taxable relationships (nexus) with newly emergent out-of-state service providers following deregulation. Without extending nexus to such suppliers, revenues will fall even further and serious 'non-neutrality' will be injected into the tax structure as different suppliers face differential tax requirements. Electricity provides a good example of such nexus complications. An out-of-state supplier could receive the customer's call for service over the internet, route electricity via the 'toll road' transmission entity, and pay the regulated local distribution firm for the use of the 'last mile' into the consumer's home or business location. Throughout this process, the out-of-state supplier has no employees, no facilities, and no other 'physical presence' in the state as required by the *Quill* (1992) standard for establishing nexus.

Such problems mean that officials must weigh the prospect of substituting away from their traditional industry specific tax structures (which have included gross receipts taxes and broad definitions of taxable property), and toward both unit (quantity)-based consumption taxes and neutral income taxes that are applicable equally to all businesses. Another critical issue is the complex assignment of the tax duties between the state and local governments, and how that assignment affects the administrative burdens facing business taxpayers in the newly competitive industries. Also, effective political action on these issues cannot normally be implemented without some degree of cooperation among the occasionally conflicting interests of the affected industries.

There is evidence (see the later section on 'The diverse forms of state tax adjustment') that the electricity and natural gas industries have been willing to accept a shift to local property valuation, even with the resulting additional administrative complexity, as a means of breaking the hold of central unit valuation that had allowed state revenue departments to tax these firms as a 'going concern'. In contrast, the telecommunications industry, feeling especially burdened by the disparate requirements of negotiating separate franchise fee and tax arrangements with the myriad of municipalities within states, seem to have preferred a more central solution by which the state assumes the taxing authority, often in exchange for an expansion of the tax and franchise fee base to include wireless and 'nonrecurring' wired services.[3] This expansion of the tax base consequently allows for a somewhat lower tax/fee rate, as well as achieving a more neutral and nondistorting tax structure within the telecommunications sector. Local jurisdictions, in turn, receive their share of the centrally collected taxes that replace the local tax or franchise fee. Although the electric and natural gas industries also face local franchise fees, there does not seem to be the same imperative to centralize the system among energy firms as is found within the telecommunications industry.

HOW SERIOUS A CHALLENGE?

Despite the extensive commentary (in both the popular press and the academic literature) regarding these dramatic changes in the telecommunications and the energy industries, the effects of deregulation on state and local tax revenues, structure, and policy have received relatively little attention compared to the controversy about the wisdom of deregulation itself.[4] With some notable exceptions (such as National Conference of State Legislatures, 1997; Walters and Cornia, 1997, and 2001; Federation of Tax Administrators (Cappellari), 1999; Cline, 2000), attention has been primarily focused on the competitive consequences and the degree to which state deregulation efforts have actually delivered the lower prices, higher service quality, and expanded consumer choice that were promised by proponents (see, for example, Borenstein, 2002).

To the extent that utility deregulation does deliver lower prices and an expansion of consumer choice by allowing the entry of service providers beyond local jurisdictional and even state boundaries, local and state governments face several direct challenges, introduced in part in the previous section:

1. Those sources of energy and telecommunications tax payments that rely on a total revenue tax base (such as franchise fees, gross receipts, consumption, sales and use taxes, and even business license fees) may

generate lower government payments due to a decline in the total revenue tax base as a result of lower retail prices (depending on the value of the price elasticity of demand in the relevant price range).

2. This transactions tax problem could be substantially worsened if legal nexus could not be established for out-of-state service providers (such as marketers), who may arguably fail to meet the *Quill* (1992) 'physical presence' requirements.[5]

3. Those sources of tax payments that depend upon asset valuations and profits (such as property and franchise taxes, and corporate income taxes) may generate substantially lower tax payments as the value of the firms providing telecommunications and energy services declines in the face of increased competition and lower prices.

4. Those local governments which have established municipal utilities stand to lose net revenue that may have also served as indirect support for general operations as competition with other service providers increases and prices fall (Hildreth et al., 1997).

However, it is not at all clear that such challenges must result or have resulted in adverse fiscal consequences for state and local governments, and not only because some of the hoped for reductions in utility prices have not (yet) materialized. In fact, the following considerations would suggest that governments have either sufficient 'defensive' policy options to exercise or that there are other compensating factors that would naturally limit the severity of this fiscal challenge:

1. State and local governments, even those which are themselves energy and telecommunications providers, are also consumers of such services and therefore stand to benefit in that role from any resulting reductions in utility prices.

2. States having relatively low cost production plants (in the energy sector) may well find those firms expanding their exports of energy under deregulation sufficient to cause a net increase rather than decrease in the total revenues (gross receipts) subject to taxation.

3. To the extent that energy and telecommunication price reductions lead to significant reductions in the cost of doing business within particular states, overall economic activity may increase sufficient to generate higher overall tax revenues even if the tax base erodes within the utility sectors themselves.

4. Certain modest policy options such as shifting from revenue-based to 'unit' (quantity)-based taxation may be able to easily immunize governments from any fall in total revenue tax bases, and to the extent that lower prices lead to even faster growth in units produced and consumed,

the unit defined tax base could well expand government revenues even without major adjustments in tax rates. As a related strategy, tax rates could be adjusted to wholly or partially compensate for any declines in the tax base.

5. Similarly, governments may find it fairly easy to solve (subject to legal clarification) any nexus threats to their tax bases by either requiring the de facto establishment of nexus as a condition for issuing business licenses to 'nondomestic' service providers, or otherwise defining physical presence as occurring whenever 'sellers' utilize the local distribution networks for the 'final stage' delivery of utility services.[6]

Therefore, a threshold issue is the very determination of the extent of the fiscal challenge that has resulted from utility deregulation and the severity of that challenge across different states. Because retail deregulation in most states is a very recent phenomenon, reliable data regarding revenue losses that might be attributed directly to industry restructuring and technological change are simply not available. But there is no presumption that deregulation of natural gas and electricity, and the technological and structural change in the telecommunications sector, raise exactly the same fiscal issues for all state and local governments. Certainly the very extent to which states have deregulated these separate industries varies greatly, with substantially more states having deregulated electricity markets than natural gas markets. While the shifts in telecommunications products apply to all states, their consequences vary with a state's tax structure (for instance, tax bases are often limited to wired technologies) and the reliance upon revenues from that sector compared to other industries. In the future, important interstate differences will also emerge in local telephone service competition. In our section after next, a 'fiscal stress index' is derived in an attempt to capture the ex ante differential vulnerabilities of states to this new economic environment that would potentially influence observed state tax policy adjustments.

FRAMEWORK FOR THE ANALYSIS

It is commonly argued that times of great uncertainty and fiscal crisis provide excellent opportunities for the implementation of more fundamental long needed tax reform (see, for example, Brunori, 2001). Hence, to the extent that deregulation has represented a serious threat to state and local governments, it has also presented a unique opportunity to address long neglected issues that have prevented states from moving toward more optimal tax structures and divisions of responsibility between state departments of revenue and those of local municipalities and counties. States will differ greatly in how far removed they are from the goal of an 'optimal tax structure'. Thus, the need for reform, as well as the likelihood for such reform will vary substantially across states.

Table 8.1 provides a possible taxonomy for evaluating how states are facing the challenge of adapting to utility deregulation. Specific examples of

Table 8.1   Overview of approaches to the fiscal challenge

Criterion	'Reform' model	'Coping' model
Focus of attention	Efficiency (forward looking): Possible new tax bases Review state/local division of authority Seek mutual gains	Distributional neutrality (backward looking): Minimize changes in overall tax burdens Concern with 'winners' and 'losers' Minimize political reactions and 'fallout'
Fiscal strategy	Seek tax system neutrality: Willing to consider a change in revenue trend line, including new revenue sources	Seek tax revenue neutrality: Stress continuity of existing revenue trend line with no change in revenue source Alternative of substituting revenue sources but retaining the existing revenue trend line Alternative of modestly new revenue trend line with minimal fine-tuning, application changes in same revenue sources
Timing	Rapid transition; Delays in moving to optimal structure primarily a logistical quest for a simultaneous adjustment of tax policy and regulatory structure so as to obtain coherent fiscal structure (e.g. Pennsylvania, New Jersey, Ohio re: electricity)	Extended transition; (Non-synchronized tax and regulatory adjustments): Tax first – deregulate later (e.g. Iowa: re electricity) Enact deregulation legislation, but condition implementation on passage of tax law changes (e.g. Oklahoma and West Virginia: electricity)

state policy adjustments are provided in our section after next, with the focus upon how the utility deregulation experience can improve our understanding of how governments can and should adapt to significant changes in their external environment. First, the concepts identified in Table 8.1 require clarification (Hildreth, 2002).

In their approach to deregulation, states might be labeled either 'reform' states or 'coping' states, depending upon whether they adopt policies that represent either a forward looking (efficiency) or a backward looking (distribution) focus. A backward looking focus highlights the winners and losers of deregulation, with efforts to design compensatory relief that will redistribute the results along a desired path. This can lead to small policy changes, rather than more fundamental ones, to limit the intensity of political reaction that could complicate the rapid movement to deregulation. The coping approach is similar to what Cline (1999) calls 'defend the status quo', in contrast to his other classifications of 'restructured utility taxes', and 'level playing field'.

Accompanying this 'distribution' focus is the fiscal strategy of tax revenue neutrality, which is the continuation of the accustomed level of tax revenues through a revision of the existing tax, or a tax substitution that maintains roughly the same revenue flow (at least during a transition period). Therefore, another characteristic of a distribution focus is an extended transition to full deregulation, with tax and regulatory adjustments handled separately in a nonsynchronized manner.

This nonsynchronicity in policy making can take two major forms. For example, Iowa changed its tax policy first, in anticipation of later electricity restructuring. But it has been unable to resolve the complexities of such restructuring, and regulatory change has yet to come to Iowa. Reversing the sequence, Oklahoma and West Virginia legislatively authorized electricity restructuring, but delayed implementation until related tax policy compromises could be reached. Those tax policy adjustments never materialized, and electricity restructuring has not been implemented.

In contrast to the backward looking distribution approach to state tax policy making following deregulation, a forward looking efficiency approach requires the establishment of a 'level playing field' to neutralize taxes as a factor in the competitive interaction among the newly expanded providers of services. The focus is also on tax changes that can generate mutual gains among the suppliers, consumers, and the governmental units affected. Therefore, all aspects of tax policy are open to review, including the tax base, tax rates, the allocation of state and local taxing authority, and the magnitude of revenues flowing to particular governmental jurisdictions. The goal is tax *system* neutrality as opposed to tax *revenue* neutrality.

Accomplishing this goal is likely to be enhanced by a rapid and relatively simultaneous consideration of both regulatory and tax policy. Even with this increased synchronicity, the full adoption of an efficiency approach is hardly guaranteed, and the result is more typically some combination of an efficiency and a distribution focus. For example, Ohio delayed any electricity authorizing legislation until related changes in tax policy could also be adopted, but while some of those tax changes were consistent with tax *system* neutrality, political realities required that tax *revenue* neutrality also played an important role (see the expanded discussion in the section after next). While not identical to Ohio, Pennsylvania's electricity restructuring legislation also directly incorporated important tax policy changes. However, among these new tax policies was the 'revenue neutral reconciliation surtax', designed to protect governmental units from any loss of revenue during a regulatory transition period. Unsurprisingly, it is difficult to find 'pure' forms of either a reform or a coping strategy.

STATE ADJUSTMENTS TO THE DEREGULATION CHALLENGE

The Scope of the Problem

Of the 50 states, 19 have not deregulated either their electricity or their natural gas industries.[7] Of the other 31 states, 12 have deregulated both segments of the energy sector (California, Illinois, Maryland, Massachusetts, Michigan, Montana, New Jersey, New Mexico, New York, Ohio, Pennsylvania, and Virginia). Eight states have deregulated natural gas but not electricity (Colorado, Georgia, Indiana, Kentucky, Nebraska, South Dakota, West Virginia and Wyoming), while the other 11 have deregulated electricity but not natural gas (Arkansas, Arizona, Connecticut, Delaware, Maine, Nevada, New Hampshire, Oregon, Rhode Island, Texas, and Washington). Since any state that has deregulated either natural gas or electricity will have faced at least some degree of resulting fiscal challenge, there are 31 states whose reactions to energy deregulation are relevant to this analysis.

The telecommunications sector presents an interesting challenge. Since the federal Telecommunications Act of 1996, states have been encouraged to move toward a competitive structure for residential phone service. However, complex issues regarding access charges for the local switching networks, and the interdependency of demonstrating adequate local competitive access for new local service entrants in order for local 'baby Bell' companies to receive FCC authorization to also provide long distance service, have delayed effective residential phone deregulation in all states. Thus, there is no simple analog to the case of the energy sector for labeling states as regulated or deregulated.

Furthermore, since the fundamental challenge to states regarding telecommunications has been technological, structural deregulation has been nearly irrelevant. That is, dramatic shifts toward wireless technologies have reduced the sales tax and franchise fee bases, which have been traditionally limited by statute to hard wired technologies. While most states have been moving into conformity with federal requirements limiting states and localities to taxing essentially only 'domestic' mobile communications (see the Mobile Telecommunications Sourcing Act, 4 USC, 116–126), the primary variability in state telecommunications tax policy has related to franchise fees, historically linked to local rights of way. For example, after earlier failed attempts, in 2000 Florida (and later Illinois) substituted a state telecommunications excise tax for the diverse municipality based franchise fee structure, along with a fundamental expansion in the tax base. By contrast, for example, Georgia has held hearings and authorized studies to consider how it might adapt to this technological challenge (including a possible Florida type solution), but it has not yet acted to implement any tax policy changes related to telecommunications.

An Informal Model of State Policy Reactions: The Research Challenge

Rather than simply document the various ways in which states have reacted to utility deregulation, of greater academic interest are the reasons why states may have chosen different strategies of adjustment to the exogenous shock of utility deregulation. Note that while some intriguing relationships may also exist between our measures of fiscal stress and the extent of deregulation, we are clearly not addressing the question of why some states have deregulated both energy sectors, while others have deregulated neither. Since the focus is on how states have reacted to changes in the utility industries, the 19 states that have deregulated neither energy industry are essentially eliminated from the analysis. However, a few of those states (such as Florida, Iowa and Oklahoma) remain of interest, since they have dealt in an interesting way with the technological challenge in telecommunications, or are useful examples of energy tax policy.

We provide no formal model of state adjustment to the fiscal challenges stemming from deregulation, but attempt to test a more informal 'fiscal stress hypothesis' (see for example, Brunori, 2001).

Fiscal stress hypothesis: States facing greater fiscal stress from utility deregulation will be more likely to adopt reform tax policy strategies, since greater fiscal challenges will expose their more substantial fiscal weaknesses and require them to adopt more comprehensive and fundamental tax reform approaches compared to states facing less fiscal stress.

One way of informally testing this hypothesis is to rate states by their degree of fiscal stress, and then examine the reactions of relatively high fiscal stress states compared to low fiscal stress states. Evidence that more fiscally stressed states tend to adopt more reform-oriented tax policy strategies compared to less fiscally stressed states would be consistent with this hypothesis. While we do not expect to find uniform evidence favoring or rejecting this hypothesis, describing state policy initiatives in this context forces us to seek systematic patterns in these adjustments that can possibly be used to predict future policy reactions as more states adopt deregulation.

The types of challenges facing states as a result of utility deregulation were identified in our first section, along with considerations that may affect the severity of such challenges. Among the factors influencing the magnitude of the challenge facing states are the following.

Components of fiscal 'stress'

1. 'Tax imbalance', or the degree to which states have been utilizing a highly unbalanced tax structure (for example, being excessively dependent upon property taxes, or sales taxes, or taxes of various types from a specific economic sector) that would then make them less flexible in coping with significant changes in any source of tax revenue (Richardson and Hildreth, 1999).
2. 'Administrative fragmentation', which might be measured as the number of counties and municipalities in a state, reflecting the potential for 'non-neutral' (and hence inefficient) setting of tax rates, tax bases and tax collection practices that may be exacerbated by deregulation (for example, utility firms have long complained about the high administrative costs in negotiating local franchise fee arrangements with so many different jurisdictions are a burden that seemed especially onerous after deregulation challenged the very premise of a monopoly franchise fee obligation).
3. The extent of the deregulation in any particular state as measured by either a discrete (0, 1, 2) measure of the number of energy sectors that have been deregulated (again, telecommunications is difficult to label at the state level as regulated or deregulated), or at least in the electricity case, by a more continuous measure of effective deregulation as measured by the 'RED (Retail Energy Deregulation) index' (see endnote 7), which varies from –10 to 100 (the highest degree of effective deregulation; see the Center for the Advancement of Energy Markets, 2001; and, Restructuring Today, 2002) .
4. 'Asset devaluation risk', defined as the proportion of the generating capacity of electricity plants that is at risk of devaluation after deregula-

tion increases competition in electricity markets (based on Walters and Cornia, 2001). States and local jurisdictions stand to lose tax revenues that are linked to the valuation of such assets.

5. 'Relative telecommunications taxation', as measured by the ratio of the effective real property tax rate in the telecommunications industry relative to that same effective tax rate applied to 'general business' (based on the 'COST' study for November 2000). While a similar measure of the relative reliance of states upon the taxation of the energy sectors would also be useful as a measure of a state's vulnerability to fundamental changes in these industries, energy data across states are not as available or reliable as that provided by the COST studies for telecommunications.

Using these criteria, a fiscal stress index was constructed for all states. Table 8.2 reports the results of these derivations for 34 states (including the 31 which have entered some phase of energy deregulation, plus three states, Florida, Oklahoma and Iowa which present interesting examples of tax policy changes). For example, while Florida is not discussed in detail in the next section (being in the 'middle' of the fiscal stress index, ranked 23rd of the 50 states), it has adopted the reform strategy of repealing its former municipal-based franchise fee structure in telecommunications and substituted a statewide 'telecommunications excise tax' with a substantial broadening of the tax base (and lower tax rate compared to franchise fees) to include not only wireless services but an expansion of the wired services subject to the tax. This approach has also been essentially adopted by Illinois, and has been considered by Georgia, and is an important example of a reform strategy applied to telecommunications.

Despite those three exceptions, the other 16 of the 19 states that have not deregulated any energy sector are excluded from Table 8.2. The states in Table 8.2 are ranked according to this stress index, from highest to lowest. Texas, New Jersey, Montana, Pennsylvania and Illinois are the five most stressed states, while the 'relevant' states of Nebraska, Colorado, Iowa, Oklahoma, and Indiana are currently the least stressed by the forces of deregulation (the nonrelevant states of Idaho, index of 1.274, and North Carolina, 3.488, are the two least stressed of the entire 50 states). The underlying data, with descriptions and sources, are reported in Appendix Table 8A1, with the derivations reported in Appendix Table 8A2, along with additional commentary regarding the methodology.

Characteristics of a reform state
In Table 8.1, we identified two types of state tax policy adjustment: the so-called reform and coping models. While any set of criteria for characterizing a state will be subject to criticism, the following factors are important to the

Table 8.2   Fiscal stress index: Selected states

34 state rank	State	Stress index	50 state rank
1	Texas	16.0423	1
2	New Jersey	14.4121	2
3	Montana	13.76	3
4	Pennsylvania	13.0472	4
5	Illinois	12.684	5
6	New York	12.2424	6
7	Arizona	11.3593	7
8	Maryland	11.2488	8
9	Ohio	10.9873	9
10	Michigan	10.6683	10
11	New Hampshire	10.512	11
12	Maine	10.4805	12
13	New Mexico	10.411	13
14	Oregon	10.0989	14
15	Delaware	9.8858	15
16	Arkansas	9.682	16
17	Virginia	9.047	17
18	South Dakota	8.9982	18
19	Wyoming	8.7922	19
20	Massachusetts	8.7104	20
21	Washington	8.3243	21
22	Nevada	8.1274	22
23	Florida	7.384	23
24	California	6.9942	25
25	Rhode Island	6.9205	27
26	Kentucky	6.9092	28
27	Connecticut	6.8965	29
28	Georgia	5.7795	34
29	West Virginia	5.7233	35
30	Indiana	5.7074	36
31	Oklahoma	5.1816	39
32	Iowa	4.957	40
33	Colorado	4.3474	42
34	Nebraska	4.1218	43
34 state average		9.1307	
50 state average		7.6324	

determination of the degree to which a state could earn the label of a reform state:

1. *Tax assignment.* The state has taken steps to review and reformulate the sharing of tax authority between the state and local (county and municipality) jurisdictions in light of the potential for a change in the optimal allocation of tax authority following the structural and technological changes in the utility sectors.
2. *Tax system neutrality*: The state has fundamentally reevaluated the tax base, tax rates, and the tax structure so as to ensure *intra-industry* tax system neutrality so that the various electricity, natural gas, or telecommunications competitors are not subjected to differential tax liabilities. This 'level playing field' requirement is necessary to avoid allowing the tax system to distort competition within any of these individual industries.
3. *Tax burden*: The state has re-evaluated the relative *inter-industry* tax burden between the utility and nonutility sectors, so that tax policy in the face of utility deregulation does not focus exclusively on the utility sector, and is able to achieve tax neutrality more broadly defined. To distinguish the inter-industry 'neutrality' considerations from the intra-industry tax system neutrality defined above, this criterion is referred to as the inter-industry relative 'tax burden'.
4. *Tax balance*: The state has addressed its overall tax structure so as to make its revenues less dependent upon any one type of tax or economic sector, and to also (directly or indirectly) make its tax structure more neutral and less distorting. A more balanced tax structure may be viewed as more efficient from the narrow view of a state 'immunizing' itself from the vicissitudes of tax base changes (such as sales revenues compared to property values), and from shifts in inter-industry economic activity (such as telecommunications declining while construction booms). But since better tax balance is also likely to be consistent with a broader concept of efficiency linked to limiting the distorting effects of taxation, it is somewhat related to 'tax system neutrality' and 'tax burden' considerations.

The next section provides a description of the tax policy developments in 21 of these states and a tentative evaluation of whether the observed tax policies of states have been consistent with the fiscal stress hypothesis.

THE DIVERSE FORMS OF STATE TAX ADJUSTMENT: THE EVIDENCE

States vary in their tax structures, a feature quite prevalent in the taxation of public utilities. As the states struggle to adjust their taxes to the realities of the market, they confront the need to redefine the tax base to cover innovations such as wireless communications and to include the separation of electric generation, transmission and distribution businesses. Moreover, the states have to assign the base of taxation and the rates that can be levied by the various taxing jurisdictions that expect revenue neutrality. While the consumer should face the same tax burden in a jurisdiction regardless of the seller, competing providers of these services and products also deserve equal tax burdens.

Accordingly, the focus turns to specific state tax activities in the context of public utility deregulation, with primary attention on tax changes related to electric industry restructuring. As defined above, *tax neutrality* refers to the goal of treating competing suppliers equally while *tax burden* relates to the goal of lessening taxes that specifically target public utilities and their commodities and services. Both of these goals fit standard public finance criteria. In contrast, there is no optimal *tax assignment*, defined as the division of tax functions between the state and its local governments, but it is rather the artifact of time and political will (McLure, 2001). These matters, however, constitute significant political hurdles for changing long standing regulatory policy in any state. Whatever the nature of the tax-related change, the impact on the total state–local tax system can potentially influence the *tax balance* between the three major tax structures (income, sales and property). Because all states are still in the early stages of deregulation, it is hard to make fine distinctions, much less to find conclusive evidence about the extent to which fiscal stress has influenced the adoption of either reform or coping tax policies strategies. And states rarely exhibit 'pure' forms of either strategy. Despite the limitations, we describe the steps that have been taken after deregulation by 21 of the states in Table 8.2. Special attention is focused upon the five most and five least stressed states, but an evaluation is provided for the other 11 states as well in an attempt to informally test the 'fiscal stress hypothesis'.[8] Despite some anomalies, the evidence is deemed generally consistent with the hypothesis.

Most Stressed States

1. Texas
Based on 1999 legislation (SB 7) that committed Texas to retail electric competition, Texas has been identified as the most deregulated retail market

for energy (Restructuring Today, 2002). Texas also enjoyed the highest number of telecommunications 'local exchange carriers' (ILECS and CLECs) of any state (Public Utility Commission of Texas, 2001). Together, these measures suggest active retail markets for previously regulated utility services, which in part is why Texas is the state 'most stressed' by the deregulation challenge.

Tax neutrality: Texas' retail electric competition legislation included a change in property valuation designed to treat competing suppliers on an equal basis. The legislation changed the valuation method from an allocation of the entire regulated company to a narrower focus on the stand-alone facility. Another change allowed nuclear power plants that became stranded investments to be evaluated at market prices (presumably lower than the regulatory value).

Prior to 1999, there was no statutory provision specifying the method and level of compensation that a Texas municipality could collect from a telecommunications provider for the use of the public right-of-way and the right to provide services within that city (franchise fees). In legislation (HB 1777) enacted in 1999, the state sought to create a mechanism to encourage competition in the provision of telecommunication services, to reduce the barriers to entry for service provision, to avoid competitive distinction in use of a public right-of-way, and to reduce the uncertainty and litigation concerning franchise fees. The law created a uniform method for certified telecommunications providers to compensate municipalities for the use of public right-of-way. Municipalities can only require CTPs to pay the fees authorized by this legislation, with the fee based on the number of access lines, not gross receipts (for the categories of residential, nonresidential, and point-to-point service). The fee is established to be revenue neutral with total revenues set at 1998 levels from franchise, license, permit and application fees and in-kind services or facilities. Pre-existing 'fee rate escalation' provisions were allowed to continue for 14 months. Moreover, the legislation limits municipalities from changing rates to increase revenues from this source, and limits appeals, audits and other related actions.

Texas is tax 'unbalanced' (it places great reliance upon the sales tax) and both telecommunications services and the residential use of gas and electricity are subject to this tax under certain conditions. The sales tax law provides that telecommunications services are subject to the state sales tax, but are exempt from all local sales taxes. However, the governing body of a city, county, transit authority, or other special purpose district may vote to impose sales taxes on telecommunications services occurring between locations within Texas. The local sales tax is collected based on where the call originates. If the origin of the call cannot be determined, then the local sales tax is based on where the call is billed. With respect to local sales and use tax on residential use of gas and electricity, only those cities that met certain conditions in 1979 are allowed to impose the tax.

Tax burden: By subjecting generation facilities to the normal appraisal valuation process, the state is taking steps to reduce the tax burden of electric generation taxpayers. The revisions to local government franchise fees and right-of-way charges also cap the tax burden that can be levied against one segment of the local economy. Other potential changes to the tax burden are unclear at this time.

Tax assignment: The electric competition law included a provision designed to hold local school districts harmless from a loss in property taxes due to a change in property valuation. The initial law protected each particular school district from a loss from what it would have been entitled to in base year 1999. Later, this provision of the law was changed to allow calculation of the 'statewide net loss', with gains in values subtracted from losses. From 2001 to 2003, the gains are limited to 30 per cent of the losses, a provision to protect against gains offsetting all losses. Accordingly, these new provisions limited the protection from any losses faced by particular school districts. Further complicating recovery, the school funding loss mechanism competes, in fourth priority, for money collected from a nonbypassable 'System Benefit Fund' fee authorized (and subsequently levied) to cover a low income mandatory electricity rate reduction, customer education, a low income weatherization program, and, only then, the school hold harmless mechanism. Needless to say, the school funding loss mechanism is not assured of funding.

Tax balance: Texas does not meet the test of a balanced tax system given its lack of an income tax, and no changes have occurred since deregulation.

Evaluation: Texas has made extensive adjustments to tax policy in the face of dramatic utility restructuring. Such policy changes have not only been sensitive to short term distributional and revenue neutrality considerations (largely limited to a transition period), but have addressed the fundamental issues of tax system neutrality (a level playing field), shifted to a less arbitrary basis for assessing franchise fees that is linked more closely to the actual costs of maintaining rights of way, and has addressed the issue of state vs. local jurisdictional tax assignment by focusing on state-wide and not merely local fiscal consequences. Texas has largely been acting as a reform state on utility tax policy.

2. New Jersey

In 1997, two years ahead of the state's comprehensive state electric industry law, New Jersey addressed related tax issues (in AB 2825).

Tax neutrality: The tax legislation repealed the 13 per cent franchise and gross receipts taxes on electric utilities (as well as regulated gas and telecommunications utilities), and established a six per cent 'energy consumption tax', with original utilities paying a transitional assessment for five years to ensure stability of revenues, with all providers (in-state as well as out-of-state) having the same tax burden. Cities were 'guaranteed' stable revenues to be rebated to them from the state tax. Furthermore, several new taxes on the industry constituted a new public utility tax pool. These taxes subjected electric utilities to the corporation business tax, electricity consumption to sales and use taxation, and ratepayers to a temporary unit rate surcharge included in the energy (per kilowatt-hour) charges of the rate schedule – termed the energy facility assessment (TEFA) tax. Additionally, energy utilities gained a unique depreciation allowance (30 year, straight line) for new capital assets.

Tax burden: New Jersey reduced the excess tax burdens that had been placed on the formally regulated electric industry. This change occurred through the repeal of the high franchise and gross receipts taxes, and by placing electric utilities subject to the corporation business tax.

Tax assignment: In 1997, a related law (c. 167) provided a new system for distribution of state aid to municipalities from the public utility tax pool. The law established the Energy Tax Receipts Property Tax Relief Fund for receipt of the public utility tax revenue and the ultimate distribution of proceeds to municipalities. While municipalities receive a guaranteed amount, the state's share varies depending upon the amount remaining after the mandatory payment to the municipalities.

Tax balance: New Jersey substituted taxes applicable to the electric utility industry and assigned them to a tax pool from which a mandatory share would be distributed to municipalities and the remaining revenues made available for use in the state's General Fund.

Evaluation: New Jersey is typically praised for its willingness to make fundamental changes in utility tax policy, and is cited by Cline (1999) as one of the 'level playing field' states. Its innovative repeal of the franchise and gross receipts taxes on electricity, and its shift to statewide alternative taxation have often been viewed as a possible model for other states. Its approach to utility taxation has been primarily reform-oriented.

3. Montana

The Montana electric restructuring law (SB 390) was enacted in 1997, but it was the Montana Electrical Generation Tax Reform Act (HB 174), enacted in 1999, that generally revised the taxation of electric utilities in Montana.

Tax neutrality: As of 1 January, 2000, all investor-owned electric utility generation facilities were transferred from a 12 per cent property tax ratio to a new class taxed at six per cent of market value. The assessed value for electrical transmission and distribution property remaining in the prior class was frozen for two years. To offset this loss, a new wholesale energy transaction tax, or WET tax, was applied to kilowatts per hour of electricity produced or consumed in Montana. Electrical production is subject to the tax whether consumed in Montana or exported to another state. Electricity consumed in Montana is subject to the WET tax whether generated in Montana or imported for consumption from another state. The WET tax is applied to electrical transmission at the rate of 0.015 cents per kilowatt-hour. There are certain exemptions to the WET tax. The transmission service provider collects the tax on a quarterly basis, with the funds deposited in the state's general fund.

Tax burden: Montana made a significant step in reducing the excess tax burden on the electric industry through the reduction in classification ratios (from 12 per cent to six per cent).

Tax assignment: As part of the electric utility reform, local governments gained a new entitlement that is funded by the state general fund (and the WET tax). Reimbursements are distributed on a semiannual basis to the county treasurer in the counties affected by a reduction in electric generation of property taxes. Distributions are based on each jurisdiction's change in assessed value of electric generation facilities and its previous year's mill levy. As a result of this reimbursement mechanism, local governments are expected to receive funds in excess of full reimbursement for the property tax changes associate with electric deregulation.

Tax balance: The effect on tax balance is unclear at this time. However, the lowering of property taxes and the introduction of the wholesale energy transaction tax is a shift in the relative use of sales vs. property taxes, in a state that has had a relatively unbalanced tax system. However, the effects on the overall tax balance within the state are not yet known.

Evaluation: Montana has made some fundamental changes in its taxation of the electricity industry, lowering the property tax rates on investor-owned generating facilities and introducing a new wholesale energy tax, which is based on quantities not revenues. Change alone does not warrant a reform label, and that particular change can be interpreted as primarily focused upon protecting tax revenues rather than ensuring tax neutrality (shifting to a tax on units consumed and away from asset values is likely to protect those revenues in the face of lower energy prices). The equal application of the WET to all electricity, whether imported or exported, is a neutral policy that also can be viewed as protecting tax revenues from market shifts. State efforts to immunize local jurisdictions from reductions in local property tax revenue are similar to New Jersey's efforts to ensure that the shift to state vs. local taxation is not unduly burdensome to local jurisdictions. Montana, therefore, represents a complex mix of reform and coping strategies.

4. Pennsylvania

Prior to the rapid ascendancy of Texas, Pennsylvania ranked as the most successful state in electric industry restructuring (Center for the Advancement of Energy Markets, 2001) based on legislation enacted in 1996 (Act 138). In 1999, additional tax changes were enacted (in Act 4).

Tax neutrality: The Pennsylvania Constitution prohibits a local property tax on public utility property. Due to this limitation, public utilities are subject to the public utilities realty tax (PURTA) collected by the state. The PURTA tax rate (30 mills) is applied to the depreciated book value of utility property that is assessed locally and reported to the state by all local taxing authorities. These local amounts are termed the realty tax equivalents (RTE) since they represent the amount of real estate taxes that could have been imposed but for the constitutional restriction. As part of the restructuring initiative, Act 4 of 1999 exempted from the definition of 'utility realty' land and improvements to land indispensable to the generation of electricity. Thus, after 1 January, 2000, the local tax roll includes generation facilities, and in so doing, places on an equal tax basis all competing generation facilities. Values are based on market value, not depreciated book value as before.

Pennsylvania has been among the most aggressive states in trying to ensure that any out-of-state suppliers do not escape taxation. 'Foreign' as well as domestic electricity generators and marketers must obtain a license from the Public Utility Commission prior to being allowed to sell electricity within the state. And before such a license is granted, those suppliers must certify that they will pay franchise fees, as well as collect and remit all sales and use taxes imposed by the state. While subject to court challenges, this strategy both ensures equal treatment of all suppliers, and protects state revenues from the potential loss of nexus regarding new competitors.

Tax burden: By removing generation facilities from the definition of 'utility realty', and therefore subjecting it to local valuation for property tax purposes, Pennsylvania promotes a shift in tax burdens away from the previously regulated industry.

Tax assignment: PURTA collections are distributed to each local taxing authority based, not on its share of statewide RTE, but rather the local share of total tax receipts (which are not limited to property taxes). This was not changed with utility deregulation. The state receives any remaining funds after distribution of RTE amounts. By subjecting generation facilities to local property taxation these properties are removed from the realty tax equivalent (RTE), and therefore from the public utility realty tax (PURTA). Currently, the basic PURTA rate fluctuates to raise enough funds to offset the RTE payments to local governments, thereby removing it as a state revenue source (except for a special PURTA rate that supports public transportation programs).

By redefining 'utility realty' to exclude land and improvements to land indispensable to the generation of electricity, local governments gained a new responsibility for tax purposes. These taxpayers were given the right to appeal their tax assessments for the past two closed tax years. Under the law, until the appeal was resolved, the taxpayer's valuation served as the amount due (even if a zero value were asserted). Taxpayers asserting (and paying) a low estimate during the appeal process incurred no penalty if they were wrong. Once the taxable values of the generation facilities are determined, the values are adjusted by assessment ratios set by the state tax equalization board to achieve statewide uniformity, although local tax rates apply. Local taxation of generation properties has led to declining values and higher property tax rates to compensate for lost revenues. This is compounded by the reduction in PURTA revenues transferred to local governments.

Tax balance: Prior to deregulation, the state budget received almost $1 billion from five state taxes on the electric utility industry, comprising about six per cent of the total General Fund and an overall effective tax rate on electric companies of ten per cent of sales (Hassell, 1997). This revenue included funds distributed to local governments to offset the loss of real estate taxes on utility realty that was precluded from local taxation by the state constitution. In confronting this nontrivial revenue situation, the state legislature placed a tax revenue neutral goal on the same level of importance as the goals of obtaining consumer benefits from competition and achieving a level playing field for the electric industry.

To hold the General Fund harmless from direct tax revenue losses, a 'Revenue Neutral Reconciliation (RNR)' surtax was instituted, with the rate to be 'capped' after a transition period. Essentially, the RNR compares the total amount of tax revenue paid by electric companies through five taxes – corporate net income tax, capital stock and franchise tax, sales and use tax, gross receipts tax and 12 mills of public utility realty tax – for a base year (1995–96) to the taxes actually received each year thereafter by the same firms, their successors and new entrants to the market. This figure is adjusted for change in the total kWh consumption of electricity for the same period. The result is a surcharge (or credit) on the gross receipts tax. The revenue neutral reconciliation feature accomplishes its purpose of preserving base year industry revenues – raising or lowering the gross receipts tax rate for electric companies depending on consumption changes.

Evaluation: Pennsylvania has been a key state for utility deregulation and a controversial state regarding tax policy. Because of its use of the RNR to protect state tax revenues, which is capped after a transition period, and its aggressive posture regarding nexus, it has been labeled as a 'defend the status quo' state by Cline (1999). But the taxation of *all* electricity facilities on a market value, not a depreciated book value basis, and its capping of the RNR surtax after a transition period, are potentially reform steps. And, of course, were nexus not to be established for out-of-state competitors, the level playing field necessary for tax system neutrality would be lost. Thus, Pennsylvania is *not* a clear example of a coping state, and reflects some important reform attributes. While it can also be considered a 'mixed' case, as was Montana, it might better be labeled as 'mildly reformist'.

5.   Illinois
In 1997, Illinois enacted legislation (Public Act 90-561) that provided for customer choice in selecting an electricity supplier.

Tax neutrality: One way the legislation promoted tax neutrality was to change the tax assessment basis for electric generating plants from original cost less depreciation to fair market value, as was the case with Pennsylvania. In addition, the legislation revisited the historical ability of Illinois cities and villages to impose an 'occupation or privileges tax' on public utilities (electricity, gas and telecommunications) of up to five per cent of the gross receipts for services provided within the corporate limits. Chicago enjoyed different limits. The 1997 electric restructuring legislation changed the legal incidence and method of calculating the new electricity privilege tax. Instead of a tax on the utility, it is levied on the end user for 'the privilege of using or consuming electricity acquired in a purchase at retail and used or consumed within the corporate limits of the municipality'. The declining ten tiered rate structure starts at 0.61 cents for the first 2,000 kWh and declines to 0.30 cents

per kWh in excess of 20 million kWh per month. A municipality may tax at a
lower rate but the same proportional relationship in the rate structure must be
maintained (and approved by the Illinois Corporation Commission). Moreover, a revenue neutral provision limits the revenues collected, until 2009,
under the municipal privilege tax to the amount that such a tax would have
generated in 1996. As such, this provision depends upon consumption data
from the utilities. Although collected from the consumer and remitted by the
deliverer to the state on behalf of the municipality, the tax remains a liability
of the deliverer to the municipality.

Tax burden: Illinois made several changes that should lessen the tax burden
on the previously regulated industries. For example, the state changed the
assessment basis for electric generation facilities. As will be explored in the
following paragraphs, the state also reformed the way local governments
could impose franchise and right-of-way fees on electricity and telecommunications firms. By structuring and limiting local powers, these changes
removed the unequal bargaining power that municipalities had in dealing
with firms that had to have local approval to conduct business.

Tax assignment: Any municipality that on a specific date in late 1997 had in
effect an existing franchise agreement with an electricity deliverer could
impose instead an 'electricity infrastructure maintenance fee'. In Chicago,
the tax is a declining tiered rate structure based on kWh delivered within its
boundaries. Smaller municipalities have a different declining tiered structure,
but with a revenue limit equivalent to the value of the compensation received
or provided under the franchise agreement. This valuation concept allows
municipalities to recover the value of free electricity, permit fees, or other
forms of compensation under pre-existing franchise agreements. Alternatively, the municipality could continue the compensation arrangements and
not impose the fee. A municipality without a pre-existing franchise agreement with an electricity deliverer can require a franchise agreement as a
condition of using a portion of the public right-of-way within the municipality. Under the legislation, the electricity infrastructure maintenance fee is
charged to the purchaser, in a separate line on the bill, and paid to the
municipality.

Illinois has struggled to design an acceptable tax structure to capture the full
range of telecommunications activity while offering simplicity for taxpayers
and revenue neutrality for taxing jurisdictions. Building on a long standing
gross receipts telecommunications excise tax on intrastate messages, the state
imposed a telecommunications infrastructure maintenance fee starting in 1998
(HB1147; Public Act 90-154) as a replacement for a personal property tax. This
new state 'infrastructure' fee is imposed on all gross charges, capturing inter-

state as well as intrastate activity. As a substitute for the franchise fee, municipalities could impose and collect a municipal infrastructure maintenance fee on
gross charges to a service address for telecommunications originating or received in the municipality. However, this municipal telecommunications
infrastructure maintenance fee was ruled unconstitutional in 2001 as it applied
to wireless retailers who did not need the rights-of-way for which the maintenance fee was targeted.

As a result of municipalities concerned with the loss of revenue due to the
court case and industry members overwhelmed by the confusing array of
local taxes and fees on telecommunications, simplifying legislation was enacted in 2002. With an effective date of 1 January, 2003, this legislation
consolidates three municipal telecommunications taxes into a single tax, with
one rate, and moves collection to the state (except for the City of Chicago
which retains local administration). The rate lid is six per cent (seven per cent
in Chicago) of gross charges for telecommunications purchased at retail –
meaning both intrastate and interstate, line and wireless. This tax replaces a
gross receipts tax on intrastate calls (limited to five per cent; six per cent in
Chicago), an alternative telecommunications tax on intra- and interstate services at the same rate limit, and the municipal infrastructure maintenance fee
on gross charges (up to one per cent; two per cent in Chicago).

Local taxing jurisdictions were impacted by a change in assessment of
electric generating plants, from original cost less depreciation to fair market
value. Legislation passed in December 1997 froze for three years (1997–99)
the then existing assessment methodology, and created a task force to consider the effect of property tax changes and recommend solutions for legislative
considerations. Although the task force suggested a slow ramp-down of assessments (and tax revenue), enabling legislation stalled. This development
forced taxing jurisdictions and owners of generating plants to negotiate any
solution.

Tax balance: The electricity restructuring legislation imposed a new 'electricity excise tax' on the privilege of using in Illinois electricity purchased for
use or consumption and not for resale, and which is deposited in the state's
general revenue fund. A declining tiered rate structure was created that started
at 0.330 per kilowatt-hour for the first 2000 kWh per month and ended at
0.202 cents per kWh in excess of 20 million kWh per month (that is, a flat
rate structure applied to municipal systems or electric cooperatives). The
supplier collects the tax revenues from the purchaser of electricity, with all
suppliers required to register with the state.

As part of the same restructuring package, the invested capital tax (which
itself had replaced an earlier personal property tax) was replaced by a 'distribution tax' because the legislature considered it a 'fairer and more equitable'

tax. The distribution tax has a tiered tax rate (increasing from 0.031 cents per kWh for the first 500 million kWh distributed per taxable calendar year, up to 0.180 cents for eight to 15 billion kWh, before declining thereafter to 0.142 cents for over 18 million kWh). There is a tax revenue ceiling (at the level estimated to have been collected under the replaced tax) after which a credit applies. For electricity distributors who are also gas distributors, there is a mechanism to avoid double taxation.

Evaluation: This extensive description shows Illinois as an excellent example of a reform state, that has attacked most of the vexing post-deregulation tax challenges, from the standards to apply to property taxation to fundamental reform in the antiquated franchise fee structure. Neutrally broad tax bases have been stressed, along with market-oriented property valuation methods, the avoidance of gross receipts bases where more appropriate alternatives can be substituted, and the relationship between state and local taxing authority has been reevaluated. Cline (1999) also considers Illinois to be an example of a 'level playing field' state.

6. New York
In New York, the Public Service Commission used its authority to issue an order in 1996 that instigated retail competition. In contrast, legislative action (Chapter 63, Laws of 2000) was required to address the complexity of taxes on natural gas and electricity that were estimated to contribute significantly to the high energy prices in the state (Klein and Doyle, 1997; Plattner, 2000; McCall, 2001).

Tax neutrality: The state repealed the 0.75 per cent gross receipts franchise tax on energy utilities retroactive to 1 January, 2000, and subjected those entities, instead, to the income-based corporate franchise tax. Moreover, the legislation phased out over five years the 2.5 per cent gross receipts tax on the transmission, transportation, and delivery of electricity and gas for commercial customers, as well as a 2.1 per cent tax on the commodity itself. For residential customers, the 2.5 per cent gross receipts tax started a phased reduction over five years until reaching a rate of two per cent at the start of 2005. A gas import tax is also phased out over five years. Manufacturers received a tax credit, effective 1 January, 2000, for the full amount of gross receipts taxes passed on to them and any gas import taxes that they paid. The legislation eliminates the sales tax on the unbundled transmission and distribution of gas and electricity over three years. Furthermore, the law imposed a compensating use tax, equal to the sales tax, on out-of-state purchased gas and electricity for use in New York as of 1 June, 2000.

Tax burden: New York greatly simplified the taxes applicable to the energy industries, probably reducing the tax burden on that sector and bringing it more into line with other industries.

Tax assignment: Absent from the legislation was any discussion of the impact of retail competition on the locally assessed property tax and local gross receipts taxes. With respect to telecommunications taxes and fees, they are just as complex as energy taxes, but, unlike energy taxes, much of the complexity remains (Office of Tax Policy Analysis, 2001).

Tax balance: Despite making significant changes in energy taxes, most of the activity occurred within the broad sales tax definition used by the US Census Bureau. Therefore, the tax balance between sales, income and property is unlikely to change significantly.

Evaluation: New York made significant legislative changes in energy taxes several years after electric restructuring was mandated by regulation action. While the delay in making tax changes is not consistent with the reform model being advanced in this chapter, New York is unique in its use of regulatory power to implement retail choice. Because of this unique institutional bifurcation of authority to make changes, a fairer evaluation would grant New York modest reform status.

7. Arizona
Arizona enacted legislation (HB 2663) in 1998 that declared electric competition to be the public policy of the state, and confirmed that the Arizona Corporation Commission (ACC) could implement that policy.

Tax neutrality: The legislation imposed on electricity suppliers the requirement to obtain a certificate from the ACC before offering electricity for sale to retail customers along with an agreement to be subject to state and local transaction privilege and use taxes. Then, the legislation modified the transaction privilege tax that is commonly referred to as a sales and use tax but actually is a tax on the privilege of doing business in the state under the utility classification (or as a telecommunications business). Specifically, the legislation clarified that the same tax base for utility classification would apply after unbundling of electric generation, transmission and distribution. The tax base is the gross proceeds of sales or gross income derived from the business. A new use tax is established for power purchased from out-of-state providers, with 20 per cent of the tax revenues shared with counties to achieve revenue neutrality.

Furthermore, the legislation prohibits cities, towns and counties from requiring franchises for electricity suppliers to provide electric generation service within their jurisdiction. These local governments may not impose rents, charges or taxes on right-of-way use for the provision of generation service, but may continue to impose them for distribution services.

Property taxes were not addressed in the original legislation. Instead, the goal of taxing generation facilities similar to manufacturing facilities in Arizona was addressed by legislation (HB 2324) passed in 2000. This legislation specified a new methodology, essentially more rapid depreciation, for valuation of electrical generation facilities not engaged in retail electric sales. While the state revenue department will continue to value improvements to land and personal property used in operating the facility, local assessors gain the job of determining land values.

Tax burden: The change in property valuation of electric generation facilities removes the excess tax burden on those properties relative to other properties.

Tax assignment: In addition to restricting the reach of local franchise and right-of-way agreements, Arizona changed some aspects of the property tax. Although local assessors gained the responsibility for determining land values for generation facilities, the change in valuation for existing facilities were phased in over two years with taxpayers expected to make 'voluntary contributions' for lost tax revenues. Owners of electric generation property receive a decline in property values of 15 per cent for tax years 2001 and 2002, to arrive at a new base valuation. These owners, however, must make a voluntary contribution to offset that loss for those years to affected counties that lose more than ten per cent of their total assessed value of all property in the county. The amount due for 2002 becomes the amount due for then next two years. The new valuation formula is repealed if any of the owners fail to pay the voluntary payments to the affected counties by the due date.

Tax balance: Arizona did not change the tax balance.

Evaluation: Arizona clarified its tax policy to accommodate the *Quill* standard in dealing with out-of-state electric suppliers, to deal with the forthcoming unbundling of the electric bill, and to promote equal property tax treatment of alternative suppliers of electricity. Both the effort to apply nexus to out-of-state suppliers and this promotion of equal property tax treatment among competitors addressed the 'level playing field issue'. Of course, extending nexus also lessened the threat of revenue loss, but the state restrictions on the powers of local government to impose burdens on electricity generators suggest that mere revenue protection was not the sole motivation for policy change. While it did make no changes in its tax balance, Arizona does not have a particularly unbalanced tax system. Thus, Arizona's policy reactions have been primarily reform-oriented.

8. Maryland

In 1999, Maryland passed comprehensive electric utility industry restructuring legislation (SB 300 and HB 703) along with companion electric and gas utility tax reform (SB 344 and HB 366).

Tax neutrality: Electric and gas generation (sales) are excluded from the 2 per cent gross receipts franchise tax, thereby only including revenues from the transmission, distribution and delivery of electricity or natural gas. Maryland imposed a distribution tax of 2.062 cents for each kilowatt-hour of electricity delivered and 0.402 cents for each dekatherm of natural gas delivered, with caps for large industrial customers.

The sales and use tax was clarified so that a taxable service includes the transmission, distribution, or delivery of electricity or natural gas. Since residential sales of energy are exempted from the sales tax, the effect was to leave the tax on business and industry. A special use tax of 0.062 cents per kilowatt-hour was imposed on electricity not distributed by a state public service company, thereby ensuring that out-of-state suppliers were subject to the tax.

Tax burden: The corporate income tax was imposed on electric and gas companies by repealing the subtraction allowed previously for gross receipts taxes paid. A new state tax credit was created to cover 60 per cent of property taxes paid on real property used to generate electricity for sale. This method is an indirect means of compensating for differential classification ratios where public utility real property is set at 100 per cent of fair market value compared to other businesses facing a tax on only 40 per cent of fair market value.

For the property tax, the legislation reclassifies poles, lines, towers and cables of a public utility as personal property rather than real property. Because personal property is not subject to the state property tax, there is a revenue loss to the state. However, this property is assessed at 100 per cent of fair market value and subject to local tax rates. Softening the tax bite for business, the legislation provided a 50 per cent exemption for personal property that is machinery or equipment used to generate electricity for sale, phased in over two years.

Tax assignment: By reclassifying poles, lines, towers and cables of a public utility as personal property rather than real property, the state lost a revenue source while local governments expanded their tax base. Offsetting this, however, the legislation provided a 50 per cent exemption for personal property that is machinery or equipment used to generate electricity for sale, phased in over two years. Special state grants, phased in over two years, were established to partially offset this loss by the 24 counties.

Tax balance: The use of income tax credits to offset property taxes paid by electric generation facilities will shift the balance between those tax sources in undeterminable ways.

Evaluation: Maryland linked utility restructuring with tax policy changes in a way that generally meets reform criteria. However, the state created 'hold harmless' transition features that protected local governments from the full impact of the change, somewhat reminiscent of Pennsylvania's use of a reconciliation tax. By imposing a per-kilowatt-hour distribution tax, while exempting firms from the two per cent gross receipts franchise tax, the tax structure was changed to better protect governments from a loss of tax revenue related to energy price reductions. The complex changes in the income and property tax rules affecting utilities may have an effect on the relative tax burden between industries, but that effect is unclear at this time. Overall, Maryland's policy reactions are not especially reform-oriented, and seem to have been primarily focused upon short term tax revenue protection typical of the coping model.

9. Ohio

Ohio delayed passage of legislation changing the electricity and gas industry regulatory structure until the necessary tax changes could also be included. The result was a comprehensive package of regulatory and tax changes (Amended Substitute Bill 3) that was enacted in June 1999.

Tax neutrality and tax burden (interrelated):   The law removed differential assessment ratios for public utilities, thereby addressing tax neutrality among competing industry members. Specifically, the taxable property of most investor-owned public utilities was assessed at 88 per cent of depreciated cost (although production equipment was assessed at 100 per cent of true value which, in turn, was defined as 50 per cent of original cost). In contrast, the tangible property of nonutility property faced an assessment ratio of 25 per cent of depreciated value. The new legislation, effective 1 January, 2001, changed electric generation property and all gas property assessment to 25 per cent of true value. It also placed 100 per cent of the value of the plant at its location, rather than the 70 per cent of value under the earlier arrangement. These changes occurred on 1 January, 2001, but affected local tax receipts starting in 2002.

Over 400 Ohio municipalities levy a personal and corporate income tax. Prior to the 1999 energy restructuring law, public utilities were exempt from the local corporate income tax. The 1999 legislation removed that exemption.

Tax assignment: Due to home rule powers, each municipality administers its own tax, thereby subjecting multi-location firms to the task of filing in numerous municipalities at the same time. To simplify the corporate income tax reporting responsibilities, subsequent legislation allows a uniform municipal income tax form, requires municipalities to publish all rules, forms and instructions on an internet website, and creates a central state website with links to all municipal income tax sites. These changes make it easier for multi-jurisdiction firms to comply with the decentralized local income tax system in Ohio.

More significantly, the taxes on electricity and natural gas consumption provide funds for two permanent tax replacement accounts, one for school districts and the other for nonschool local governments. All the natural gas tax revenues flow to the two dedicated funds. However, only 37 per cent of the electricity tax goes to the same two accounts. The remaining shares replace the repealed state gross receipts tax; the state General Fund receives 60 per cent of the electricity tax and the remaining three per cent is directed to existing local government transfer accounts. Subsequently, the General Assembly 'froze' at zero, for two years, the three per cent transfer designed for the existing local government transfer accounts.

Tax balance: Because the reduction in assessment rates reduces the property tax revenues for schools and other local governments, the restructuring legislation included provisions that obligate the state to fully reimburse losses during a five to 15 year transition period. Funding this 'hold harmless' provision is an excise tax on the amount of electricity distributed to electricity customers in the state. This new tax is levied on the electric distribution company and is measured by kilowatt-hours of consumption of each customer, with the rate decreasing with consumption. A similar tax on natural gas consumption was imposed a year later.

Evaluation: Ohio enacted comprehensive tax and regulatory changes in one extensive piece of legislation. The full impact of the changes conforms to our reform model, despite incorporating one of the most detailed revenue neutrality features of any state. Since our criteria for being designated a coping state include the nearly exclusive focus on preserving the status quo, limiting action primarily to revenue protection, these revenue neutrality features should not overwhelm the otherwise comprehensive and largely reform nature of Ohio's legislation.

10. Michigan

Following an earlier attempt by the Michigan Public Service Commission to use its existing authority to push for electric industry restructuring that was rebuffed by the state's Supreme Court, legislation (Public Acts 141 and 142) was enacted in 2000 which provided retail choice of electricity suppliers beginning in 2002.

Tax neutrality: Due to a mandatory electricity rate reduction contained in the legislation, the fiscal impact was expected to negatively affect state and local sales tax collections since electricity and natural gas are subject to the tax. From the state's sales tax, the loss of revenue ripples to the school aid fund (which receives 60 per cent of the dedicated amount), local revenue sharing (36 per cent), and the state's general fund (four per cent). There were no provisions for revenue loss recovery. An additional tax concern focused on local sales tax collections. Under the original scheme, the Michigan Public Service Commission ruled that it could not help cities collect local sales taxes from direct access suppliers. This potential problem was erased in the retail choice legislation: 'The commission also shall require alternative electric suppliers to agree that they will collect and remit to local units of government all applicable users, sales and use taxes [Public Act 141, Section 10a(2)].' A larger issue remained to be solved, namely the effect of unbundled bills. Since the state's sales tax law does not define the price of electricity as the price of generation, transmission, distribution, and related charges, the tax might not be assessable against the parts of the bill that are not generation-related. Local governments failed in their attempt to amend the retail choice legislation to protect local governments from a loss of personal property tax losses arising from accelerated depreciation rules adopted by the Michigan Tax Commission.

Tax burden: Because there is little change in state tax policy regarding these previously regulated industries, their tax burden is unlikely to alter significantly.

Tax assignment: During the implementing period, a tax assignment question arose due to Michigan's Constitution, which authorizes local governments to grant public utilities right-of-way access and for cities and townships to award franchises to public utilities. The restructuring legislation allows consumers to select an 'alternative electric supplier' (AES) to provide electric generation service, with the AES using the existing transmission lines and the local distribution company to reach the retail customer. Since the restructuring legislation did not exclude the AES from the definition as a 'public utility', local governments were able to impose on the AES a requirement to have an executed contract with a customer in their area before receiving a franchise. This situation emerged as a barrier to entry when a legally approved franchise itself became a prerequisite for gaining access as a supplier to the existing transmission and distribution companies. In 2001, corrected legislation (SB 446, Public Act 48) was enacted to exclude the AES from the definition of a public utility, therefore exempting the AES from the franchise reach of local governments. A rationale for amending the original retail competition legislation this way was to prevent a form of double taxation by precluding a local jurisdiction from charging a public utility for its transmission over the utility's rights-of-way and also charging an AES for transmission over the same lines.

Tax balance: Little change is expected as a result of any of these policy changes.

Evaluation: Michigan devoted most of its effort to structuring the taxing authority of local governments. While this exhibits a reform-oriented willingness to address the proper scope of taxing authority of local governments vs. the state, no important successes were achieved in moving the state to a more efficient overall tax system. Thus, Michigan represents a mixed case, with no clear credentials for being designated a reform state.

Least Stressed States

The group of states that are 'least stressed' are reviewed in somewhat briefer form (without the separate subsections) starting in reverse order with Nebraska, the least stressed of all the states that have deregulated at least one of the energy industries. Since Oklahoma and Iowa are unique cases (not having yet deregulated either energy industry), they are discussed last.

1.   Nebraska
Nebraska is unique in the United States in that all the electric utilities are exclusively publicly owned and operated, with rates regulated by the controlling authorities of the various entities. With low consumer rates and exclusive retail service territories, there has been little interest in retail competition. The unicameral legislature adopted legislation in 2000 (LB 901) that stated that it is '... the policy of the state to prepare for an evolving retail electricity market if certain conditions are met which indicate that retail competition is in the best interests of the citizens of the state'. To monitor the five specific conditions, the legislation created an ongoing power review board with the requirement to report annually to the governor and legislature. Nebraska's 'conditions certain' approach to retail competition places a strong bias on

maintaining the current regulatory scheme. Accordingly, electricity provision remains unchanged in Nebraska, and no steps have been taken to consider electricity tax policy in light of the potential for future restructuring, as anticipated by the legislature.

Nebraska is labeled as having deregulated natural gas, because of the establishment of a pilot program for moving toward at least partial unbundling. But progress has been slow and there have also been no known shifts in energy tax policy. To the extent that future natural gas marketers are located outside the state, current state law regarding sales tax permits may, despite the *Quill* (1992) nexus standard, be thought to limit revenue losses. That is, current law lists six criteria for being required to obtain a sales tax permit, *any one* of which would trigger the requirement. Since one of those six is 'soliciting retail sales from residents of this state on a continuous basis through the media', it would appear easy to apply current retail sales tax law to those marketers. Of course, there are other tax considerations beyond sales. But existing statutes combined with the slow pace of effective deregulation have apparently provided limited motivation for tax policy review and possible modification.

Evaluation: Since Nebraska has taken minimal deregulation action, the fact that no tax policy changes have been made is not surprising (although other states *have* at times addressed utility tax issues in advance of actual deregulation). Thus, while it might be viewed as a 'coping' state due to its lack of action, absence of action alone does not warrant that classification. Nebraska essentially provides no evidence about its approach to utility tax policy in reaction to utility restructuring.

2. Colorado

Pursuant to legislation (SB 152), a broad-based electricity advisory panel issued its 15-month study in November 1999, based in part on a comprehensive analysis performed by independent experts. Short of the statutorily required two thirds vote, a majority of its members concluded that there was '... clear and significant evidence that restructuring of the retail electric industry in Colorado is not in the public interest'. Comments contained in the report noted that the state and local governments rely on the sales tax collected on the sale of electricity and that any change should clarify that sales tax occurs where the electricity is consumed. Complicating any tax changes in Colorado is the TABOR Amendment that places substantive limits on the amount of revenues that governments can keep and spend, and procedural requirements for voter approval for governments to raise taxes or to keep revenues in excess of the cap. Accordingly, in Colorado, any tax changes attendant on utility deregulation run into strict constitutional limits. Other than requiring unbundled billing, little else has happened on electric industry restructuring.

In contrast, telephone competition was legislatively authorized in 1995, with local monopoly service lifted the following year. Also, Colorado is one of the seven 'second tier' states to move toward implementation of statewide natural gas unbundling (six others, including the District of Columbia, initiating full 100 per cent gas unbundling are the 'first tier'). However, the 1999 Colorado Retail Competition Act only allowed companies to unbundle natural gas services on a voluntary basis, by submitting a plan to the state after one third of the utility's customers have chosen an alternate supplier. To date, apparently no company has presented a plan to the Public Utility Commission to unbundle services for residential customers. No tax policy changes have been identified related to either natural gas or telecommunications.

Evaluation: The absence of tax policy changes in Colorado is more reflective of a coping tax strategy than was true of Nebraska, where deregulation has hardly occurred. While deregulation has also been limited in Colorado, deregulation steps have been taken in both natural gas and telecommunications. At the very least, Colorado cannot be considered to be a reform state, and given the apparent absence of any tax policy review, the coping classification is not unwarranted.

3. Indiana

Legislative efforts have failed repeatedly to enact retail electricity competition in Indiana. A report by the Indiana Utility Regulatory Commission in 1997 noted that 2.1 per cent of the total property tax levied in the state was electric utility-related, but 60 per cent of that total was concentrated in four counties. All for-profit firms doing business in Indiana are required to compute taxes due under the single rate gross receipts tax (GRT) and the income tax and remit the higher of the two. To achieve intra-industry neutrality, the state would have to clarify its taxes to permit tax assessment on interstate receipts generated by out-of-state businesses making electricity sales to Indiana consumers. Indiana has not yet addressed these matters.

Indiana has, however, established a pilot program for partial unbundling of natural gas. However, as is typical of most states regarding natural gas deregulation (especially in contrast to electricity), no comprehensive natural gas competition plan exists. Current Indiana natural gas tax policy (see Barents Group, 1999) includes a 0.15 per cent gross receipts 'regulatory fee', and the same income tax requirements as facing other companies. Natural gas sold for residential use is subject to the customary five per cent state sales tax, but industrial use natural gas is exempt. Regarding property taxation, unit valuation of each company applies, including apportionment of interstate companies, and is subject to tax at local rates. However, no known changes have occurred in this utility tax structure since Indiana established its natural gas deregulation pilot program, although the current tax structure is not unduly burdensome on natural gas versus other industries.

Evaluation: The absence of tax policy changes in an already reasonably balanced (that is, no undue tax burden) natural gas industry should not be viewed as an active coping strategy. Like Nebraska, it is more reflective of an absence to date of sufficient data to utilize Indiana as evidence either favoring or conflicting with the fiscal stress hypothesis. The slow pace of actual deregulation also limits any motivation to take action, although again, a truly reform state would begin adjusting its tax policy in anticipation of pending industry restructuring.

4. Georgia

While Georgia has not authorized retail competition of electricity, it has deregulated natural gas (The Natural Gas Competition and Deregulation Act, 1997), with all residential retail consumers purchasing gas directly from certified markets as of 1 October, 1999. In fact, Georgia took the most unique approach of any state in handling 'default service' to customers not choosing an alternate gas supplier, by proportionally assigning those customers to marketers based on the market shares of those marketers among customers making an active choice. Georgia also passed Senate Bill 137 in 1995 designed to 'open up competition in the local telephone market in Georgia'. As with other states, effective local telephone competition has been tied more to FCC regulatory action linked to the federal 1996 Telecommunications Act, than to such state legislation. Following just such a 2002 ruling by the FCC regarding BellSouth's access charges and other efforts to open local service to new entrants, local residential telephone competition is only now slowly beginning to emerge in Georgia. Disillusionment with the effects of natural gas deregulation has led to substantial modifications in the original legislation (including a 'bill of rights for natural gas consumers'), and as with much of the country, the momentum is more toward *re-regulation* than any further deregulation.

With respect to electricity, a 1998 staff report of the Public Service Commission recognized the need to give equitable tax treatment to all competitors. According to that report, Georgia subjects generating fuel to the sales and use tax. This gives an advantage to suppliers producing electricity outside Georgia. An additional inequity arises from having local franchise fees based on gross receipts of unbundled energy charge and services since out-of-state suppliers would face only distribution charges. Competition also could impact the local property tax. Therefore, the PSC staff concluded that tax reform would need to accompany any restructuring proposal.

Regarding natural gas deregulation, the state reacted promptly to projections that a failure to extend sales and use taxation to transportation charges associated with the newly competitive sale of natural gas (estimated to be as high as $24 million if the approximately 60 per cent of the total gross price of natural gas linked to transportation were to be exempt). By establishing 'general principles of law' that allowed transportation charges to be taxed, the feared revenue loss was avoided. Similarly, the still regulated final gas distribution company (Atlanta Gas and Light) negotiated a change in the franchise fee base with the Georgia Municipal Association (GMA) to largely immunize municipalities from any potential loss in franchise revenue as a result of anticipated declines in retail prices. The base was changed from gross receipts to a complex formula related to 'design day capacity', intended to shift the basis for 'taxation' from revenues to volumes (units delivered).

Evaluation: Despite Georgia's surprising creativity in initially structuring natural gas deregulation, its tax policy changes primarily represented 'coping' strategies designed to guarantee revenue neutrality, not tax system neutrality. Further evidence of the inability of Georgia to move toward a more reformist approach to post-deregulation tax policy was the well intentioned, but ultimately ineffectual 'Joint study committee on franchise fees and conditions, rights-of-way, and tax implications of competitive markets', which authorized a study and held hearings on how to more fundamentally reform the franchise fee system in Georgia. However, except for encouraging all of the parties (energy and telecommunications companies, municipalities, counties, and consumer groups) to seek a mutually acceptable solution and then come to the legislature with a plan, no action was taken. Efforts among those parties, pushed primarily by telecommunications companies and to a lesser extent by GMA and the Association of County Commissioners of Georgia, to develop a proposal (possibly modeled after Florida's creation of a statewide tax to replace local franchise fees) have been encouraging, but not yet successful.

5. West Virginia
In 1998, the legislature enacted HB 4277 which authorized the Public Service Commission to consider whether restructuring was in the public interest and if so, to submit a restructuring plan for legislative approval. In January 2000, the Public Service Commission issued a plan for restructuring which the West Virginia legislature conditionally approved pending tax law changes. Offsetting the revenue loss from the state's unique Business and Occupation (B&O) tax on generation capacity proved difficult, much less the plan for a transaction tax on energy consumption. Before those issues could be resolved, California's problems intervened. Currently, electric industry restructuring is on hold pending further study.

By contrast, West Virginia was one of the earliest states to establish residential natural gas unbundling, but as with the other states, only very limited or no action to change its utility tax policy can be found in reviewing state tax laws and Department of Revenue guidelines. The only apparent change is the phasing out of the property tax on intangible property. Barents Group (1999) reports West Virginia's natural gas tax policy as including a B&O tax of $4.29 per $100 gross income, not including pipeline companies, and a corporate income tax (nine per cent) and corporate franchise tax (at 0.7 per cent) based on net equity, identical to that imposed on other industries. Real and personal property is assessed at the state level based on unit value, with an assessment ratio of 60 per cent. Natural gas is treated very favorably in that it is not subject to sales taxes, but municipalities have the right to impose and collect a public utility tax of no more than two per cent of the 'amount rendered for public utility services'.

Evaluation: Existing natural gas tax policy favors natural gas in exempting it from the sales tax, and treats the industry no differently than others regarding corporate income, franchise and property taxes. While municipalities can impose special public utility taxes, there is no evidence that existing natural gas taxation is unduly burdensome. Surprisingly, as one of the earlier states to consider natural gas deregulation, it has neither been noteworthy in terms of effective deregulation, nor in reviewing tax policy in light of restructuring. Reviews of state developments in natural gas competition do not identify West Virginia (as opposed to states like Pennsylvania, New Jersey, Montana, Ohio, California, Massachusetts and Georgia; see Alexander, 2000). Again, while it is not clearly behaving as a coping state, there is also no evidence of a forward looking assessment of potential tax challenges typical of the reform approach.

6.   Kentucky

Kentucky has not approved retail electric competition, but under legislative charter an independent study was conducted on the state and local tax impact of deregulation in the electric utility, natural gas, and telecommunications industries (Barents Group, 1999). The state's tax policies directly in the path of retail competition include central assessment of utility property, a sales tax on retail sales of gas and electricity, local school district utility gross receipts taxes, and local government franchise fees.

Evaluation: Since Kentucky has not acted on utility industry restructuring or addressed its significant tax policy issues attendant to regulatory policy, the state either should be considered to provide no compelling evidence as to its tax policy, or arguably should be labeled a coping state.

7. Connecticut

In 1998, Connecticut enacted legislation (Substitute HB 5005) that restructured the electric industry to permit customer choice starting in 2000. A provision of that legislation created payments in lieu of taxes ('PILOTs') that entitled municipalities to a partial reimbursement for property tax revenues on generating plants that would be lost as a direct result of industry restructuring. Losses had to occur before assessment year 2005. Reimbursement was set at 90 per cent of the revenue loss in the first year, declining by ten per cent per year over the next nine years. Offsetting the losses would be any gains in property tax revenues from new generating plants. Reimbursements under this provision are to come from a system benefit charge levied against nearly all customers taking power off the grid. Thus far, however, the reimbursement provision has not been utilized.

In advancing a revenue neutral goal, the restructuring legislation shifted the utility gross earnings tax (GET) from generation by increasing the GET on all distribution and transmission services from four per cent on revenues earned from residential customers to 6.8 per cent. The law changed the tax from five per cent for all commercial customers (with manufacturers exempt) to 8.5 per cent.

Evaluation: Connecticut followed a revenue neutrality path, with limited attention given to tax system neutrality. Therefore, it conforms primarily to the coping strategy.

8. Rhode Island

Despite being the first state to introduce retail competition, Rhode Island's 1996 legislation (HB 8124) prompted few customers to switch suppliers so new changes were instituted (HB 7786) in 2002. Although neither piece of legislation made substantive tax changes, other steps were taken to improve state tax policy that promoted tax neutrality. Existing generation facilities were exempt from the local inventory tax under a manufacturing exemption, but they entered into agreements to pay an in-lieu of fee to the local government. After July 1997, new generation facilities were subjected to the inventory tax. Beginning in July 1999, however, the local government wholesale and retail inventory tax was required to be phased out by ten per cent per year for ten years, with state revenue sharing allocations increased to cover the revenue loss.

Evaluation: While Rhode Island led the country in initiating electric industry restructuring, its low jurisdictional fragmentation, relatively balanced tax system, limited generating capacity subject to devaluation risk, failure to deregulate natural gas, and surprisingly slow pace in actually implementing more consumer choice limited the degree of fiscal stress that it has faced. Yet, despite this fact it has taken important steps in correcting tax inequities related to utilities. Accordingly, it meets the criteria for following the reform model.

9. California

California's restructuring of the electricity utility regulatory structure (AB 1890) was enacted into law unanimously in September 1996, with the effective date of competition in 1998. With the onset of significant energy shortages and amazing price escalations that riled California in mid 2000 and early 2001, state policy makers re-instituted utility regulation in the Spring of 2001. Despite these significant shifts in regulatory policy, there was little need for tax system changes. The one exception concerned the property tax. California's balanced tax system masks a property tax system that caps the growth of the tax base and imposes severe limits on tax rate changes.

A tax policy tried during the short period of deregulation, but which was recently reversed, is local assessment of power generation facilities. The California Board of Equalization adopted Rule 905 in 1999 to allow generating facilities not owned by regulated utilities to be locally, instead of centrally, assessed. This move fostered neutrality among competing suppliers.

In California, local property assessment means that each generating facility is separately assessed, not valued as a unit. Moreover, additions to locally determined taxable values are limited to two per cent growth per year as prescribed by Proposition 13. In contrast, state-assessed property does not face similar limits. Once the state's energy plight took center stage in 2001, and the relatively low taxable value assigned locally to what were now very profitable generating properties became widely known, some state policy makers clamored for central assessment again. Adding complexity to the issue is the distribution mechanism of the revenues raised. If a facility is state-assessed, its value is part of the unitary value that is allocated to a countywide pool, with all taxing agencies in the county sharing in the revenue based on a distribution formula. However, if a facility is locally assessed, the total revenue generated accrues only to the taxing units with an imposed tax on that parcel. At the height of the California energy market debacle, complaints arose due to low local tax assessments despite high market prices for energy facilities. In response, the Franchise Tax Board reasserted state assessment, but delayed action until 1 January, 2003 to allow the legislature time to craft an alternative distribution mechanism (Pratt, 2001). In 2002, the California legislature enacted legislation (AB 81) that repealed Rule 905 but allocated revenues based on facility location rather than countywide under the old state distribution system. This aborted change in tax assignment reverses an attempt to foster neutrality among competing suppliers.

Evaluation: California is unique in that it introduced sweeping industry restructuring (in fact, other states emulated its policies) only to pull back once the rules of the resulting market were found seriously deficient. Therefore, if one were evaluating its status as a reform state regarding regulatory policy, it would raise questions about the stability of such a commitment to reform. However, the relevant issue is its status regarding tax policy in the face of deregulation. Its primary tax policy initiative was to shift to local assessment of electric power generating facilities, which moved electricity into line with the treatment of other industries (an apparent improvement in tax burden), and potentially also improved tax neutrality within the industry. Similar to its inconsistency on regulatory policy, this tax policy change was reversed, after fears arose about the potential loss of revenues from the electric industry. While it is true that as an already tax balanced state, it did not face as many tax policy challenges as some states, its limited and ultimately contradictory tax policy moves are inconsistent with being a reform state. Thus it is considered to have adopted the coping policy model.

10. Oklahoma

In 1997, Oklahoma mandated retail competition by 1 July, 2002. That same law (Senate Bill 500) assigned to a task force the job of formulating a 'fair and equal basis' of taxation and the obligation to ensure 'that tax revenues derived by municipalities will not be adversely impacted as a result of restructuring'. More importantly, the legislation stated: '[I]n the event a uniform tax policy which allows all competitors to be taxed on a fair and equal basis has not been established on or before 1 July, 2002, the effective date for implementing customer choice shall be extended until such time as a uniform tax policy has been established.' Task force discussions focused on the feasibility of a uniform consumption tax as a means of overcoming significant property tax and local franchise tax hurdles. By the task force's 1 October, 1999 statutory deadline, however, the group failed to achieve consensus and returned the matter back to the state legislature (Oklahoma Joint Electric Utility Task Force, 1999). In May 2001, at the height of the California energy shortage, another law (SB 440) was passed that placed all matters with another task force and froze implementation of consumer choice of retail electric energy suppliers until the legislature adopted enabling legislation

Evaluation: Inability to gain consensus on tax policy forestalled timely introduction of electric restructuring. The delay allowed the California debacle to overwhelm any local plans to move forward with deregulation. However, Oklahoma is an intriguing case. While the initial legislation authorizing deregulation identified two potentially conflicting criteria to move forward with deregulation implementation (a 'fair' tax system, *and* revenue protection for local governments), the absolute requirement that a task force find a way to ensure that all competitors be taxed on a 'fair and equal basis' was an admirable example of placing tax system neutrality above mere tax revenue neutrality. The fact that electricity deregulation was then sacrificed when such a tax goal could not be reached may be viewed as either lucky or tragic in light of some recent deregulation experience. However, Oklahoma's stress on tax neutrality justifies a tax policy reform label, despite the actual lack of a policy change.

11. Iowa

Iowa presents another interesting challenge, since it addressed its tax system problems, but has not resolved the broader issue of industry restructuring. The stated purpose of the 1988 tax legislation (Senate File 2416) was: 'to replace property taxes imposed on electric and natural gas companies, electric cooperatives and municipal utilities with a system of taxation that will enable such entities to effectively compete in a competitive marketplace, while preserving revenue neutrality and debt capacity for local governments and taxpayers'. The goal was advanced by exempting entities involved primarily in the production, delivery and transmission of electricity and natural gas within the state from the local property tax. Instead of the property tax, the state enacted a 'replacement tax' that includes an excise tax based on the per-kilowatt-hour generation, per-kilowatt-hour delivery tax and an electricity transmission tax based on pole miles. The delivery tax is based on a utility's prior property tax liability, and is net of the utility's transmission and generation replacement tax liability.

Complicating the use of a replacement for the local property tax was the need to protect the property tax values that secure local government debt and the tax revenues that flow into property tax-dedicated accounts. To meet the revenue flow challenge, Iowa defined the replacement tax as a property tax for receipt purposes. Specifically, '[t]he replacement tax ... remitted to a county treasurer ... shall be treated as a property tax when received and shall be disposed of ... as taxes on real estate (Iowa Code, Section 437A.15).'

Fearing that erosion of the property tax base would harm the debt capacity of local governments, the state agreed to continue the valuation of property used in the generation, transmission and delivery of electricity and natural gas. This property is subject to a statewide property tax of three cents per thousand dollars. Since these property tax receipts (about $140 000) are for the state's General Fund to cover administrative costs, the rationale was not to generate state revenues, but rather to preserve the property tax valuation base for calculating local debt capacity.

Iowa designed a transition surcharge – the property tax equivalent tax – for three years to ensure that the replacement tax on generation, transmission and distribution activities produced equivalent amounts to the calculated utility property tax equivalent. Consistent with the revenue neutral aspect of the restructuring legislation, however, tax credits offset any overpayment of the replacement tax. For fiscal year 2002 budgets (1 January, 2000 valuations), the replacement tax generated $140.96 million, before tax credits, or four tenths of one per cent more than the property equivalent tax of $139.6 million. Within that total, however, private gas and electric firms were the only industry segments facing an aggregate higher replacement tax than the property equivalent tax. Assuming all else is equal and the same pattern holds at the conclusion of the three year transition period, the replacement tax is likely to generate more revenues than the previous property tax on utilities.

Evaluation: Iowa is a good example of the fact that considerable change in tax policy need not justify a tax reform label. While it admirably attacked a wide variety of tax complexities created by the prospect of deregulation, most of these actions were devoted to the dogged determination to avoid any change in the tax revenues flowing from the electricity industry. It thus reflects what Cline (1999) would call a 'maintain the status quo' approach, despite the fascinating array of policy initiatives and the admirable recognition that deregulation should not be introduced without a careful consideration of the fiscal system consequences.

CONCLUSIONS

States vary greatly in their tax policies regarding the energy and telecommunication industries, and describing the intricacies of those policies is a daunting task. In an attempt to focus on important themes and identify potentially testable propositions, the fiscal stress hypothesis was proposed. According to this hypothesis, states that are especially likely to be confronted with serious fiscal and tax policy challenges following the introduction of retail utility competition are more likely to confront that challenge by adopting more forward looking and fundamental 'reform' tax policies, as opposed to merely 'coping' strategies (Table 8.1). In addition to describing the variety of tax policy reactions among the states, special focus was placed on those states having an especially high and an especially low 'fiscal stress index' (Table 8.2).

In part because those states facing low fiscal stress also had adopted only limited deregulatory policies, while those states facing high fiscal stress had almost uniformly adopted both effective electricity and natural gas deregulation policies, this hypothesis was difficult to 'test'. However, it was not inevitable that high fiscal stress states would have quite different deregulation histories than low fiscal stress states. The measurement of fiscal stress included only two components directly linked to deregulation status, and four components that were independent of that experience (jurisdictional fragmentation, tax imbalance, percentage of generating assets at risk of devaluation, and relative telecommunications tax rates). However, there is tentative evidence favoring the fiscal stress hypothesis. Of the five most fiscally stressed states, three are following reform tax strategies (Texas, New Jersey and Illinois), while Pennsylvania and Montana are more problematic. However, even those two states have engaged in some reform strategies, with Pennsylvania possibly being labeled as 'mildly' reformist, despite some controversy about its approach. Extending the scope of states beyond those five most fiscally stressed examples, the other 'top ten' states provide two good examples of a reform approach (Ohio and Arizona), one modest reform example (New York), one mixed case too conflicting to label (Michigan), and one seemingly legitimate case of the coping approach to tax policy (Maryland). Thus, one might conclude that at least 60 per cent of the most fiscally stressed states have adopted primarily a reform approach to deregulatory tax policy.

The primary observation that can be made about the five states with the lowest degree of fiscal stress related to deregulation is that none of them are clearly behaving as reform states. Because none of these states have deregulated electricity, all of them are of interest primarily because they have taken some steps to deregulate natural gas (or to some degree telecommunications). However, natural gas deregulation is much more limited nationally than electricity deregulation, and the slowness of developing effective competition in all of these states except Georgia, perhaps makes it inevitable that no fundamental reassessment of tax policy will have occurred in most of these states.

By contrast, Georgia has made some changes in tax policy regarding the natural gas industry, but those changes can be viewed as primarily designed to protect existing tax and franchise fee revenues rather than attacking more fundamental issues. This has also been true in Georgia's lack of success to date in addressing the ongoing pressures, primarily from the wired telecommunications industry, to change its franchise fee structure in light of the Florida model of telecommunications tax reform.

Moving beyond the five least stressed states, there are some states that have moved to deregulate electricity. We concluded that Rhode Island and Oklahoma could be considered reform states, while Iowa, California, and Connecticut were mostly following coping strategies, and Kentucky provided no real evidence as to its tax policy approach. Thus, although not all low stress states followed coping strategies, a substantially lower proportion of those states behaved as reform states compared to the high stress states.

In that sense, there is evidence favoring the fiscal stress hypothesis (although some might disagree with our individual state evaluations). However there is also conflicting evidence. The fact that Rhode Island is a relatively low fiscally stressed state, yet has largely adopted reform tax policy strategies in the face of its early electricity deregulation is clearly an important exception. Furthermore, both Florida and Illinois have adopted similar reform strategies regarding telecommunications taxation, even though Florida ranks only 23rd in fiscal stress, while Illinois is the fifth most stressed state. That example, too, does not suggest a close correlation between fiscal stress and reform behavior. Also, there is a similar incidence of reform strategies among the top five most fiscally stressed states, and the next five most stressed states, providing some caution about the strength of the hypothesis.

While it had been anticipated that more and more states would move toward utility restructuring, and hence provide a richer database for the analysis, recent developments have substantially reversed the momentum for such restructuring. However, the exploratory model evaluated here can be one of the tools of analysis for exploring the complex issue of tax policy in the face of future eventual utility deregulation. Whether the concept of fiscal stress, and the proposed distinctions between reform and coping tax policy models, will be useful in explaining those ongoing developments will require the maturation of state tax policies, and further research.

APPENDIX

As discussed in the text, *ceteris paribus,* a state will face *greater* fiscal stress from utility deregulation and technological change the *greater* is its (1) degree of jurisdictional fragmentation; (2) degree of tax structure *imbalance*; (3) the extent of effective utility deregulation, measured *both* as a discrete 'regulated/deregulated' characteristic, and where data are available, by a more continuous 'effective consumer choice' score as provided by the RED index in electricity; (4) proportion of generating capacity subject to devaluation; and (5) degree of taxation of telecommunications real property relative to other business real property. Table 8.A1 provides background data regarding these measures for all states, followed by the demonstration in Table 8.A2 of the derivation of a fiscal stress index.

Table 8.A1 serves as the data source for the derivation of a 'stress index', intended to reflect the vulnerability of states to the anticipated effects of deregulation and utility industry restructuring. It incorporates the factors identified above, and applies them as follows. Continuous measures such as the Table 8.A1 fragmentation index, the RED index and the percentage of property (generating capacity) subject to devaluation risk, require that each state's measure be normalized by dividing the individual state value by the average value for all states (averages of 126.451 for fragmentation, 16.64 for the RED index, and 39.38 for percentage property). Those adjusted measures are reported in columns 3, 5 and 7 of Table 8.A2 as adjusted fragmentation, adjusted RED, and adjusted property risk. This transformation neutralizes the scaling differences across these measures, and allows them to be added. The telecommunications tax measure is already a ratio, and any further modification of that measure relative to the state average generates only trivially different values.

To make the discrete variables more comparable to these 'adjusted' continuous values, and to better reflect their role in creating fiscal stress, the following simple transformations are made to the values in Table 8.A1. If a state has a very balanced tax structure (rated as a 1), that tax structure does not contribute anything to fiscal stress following deregulation, so it receives a 0 stress 'score'. A state with a good but not excellent degree of tax balance (rated as a 2 in Table 8.A1) receives a stress score of 2, and unbalanced states (regardless of the particular tax that is excessively relied upon, in other words, Table 8.A1 ratings of 3, 4, or 5) are given a stress score of 4 in the 'Adj. Tax' column. Similarly, any state that has deregulated neither natural gas nor electricity ('n' in Table 8.A1) receives a 0 stress score in Table 8.A2 'Deregulate' column, while a state that has deregulated one of the two energy sectors (either a 'g' or an 'e') receives a 2 stress score. If both energy sectors are deregulated ('eg') a stress score of 4 is given.

While Table 8.A1 provides data for all 50 states, Table 8.A2 is limited to only those 34 states that are of particular interest, that is all states that have deregulated at least one of the energy sectors, plus three states (Florida, Oklahoma, and Iowa) that have dealt with either telecommunications or energy issues in especially interesting ways.

Other variations on constructing this index are clearly possible. However, several alternatives did not substantially change this ranking, or were conceptually flawed. For example, it might be thought that jurisdictional fragmentation would require some adjustment for state population. However, measures of 'the number of local governments per capita' would have identified large area, low population states like North and South Dakota, Nebraska, Iowa and Kansas as the most 'highly fragmented' states, even though any energy or telecommunications companies having to negotiate, for example, franchise fee contracts with local municipalities (and at times with counties) would find most troublesome the total number of separate contracts to negotiate, not the populations involved. We are confident that the ranking in Table 8.A2 captures the essential differences across states in terms of their fiscal vulnerability and the tax policy challenge from utility restructuring, including the extent to which effective deregulation has actually been occurring in those states.

Table 8.A1 Important characteristics of states

State	# Units	Local tax	Frag. index	Tax bal.	RED index	Dereg.	% Prop.	Tel. tax	GB tax	Tel. ratio
AL	513	0.1201	61.61	3	–5	n	46	1.44	0.9	1.6
AK	161	0.3855	62.07	5	0	n	29	0.32	0.32	1
AZ	102	0.2804	28.6	3	43	e	61	4.2	4.2	1
AR	566	0.1043	59.03	3	17	e	47	0.81	0.81	1
CA	528	0.2242	118.38	1	10	eg	18	1.1	1.1	1
CO	331	0.29	95.99	1	–5	g	35	2.29	2.29	1
CT	30	0.3476	10.43	1	36	e	65	3.56	3.56	1
DE	60	0.1417	8.5	5	30	e	40	1.41	1.41	1
FL	460	0.3553	163.44	3	0	n	43	2.3	2.3	1
GA	691	0.2577	178.07	1	0	g	54	1.35	1.35	1
HI	4	0.1591	0.64	3	0	n	49	0	0.93	0
ID	244	0.2716	66.27	1	–5	n	2	1.7	1.7	1
IL	1390	0.385	535.15	1	30	eg	61	5.5	5	1.1
IN	660	0.3322	219.25	1	0	g	47	2.2	2.81	0.78
IA	1049	0.332	348.27	1	1	n	45	2.51	2.51	1
KS	732	0.2975	217.77	1	0	n	30	3.85	2.92	1.32
KY	553	0.1478	81.73	2	2	g	45	1.17	1.17	1
LA	362	0.1635	59.19	3	–5	n	17	2.67	3.9	2.67
ME	38	0.3685	14	2	64	e	60	2.49	2.49	1
MD	179	0.2436	43.6	1	53	eg	48	4.65	1.86	2.5
MA	56	0.3278	18.36	1	42	eg	41	3.22	3.22	1
MI	617	0.2435	150.24	1	53	eg	51	2.52	2.52	1
MN	941	0.2619	246.45	1	–5	n	56	4.25	4.25	1

MS	377	0.2331	87.88	3	-5	n	34	2.32	2.32	1
MO	1058	0.258	272.96	1	0	n	46	1.87	1.87	1
MT	182	0.3247	59.1	5	40	eg	35	4.5	2.25	2
NE	628	0.3469	217.85	1	-10	g	0	2.05	2.05	1
NV	35	0.2351	8.23	3	5	e	30	1.11	1.11	1
NH	23	0.6475	14.89	4	40	e	39	2.78	2.78	1
NJ	345	0.4542	156.7	4	50	eg	46	3.66	3.66	1
NM	132	0.1305	17.23	3	6	eg	36	0.95	0.95	
NY	672	0.307	206.3	1	61	eg	51	2.83	1.71	1.65
NC	627	0.2149	134.74	1	0	n	56	0.85	0.85	1
ND	416	0.2996	124.63	5	1	n	6	0	2.25	0
OH	1029	0.2886	296.97	1	39	eg	51	2.98	2.98	1
OK	669	0.1691	113.13	2	-1	n	18	2.16	1.14	1.89
OR	276	0.3126	86.28	5	25	e	36	1.2	1.2	1
PA	1089	0.2721	296.32	1	67	eg	57	3.6	2.93	1.23
RI	8	0.4018	3.21	2	29	e	6	3.4	3.4	1
SC	315	0.2785	87.73	1	0	n	60	2.91	2.91	1
SD	375	0.3741	140.29	3	0	g	35	2.45	2.45	1
TN	436	0.2326	101.41	3	0	n	0	3.84	1.95	1.97
TX	1431	0.3967	567.68	3	69	e	16	2.6	2.6	1
UT	259	0.2305	59.7	2	0	n	44	1.23	1.23	
VT	63	0.2129	13.41	2	5	n	60	2.37	1	2.37
VA	326	0.3143	102.46	1	34	eg	47	1.33	1.33	1
WA	314	0.2153	67.6	3	3	e	24	1.42	1.42	1
WV	287	0.1947	55.88	1	18	g	50	1.4	1.5	0.93
WI	655	0.3125	204.69	1	0	n	46	2.75	2.7	1.02
WY	120	0.3188	38.26	5	0	g	50	0.79	0.65	1.22

Notes to Table 8.A1:

1. The '# units' refers to the sum of all county and municipal governments within a state in 1997 (US Census Bureau, *1997 Census of Governments, Government Organization*, Series GC07(1); See also *Statistical Abstract of the United States, 1999* (Table 501).

2. 'Local tax' refers to the local property tax and local public utility selective sales taxes as a percentage (12 per cent = .12) of all state *and* local government taxes for 1998–99. It is intended to measure the relative burden of local taxation vs. state taxation. Data sources include the US Census Bureau, *Census of Governments*, accessible at http://www.census.gov/govs/www/estimate.html

3. 'Frag. index' is the product of the '# of units' and the 'local tax' and is intended to reflect a 'weighted' measure of the degree of administrative fragmentation in a state. Since the potential administrative and efficiency costs of having many jurisdictions will be greater if local taxation is more important, this interaction term reflects both of those factors.

4. 'Tax bal.' refers to the degree of tax balance within a state in 1997–98, coded as 1 through 5, with 1 and 2 being the most balanced among income, sales, property and other taxes, while excessive reliance upon a particular type of tax is indicated by 3 (sales), 4 (property) and 5 ('other'). A state earning a '1' has each type of taxation representing greater than 20 per cent but less than 40 per cent of total state revenues; and a '2' indicates a state with each type of tax constituting between 15 per cent and 45 per cent of state revenues. The imbalanced states fall outside of those boundaries. Source: US Census Bureau, *Census of Governments*, accessible at http://www.census.gov/govs/www/estimate.html Note that the rating for some states can be sensitive to the particular year chosen, but for the most important states in this study, their tax balance ratings were mostly stable over time.

5. 'RED' index is the score given by the Center for the Advancement of Energy Markets to states regarding the degree to which they have unbundled retail electricity provision and created consumer choice. While a score of 100 is the highest available, a score of 0 is not the lowest. Modestly negative scores are given to states that have 'explicitly rejected consumer choice' in their electricity policy, or have a majority of their generating capacity government owned. A 'neutral' 0 score is more commonly given to states that have not taken steps to deregulate electricity and are merely following the 'traditional' set of electricity regulation policies.

6. 'Dereg.' identifies states as having deregulated natural gas (g), electricity (e), both gas and electricity (eg), or neither energy source (n) as of 2002 according to the Energy Information Administration.

7. '% Prop.' refers to the 'proportion of electric generating capacity at risk of devaluation' as a result of competition and pricing changes following deregulation (from Walters and Cornia, *State Tax Notes*, 6 November 2001).

8. 'Tel. tax' (telecommunications real property tax rates) and (9) 'GB tax' (general business real property tax rates), are reported by the Committee on State Taxation (COST) for November 2000, *Report on State Taxation, 50-State Study and Report on Telecommunications Taxation*. Note that similar, but slightly different tax rates were reported in the September 1999 COST study as reported by Cline (2000: 775, Appendix Table A-1). Note also that supplemental revised data on the *total* tax burdens of telecommunications relative to general business were constructed by COST for 2001, and reported in the *Tax Management Multistate Tax Report*, (Vol. 9, No. 4), 26 April 2002, reporting a substantially higher total average state telecommunications tax 'burden' of 13.9 per cent vs. about 7.5 per cent for general business.

9. 'Tel. ratio' is then the simple ratio of the telecommunications real property tax rate to the general business real property tax rate.

Table 8.A2   Derivation of fiscal stress index for selected states

Rank	State	Adj. Frag.	Adj. Tax	Adj. RED	Dereg.	Adj. Prop. risk	Tel. tax	Stress index
1	TX	4.489	4	4.147	2	0.406	1	16.042
2	NJ	1.239	4	3.005	4	1.168	1	14.412
3	MT	0.467	4	2.404	4	0.889	2	13.76
4	PA	2.343	0	4.026	4	1.447	1.23	13.046
5	IL	4.232	0	1.803	4	1.549	1.1	12.684
6	NY	1.631	0	3.666	4	1.295	1.65	12.242
7	AZ	0.226	4	2.584	2	1.549	1	11.359
8	MD	0.345	0	3.185	4	1.219	2.5	11.249
9	OH	2.349	0	2.344	4	1.295	1	10.988
10	MI	1.188	0	3.185	4	1.295	1	10.668
11	NH	0.118	4	2.404	2	0.99	1	10.512
12	ME	0.111	2	3.846	2	1.524	1	10.481
13	NM	0.136	4	0.361	4	0.914	1	10.411
14	OR	0.682	4	1.502	2	0.914	1	10.098
15	DE	0.067	4	1.803	2	1.016	1	9.886
16	AR	0.467	4	1.022	2	1.193	1	9.682
17	VA	0.81	0	2.043	4	1.193	1	9.046
18	SD	1.109	4	0	2	0.889	1	8.998
19	WY	0.303	4	0	2	1.27	1.22	8.793
20	MA	0.145	0	2.524	4	1.041	1	8.71
21	WA	0.535	4	0.18	2	0.609	1	8.324
22	NV	0.065	4	0.3	2	0.762	1	8.127
23	FL	1.293	4	0	0	1.092	1	7.385
24	CA	0.936	0	0.601	4	0.457	1	6.994
25	RI	0.025	2	1.743	2	0.152	1	6.92
26	KY	0.646	2	0.12	2	1.143	1	6.909
27	CT	0.082	0	2.163	2	1.651	1	6.896
28	GA	1.408	0	0	2	1.371	1	5.779
29	WV	0.442	0	1.082	2	1.27	0.93	5.724
30	IN	1.734	0	0	2	1.193	0.78	5.707
31	OK	0.895	2	−0.06	0	0.457	1.89	5.182
32	IA	2.754	0	0.06	0	1.143	1	4.957
33	CO	0.759	0	−0.3	2	0.889	1	4.348
34	NE	1.723	0	−0.601	2	0	1	4.122

NOTES

1. For example, among the very first states to enact electricity restructuring legislation (as early as 1996) were Rhode Island, Massachusetts, Maine, California, Pennsylvania, Illinois and New Hampshire – all with 'total average revenue per kilowatt-hour' substantially higher than the national average (ranging from 17 per cent higher in Pennsylvania to 77 per cent higher in New Hampshire). See Department of Energy, 'Status of restructuring activities by state, as of 2 December 1997', and comparison of electricity prices, at www.eia.doe.gov/cneaf/ electricity/esr/esr_sum.html
2. This consensus would be seriously challenged by the California energy debacle of 2000–01, which raised the possibility that the separation of generation from distribution could increase the market power of suppliers, at least in the absence of better rules then in place in California's 'deregulated' market.
3. 'Franchise fees' (in contrast to franchise taxes) are taxlike charges based normally on gross receipts that are paid (or collected by) energy and telecommunications firms as 'compensation' for the rights-of-way and other costs incurred by municipal (and in the case of cable television, county) governments in 'maintaining' such rights-of-way and coping with the disruptions of utility construction and other uses of public facilities and roadways. They are typically 'negotiated' with individual local governments. They have traditionally been justified as a kind of quid pro quo for utilities having a monopoly franchise, and are thus potentially irrelevant in a deregulated world where monopoly franchises are gradually eliminated.
4. However, these issues are a frequent program topic at the annual Wichita Program on Appraisal for Ad Valorem Taxation of Communications, Energy and Transportation Properties that attracts industry tax professionals and state and local revenue officials from around the country (http://appraisal.wichita.edu). The Institute for Professionals in Taxation sales tax symposium held in Sarasota, Florida in January 2000 included a session on taxation of transactions under electric deregulation, and the annual conferences of groups such as the National Tax Association occasionally include panels and papers on the topics. Individual states and localities have certainly demonstrated concern as evidenced by state specific analyses (for example, Klein and Doyle, 1997; Barents Group, 1999), city impact studies (for example, Carl Vinson Institute, 1999), state policy conferences (for example, Seaman, 2000), and legislative testimony (for example, Seaman, 1999).
5. The Georgia Municipal Association provides an example of the significant potential franchise fee revenue loss to a single city from only one taxpayer due to the combination of price reductions and nexus problems (1997; see also Seaman, 1999, p. 9). In fiscal year 1997, Gainesville, Georgia received $1.392 million in franchise fee revenue from Georgia Power Company alone. Assuming (1) 22.5 per cent of such revenue stemmed from electricity generation, subject to new competition; (2) a 20 per cent drop in gross electricity revenues due to price reductions (admittedly an 'optimistic' assumption of consumer benefits from deregulation); and (3) a 30 per cent diversion of business to non-Georgia generating companies lacking state nexus, the loss of franchise fee revenue would be as high as 25.4 per cent. That is, the $313 220 of original revenue from generation is reduced first by 20 per cent and then again by 30 per cent to yield $175 403 in remaining generation revenue. Meanwhile, the $1 707 869 of such fees originally derived from distribution (which remains regulated) falls only by the 20 per cent linked to price reductions, yielding a remaining $863 095 in distribution revenue. This total revenue of $1.0385 million is $.3535 million lower than the original $1.392 million – a loss of 25.4 per cent. States face broader potential losses from other types of utility taxes applied not to only one company, but to the entire energy and telecommunications industries.
6. New Jersey requires energy sellers to have an office in the state while Pennsylvania requires state registration as a precondition for providing the service. Creative means of establishing nexus have not been tested in the courts and may be held to be unconstitutional infringements of interstate commerce under *Quill* (1992).
7. Since many states are in a transition stage of deregulation, a state is considered to have

deregulated its electricity sector if legislation has been passed or a regulatory ordered issue to deregulate the industry, and if the Center for the Advancement of Energy Markets has identified it as having a 'RED' (Retail Energy Deregulation) index score greater than zero. Oklahoma had passed contingency legislation to deregulate electricity, but deregulation was never implemented. In the natural gas case, a state is considered to be deregulated if it has at least established a 'pilot program' that creates at least 'partial' unbundling. Note that both Delaware and Wisconsin had earlier established a pilot program, which was then discontinued. They are thus labeled as regulated.

8.   Most of the material used in constructing these state summaries is available on the web. For example, substantial information on electric industry restructuring is available from the Energy Information Agency at http://www.eia.doe.gov/cneaf/ electricity/chg_str/regmap.html. Supplemental information is available at the web site of the National Association of Regulatory Utility Commissions (www.naruc.whatsup.net). Legislative analyses and related fiscal notes provided further guidance, as did documents from various state Departments of Revenue, Public Service Commissions, and state budgetary reports. Since the focus was on state *tax policy* reactions to *given* features of utility industry restructuring, we did not elaborate on issues of mandatory rate reductions, stranded cost recovery charges, and other energy pricing and transition issues addressed in the deregulation legislation, although in some cases those issues can affect specific tax collections and raise interesting tax policy questions. Such decisions about how to limit the scope of the analysis can always be questioned. For example, if a sales tax is not allowed on a surcharge to recover stranded costs, but those costs were previously taxed under the regulatory pricing scheme, sales tax collections could be negatively affected. Thus, the policy decision regarding whether to apply sales taxation to stranded costs could be an important feature of post-deregulation tax policy.

REFERENCES

Alexander, Barbara A. (2000), 'Retail natural gas competition for residential and small commercial customers: A summary of recent state developments', presented on behalf of the Colorado Office of Consumer Counsel, June: 1–7 (available at the website of the Colorado Department of Revenue).

Barents Group (1999), *State and Local Impacts of Deregulation in Kentucky's Utility Industries*, prepared for Kentucky Task Force on Utility Tax Policy, available at: www.ofmeaweb.fi.state.ky.us/utility/tax/barantsfinal.pdf

Borenstein, Severin (2002), 'The trouble with electricity markets: Understanding California's restructuring disaster', *Journal of Economic Perspectives*, 16(1): 191–211.

Brunori, David (2001), *State Tax Policy: A Political Perspective*, Washington, DC: Urban Institute Press.

Carl Vinson Institute of Government (1999), 'An analysis of the financial impacts of gas and electricity deregulation on the city of Moultrie, Georgia', prepared for Moultrie City Council. University of Georgia, Applied Research and Publications Division, October.

Center for the Advancement of Energy Markets (2001), 'Retail energy deregulation (RED) index', downloaded from: www.caem.org

Cline, Robert (1999), 'How are states changing their tax systems in response to utility deregulation?', Supplemental Proceedings of the 29th Annual Wichita Program on Appraisal for Ad Valorem Taxation of Communications, Energy and Transportation Properties, Wichita State University, pp. 1–17.

Cline, Robert (2000), 'Reducing out-of-line telecommunications taxes: State responses to increased competition', Proceedings of the 30th Annual Wichita Program on Appraisal for Ad Valorem Taxation of Communications, Energy and Transportation Properties, Wichita State University, reprinted in *State Tax Notes*, 18 September, 2000: 769–75.

Consumer Reports (2002), 'Deregulated: Airlines, banking, cable TV, telephones, electricity: A feature report', July: 1–4, available at: www.consumerreports. org

Federation of Tax Administrators (John Cappellari) (1999), 'Electric utility taxation under deregulation', *State Tax Notes*, 18 January: 177–94.

Hassell, C. Daniel (1997), 'Switching on competition: The tax implications of consumer choice in Pennsylvania', *State Tax Notes*, 13(3), 21 July: 179–84.

Hildreth, W. Bartley (2002), 'State and local tax transitions during electric industry restructuring', Paper presented to the Association for Budgeting and Financial Management, 15 January, Washington, DC.

Hildreth, W. Bartley, John D. Wong and H. Edward Flentje (1997), 'Implications of retail competition for Kansas municipal electric utilities and municipalities', Proceedings of the Ninetieth Annual Conference of the National Tax Association, Washington, DC: National Tax Association.

Joskow, Paul L. (1997), 'Restructuring, competition, and regulatory reform in the US electricity sector', *Journal of Economic Perspectives*, 11(3), Summer: 119–38.

Klein, Mark S. and Christopher L. Doyle (1997), 'New York's energy taxes: Recent interpretations provide little light, no heat', *State Tax Notes*, 13(2), 14 July: 113–22.

McCall, H. Carl (2001), *Electric Deregulation in New York State: The Need for a Comprehensive Plan*, New York, NY: Office of the State Comptroller.

McLure, Charles E. Jr. (2001), 'The tax assignment problem: Ruminations on how theory and practice depend on history', *National Tax Journal*, 54(2): 339–63.

National Conference of State Legislatures (1997), Series of eight reports on 'Tax implications of electric industry restructuring, the NCSL partnership on state and local taxation of the electric industry', NCSL marketing department, 1560 Broadway, Suite 700, Denver, CO.

Office of Tax Policy Analysis (2001), *Local Telecommunications Taxes and Fees in New York State*. New York, NY: Department of Taxation and Finance, available at: http://www.tax.state.ny.us/statistics/Policy-Special/telco00/ Telco00 Contents.htm. Oklahoma Joint Electric Utility Task Force, Revenue and Taxation Working Group (1999), final report.

Oklahoma Corporation Commission (1999), *Final Report of the Joint Electric Utility Task Force*, 29 September, Oklahoma City.

Plattner, Robert D. (2000), 'State enacts sweeping changes in energy taxation', *State Tax Notes*, 22 May: 1753.

Pratt, Allison (2001). 'BOE gives final approval to state power assessment', *State Tax Notes*, 22(10), 3 December: 711.

Public Utility Commission of Texas (2001), 'Scope of competition in telecommunications: Markets of Texas, Report to the 77th Texas Legislature', available at: http://www.puc.state.tx.us/telecomm/reports/scope/ 2001scope tel.pdf (Table 1, p. 27).

Quill Corporation v. *North Dakota* (1992), 504 US 298.

Reeb, Donald J. and Edward T. Howe (1985), 'State and local taxation of electric utilities: a study of the record', in Michael A. Crew (ed.), *Analyzing the Impact of Regulatory Change in Public Utilities*, Lexington, MA: Lexington Books, pp. 59–74.

Restructuring Today (2002), 'CAEM's Malloy picks England/Wales as world leader', *Restructuring Today*, 3 May: 1–3.

Richardson, James A. and W. Bartley Hildreth (1999), 'Economic principles of taxation', in W. Bartley Hildreth and James A. Richardson (eds), *Handbook on Taxation*, New York, NY: Marcel Dekker, Inc., pp. 21–30.

Seaman, Bruce (1999), *An Analysis of Franchise Fees in Georgia*, Fiscal Research Program, Andrew Young School of Policy Studies, Georgia State University, Atlanta, Georgia. FRP report No. 34, August: 1–13.

Seaman, Bruce (2000), 'Taxation of transactions under electric deregulation', Presentation to the Joint Sales Tax Seminar, 'Transaction Taxation and Electronic Commerce', National Tax Association, 24–5 January, Sarasota, FL.

Telecommunications Tax Task Force of the Council on State Taxation (2002), 'Supplement to 2001 state study and report on telecommunications taxation', *Tax Management Multistate Tax Report*, 9(4), 26 April: 275–7.

Walters, Lawrence C. and Gary C. Cornia (1997), 'The implications of utility and telecommunications deregulation for local finance', *State and Local Government Review*, 29(3): 172–87.

Walters, Lawrence C. and Gary C. Cornia (2001), 'Electric utility deregulation and school finance in the United States', *Journal of Education Finance*, Spring, 2001, reprinted in *State Tax Notes*, 26 November 2001, 22(9): 677–90.

9. Globalization and state–local government finances*

James Alm, Jill Ann Holman, and Rebecca M. Neumann

INTRODUCTION

There is little question that state and local (SL) governments in the United States face enormous challenges in the new millennium. Changing demographics – the ageing of the population, a change in its racial and ethnic composition, a shift in the rate of household formation, and the movement of individuals across jurisdictions – will change both the demands for SL expenditures and the ability of SL governments to finance these expenditures. The potential for continued devolution of responsibilities to SL governments will require these governments to adapt to increased, or at least, altered, responsibilities. Persistent growth in the consumption of difficult-to-tax services will strain SL sales taxes, as will the already massive and still projected explosion in electronic commerce. Importantly, increased integration of the world's economy will create challenges for governments at all levels, both in the United States and abroad. The purpose of this chapter is to focus on these last effects, the impacts of globalization on SL finances.

A common and widely accepted view is that globalization will dramatically reduce the ability of a government to collect its taxes and to set any of its policies independently of market forces and of policies in other jurisdictions. If labor and capital (and even consumption) can move easily from one jurisdiction to another, then any attempt to tax these factors more heavily than one's neighbors will lead to a 'vanishing taxpayer' as labor and capital flee from high to low tax regions. Analysts differ on whether this development is a positive or a negative one. However, few question that globalization has led, and will continue to lead, to a significant reduction in the autonomy of governments.

It is our purpose here to explore the impacts of globalization on SL government finances in the United States. We make two basic points. *First*, the actual evidence on the predicted effects of globalization – its impacts upon the narrow issue of SL taxes and upon the broader issue of government autonomy – is suggestive, but it is also quite preliminary and somewhat mixed. *Second*, and more importantly, while globalization obviously limits the choices that governments can make in some areas, it also creates opportunities that governments can exploit in other areas. After all, with greater resource mobility, governments arguably have more power to influence the locational decisions of firms, workers, and consumers. Governments that succeed in their choices will be the ones that have well grounded and credible institutions, that are better able to match taxes with expenditures, and that are better able to give taxpayers the services that they wish for the taxes they pay. In short, we argue that globalization may well enhance, not diminish, the power of those SL governments that are able to provide the type of environment that its constituents desire.[1]

In the next section we define 'globalization' and discuss various indicators of its trends. We then examine some long and short term developments in government finances, including SL governments in the United States and governments in other parts of the world. In the following section we present some initial 'speculations' on the effects of globalization and SL finances, and we then present some results from a more rigorous but stylized model of government. Our conclusions are discussed in the final section.

'GLOBALIZATION': DEFINITIONS AND TRENDS

Globalization can be difficult to define. Some describe globalization as liberalization of trade flows and capital flows, including deregulation of the banking sector (Fox, 1998; Grunberg, 1998). Others focus on increased factor mobility as a sign of integration among countries (Grubert, 1998). Globalization could also be defined by the conditions that contribute to increased economic integration, such as improved technology advances, lower communication costs, increased information flows, and reduced transportation costs, all of which make outsourcing and production shifting cheaper and easier. The Organization for Economic Cooperation and Development (OECD, 2001a) characterizes globalization as the 'internationalization of production and sales and new forms of delivering goods and services to consumers across countries, new developments in information and communications technologies, and the growing importance of e-commerce'. We focus on several specific trends indicating increased globalization across economies to examine the impact of globalization on the SL level. Our working definition of 'globalization' is increased factor mobility across countries and across regions within a country.

One indicator of globalization is advances in communication technologies. According to the World Bank (1999), the number of internet hosts around the world increased from under one million in 1990 to nearly 50 million at the end of the 1990s. Such advances have made it easier to monitor events in distant locations, and have also made it easier to transmit information instantly around the world.

Table 9.1   World trade and taxes, 1960–1995

	Year				
Measure	**1960**	**1970**	**1980**	**1990**	**1995**
World trade[a]	24.5	27.1	38.8	37.9	42.5
World trade taxes[b]	NA	17.6[c]	14.9	13.4	7.9

Notes:
[a] 'World trade' is defined as the sum of exports and imports of goods and services, and is expressed as a per cent of gross domestic product.
[b] 'World trade taxes' include import duties, export duties, profits on export or import monopolies, exchange profits, and exchange taxes, and are expressed as a per cent of current revenues.
[c] World trade taxes are for 1973.

Source: World Bank (1998).

Another indicator is the increase in world trade. Table 9.1 shows that over the last 40 years trade increased as a share of gross domestic product (GDP), a trend that has become increasingly strong in recent years. In the 1990s, trade volume growth (seven per cent per year) far outpaced growth in real GDP (three per cent per year). This trend continued in the late 1990s and through 2002. The OECD (2001a) reports that the ratio of trade in goods and services to GDP (measured in volume terms as world exports relative to GDP) increased from about 19 per cent in 1995 to 23 per cent in 1999, and on average OECD trade grew in value terms at around 8.5 per cent per year during the last 15 years. Globalization is also revealed in increased trade liberalization and financial liberalization across countries. Table 9.1 shows that taxes on international trade have fallen significantly over the last 20 years.

Moreover, global economic integration is evident in the increased size and importance of private capital flows to developing countries. The World Bank (1998) reports that official development finance declined during the 1990s, while private debt and equity flows grew spectacularly (Figure 9.1). Private flows as a per cent of total flows were only 43 per cent in 1990, and grew to 85 per cent in 1997. The volume of cross-border transactions in bonds and equities also exploded in the last 20 years, as have foreign exchange transac-

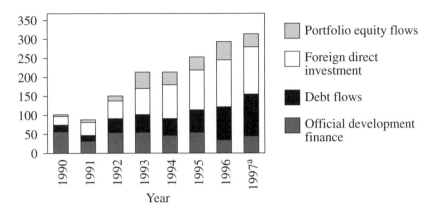

Notes:
Developing countries are defined as low and middle income countries with 1995 per capita incomes of less than $765 (low) and $9,385 (middle).
[a] Preliminary.

Source: World Bank (1998).

Figure 9.1 Net long-term resource flows to developing countries, 1990–1997 (in billions of US dollars)

tions. For example, for Japan, Germany, and the United States, international transactions in bonds and equities have grown from 15 per cent of total output to nearly 600 per cent of total output (Daniels and Van Hoose, 2002). The increase in international transactions in financial assets has far outpaced the growth in trade. From 1979 to 1998, the annual turnover of foreign exchange grew from 12 times the volume of world exports of goods to 70 times the volume of world exports (Daniels and Van Hoose, 2002). Much of this foreign exchange turnover is conducted for international portfolio rebalancing. Gross international capital flows have risen to about six times the level of net flows. Therefore, even countries with small net capital flows may experience substantial inflows and outflows of capital (International Monetary Fund, 2001).

SOME TRENDS IN GOVERNMENT FINANCES

While our measures of globalization focus on the integration of the world economy, we are mainly interested in the effects of globalization on SL governments. Accordingly, we next present trends in government finances, in the level of taxes (and expenditures), in the structure of taxes, and in average tax rates for different types of taxes.[2] We also examine the evidence for the United States and for other countries.

If globalization makes it more difficult to tax mobile factors, then taxes on mobile factors should diminish, and those on immobile factors should increase, with globalization. However, the evidence here is somewhat mixed. Consider first the changes in SL taxation in the United States over the last 90 years. The burden of property taxes is generally (though not entirely correctly) viewed as falling on immobile factors, especially land, while consumption taxes are seen as falling on consumers and income taxes are borne by factor owners. However, Table 9.2 shows that, as a percentage of total tax revenues at the state and local level, property taxes have in fact fallen while sales and income taxes have risen over this period. Although not shown in Table 9.2, SL reliance upon user fees has increased, especially in the last several decades.

Table 9.2   Changing importance of major state and local taxes in the United States, 1902–1992

| Year | Per cent of total tax revenues, type of tax | | | |
	Property tax	Sales taxes	Income taxes	Other
1902	82.1	3.3	0.0	14.6
1927	77.7	7.7	2.7	11.9
1950	46.2	32.4	8.7	12.7
1970	39.3	34.9	16.7	9.1
1992	32.1	35.3	25.0	7.6

Source: Vedder (1999).

The composition of taxes has also changed at the national level, perhaps in response to tax competition across countries. In particular, governments compete to attract inflows of capital, especially inflows of foreign direct investment. As a result, governments have been lowering corporate income tax rates, while relying more on personal income taxes and a variety of indirect taxes.

While the reliance on different types of taxes has changed, the shares of tax revenues for state versus local governments in the United States have been little altered. Table 9.3 shows that state (local) governments collected about 60 (40) per cent of total SL taxes both in 1980 and 1995. Table 9.3 also indicates that local governments rely primarily on property taxes, while states rely more on sales taxes and income (especially individual income) taxes. These shares were little changed over the period.

Table 9.3   State and local taxes in the United States, 1980 and 1995

Type of tax	1980	1995
Total state and local taxes (in billions of dollars)	223	661
State, per cent of total	61.4	60.5
Local, per cent of total	38.6	39.5
Property taxes		
State, per cent of total state and local taxes	1.4	1.5
Local, per cent of total state and local taxes	29.6	29.3
Individual income taxes		
State, per cent of total state and local taxes	16.6	19.1
Local, per cent of total state and local taxes	2.2	1.8
Corporate income taxes		
State, per cent of total state and local taxes	5.8	4.4
Local, per cent of total state and local taxes	0.0	0.3
Sales taxes		
State, per cent of total state and local taxes	30.5	29.1
Local, per cent of total state and local taxes	5.4	6.1

Source: United States Bureau of the Census (1998).

In theory, an increase in factor mobility should lead to some convergence of tax rates across governments. In fact, however, the evidence on tax rate convergence is mixed. Consider first tax rate convergence across nations. Mendoza et al. (1997) calculate effective tax rates for consumption, capital income, and labor income taxes for a number of developed economies for 1970, 1980 and 1990 (Table 9.4). They find that the average tax rates for the various taxes, as well as the standard deviations, are surprisingly similar for the three years, despite the increased integration of economies over this period. Ault (1997) and Messere (1998) also find that the tax systems of industrialized countries retain remarkable and sustained diversity. Carey and Tchilinguirian (2000) calculate average effective tax rates (AETRs) on capital, labor, and consumption for OECD countries, updating the original methodology as used by Mendoza et al. (1994). They find that in OECD countries for 1991 to 1997, the AETR on capital was on average 34.7 per cent, the AETR on labor was 36.8 per cent, and the AETR on consumption was 16.4 per cent. As for the trends in AETRs, they show that the average

Table 9.4   Average effective tax rates on consumption and on factor incomes, country averages[a], 1970–1990

	Mean	**Standard deviation**
Consumption tax rates		
1970	15.23	7.23
1980	15.06	8.41
1990	17.56	8.96
Capital income tax rates		
1970	30.55	13.85
1980	34.74	12.88
1990	38.99	13.62
Labor income tax rates		
1970	25.76	7.40
1980	32.30	8.56
1990	36.77	9.93

Note: [a] The AETRs are computed from effective tax rates on factor incomes and consumption (see www.econ.duke.edu/~mendozae).

Source: Mendoza et al. (1997).

annual changes in AETRs on capital and consumption were in each case 0.2 per cent, while the average annual change on labor was 0.3 per cent. Thus, they conclude that OECD countries have focused the increase in the overall tax burden on labor, the least mobile factor of production. Across OECD countries since 1990, they also find a narrowing in the distribution of AETRs on capital (and, to a lesser extent, on consumption), but not on labor.

In contrast, Edmiston (2002) calculates annual sample statistics from effective tax rates on consumption, labor, gross capital, and net capital, as well as statutory rates on corporate income and personal income, for the 15 EU countries over the period 1970–2001. With the exception of the individual income tax rate, there was a clear downward trend in the relative variances, defined as the variance divided by the mean tax rate.

Patterns of convergence in tax rates arguably should be more evident in the United States, where factors are more mobile than they are across countries. Again, however, tax rates across the states have not converged (Federation of Tax Administrators, 1999). As indicated in Table 9.5 at the end of the chapter, even now state individual income tax rates range from a low of less than one per cent in Iowa, Ohio, and Oklahoma to 12 per cent in the highest tax bracket in North Dakota; several states (Alaska, Florida, Nevada, South Dakota, Texas, Washington, and Wyoming) do not impose any income tax. State corporate income tax rates have also not converged, varying from one per cent in Alaska and Arkansas to 12 per cent in Iowa, and the states still differ significantly in the factors and formulae used to apportion income. Several states (Nevada, South Dakota, Washington, and Wyoming) have no corporate income tax, and several other states (Michigan and Texas) impose an alternative form of business tax. There is also much variation in general sales tax rates (zero to seven per cent), gasoline taxes (7.5 to 32 cents per gallon), and cigarette taxes (2.5 to 100 cents per pack). Consideration of purely local taxes would add further to the variation. There is little evidence of any recent change in these patterns.

As for the level of tax collections or, more broadly, the size of government, it is argued that increased globalization will reduce government spending because it limits the ability of government to collect taxes. Even here the evidence is not supportive of the idea of a government that is powerless in the face of increasing globalization. Over the last century, and also over the last several decades, total government spending in nearly all industrialized countries has grown, from an average of well under ten per cent of GDP before 1900 to now nearly half of GDP across these countries (International Monetary Fund, 1998). Figure 9.2 shows that the OECD average tax-to-GDP ratio rose by 3.5 percentage points from 1985 to 1999 and by 6.2 percentage points from 1975 to 1999. Most recently, the OECD average tax-to-GDP ratio actually rose from 36.9 per cent in 1998 to 37.3 per cent in 1999, largely

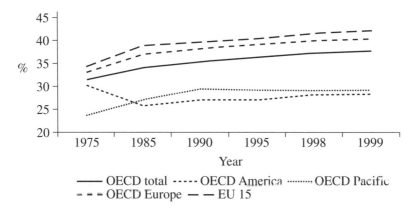

Source: OECD (2001b).

Figure 9.2   Total tax revenue, percentage of GDP, 1975–1999

reflecting strong worldwide economic growth as countries also made some recent moves to cut tax rates. Focusing on the various regions within the OECD, Figure 9.2 shows that the European and Pacific regions followed similar patterns as that for the OECD as a whole. Total tax revenues were lower in 1999 than in 1975 in OECD America, which includes Canada, Mexico, and the United States, but increased over the period 1985 to 1999.

These averages, however, mask a great deal of variation. From 1985 to 1999, 12 OECD countries had a reduction in their tax-to-GDP ratios while 18 had increases (OECD, 2001b). Over this period, general consumption tax revenues and social security contributions accounted for most of the rise in the tax-to-GDP ratios. Social security contributions have been relatively constant since 1996, indicating that most of the increase has come from growth in general consumption tax revenues. These increases have been partly offset by reduced revenues from taxes on specific goods and services like tobacco (OECD, 2001b). Figure 9.3 shows taxes on income and profits relative to GDP. From 1975 to 1999, tax revenues for the OECD as a whole grew relative to GDP. Again, however, there is a great deal of variation across different regions. The European regions have seen steady growth in taxes on income and profits. Taxes on income and profits for OECD America were lower in 1999 than they were in 1975, but have grown steadily since 1985. Taxes on income and profits in OECD Pacific peaked in 1990 and have fallen steadily since then.

Further variations in tax collections across countries are evident in taxes imposed on wage earners. The tax wedge on labor, or the difference between what employers pay out and what employees take home, varies widely across

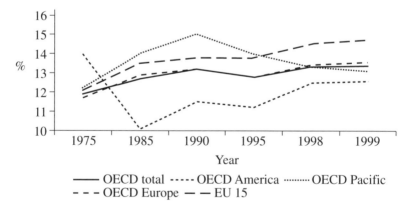

Source: OECD (2001b).

Figure 9.3   Taxes on income and profits, percentage of GDP, 1975–1999

countries. For a single worker, the wedge ranges from a low of 14 per cent in Mexico and 16 per cent in Korea to 52 per cent in Germany and 57 per cent in Belgium. For a married couple, the range is similar, from negative two per cent in Iceland and 11 per cent in Luxembourg to 41 per cent in Belgium and 44 per cent in Sweden (OECD, 2000). Some of these taxes have come down; for example, Belgium, Germany, Sweden, Austria, and Italy have lowered tax wedges by about one per cent for most categories of wage earners. Nevertheless, these numbers provide evidence that some of the arguably most open economies continue to have some of the highest tax rates. *The Economist* (2001) notes that two of the most open international economies, Sweden and Denmark, have remarkably high tax collections, 57 per cent and 53 per cent of GDP, respectively.

On balance then, the evidence clearly suggests that globalization, however measured, is on the rise.[3] However, the effects of globalization on government finances are a good bit harder to discern. In the United States, in fact, government spending has risen steadily over the last century, and has risen at all levels of government. Especially in the 1990s, at a time when the spread of globalization was thought to be particularly dramatic, government spending by local, state, and federal governments in the United States continued upward, fed by a huge – and largely unpredicted – surge in tax revenues. Government spending has risen even more dramatically in Europe, at a time when these economies have become arguably more open and more interconnected. Of course, it may well be that there has not been sufficient time for many of the effects of globalization to be felt fully. Still, these data give at least an initial reason for retaining some skepticism about the supposed effects of globalization.

THE EFFECTS OF GLOBALIZATION ON STATE AND LOCAL GOVERNMENT FINANCES: SOME INITIAL SPECULATIONS

State and local tax systems were originally designed for a world in which production and consumption were primarily of *tangible goods*, in which the sale and consumption of these goods generally occurred in the *same location*, and in which the factors of production used to make the goods were for the most part *immobile*. In such a world, taxation was a fairly straightforward exercise. Sales and excise taxes could be imposed on the tangible goods that were consumed, by the government in the jurisdiction in which consumption (or production) occurred. Similarly, income and property taxes could be imposed on factors where they lived and worked without fear that taxes would drive the factors elsewhere. In making these tax decisions, a government in one jurisdiction had no need to consider how its actions would affect the governments in other jurisdictions because tax bases were largely immobile.

There is little doubt that, in principle, globalization changes things, and changes them dramatically. First, as noted earlier, globalization implies that tax bases are significantly more mobile. With integrated national and world markets, factors of production are obviously able to move more easily from one jurisdiction to another. For example, businesses have more flexibility in choosing where to locate because communication and transportation costs have been slashed. Further, some forms of production activity require little in the way of traditional capital and labor, so that physical location becomes less important. Labor, especially skilled labor, also becomes more mobile in this environment. Likewise, financial capital is able to flow quickly across local, state, and national boundaries.

Clearly, if factors of production can move easily from one location to another, then the ability of a government to tax these factors is greatly diminished. A government that raises its tax rates above those of other juris-dictions risks losing its tax base to these areas. Particularly in the case of income from capital, there is much speculation that taxation will become increasingly problematic (Mintz, 1992). In fact, there is some empirical evi-dence that factors are responding to these types of tax considerations (Grubert, 1998; Hines, 1999).

Increased mobility is not limited to factors of production. Consumers are also able to plan their consumption according to tax considerations, and consumption does not necessarily occur in the jurisdiction in which a tax-payer resides. A jurisdiction that attempts to tax, say, gasoline more heavily than in surrounding areas will find that consumers will purchase elsewhere. Similarly, individuals can now purchase most types of products over the internet and thereby avoid paying some (or even all) sales taxes. Additionally, there has been increased consumption of services and intangible goods, both of which are much more difficult to tax than tangible goods.[4] This is espec-ially true within domestic economies. Services contribute a minor role in international trade (about 20 per cent) but contribute a great deal to domestic GDP. For the G7 countries, the proportion of total production contributed by services is about 55 to 65 per cent, and continues to rise relative to declining agriculture and industry shares (OECD, 2001a). From 1995 to 1999, G7 trade in total services grew at an average annual rate of change of three per cent. Of this, trade in computer and information services, which are some of the more difficult services to measure and therefore to tax, grew at an annual rate of 14 to 15 per cent. Other fast growing services include financial services, and royalties and license fees (OECD, 2001a). The once tight link between the location of sales and the location of consumption is now quite loose.

Second, and relatedly, globalization implies that the measurement, identification, and assignment of tax bases are much more difficult.[5] Consider a typical multistate (or multinational) business. The product that the firm makes may be designed in one or more jurisdictions; the firm may use inputs purchased in multiple jurisdictions; the product may be produced in several places and assembled in a still different location; and the final good may be sold in multiple locations. Because the business operates in multiple jurisdictions, the firm has considerable leeway to manipulate prices to minimize its tax liabilities. This latter problem is well known, but its severity has increased with the enormous expansion in the number of firms operating in multiple jurisdictions.

Likewise, consider an individual whose income comes from multiple sources. A global income tax requires that income from these sources be aggregated. However, it is easy for an individual to hide, say, interest income from multiple areas. In the absence of information sharing across governments, the ability of a state or local government to identify incomes from other jurisdictions is quite limited.

Consider finally a consumer who can purchase goods and services in at least two different ways: from traditional local merchants or from company websites. In the former case, identification, measurement, and assignment of the tax base are straightforward. In the latter case, they are not. Application of sales taxes in this new environment poses considerable problems for governments.

How will SL governments respond to these various pressures, especially in their tax choices? Most importantly, globalization implies that the ability of any government to choose its tax policies independently of those in other jurisdictions is greatly curtailed. In the presence of mobile tax bases, a single government's choice of tax policies will have effects beyond its own borders and will be affected by the actions of other jurisdictions. In short, tax competition will increase, and this increase will have a number of effects.

The *level* of tax rates seems likely to decline. In particular, if tax bases can move easily from one jurisdiction to another, then they will flow from high tax to low tax areas. Owners of capital, skilled labor, and consumers will become increasingly sensitive to tax differentials in their locational decisions. As a consequence, it is commonly argued that governments will face increasing pressures to compete with one another by reducing tax rates or by offering special tax incentives, in order to attract and to retain the various tax bases. For example, when a government reduces its tax rates on capital income, it thereby attracts capital flows from other jurisdictions, and in doing so the government benefits its own jurisdiction. However, the government's action also imposes costs – or negative externalities – on the jurisdictions that lose factors of production, and it risks generating similar tax cutting responses from those governments. With tax competition, there could well be what some have referred to as a 'race to the bottom', in which overall tax collections decline precipitously as SL governments compete to attract or to retain their tax bases.[6]

As noted earlier, however, the evidence here is mixed. Tax collections by SL governments have in fact risen greatly in the last decade, at precisely the time that globalization has increased.[7] Overall, SL government spending has continued to rise over this period. Of course, it may be too early to discern the effects of taxation on government, and even a small negative impact on tax collections could create significant problems for some SL governments.

The *composition* of SL taxes could also change as a result of increased difficulty in taxing mobile tax bases. The overall tax burden from income taxes on mobile tax bases like capital and skilled labor will likely decline across governments; tax rates on these factors should also flatten and converge. In contrast, taxes on immobile bases – unskilled labor, physical capital, and property – should increase.[8] Charges and fees for specific services should rise in importance because these tax bases are largely immobile. SL governments may turn more frequently to 'sin taxes' on alcohol and cigarettes, to environmental or 'green taxes', and to lotteries, in attempts to replace lost revenues from mobile bases. There is some empirical evidence that such taxes fall more heavily on lower income individuals.

The *form* of SL sales taxes is also likely to change. State and local governments may well decide that a destination-based consumption tax that is collected by the federal government and distributed to state and local governments would be preferable to further erosion in their sales tax collections. Alternatively, they may agree among themselves to apply a uniform state sales tax. They may even radically reform the sales tax by moving toward a consumption-based, uniform rate, destination principle sales tax, as advocated by McLure (1997a) and Fox and Murray (1997).

These latter changes suggest more broadly that SL governments may attempt greater *harmonization* (or at least *coordination*) of their tax systems, in an attempt to reduce the negative fiscal externalities that one government's decisions impose upon other governments. Such harmonization implies that there should be some *convergence* in tax rates across SL governments, and also in the definitions of tax bases. With harmonization, SL autonomy in tax policy will obviously diminish.[9]

Overall, these compositional changes imply that SL tax systems will likely become more regressive than at present. If taxes on capital and skilled labor decline, if sin taxes, income taxes on unskilled labor, and lotteries all increase, and if marginal income tax rates flatten, then SL governments will find it quite difficult to maintain any progressivity in their tax systems. Together with an expected decline in overall revenues, the ability of SL governments to redistribute income to lower income individuals will likely diminish.

As discussed earlier, there have been some changes in SL tax policies along these lines. However, to date these changes have been minimal. While the economics of these changes is certainly plausible, the process by which they occur seems slow, erratic, and uncertain. The next section presents the main results of a rigorous but highly stylized model of government choices that suggests that governments are not as powerless as these initial speculations would suggest.

THE EFFECTS OF GLOBALIZATION ON STATE AND LOCAL GOVERNMENT FINANCES: SOME RESULTS FROM A STYLIZED MODEL

As suggested by the previous section, a basic analysis of globalization predicts that greater factor mobility will lead eventually to lower, more regressive, and less variable tax rates. However, much of this analysis is speculative and relies on analysis of a small open economy. By contrast, consider two open economies that trade with one another, each of which has a government that taxes labor, capital, and consumption. By introducing different degrees of tax base mobility, such a stylized model allows us to examine how globalization affects the ability of a government to tax its tax bases and also how globalization affects the mix of its taxes.[10]

To be precise, consider a standard dynamic neoclassical two-country model with two factors of production and a representative agent in each country. The home country uses its factors of production (capital and labor) to produce and export a commodity (denoted X), and the foreign country similarly uses both factors to produce and export Y; the production function in each country is characterized by constant returns to scale. Factors are fully employed and are paid the value of their marginal product; also, prices are perfectly flexible, and all markets – both domestic and international – are assumed to clear. A 'representative agent' in each country chooses the amount of capital and labor to supply to production in both countries and the amount of domestic and foreign goods to consume, and each agent faces a labor-leisure choice. Agents make these choices to maximize the discounted sum of utility over the infinite horizon. The government in each country can impose taxes on both factors of production and on consumption. The model is dynamic, and is solved using numerical steady state methods.

We examine several different scenarios, each of which corresponds to different degrees of factor mobility. In our initial scenario, there is free trade of goods, and capital and labor are assumed to be immobile across countries.[11] We then introduce 'globalization' by allowing for factor mobility, and different degrees of globalization are also considered. In all cases, we calculate the responsiveness of the tax bases – consumption, capital, and labor – with respect to a ten per cent change in the tax rate on consumption, on capital, or on labor. Table 9.6 provides a summary of the basic results from our numerical analyses comparing factor immobility to factor mobility under different tax scenarios.

For example, consider the effects of home country taxation of capital, comparing the results when both capital and labor are immobile versus when both are mobile (the top section of Table 9.6). The response of domestic capital is similar regardless of factor mobility. Table 9.6 shows that domestic capital (Kx) falls 14 per cent when factors are immobile and 17 per cent when factors are allowed to flow freely across borders. Overall, capital accumulated by domestic factors falls less when capital is taxed and factors are mobile. Also in response to the tax on domestic capital, domestic labor rises one per cent when factors are immobile and also rises one per cent when factors are mobile. Overall, hours worked by domestic factors rise less when factors can choose the country in which they work. Government revenues are cut in half when factors are mobile and only home capital is taxed; however, if the home government is able to tax both home and foreign capital used in home production, then home government revenues are unaffected by factor mobility. As can be seen in the middle section of Table 9.6, a largely similar conclusion emerges when the home country taxes labor, with or without factor mobility. The bottom section of Table 9.6 shows that factors do not respond to changes in consumption taxes regardless of factor mobility. As one would expect, consumption falls when it is taxed, and it falls in an identical fashion regardless of factor mobility.

Allowing for different degrees of factor mobility indicates the direct effects of increasing globalization, and, as we have seen, home government revenue tends to decline as factor mobility increases. We can also indirectly vary the degree of factor mobility by varying the degree of substitutability of factors across the production processes in the two countries. We do not report these numerical results here. However, when the degree of substitutability between foreign and domestic factors is low, the decline in government revenue from increasing substitutability is relatively small. By contrast, when the degree of substitutability between factors is high, the decline in government revenue from increasing substitutability is relatively large. Therefore, when there are smaller substitution possibilities in production, the response of government revenues to increased factor mobility tends to be smaller.

Overall, our numerical results indicate that there is clearly some shifting of factors to escape the relatively higher tax burden imposed on domestic production; that is, factors of production that are free to move in response to tax differentials do in fact relocate to escape taxation. However, even in this stylized world there is little evidence of a 'vanishing taxpayer'. Government revenue declines with greater mobility, but government largely retains the ability to collect taxes. Perhaps surprisingly, the amount of revenues collected remains largely the same, at least in some circumstances, whether factors are mobile or immobile. Even when only one government assesses a tax and the other government does not, factors are mobile, and factors are substitutes in production, it is nevertheless the case that both countries continue to produce and consume at largely similar levels whether factors are mobile or immobile.

CONCLUSIONS: IS GLOBALIZATION 'GOOD' OR 'BAD' FOR STATE AND LOCAL GOVERNMENTS?

Regardless of agreement or disagreement on the broad effects of globalization on SL finances, and the responses of SL governments to them, observers are likely to differ on whether these changes are desirable. It is this last issue that we consider in our conclusions.

At one end of the spectrum are those who believe that a reduction in the power of government, including SL governments, is clearly negative. In their view, government is needed to correct the shortcomings of markets, to provide essential goods and services not provided by the market, and to redistribute income. If globalization means that government cannot perform these essential functions, then globalization is clearly harmful. At the other end of the spectrum are those who see most government interventions in markets as inefficient, even inequitable. In this view, if globalization and its concomitant effects limit the ability of governments to meddle in markets, then there are clear benefits from globalization.

We argue here that neither view is quite accurate, for two reasons. *First*, as noted at several points, the evidence on the effects of globalization is unclear. At least at the present time, there is little empirical – or theoretical – evidence that SL governments cannot collect taxes, that they are losing their fiscal autonomy, that their tax rates and bases are converging, that their tax systems are becoming more regressive, and that their expenditures are falling in total or changing in composition. The empirical evidence could well change, but for now it is largely inconclusive, even perhaps negative, on the predicted impacts of globalization on SL governments.

Second, and more importantly, we believe that much of the current discussion of the effects of globalization on SL governments ignores an important consideration: globalization both limits and expands the choices that governments can make. With greater factor and tax base mobility, governments have

Table 9.5 State tax rates, 1999

State	General sales tax: Rate (%)	Gasoline tax: Cents per gallon	Cigarette tax: Cents per pack	Individual income tax: Range of rates (%)/ number of brackets	Corporate income tax: Range of rates (%)
Alabama	4.0	18.0 cents	16.5 cents	2.0–5.0//3	5.0
Alaska	No state tax	8.0	100	No state tax	1.0–9.4
Arizona	5.0	18.0	58	2.87–5.04//5	8.0
Arkansas	4.625	19.7	31.5	1.0–7.0//6	1.0–6.5
California	6.0	18.0	87	1.0–9.3/6	8.84
Colorado	3.0	22.0	20	5.0//1	5.0
Connecticut	6.0	32.0	50	3.0–4.5//2	8.5
Delaware	No state tax	23.0	24	2.6–6.4//7	8.7
Florida	6.0	13.1	33.9	No state tax	5.5
Georgia	4.0	7.5	12	1.0–6.0//6	6.0
Hawaii	4.0	16.0	100	1.6–8.75/8	4.4–6.4
Idaho	5.0	26.0	28	2.0–8.2/8	8.0
Illinois	6.25	19.3	58	3.0//1	7.3
Indiana	5.0	15.0	15.5	3.4//1	7.9
Iowa	5.0	20.0	36	0.36–8.98//9	6.0–12.0
Kansas	4.90	20.0	24	4.10–6.45//3	4.0
Kentucky	6.0	16.4	3	2.0–6.0//5	4.0–8.25
Louisiana	4.0	20.0	20	2.0–6.0//3	4.0–8.0
Maine	5.5	19.0	74	2.0–8.5//4	3.5–8.93
Maryland	5.0	23.5	66	2.0–4.85//4	7.0
Massachusetts	5.0	21.0	76	5.95//1	9.5
Michigan	6.0	19.0	75	4.4//1	State 'business activities tax'
Minnesota	6.5	20.0	48	6.0–8.5//3	9.8
Mississippi	7.0	18.4	18	3.0–5.0//3	3.0–5.0

State				
Missouri	4.225	17.05	17	1.5–6.0//10	6.25
Montana	No state tax	27.0	18	2.0–11.0//10	6.75
Nebraska	5.0	25.0	34	2.51–6.68//4	5.58–7.81
Nevada	6.5	24.0	35	No state tax	No state tax
New Hampshire	No state tax	18.7	52	State tax on dividends and interest only	7.0
New Jersey	6.0	10.5	80	1.4–6.37//6	9.0
New Mexico	5.0	18.0	21	1.7–8.2//7	4.8–7.6
New York	4.0	8.0	56	4.0–6.85//5	9.0
North Carolina	4.0	21.6	5	6.0–7.75//3	7.0
North Dakota	5.0	21.0	44	2.67–12.0//8	3.0–10.5
Ohio	5.0	22.0	24	0.673–6.799//9	5.1–8.5
Oklahoma	4.5	17.0	23	0.5–6.75//8	6.0
Oregon	No state tax	24.0	68	5.0–9.0//3	6.6
Pennsylvania	6.0	30.77	31	2.8//1	9.99
Rhode Island	7.0	29.0	71	26.5% of federal liability	9.0
South Carolina	5.0	16.0	7	2.5–7.0//6	5.0
South Dakota	4.0	22.0	33	No state tax	No state tax
Tennessee	6.0	21.4	13	State tax on dividends and interest only	6.0
Texas	6.25	20.0	41	No state tax	State 'franchise tax'
Utah	4.75	24.75	51.5	2.3–7.0/6	5.0
Vermont	5.0	20.0	44	25% of federal liability	7.0–9.75
Virginia	3.5	17.5	2.5	2.0–5.75//4	6.0
Washington	6.5	23.0	82.5	No state tax	No state tax
West Virginia	6.0	25.35	17	3.0–6.5//5	9.0
Wisconsin	5.0	25.8	59	4.77–6.77//3	7.9
Wyoming	4.0	14.0	12	No state tax	No state tax
District of Columbia	5.75	20.0	65	6.0–9.5/3	9.975

Source: Federation of Tax Administrators (1999).

more power to influence the locational decisions of firms, workers, and consumers. Those governments that succeed in these choices will be the ones who are better able to match taxes with expenditures, who are better able to give taxpayers the services that they wish for the taxes they pay. Previous research has focused mainly on the negative fiscal externalities of tax competition. It is only relatively recently that the positive effects of tax and, especially, of expenditure competition have begun to be considered in analytical models of SL government behavior (McLure, 1986; Wilson, 1999). It is these positive effects that we believe deserve more emphasis, effects that are present independently of any impact of globalization on the size of government per se.

To illustrate, consider a world in which all factors of production are completely mobile, there are no transportation or communication costs, and there is a single national market for all goods and services. It might seem that no government at any level would be able to impose taxes in such a hypothetical world because any taxes would lead to the immediate outflow of the tax base from the jurisdiction. Put differently, it might appear that the 'vanishing taxpayer' would lead inexorably to the virtual disappearance of government.

Of course, complete taxpayer mobility does not now, and will never fully, exist. Even so, this view is surely wrong. Individuals value the goods and services that SL governments provide, and they are willing to pay for them. As originally argued by Tiebout (1956), individuals will 'vote with their feet' by moving to those jurisdictions in which governments provide services that residents value. Indeed, SL governments will be encouraged, even required, to make their communities as attractive as possible: by providing uncongested roads, a clean environment, pleasant parks, quality schools, safe neighborhoods, and the like, all with a tax burden that individuals deem responsible and appropriate. If individuals value redistribution, as many certainly do, then even programs for the poor would survive, albeit at smaller levels than currently.

In sum, then, even in an increasingly integrated global economy SL governments will still exist, they will still impose taxes, and they will still make expenditures. There is no question that these decisions will be circumscribed by the possibility of a 'vanishing taxpayer'. However, the existence of such a taxpayer also creates opportunities, by giving SL governments the potential to influence these locational decisions. SL governments whose prior performance has been poor will have little credibility in making policy decisions; the response to those governments with sound institutions will be quite different. The forces unleashed by globalization will therefore create pressures on all SL governments to establish these institutions. Those governments that succeed in these choices will be the ones who are better able to match taxes with expenditures, or are better able to give taxpayers the services they desire for the taxes they wish to pay. The challenge for SL governments is to recognize and to act upon the benefits and the costs that globalization creates.

Table 9.6   Tax base responses for immobile versus mobile factors[a]

Percentage change in base	Response to a 10% tax on Kx when factors are immobile	Response to a 10% tax on Kx when factors are mobile
Percentage change in Cx	–5.78%	–3.20%
Percentage change in Cy	0	–0.50
Percentage change in Kx	–14.06	–16.59
Percentage change in Lx	1.02	1.12
Percentage change in Ky	–	–0.05
Percentage change in Ly	–	0.56
Percentage change in K	–	–8.32
Percentage change in L	–	0.84
Change in g	2.48	1.20

	Response to a 10% tax on Lx when factors are immobile	Response to a 10% tax on Lx when factors are mobile
Percentage change in Cx	–9.70%	–7.26%
Percentage change in Cy	0	–2.26
Percentage change in Kx	–1.14	–0.81
Percentage change in Lx	–1.16	–6.24
Percentage change in Ky	–	0.13
Percentage change in Ly	–	5.12
Percentage change in K	–	–0.34
Percentage change in L	–	–0.51
Change in g	4.77	2.33

	Response to a 10% tax on Cx and Cy when factors are immobile	Response to a 10% tax on Cx and Cy when factors are mobile
Percentage change in Cx	–9.09%	–9.09%
Percentage change in Cy	–9.09	–9.09
Percentage change in Kx	0	0
Percentage change in Lx	0	0
Percentage change in Ky	–	0
Percentage change in Ly	–	0
Percentage change in K	–	0
Percentage change in L	–	0
Change in g	5.06	5.06

Note: [a]   Kx and Lx are home capital and labor supplied to home production; Ky and Ly are home capital and labor supplied to foreign production; K is defined as Kx + Ky; L is defined as Lx + Ly; Cx and Cy are domestic consumption of the home and foreign goods; and domestic government revenue is denoted g. Note that, when factors are immobile, the percentage change in K (or in L) is simply the percentage change in Kx (or in Lx). See Neumann et al. (2002) for further discussion.

NOTES

* An earlier version of this chapter was presented at the National Tax Association 92nd Annual Conference on Taxation in October 1999. We are grateful for helpful comments from Roy Bahl and Helen Ladd. Please address all correspondence to James Alm.
1. Similar themes on the future evolution of the role of government can be found in various issues of *The Economist* (1997, 2001), from which we have benefited.
2. For a more detailed discussion of these recent trends, see Fox (1998), Tannenwald (1998), and Vedder (1999). For an earlier but still relevant discussion, see Bahl (1984).
3. Frankel (2000) argues that the extent of globalization has been exaggerated and that much of the post World War Two trends in globalization are merely a return to the level of integration achieved prior to World War One. Further, he contends that the process of globalization is far from complete and important barriers remain. Such barriers include national borders and geography, differences in currencies, languages, political systems, and customs, as well as tariff and nontariff trade barriers.
4. For a discussion of these other effects, see McLure (1997a), Fox and Murray (1997), and Hellerstein (1997).
5. McLure (1997b) and King (1997) make a similar point. For example, King (1997) refers to the 'observability' and the 'verifiability' of the technology of tax administration.
6. For a comprehensive review of the tax competition literature, see Wilson (1999).
7. See, for example, Hawkins and Eppright (1999) for the case of Florida.
8. Youngman (1999) argues that property taxes, especially property taxes on an immovable base, are an attractive tax base for SL governments.
9. For further discussion of harmonization, see Tanzi (1995).
10. See Neumann et al. (2002) for a complete discussion and analysis.
11. Obviously, a closed economy with no trade in goods and immobile factors allows governments the most freedom to tax consumption and factors without consideration of mobility into or out of the country.

REFERENCES

Ault, Hugh J. (1997), *Comparative Income Taxation: A Structural Analysis*, The Hague: Kluwer Law International/International Fiscal Association.

Bahl, Roy (1984), *Financing State and Local Government in the 1980s*, New York, NY: Oxford University Press.

Carey, David and Harry Tchilinguirian (2000), 'Average effective tax rates on capital, labor, and consumption', *OECD Economics Department Working Papers*, No. 258.

Daniels, Joseph P. and David D. Van Hoose (2002), *International Monetary and Financial Economics*, Cincinnati, OH: South-Western Publishing.

The Economist (1997), 'The future of the state', *A Survey of the World Economy*, 20 September.

The Economist (2001), 'Is government disappearing?', *A Survey of Globalization*, 29 September.

Edmiston, Kelly (2002), 'Patterns of effective and statutory tax rates in the EU, 2002', Andrew Young School of Policy Studies, Georgia State University, Working paper.

Federation of Tax Administrators (1999), http://www.taxadmin.org

Fox, William F. (1998), 'Reengineering state and local revenue structures for the new economy', *Proceedings of the Nineteenth Annual Conference on Taxation*, November 1997, Chicago, IL, pp. 95–105.

Fox, William F. and Matthew N. Murray (1997), 'The sales tax and electronic commerce: So what's new?', *National Tax Journal*, 50(3): 573–92.

Frankel, Jeffrey A. (2000), 'Globalization of the economy', NBER Working paper No. 7858.

Grubert, Harry (1998), 'Has globalization transformed the behavior of governments and taxpayers?', *Proceedings of the Ninetieth Annual Conference on Taxation*, November 1997, Chicago, IL, pp. 237–9.

Grunberg, Isabelle (1998), 'Double jeopardy: globalization, liberalization, and the fiscal squeeze', *World Development*, 26(4): 591–605.

Hawkins, Richard R. and David R. Eppright (1999), 'Economic structure and the sales tax threat in Florida from electronic commerce', Paper presented at the National Tax Association 92nd Annual Conference on Taxation, Atlanta, GA, November 1997.

Hellerstein, Walter (1997), 'Transaction taxes and electronic commerce: Designing state taxes that work in an interstate environment', *National Tax Journal*, 50(3): 593–602.

Hines, James R. Jr. (1999), 'Lessons from behavioral responses to international taxation', *National Tax Journal*, 52(2): 305–22.

International Monetary Fund (1998), *Government Finance Statistics Yearbook*, Washington, DC: The International Monetary Fund.

International Monetary Fund (2001), 'IMF report confirms dominant US position as recipient of international capital flows', *IMF Survey*, 30 July: 252–3.

King, Mervyn (1997), 'Tax systems in the 21st century', in *Visions of the Tax Systems of the 21st Century*, The Hague: Kluwer Law International/International Fiscal Association, pp. 53–64.

McLure, Charles E. Jr. (1986), 'Tax competition: Is what's good for the private goose also good for the public gander?', *National Tax Journal*, 39(3): 341–8.

McLure, Charles E. Jr. (1997a), 'Electronic commerce, state sales taxation, and intergovernmental fiscal relations', *National Tax Journal*, 50(4): 731–49.

McLure, Charles E., Jr. (1997b), 'Tax policies for the 21st century', in *Visions of the Tax Systems of the 21st Century*, The Hague: Kluwer Law International/International Fiscal Association, pp. 9–52.

Mendoza, E.G., G. Milesi-Ferretti and P. Asea (1997), 'On the ineffectiveness of tax policy in altering long-run growth', *Journal of Public Economics*, 66(1), 99–126.

Mendoza, E.G., A. Razin and Linda L. Tesar (1994), 'Effective tax rates in macroeconomics: Cross-country estimates of tax rates on factor incomes and consumption', NBER Working paper No. 4864.

Messere, Ken (ed.) (1998), *The Tax System in Industrialized Countries*, New York, NY: Oxford University Press.

Mintz, Jack (1992), 'Is there a future for capital income taxation?', University of Toronto, Department of Economics Working paper.

Neumann, Rebecca M., Jill Ann Holman and James Alm (2002), 'Globalization and tax policy', Department of Economics, University of Wisconsin-Milwaukee, Working paper.

Organization for Economic Cooperation and Development (OECD) (2000), 'Taxes paid by wage earners in OECD countries', Paris: OECD.

Organization for Economic Cooperation and Development (OECD) (2001a), 'Trade in goods and services: Statistical trends and measurement challenges', *Statistics Brief*, No.1, 1 October, Paris: OECD.

Organization for Economic Cooperation and Development (OECD) (2001b), *Revenue Statistics 1965–2000*, Paris: OECD.

Tannenwald, Robert (1998), 'Come the devolution, will states be able to respond?', *New England Economic Review*, May/June: 53–73.

Tanzi, Vito (1995), *Taxation in an Integrating World*, Washington, DC: The Brookings Institution.

Tiebout, Charles M. (1956), 'A pure theory of local expenditures', *The Journal of Political Economy*, 64(3): 416–24.

United States Bureau of the Census (1998), 'State and local government finances and employment', *Statistical Abstract of the United States*, Washington, DC.

Vedder, Richard K. (1999), 'State and local taxation and economic growth: Lessons for federal tax reform', Prepared for the Joint Economic Committee (http://www.senate.gov/comm/jec/general/sta&loc.html)

Wilson, John Douglas (1999), 'Theories of tax competition', *National Tax Journal*, 52(2): 269–304.

World Bank (1998), *World Development Indicators*, Washington, DC: The World Bank.

World Bank (1999), *The World Development Report 1999/2000 – Entering the 21st Century*, New York, NY: Oxford University Press for The World Bank.

Youngman, Joan M. (1999), 'Property taxes in an age of globalization', *The Journal of Property Tax Assessment and Administration*, 4(3), 41–49.

10. Urban sprawl and the finances of state and local governments[1]

Therese J. McGuire and David L. Sjoquist

INTRODUCTION

Concern over the rate of spatial growth of urban areas has become a significant national political issue and a major development issue in many urban areas. An often cited statistic, typically presented as evidence of sprawl, is that between 1960 and 1990 the urban population in the United States increased by 50 per cent while the amount of developed land more than doubled (Benefield et al., 1999).

While much has been written about the causes and consequences of sprawl, little attention has been paid to the implications of sprawl for the finances of state and local government. There are at least two possible channels for sprawl to affect the finances of state and local governments. First, if the causes of sprawl include market failures or government policies, there may be a role for governmental corrective action. Second, sprawl may affect the costs of and revenue sources for the public provision of goods and services. This chapter considers the potential effects that sprawl might have on the finances of state and local governments and the possible policies that might be adopted to address the causes and consequences of sprawl.

The chapter is organized as follows: first we discuss what is meant by sprawl and how pronounced it is. We then discuss possible causes of sprawl, and then the consequences of sprawl for state and local government expenditures and revenues. In the following section we consider the pressures to address sprawl faced by state and local governments and the fiscal policies that they might choose to adopt to address sprawl and its consequences. In the final section we draw some conclusions.

WHAT IS SPRAWL AND HOW EXTENSIVE IS IT?

While the news coverage and public dialogue of sprawl would suggest it is a new issue or force, it is certainly not a new concept. Hess et al. (2001), for example, found the concept used as early as 1938 by Buttenheim and Cornick (1938). Despite its age, there is no consensus definition of sprawl.

What is Sprawl?

Some individuals associate sprawl with any expansion of the developed land of an urban area. But, in metropolitan areas with growing populations it would only be normal for additional land development to occur to accommodate the larger population.

Burchell et al. (1998), as an outcome of their extensive review of the literature, suggest that sprawl needs to be viewed as having many of ten characteristics, including low density, leapfrog development, and widespread commercial strip development (p. 124). Galster et al. (2000) review the literature on sprawl and find that the definitions of sprawl can be grouped into six general categories. Based on their review of the literature, they propose that sprawl be defined as a pattern of land use that exhibits some combination of eight distinct dimensions including low density, discontinuity of development, and little open space within the urban area.

For our purposes, we consider development patterns to be economically efficient if they are produced by a perfectly competitive market in the absence of distortions created by externalities or public policies. Sprawl, then, is a situation in which such distortions exist and the result is an urbanized area that is larger and a population density that is lower than are socially desirable.

The Magnitude of Sprawl

While we consider sprawl to be a situation in which expansion of the urbanized area is 'excessive', measuring sprawl according to this concept would be exceedingly difficult. Most authors measure the degree of sprawl as some variant of density. Dye and McGuire (2000), for example, consider four measures: share of the population outside the urban core relative to the total population of the metropolitan area; the share of urbanized land area relative to total land area of the metropolitan area; the annual growth in urbanized land area; and the population density of the suburban area relative to the population density of the total metropolitan area. Dye and McGuire examined over 100 large metropolitan areas and found that the mean share of total land area that lies in the Census-defined urbanized land area (population density greater than 1000 persons per square mile) increased from 0.07 in 1970 to 0.14 in 1990, indicating that the share of land in these metropolitan areas that was highly developed had doubled.

Galster et al. (2000) applied their definition to 13 metropolitan areas and ranked them from least sprawling to most sprawling. The resulting ranking, from least to most sprawling is: New York, Philadelphia, Chicago, Boston, Los Angeles, San Francisco, Houston, Washington, DC, Dallas, Denver, Detroit, Miami, and Atlanta.

A recent report from the Brookings Institution (Fulton et al., 2001) considers an area as sprawling if the consumption of land increases faster than population. Between 1982 and 1997, they found that urbanized land in the United States increased 47 per cent, while the US population increased 17 per cent (p. 4).[2] Metropolitan density declined from 5.00 persons per urbanized acre in 1982 to 4.22 persons per urbanized acre in 1997, or by 15.6 per cent. Table 10.1 shows the distribution of changes in density in metropolitan areas. All but 16 of the 281 metropolitan areas in their sample experienced declines in density.

Table 10.1 Percentage change in density, 1982–1997

Percentage change	Number of metropolitan areas
>25% decline	88
10–25% decline	138
0–10% decline	39
0–10% increase	9
>10% increase	7

Source: Fulton et al. (2001, p. 5).

Fulton et al. (2001) calculated the ratio of the percentage change in urbanized land divided by the percentage change in population, with higher values of this ratio implying greater sprawl. Ranking regions from least to most sprawling yields the following order: West, South, Midwest, and Northeast; the ratios are, respectively, 1.52, 2.68, 4.54, and 5.67 (Table 10.2). This result

Table 10.2 Percentage change in urbanized land and population, 1982–1997

Census region	Change in land	Change in population	Ratio of percentage change in land to percentage change in population
West	48.4	32.2	1.52
South	59.6	22.2	2.68
Midwest	32.2	7.1	4.54
Northeast	39.1	6.9	5.67

Source: Fulton, et al. (2001).

Table 10.3 Population, land area, and population density of the 20 largest urbanized areas, 1960–1990

(Pop. 2000)	Percentage change, 1960–1990				Population density of urbanized area (1000s per sq. mi.)		
	Urban population	Urbanized land area	Central city population	Suburban population	1960	1990	Change
Rust belt							
1 New York, NY 20,119,458	14	57	-6	27	7.46	5.41	-2.05
2 Chicago, IL 8,272,768	14	65	-22	68	6.21	4.29	-1.92
3 Boston, MA 6,057,826	15	73	-18	28	4.68	3.11	-1.56
4 Philadelphia, PA 5,100,931	16	95	-21	39	6.09	3.63	-2.47
5 Washington, DC 4,923,153	86	177	-21	126	5.31	3.56	-1.75
6 Detroit, MI 4,441,551	5	53	-38	38	4.83	3.30	-1.53
7 Minneapolis-St. Paul, MN 2,968,806	51	62	-20	123	2.10	1.96	-0.14
8 St. Louis, MO 2,603,607	17	125	-47	46	5.16	2.67	-2.49
9 Baltimore, MD 2,552,994	33	169	-22	87	6.44	3.19	-3.25
10 Pittsburgh, PA 2,358,695	-7	48	-39	-3	3.44	2.16	-1.28

Sun belt

1	Los Angeles, CA 9,519,338	76	43	41	51	4.74	5.80	1.06
2	Dallas-Fort Worth, TX 5,221,801	123	57	40	246	1.56	2.22	0.66
3	Houston, TX 4,177,646	155	173	81	281	2.65	2.46	-0.18
4	San Francisco-Oakland, CA 4,123,740	49	54	1	66	4.27	4.15	-0.12
5	Atlanta, GA 4,112,198	181	362	-19	211	3.13	1.90	-1.23
6	Phoenix, AZ 3,251,876	263	198	125	335	2.22	2.71	0.48
7	San Diego, CA 2,813,833	181	150	94	202	3.03	3.40	0.37
8	Seattle, WA 2,414,615	102	147	-7	166	3.63	2.97	-0.66
9	Tampa, FL 2,395,997	173	197	2	228	2.87	2.63	-0.24
10	Miami, FL 2,253,362	125	93	23	145	4.66	5.43	0.77

Notes:
Twenty largest urbanized areas by 1990 population.
Central city is the city or cities named.
Suburban is the difference between the urbanized area's corresponding metropolitan area and the central city. The 1999 metropolitan boundaries are used for both 1960 and 1990 data.

runs counter to what we believe to be the common perception, that is, that sprawl is an issue in the South and West. This perception is due, no doubt, to the fact that the metropolitan areas of the South and West have experienced relatively fast population growth. While land consumption for development in the Midwest and Northeast has been small in absolute terms, it has been large relative to population growth.

Viewing sprawl as some combination of a decrease in population density, an expansion of developed land area, and an emptying out of the center in favor of the periphery, we present in Table 10.3 descriptive statistics for the 20 largest urbanized areas and their corresponding metropolitan areas. We divide the 20 cities into ten 'rust belt' cities (located in the Midwest and the Northeast) and ten 'sun belt' cities (located in the South and the West).

The rust belt cities all experienced greater expansions of their urbanized land areas than of their urban populations between 1960 and 1990, resulting in declines in their population densities. These metropolitan areas also uniformly experienced declines in their central city populations over this period.[3] These cities are not the ones that come immediately to mind when the topic is sprawl. Nonetheless, from St. Louis to Baltimore, the cities of the Northeast and the Midwest experienced some of the classic symptoms of sprawl over the 30 year period: declining population density, much more rapid population growth on the periphery relative to the center, and growth of the developed land area.

The sun belt cities' experiences were more variable; still there were some remarkable contrasts with the rust belt cities. First, population increased faster than the urbanized land area in half of the sun belt cities, resulting in an increase in population density for these metropolitan areas. In addition, several metropolitan areas (Los Angeles, Dallas-Fort Worth, Houston, Phoenix, and San Diego) witnessed robust growth in the population of their central cities, both absolutely and in comparison to their suburbs. Among the sun belt cities, the experience of Atlanta, the poster child for sprawl, was the most similar to the rust belt cities: declining population density and an emptying out of the center relative to the periphery.

CAUSES OF SPRAWL

Forces driving land use patterns can be categorized into three groups: factors increasing the demand for land at the urban fringe, market failures, and public policies.

Factors Increasing the Demand for Land at the Urban Fringe

In simple terms, land at the urban fringe is demanded by farmers and by developers.[4] The more productive is land in agricultural use, the greater its value to farmers, and thus the higher the price developers will have to pay to acquire the land. To the extent that demand for development increases, it is expected that developers will bid away more land from agricultural uses.

There are three main economic forces affecting the demand for land and thus the development of land on or beyond the fringe of urban areas: population growth, rising income, and falling commuting costs (Mieszkowski and Mills, 1993; Brueckner, 2000, 2001b). In addition, changes in communication technology may have reduced the importance of spatial proximity in production, thereby increasing the demand for land on the urban fringe.

Population growth
Certainly, as population increases, additional land will be absorbed to accommodate this growth. Between 1980 and 2000, the population of metropolitan areas increased by 27.4 per cent. Thus, assuming no change in density, land used for urban development would have increased by 27.4 per cent.

Rising income
Rising household income increases the demand for most goods, including land and housing. Thus, even in the absence of population growth, growth in income will lead households to occupy larger tracts of land. Empirical studies suggest that the income elasticity of the demand for housing size is 0.46 (O'Sullivan, 2000, p. 392), while the income elasticity of demand for the land component of housing services has been estimated to be 0.32 (Witte et al., 1979). Margo (1992) finds that 40 per cent of suburbanization between 1950 and 1980 can be explained by increases in household income.

Falling commuting costs
Automobiles and the development of the interstate highway system substantially reduced the cost of commuting by increasing speed and thus reducing the time it takes to travel between residence and workplace. This allowed individuals to live further from their place of work. Evidence of these trends is found in the Nationwide Personal Transportation Survey (US Department of Transportation, 1997). The survey, conducted in 1990, found that between 1983 and 1990 commuting distance in suburban areas increased about 27 per cent, while commuting speed increased 16 per cent. For central city areas, commuting distance increased 20 per cent and commuting speeds increased by 26 per cent (pp. 154–5). This increased speed can be attributed to an increase in highway capacity through construction of more urban freeways

and improved transportation technology, but also a shift away from slower public transit and an increase in less congested reverse commuting. The increase in speed should lead households to be willing to live further from their worksite and to pay more for a residential tract at the urban fringe. Hence, developers will outbid farmers for land on the urban fringe and hence will acquire more agricultural land.

Brueckner and Fansler (1983) provide some evidence that existing levels of density are a result of these market forces. Consistent with what we argued above they predict that the size of an urban spatial area should be related positively to population and income and negatively to transportation costs and the price of land at the urban fringe. They find empirical support for their predictions; metropolitan areas with larger populations, higher incomes, lower transportation costs, and lower values of agricultural land occupy greater amounts of land.

Changes in communication technology
Another possible cause of the change in land use patterns is a decline in the importance of spatial proximity. Historically for many industries it was thought that a company would be more productive if it located in close proximity with other businesses in the industry. Likewise, it was thought that productivity would be higher if the divisions of a firm were located at the same site. Some have speculated that improvements in communications (faxes, e-mail, internet, cell phones, and so on) may have reduced the importance of spatial proximity for firm productivity. Thus, just as manufacturing firms could seek suburban and ex-urban sites when they were no longer tied to rivers for power or railroads for transportation, it may be less important for firms and their divisions to be as spatially close to other firms. The result is that many firms and divisions are no longer restricted to major commercial centers, and thus have become more dispersed. There is anecdotal evidence that many firms have moved back-office functions out of the central city, but there is little systematic evidence as to the magnitude of the importance of changing communication technology on the spatial proximity of firms.[5]

Market Failures

As long as the land market is perfectly competitive, economists argue that the pattern of development and the amount of land that is developed is efficient and thus there should be no concern about sprawl. To the extent that market distortions exist, however, the amount of urban land developed may be excessive or the pattern of development may be inefficient.

An important market imperfection is that open space on the fringe of urban areas may have value beyond its private value. Society may value the diversity of species and ecosystems associated with open space, the contribution of open space to clean air and water, and the potential uses of open space for public parks and rights-of-way. In the presence of such external benefits, the market price for land on the urban fringe is too low and more land will be converted from open space/agricultural use to urban development use than is socially optimal.

Another important market failure results from individuals making choices about commuting based on the private costs of travel. However, when a car enters the transportation network during rush hour, it slows the flow of traffic thereby increasing the time other drivers have to spend commuting. In addition, cars generate air pollution, which imposes additional costs on others. Commuters do not bear these congestion and pollution costs that they impose on others, and hence have no incentive to consider these costs when they make commuting decisions. Because individuals do not consider the full cost of using their cars, they will live further from their worksite and commute further than is optimal. The result is lower density than is optimal.

Public Policies

There are several ways in which public policies affect land use patterns. First, there are various subsidy programs that encourage low density development. The federal income tax system provides a substantial incentive for owner-occupied housing; the resulting lower effective price of housing services encourages larger lots and homes.

Public infrastructure is also subsidized. Federal subsidies in the 1960s, 1970s, and early 1980s meant that the price that developers paid for infrastructure was less than marginal cost, and thus geographic expansion was encouraged. Transportation, both mass transit and interstate highways, is also heavily subsidized, leading to a more extensive transportation network than may be efficient. The result is to lower the cost of transportation, which encourages longer commutes.

Governments typically fail to charge developers the full cost of public infrastructure needed to serve new developments. An issue that has received a great deal of attention is the additional cost of the infrastructure needed to serve less dense development patterns. To the extent that the cost of infrastructure and service delivery are negatively related to density and that these costs are not fully borne by the new development, there is an incentive for development to be less dense than is efficient. In most urban areas, infrastructure and public services are paid for through property taxes levied on all property. Thus, the pricing of infrastructure is averaged over all property taxpayers and therefore the infrastructure cost of development paid by the new development is less than the marginal cost of the public infrastructure.

Furthermore, since land being developed on the fringe of the urban area commands a lower price than in the more centralized and previously developed areas, property tax financing of infrastructure for new development results in an infrastructure price that is even lower than the average across all properties. This provides an incentive for less dense development and for extending the urban fringe.[6]

The use of property taxes results in less dense development than if a nondistortionary tax was used to finance public services. The property tax is levied on land and buildings, so compared to a pure land tax, the property tax results in development that is less land intensive (Nechyba, 1998). Brueckner (2001a) explores this issue by considering an urban area with a fixed population within a standard urban model and shows that the property tax leads to sprawl, in other words a decrease in overall density resulting from an expansion of the urban area beyond what is economically efficient in order to accommodate the fixed population.

Another public policy associated with sprawl is government regulation of land use. Suburban land use is dominated by zoning and subdivision ordinances that have substantial effects on land use. Zoning and subdivision ordinances frequently require large lots, discourage multifamily housing, and mandate large parking lots for commercial and retailing developments.[7]

The existence of a large number of municipalities allows individuals a wide range of public services packages from which to choose, and the interjurisdictional competition that results encourages governments to be more efficient. However, the greater the number of local governments within an urban area, the greater the competition for the property tax base. To the extent that communities on or beyond the urban fringe use incentives to encourage and promote the development of land before it otherwise would be efficient, tax base competition leads to an expansion of the urban area beyond what would be driven by market forces. In addition, the greater the number of local governments, the more difficult it is to adopt policies that might control sprawl because of the problems that arise in coordinating policies across a large numbers of jurisdictions. Fulton et al. (2001) find that sprawl is associated with metropolitan areas in which the average population of local governments is smaller. Dye and McGuire (2000) find that sprawl is positively associated with the number of local governments in an area.

THE EFFECTS OF SPRAWL AND CONSEQUENCES FOR STATE AND LOCAL GOVERNMENT FINANCES

As Ewing (1994) points out, it is not sprawl itself that is undesirable, but the negative impacts associated with sprawl. The extensive literature survey by

Burchell et al. (1998) uncovered 27 alleged negative impacts of sprawl and 14 alleged positive impacts. Conflicting arguments can be found in the literature regarding several of the suggested effects of sprawl; for example, there is research alleging that sprawl increases commuting times and other research alleging that it reduces commuting times. For many of the alleged effects, there is little evidence demonstrating a causal relationship with sprawl.

In this section we explore how sprawl might be expected to affect the expenditures and revenues of state and local governments. In the next section we consider the policies that state and local governments might consider to address sprawl.

Increased Cost of Public Infrastructure

It is commonly argued that less dense development results in a higher cost of providing public infrastructure.

Highway and street networks
Consider the effect of density on the cost of providing a commuter highway network. Consider two cities of radius r and 2r, each with the same population evenly distributed over the space of the city and with all employment located at the center. The density in the larger city will be one quarter the density of the smaller city. Suppose that the highway system starts at the edge of the city and expands as it reaches the center of the city in order to handle the increasing number of drivers. Essentially, the highway system will be shaped like a set of cones. If the radius of the city doubles, the size of the cone, that is, the number of lane miles, will also double.[8]

The neighborhood streets required to get commuters to the highways will also have to increase. If the density of neighborhood streets in the city with radius 2r has to be the same as in the city of radius r, then the miles of neighborhood streets will have to be four times as large in the city of radius 2r as in the city of radius r.[9]

These calculations are based on the assumption that all commutes are to the center of the city. If sprawl also results in a dispersal of employment locations, then sprawl might not result in longer commutes or reduced accessibility. However, actual development patterns have separated trip destinations such as residence, employment, and shopping, and thus commuting distances have increased over time. The Nationwide Personal Transportation Survey, conducted in 1990, found that the average distance traveled each day was 29 miles, an increase from 26 miles in 1977, and from about 24 miles in 1969 (US Department of Transportation, 1997, p. 148).

Public transit
To be cost-effective, public transit requires high residential and employment densities in order to generate sufficient trips. In addition, public bus transit is more cost-effective if the bus lines can be focused on a limited set of destinations, such as a central business district (CBD). Even if employment remains in the CBD, a less dense population requires longer bus routes to collect the same volume of riders. Thus, if sprawl results in lower population density and in numerous and widely dispersed employment centers, then public transit becomes a more costly option.

Water and sewer lines
The cost of water and sewer lines will also increase with lower density. Consider a square city subdivided into B square blocks of length L, with lots fronting all sides of the block. Assume that there must be one water line and one sewer line under every street, that is, one line can serve houses on both sides of the street. Consider an alternative city with the same population and block size, but with lot sizes that are twice as big; density in the new city will be half of what it was in the old city and the number of blocks will double. The total distance of the water and sewer lines that have to be installed in the new city will be slightly less than twice what it was in the more dense city.[10] The implication is that the cost of installing and maintaining water and sewer lines will nearly double.

Existing studies
The above calculations assume that all commutes are to the center of the urban area and that block sizes are fixed. An alternative approach to exploring the relationship between land use patterns and infrastructure is to consider the effect of alternative development patterns on the cost of infrastructure. The Office of Technology Assessment (US Congress, 1995), for example, estimated that sprawl increased the cost of infrastructure from ten per cent to 20 per cent. It cited one study that found that the cost of providing infrastructure for a house in a scattered, outlying development was 40 per cent higher than for a house in the core area of the city.

Burchell (1997) estimated the future infrastructure cost required by the growth in South Carolina for the period 1995 to 2015, and argued that if current development patterns continue, statewide infrastructure costs will be $56 billion, or $750 per person per year, half of which would be for road construction. He estimated that about ten per cent of this could be saved by adopting a more compact development pattern; most of the infrastructure cost is related to growth, regardless of the pattern of development.

The State of the Cities 1999 (US Department of Housing and Urban Development, 1999) reported that, 'Road costs are 25 per cent to 33 per cent higher and utility costs are 18 per cent to 25 per cent higher in communities marked by sprawl than in sprawl-free communities.'

These types of studies are not without flaws. For example, Altshuler and Gómez-Ibáñez (1993) point out that studies of fiscal impacts of alternative development patterns do not always use appropriate cost concepts or measures. Some of these studies assume that different residential density will lead to different household demographics, thereby confounding the effects on infrastructure costs of different densities with the effects of different demographics. Furthermore, the studies usually assume no difference in the level of service or in the technology used across developments of different densities. However, at low density streets could be narrower since there will be less traffic, and sidewalks could be built on only one side of the street since there will be fewer pedestrians.

Increased Operation Costs

There are several public services whose costs are likely to increase with lower density. Consider communities with the same population (both in size and characteristics) and the same quality of public services, but with different densities. To maintain the same quality the response times for police, fire, and EMS need to be the same for both densities. Lower density will require more fire stations to ensure the same response time. There will have to be more police patrols to ensure the same response time and that each house and commercial building get patrolled the same number of times. Since traffic congestion will be less when density is less, the percentage increase in costs should be less than the percentage decrease in density.

The costs of collecting solid waste, of street cleaning, and of snow plowing could also be higher. Garbage collection costs vary directly with distance (and speed) between pickup stops and the amount of trash collected. Since the latter will not change with density, the costs will not increase at the same rate that density decreases. Street cleaning and snow removal, however, vary in proportion to the miles of road. As noted above, the number of miles of road could increase at close to the same percentage that density falls. With lower density, however, there will be fewer cars per mile of road to interfere with the operations, which should increase speed.

Sprawl should have little effect on the costs of other services. Assuming that park space is the same regardless of density, the cost of parks and recreation should be unaffected, although land prices may be higher with higher density. On the other hand, with larger residential lots, the demand for public parks may be reduced. Education, other than the cost of transporting students, is also unlikely to be affected by density. Likewise, there is no reason to expect that the costs of functions such as courts, jails, and general government would be affected by density.

Increased density may change the characteristics of the community in ways other than geographic size, ways that might increase the costs of public provision. Denser cities may have taller buildings and more congestion, both of which increase the cost of providing certain public services, and there is a greater likelihood that fires might spread to surrounding buildings, so that more fire protection is needed.

Empirical studies of the cost of service provision suggest that per capita service costs are U-shaped with respect to density (Ladd, 1998). In such studies it is difficult to sort out the direct effect of density from the effect of other factors such as population characteristics associated with denser cities. However, if all cities were to be more dense, presumably there would be no additional sorting of individuals across cities based on factors associated with higher density, and thus the demographics of the cities would not change.

Property Taxes

Sprawl will have an effect on the property tax base and the effect may differ by the geographic location of the jurisdiction. Suppose that the price of land at the edge of the urban area decreases. Assume that the urban population does not change and that there are no other distortions. Within the context of a standard monocentric urban model the decrease in the price of land at the urban fringe will cause the urban area to expand. It is easy to show that the land value gradient will shift down and will equal the new, lower price of undeveloped land at a greater distance from the city center. The result is that within the original urban area, the total value of land will fall, and thus, the land value of the property tax base will fall. Because there is more land within the now expanded urban area, the total land value could increase.

Since the price of land has fallen, the production of goods and services will become less capital intensive, meaning that the total value of improvements should also fall. Furthermore, some of the existing capital should be relocated to the previously undeveloped land. Unless the income effect from the fall in land prices results in a substantial increase in the demand and hence production of local goods and services, including housing, the total value of the property tax base within the pre-existing urban area will fall.

The second aspect of the change in the value of the property tax base is how the change will be distributed across the urban area. Without putting some structure on the utility function in the monocentric model, the model does not yield a definite prediction regarding the percentage change in land value across the urban area. However, it is a common perception that commercial and industrial development is more dispersed with sprawl. Rather than all nonresidential property located in the CBD or in a few nodes, under sprawl this property will likely be distributed more uniformly across the urban area. This will provide more suburban jurisdictions with a nonresidential property tax base and decrease the property tax base in the central city.

We crudely explored this issue by investigating how the distribution of the property tax base changed over time as the Atlanta urban area expanded. We estimated a property tax gradient for 1970 and for 1999 using as the unit of observation per capita property tax base, at the county level, for the 20-county Atlanta MSA. If sprawl reduces density and extends the boundaries of the urbanized area, then the gradient should become flatter with sprawl. However, we found the value of the gradient became slightly steeper, although the change was not statistically significant.

Quality of Life

There are many ways that sprawl affects the quality of life. State and local governments may be called upon to address these consequences of sprawl.

Central city costs

To the extent that sprawl is the result of migration of central city residents to more distant suburbs, there are clear implications for the central city. Central cities have fixed infrastructure that has to be maintained. With out-migration of central city residents to the suburbs, the remaining central city residents will each have to bear a greater share of these maintenance costs. Furthermore, if the households who move to the suburbs are higher income households, then the tax base per capita in the central part of the urban area will likely decrease.

Environmental problems

Sprawl is also associated with environmental issues. Longer commutes associated with low density development contribute to air pollution. Low density development also increases water runoff since the larger the land area that is covered, the greater the water runoff. For example, parking lots generate almost 16 times as much runoff as undeveloped land. Sprawling low rise shopping centers and office parks increase the land that is paved and therefore the amount of runoff (Hirschhorn, 2000). The result is increased costs of waste water treatment and greater health care costs from air pollution.

Psychic costs

Authors have also associated sprawl with psychic costs such as unaesthetic development and loss of community. Many authors decry the proliferation of strip malls and big box stores. Some authors associate the traditional suburban subdivision with an increase in the isolation of households, leading to a loss of community. It is argued that this loss of community is compounded by the increased time spent in automobiles commuting to work and running errands. To the extent that this is true, it may reduce the time individuals spend volunteering in the community and increase the need for local governments to take on the functions that the volunteers would otherwise have performed.

POSSIBLE STATE AND LOCAL POLICIES TO ADDRESS SPRAWL

Growing concerns about sprawl and its consequences have pushed it to a prominent place on the political agenda and therefore put pressure on state and local governments to take action. Katz and Bernstein (1998) argue that broad based coalitions are being formed among a diverse set of interest groups, all of which, in Katz and Bernstein's view, have something to lose as sprawl accelerates. 'These constituencies reject the conventional wisdom that current growth patterns are inevitable – the result only of invisible market forces and consumer preferences. Rather, they are focusing more on the role that government policies – spending program, tax expenditures, and regulatory and administrative actions – play in shaping our communities and, by extension, our lives' (Katz and Bernstein, 1998, p 5). Leo et al. (1998) discuss in detail the various interest groups that have found common ground in their concern over sprawl: local businesses because they see the consequences of sprawl as detrimental to the local business climate and view smart growth as a means of opening up development opportunities; environmentalists who have come to realize that policies that control sprawl are in line with their growing interests in the urban environment; and agricultural interests because anti-sprawl policies are seen as a means of limiting the conservation of farm land as well as the pressures that urban development place on the activities of surrounding farms.

Sprawl has also become an issue high on the public's agenda. For example, in a Pew Center for Civic Journalism national survey in October 1999, sprawl and crime were ranked first as the most important problems facing the respondent's community (Williams, 2000). Sprawl is ranked as more of a problem among suburbanites, whites, and those with higher education.

This political pressure is forcing state and local governments to address sprawl and the consequences of current development patterns. The interest groups have lobbied governments to control sprawl through the use of growth management policies, impact fees, reduction of residential growth, and the purchase of land to preserve open space. By one count, in 2001, there were

240 smart growth initiatives being considered across the county (Gosling, 2001).[11]

Policies to address sprawl can be broadly categorized into two groups. The first set of policies is aimed at directly preventing sprawl, and include growth controls and regional growth management. The second set includes policies that are intended to discourage sprawl by correcting market failures through providing proper incentives and eliminating market distorting public programs and policies.

Regulatory Policies

Growth control policies implicitly assume that sprawl and its consequences are the result of population growth. Thus, the argument goes, by limiting growth sprawl can be controlled. However, growth control policies have largely been discredited as short sighted and ineffective (Downs, 1994).

Growth management policies, which aim to direct growth to certain areas and away from others, have been strongly endorsed, particularly by planners (Nelson, 1999, 2000). The policies include regional planning or regional review of local planning and zoning,[12] restricting or steering development to areas that are served by appropriate public infrastructure, urban growth boundaries, and green belts.[13] Several states have enacted legislation requiring regional planning, although the strength of these laws varies widely across states (Gale, 1992). Oregon established the most widely noted urban growth boundary around Portland in 1973 (Abbott, 1997), but growth boundaries have also been established around other cities (Easterly, 1992; Lang and Hornburg, 1997). Green belts have been created in Seattle and Boulder (Nelson, 1986).

As we discussed above, and as most students of urban land markets agree, urban land markets are not perfectly competitive, and thus development patterns are not economically efficient. Proponents of growth management policies argue, at least implicitly, that the solution to this inefficiency is through control of the development process. Such policies as growth boundaries are, however, very blunt policy instruments. Growth boundaries essentially replace market determination of how the boundaries of an urban area are set or adjusted to accommodate population growth with a planner's vision of the most desirable pattern of development. If growth boundaries are drawn tightly around the developed area, or not allowed to expand with increases in population, then development is constrained to a land mass that can be too restrictive. On the other hand, the boundary could be drawn so far out that it has no effect on development patterns.

In 1979, Mills (1979) noted that there had been very little scholarly analysis of land use controls, by which he meant zoning. The same could be said today regarding growth management tools such as growth boundaries. Hence we know very little about the effects of urban growth boundaries.

From a theoretical perspective, since growth boundaries, if binding, reduce the supply of land available for development, they should result in an increase in the price of land throughout the urban area, an increase in residential density, and an increase in the concentration of commercial development in the central city. There is some empirical evidence that residential density in Portland has increased and trip times have been reduced, but at the expense of an increase in housing prices (Nelson, 1999). Nelson et al. (2002) reviewed the literature on the effect of growth management policies on land and housing prices, and found that land prices are positively affected by urban growth boundaries. However, they argue that the increase in land value might be due to an increase in housing demand resulting from the increased desirability of the urban environment in communities that control sprawl, and not just from restrictions on the availability of land.

Policies to Correct Market Imperfections and Misguided Government Policies

An alternative approach to growth management is to adopt policies that correct the imperfections that lead to sprawl. We consider each of the causes of sprawl and identify possible policies (all of which are discussed at length by others) to address each cause.

Open space is undervalued

There are two issues associated with open land: the land on the urban fringe and interior open space. Consider land on the urban fringe. As discussed above, if the social value of open space on the urban fringe exceeds the market price, then more land will be converted from open space/agricultural use to urban development than is socially optimal. An obvious policy is to adopt a development tax set equal to the external costs of converting agricultural land to developed land. In other words, impose a tax equal to the dollar value of the social benefits to residents from the open space that would be eliminated by the development.

The obvious difficulty is determining the social value of land that may be converted from agricultural use to development purposes. It is unlikely that a uniform development tax would be appropriate for all land in all urban areas. It is likely that certain types of land will have greater social value; for example, a tract of land that contains a river may have greater social value than an open field. Furthermore, to the extent that the value of open space accrues to all residents, that is, the externality is of a public good variety, then the development tax should increase with the population of the area.

There have been very few efforts to estimate the social value of open space. López, Shah, and Altobello (1994) use data from previous studies to calculate the marginal social value of open space and find values that range from $12 to $103 per acre depending on the location.

One method that is currently being used to measure social values is contingent valuation, a method that relies on individual responses to questions about willingness to pay for a reduction in an externality.[14] Brueckner (2001b) argues that the methods available to estimate such social values are not sufficiently creditable that they can be a reliable basis for policy. Thus, in setting such a development tax, a policy maker may just as easily set too low or too high a tax, both of which would produce economic inefficiencies. It is not clear, however, whether imposing no tax would be socially preferred to levying a tax that may be calculated incorrectly.

An alternative to taxing development is to subsidize farmers, for example, by reducing property taxes, to encourage them not to sell their land to developers. Every state already has a program that in one way or another reduces property taxes on certain agricultural land. These programs include applying a lower assessment ratio on agricultural land, using use value rather than fair market value, and levying reduced tax rates in return for long term agreements not to convert the use of the land. Studies of the effect of use-value assessment on the retardation of farm land conversions have found the impact to be slight; see Chicoine, Sonka, and Doty (1982) and the references they cite. More recently however, Morris (1998) found that preferential assessment of farmland reduced the loss of farmland by about ten per cent relative to the base case. But the issue of determining the appropriate magnitude of the subsidy remains.

The above policy is concerned with the pace at which agricultural/open land on the urban fringe is converted to developed uses. But there clearly is a desire to retain open space within the urban area. Land for public open space should be acquired by the government. However, since parks are a public good and if they are provided by multiple local governments, park space may be undersupplied. Small local governments will consider the benefits to their taxpayers, who are a small percentage of the metropolitan area's population. Because each local government will face the full price of acquiring land, it will likely purchase less open space than is socially optimal. Thus, there may be a role for a regional government in the provision of public open space.

While public parks are one form of open space, privately owned common areas are another. It is argued, for example, that instead of building ten houses, each on half acre lots, it would be environmentally advantageous if the houses were clustered on two acres, with three acres set aside for common open space. To preserve a set of geographically dispersed private open spaces within the interior of the urban area, however, would seem to require a very complicated developmental tax or subsidy policy. Such a policy would have to reflect the size, the location, and the environmental sensitivity of multiple tracts of open space.

Distortions caused by the property tax

If the property tax results in distortions leading to excessive expansion of the urban area, an obvious policy option is to replace the current property tax with a land value tax. While land value taxation is used in several countries, there is no jurisdiction in the United States that has shifted to a land value tax. Several jurisdictions have adopted a split rate property tax in which land is taxed at a higher rate than improvements. A study by Oates and Schwab (1997) found that the split rate property tax in Pittsburgh may have lead to increased development in the central city. Land value taxation has been extensively discussed elsewhere (Bahl and Linn, 1992; Netzer, 1998; Tideman, 1998) and thus is not further pursued here.

Mispricing of public infrastructure

The economic solution to inappropriate pricing of public infrastructure is to charge new development the full cost of providing the infrastructure. In an effort to impose such costs, many local governments impose impact fees on new developments. Typically, the impact fees are calculated by a formula derived from estimates of the differences in the cost of public infrastructure for different types of development. Altshuler and Gómez-Ibáñez (1993), who provide an extensive discussion of impact fees and other forms of development exactions, point out that many of the attempts to estimate these costs are flawed. Furthermore, impact fees are usually based on average costs, not marginal costs. Thus, impact fees are usually the same for an infill development that simply has to connect to the existing water and sewer systems and for a development on the urban fringe that requires an extension of the public infrastructure. The appropriate cost concept is the marginal infrastructure cost of the development. Thus, while impact fees are widely used, their design is often inconsistent with economically efficient pricing of public infrastructure.

On the theoretical side, Breuckner (1997) explores the effects of three different schemes for financing infrastructure required by new development. The first scheme is impact fees, where the incremental cost is borne by the developer. The second scheme is an arrangement under which the infrastructure cost is shared among all landowners and is paid at the time of development. The third scheme is like the second one, except the cost is financed by infinite maturity bonds. He analyses the three schemes in an urban growth model. He finds that impact fees restrict growth over the other two options as long as the marginal infrastructure cost is greater than the average cost and the population growth rate is less than the interest rate.

There has been little empirical work on the effect of impact fees. Other than a paper by Skidmore and Peddle (1998), who found that impact fees in DuPage County, Illinois, reduced residential development, we found no recent empirical analysis of the effect of impact fees on development patterns. Yinger (1998) cites two studies that explore the effect of impact fees on the price of housing. Both studies obtain the surprising result that the price of a house increases by two to three times the value of the impact fee. The implication is that there is substantial overshifting of impact fees to the purchaser of the home.

Mispricing of road use

Individuals make choices about commuting based on the private costs of travel such as the cost of time. Since commuters do not bear the costs of congestion and air pollution imposed on others, they have no incentive to consider these costs. For example, when another car enters traffic during rush hour, it further slows the flow of traffic, thereby increasing the time everyone else has to spend commuting. But the driver considers only his commute time, not the effect he has on everyone else. Because of this situation, individuals choose to drive longer distances than are optimal. One solution to this problem is to charge drivers for the cost they impose on other drivers, in other words, to impose congestion fees.

Optimal congestion fees should be set equal to the costs that the driver imposes on everyone else. The appropriate fee depends on the volume of traffic on the segment of the transportation system used. The toll should not be imposed just for the use of highways, since congestion also occurs on surface streets, and imposing a toll just on the use of highways would encourage drivers to shift from the highway to surface streets. The congestion toll provides an incentive for individuals to shorten the commuting trip, to shift to a time when the toll is lower, and to switch to an alternative mode of transportation.

Much research has been directed at determining the appropriate magnitude of a congestion toll. Decorla-Souza and Kane (1992), for example, estimate that the marginal social cost of congestion is between $0.34 to $0.56 (in 2000 prices) per vehicle mile, while Small (1997) estimates that the air pollution cost of urban transportation is between $0.007 and $0.037 per vehicle mile. Congestion fees are used in several places, particularly outside the United States, and there are a variety of ways that they can be imposed, some more practical than others, and some more politically acceptable than others (Small, et al., 1989).

One effect of congestion fees should be to reduce the number of miles traveled, which should also result in a reduction in air pollution. To the extent that commuting trips are directed to the CBD, then reductions in commuting distance imply residing closer to the CBD, which in turn implies greater density. However, not all worksites are located in the CBD but are spread throughout the metropolitan area. Suppose that employment centers remain fixed and individuals move their place of residences in order to be closer to their particular place of employment. In that situation will density increase and will the developed area be smaller? If more individuals commute into the CBD than reverse commute, then this rearranging of residences should result in an increase in the central city population. At the same time, individuals will locate closer to other employment centers, increasing density around those centers. However, it is not clear that the urban area will be smaller, although there may be places within the urban area that will be less developed.

Related to the use of the transportation system is the cost of parking at work. Free parking encourages commuting. Requiring firms to charge employees for parking, or to pay employees who do not use the parking lot, would correct the distortion caused by free parking. The effect would be to reduce the number of commuters, thereby reducing congestion.

Competition among jurisdictions

Jurisdictional competition for tax base, either in the form of commercial development or housing types that contribute more in taxes than they cost in services, is thought to cause sprawl. This would occur if jurisdictions at or beyond the urban boundary provide incentives that lead to land being developed sooner than would be economically efficient.

Such competition could be reduced by implementing a tax base or tax revenue sharing arrangement within the urban and ex-urban areas. The principal example of tax base sharing is the program in the Minneapolis-St. Paul metropolitan area, implemented in the 1970s. Under this legislation, in the Twin Cities area 40 per cent of the increase in commercial-industrial property tax value goes into a regional pool to be shared by all taxing jurisdictions in the area. The sharing formula is based directly on population and inversely on relative property tax base per capita.

Tax base sharing was enacted to reduce fiscal disparities[15] and to encourage more sensible land use decisions. To the extent that a jurisdiction's tax base does not increase by the full property value of the businesses that locate within its boundaries, interjurisdictional competition for nonresidential tax base should be reduced. With the Twin Cities program, local governments still compete for the 60 per cent of the increase in the commercial-industrial base that is not shared.

Another tax base sharing program is illustrated by the Hackensack Meadowlands Development and Reclamation Act in New Jersey. This program differs from the Minnesota program in how the shared tax base pool is distributed. There are three factors used. First, jurisdictions that take tracts of land off of their property tax roll for public purposes (such as, wetlands) receive in-lieu-of-tax payments. Second, a municipality gets a payment for land zoned for residential purposes to compensate for increased student enrollments. Finally, the remaining shared tax base is allocated on the basis of land area. By tying the distribution to actual land use, the tax base sharing program should have more influence on land use decisions than does the Minnesota sharing arrangement.

There has been little research on whether tax base sharing has had an effect on land use decisions. In one published paper, Reschovsky (1980) reports that he found little evidence that tax base sharing had an effect on land use patterns; but the Minnesota program was still relatively new at the time of the study. Luce (1998), however, draws the same conclusion, noting that the use of tax increment financing suggests that local competition for business is still intense.

A second approach to tax competition is to reduce the number of local governments. The greater the number of local governments, the more likely it is that they will try to compete for tax base and try to exclude households with high service costs. Thus, reducing the number of local governments or shifting certain services to regional governments, should reduce this form of competition.

To the extent that this incentive is operable, we should expect that metropolitan areas with few relatively large jurisdictions should have experienced less sprawl than in metropolitan areas with a large number of smaller jurisdictions in which the well-to-do are able to isolate themselves. Dye and McGuire (2000) find some evidence that metropolitan areas with a greater number of local governments are more sprawled.

While such schemes may reduce the incentive of high income households to move to the urban fringe, the likelihood of implementing such schemes is very low since political opposition would likely be fierce. Orfield (1998) provides an account of the political struggle to implement tax base sharing in the Minneapolis-St. Paul area and argues that to pass such legislation requires that there be more winners than losers. Orfield (1997) argues that a coalition of the central city and older, inner ring suburbs should be able to find sufficient common ground and be sufficiently large to get legislation passed.

Zoning and subdivision ordinances
It has been widely argued that existing zoning and land use regulations create incentives for sprawl. Thus, the obvious solution is to change these laws and ordinances (Downs, 1994). Another option is regional coordination and rationalization of local land use planning. Such centralization of growth management or mandated changes in local zoning ordinances is opposed by local jurisdictions since they do not want to give up local control of growth.

SUMMARY AND CONCLUSIONS

The finances of state and local governments can be affected by sprawl in many ways. The costs of providing highway and street networks, public transit, water and sewer infrastructure, and many city services such as police, fire, sanitation and EMS services increase as density falls and the urban area increases for a given population. The level and geographic distribution of the property tax base may also be affected by sprawl. In addition, state and local governments may be called upon to correct market imperfections and mis-guided government policies that lead to sprawl.

The two most important market imperfections associated with sprawl are that the social value of open space may be greater than the private value and that the social costs of commuting may exceed the private costs. Policies to address the former include fees or taxes on development, subsidies to farm-ers, and public acquisition of land at the urban fringe or open land in the interior of the urban area. Congestion fees are the obvious response to the external costs imposed by drivers when they enter congested highway net-works. State and local governments have all of these tools at their disposal.

It can be argued that local government reliance on the property tax also contributes to sprawl both because the property tax results in less dense development than a land tax and because it results in average cost pricing of public infrastructure for new development. Shifting toward a land tax and imposing properly-calculated impact fees would address these potential self-inflicted causes of sprawl.

Finally, through the proliferation of local governments and the zoning laws exercised by them, regional cooperation to address sprawl can be difficult. Regional government and a centralization of land use decisions are the obvi-ous, although highly unpopular, solutions to sprawl. If the perception is that the social costs of sprawl have become unacceptable, then state and local governments will be compelled to consider a combination of many of the policies discussed herein.

NOTES

1. This chapter has benefitted from the comments of Ben Scafidi and Geoffrey Turnbull, and the technical assistance of Diane McCarthy.
2. They use urbanized land as estimated by the National Resources Inventory, not urbanized area as measured by the Bureau of the Census.
3. Population data for 2000 indicate that many central cities in these metropolitan areas experienced a turnaround in the decade of the 1990s. The central city population growth rate was positive for New York, Chicago, Boston, and Minneapolis-St. Paul.
4. By developers we mean anyone wanting to acquire land in order to build housing or commercial or industrial facilities.

5. Glaeser and Kahn (2001) discuss the decentralization of industry in urban areas.
6. Brueckner (2001a) explores the effect on spatial form of charging developers a tax equal to the average cost of infrastructure rather than the marginal cost.
7. Leinberger (1998) claims that a neighborhood commercial center will 'always be built on a 12- to 15-acre site, with 20 per cent of space set aside for building and the remaining 80 per cent dedicated to parking' (36). He also claims that for every 1000 square feet of office space, 1500 square feet of parking will be provided, and for every 1000 square feet of restaurant seating space, parking will require 3500 square feet.
8. The size of the cone will be rM/2, where r is the radius and M is the width of the road at the center of the city. M is the same regardless of r for a given population. Doubling r doubles the size of the cone.
9. The area of the city is πr^2. So doubling r, quadruples the area.
10. The percentage increase in the miles of water and sewer lines will approach the percentage increase in the number of blocks as the number of blocks approaches infinity.
11. For a summary of many of the policies that have been adopted by state and local governments to restrict the spatial expansion of cities see Brueckner (2001b).
12. Gale (1992) discusses the characteristics of eight state-sponsored growth management programs, while Glickfeld and Levine (1992) discuss the adoption of such programs in California.
13. Growth boundaries and green belts are ways to restrict the geographic expansion of urban development.
14. For a discussion of contingent valuation see Diamond and Hausman (1994).
15. Fisher (1981) and Fox (1981) discuss the flaws in the design of the Minnesota program in terms of how it addresses fiscal disparities.

REFERENCES

Abbott, Carl (1997), 'The Portland region: Where city and suburbs talk to each other – and often agree', *Housing Policy Debate*, 8(1): 11–51.

Altshuler, Alan A. and Josè A. Gómez-Ibáñez (1993), *Regulation for Revenue: The Political Economy of Land Use Exactions*, Washington, DC: The Brookings Institution and Cambridge, MA: Lincoln Institute of Land Policy.

Bahl, Roy and Johannes F. Linn (1992), *Urban Public Finance in Developing Countries*, New York, NY: Cambridge University Press.

Benefield, F. Kaid, Matthew D. Raimi and Donald D.T. Chen (1999), *Once There Were Greenfields*, New York, NY: Natural Resources Defense Council.

Brueckner, Jan K. (1997), 'Infrastructure financing and urban development: The economics of impact fees', *Journal of Public Economics*, 66: 383–407.

Brueckner, Jan K. (2000), 'Urban sprawl: diagnosis and remedies', *International Regional Science Review*, 23(2): 160–71.

Brueckner, Jan K. (2001a), 'Property taxation and urban sprawl', in Wallace E. Oates (ed.), *Property Taxation and Local Government Finance*, Cambridge, MA: Lincoln Institute of Land Policy, pp. 153–72.

Brueckner, Jan K. (2001b), 'Urban sprawl: lessons from urban economics', in William G. Gale and Janet Rothenberg Pack (eds), *Brookings-Wharton Papers on Urban Affairs*, Washington, DC: The Brookings Institution, pp. 65–89.

Brueckner, Jan K. and David A. Fansler (1983), 'The economics of urban sprawl: Theory and evidence on the spatial size of cities', *Review of Economics and Statistics*, 65(3): 479–82.

Burchell, Robert W. (1997), *South Carolina Infrastructure Study: Projection of*

Statewide Infrastructure Costs 1995–2015, New Brunswick, NJ: Center for Urban Policy Research, Rutgers University.

Burchell, Robert W., Naveed A. Shad, David Listokin, Hilary Phillips, Anthony Downs, Samuel Seskin, Judy S. Davis, Terry Moore, David Helton and Michelle Gall (1998), *Cost of Sprawl – Revisited*, Washington, DC: National Transportation Research Board/National Research Council.

Buttenheim, H.S. and P.H. Cornick (1938), 'Land reserves for American cities', *The Journal of Land and Public Utility Economics*, 14: 254–65.

Chicoine, David L., Steven T. Sonka and Robert D. Doty (1982), 'The effects of farm property tax relief programs on farm financial conditions', *Land Economics*, 58(4): 516–23.

Decorla-Souza, Patrick and Anthony Kane (1992), 'Peak period tolls: Precepts and prospects', *Transportation*, 19: 291–311.

Diamond, Peter and Jerry Hausman (1994), 'Is some number better than no number?', *Journal of Economic Perspectives*, 8: 45–64.

Downs, Anthony (1994), *New Visions for Metropolitan America*, Washington, DC: The Brookings Institution.

Dye, Richard F. and Therese J. McGuire (2000), 'Property taxes, schools, and sprawl', *State Tax Notes*, 29 May: 1899–1908.

Easterly, V. Gail (1992), *Staying Inside the Lines: Urban Growth Boundaries*, Chicago, IL: American Planning Association.

Ewing, Reid H. (1994), 'Characteristics, causes, and effects of sprawl: A literature review', *Environmental and Urban Issues*, Winter: 1–15.

Fisher, Peter S. (1981), 'State equalizing aids and metropolitan tax base sharing: A comparative analysis', *Public Finance Quarterly*, 9(4): 449–70.

Fox, William F. (1981), 'An evaluation of metropolitan tax-base sharing: A comment', *National Tax Journal*, 34(2): 275–9.

Fulton, William, Rolf Pendall, Mai Nguyen and Alicia Harrison (2001), *Who Sprawls Most? How Growth Patterns Differ Across the US*, Washington, DC: The Brookings Institution, Center on Urban & Metropolitan Policy, Survey Series.

Gale, Dennis E. (1992), 'Eight state-sponsored growth management programs: A comparative analysis', *Journal of the American Planning Association*, 58(4): 425–9.

Galster, George, Royce Hanson, Hal Wolman, Stephan Colemen and Jason Freihage (2000), 'Wrestling sprawl to the ground: Defining and measuring an elusive concept', *Housing Facts and Findings*, 2(4): 3–5.

Glaeser, Edward L. and Matthew E. Kahn (2001), 'Decentralized employment and the transformation of the American city', in William G. Gale and Janet Rothenberg Pack (eds), *Brookings-Wharton Papers on Urban Affairs*, Washington, DC: The Brookings Institution, pp. 1–63.

Glickfeld, Madelyn and Ned Levine (1992), *Regional Growth … Local Reaction: The Enactment and Effects of Local Growth Control and Management Measures in California*, Cambridge, MA: Lincoln Institute of Land Policy.

Gosling, John (2001), 'Debating density', *Urban Land*, 20(8): 14–19.

Hess, George R., Salinda S. Daley, Becky K. Dennison, Sharon R. Lubkin, Robert P. McGuinn, Vanessa Z. Morin, Kevin M. Potter, Rick E. Savage, Wade G. Sheldon, Chris M. Snow and Beth M. Wrege (2001), 'Just what is sprawl, anyway?', Unpublished paper, Forestry Department, North Carolina State University, www4.ncsu.edu: 8030/~grhess/papers/sprawl.pdf

Hirschhorn, Joel S. (2000), *Quality of Life in the New Economy*, Washington, DC: National Governors Association.

Katz, Bruce and Scott Bernstein (1998), 'The new metropolitan agenda', *Brookings Review*, 16(4): 4–7.

Ladd, Helen F. (1998), 'Land use regulation as a fiscal tool', in Helen F. Ladd (ed.), *Local Government Tax and Land Use Policies in the United States: Understanding the Links*, Cheltenham, UK and Northampton, MA: Edward Elgar, pp. 55–81.

Lang, Robert E. and Steven P. Hornburg (1997), 'Planning Portland style: Pitfalls and possibilities', *Housing Policy Debate*, 8(1): 1–10.

Leinberger, Christopher (1998), 'The market and metropolitanism: Questioning forty years of development practices', *Brookings Review*, 16(4): 35–6.

Leo, Christopher, with Mary Ann Beavis, Andrew Carver and Robyne Turner (1998), 'Is urban sprawl back on the political agenda? Local growth control, regional growth management, and politics', *Urban Affairs Review*, 34(2): 179–212.

López, Rigoberto, Farhed Shah and Marilyn Attolbello (1994), 'Amenity benefits and the optimal allocation of land', *Land Economics*, 70(1): 53–62.

Luce, Thomas F. Jr. (1998), 'Regional tax base sharing: The Twin Cities experience', in Helen F. Ladd (ed.), *Local Government Tax and Land Use Policy in the United States: Understanding the Links*, Cheltenham, UK and Northampton, MA: Edward Elgar, pp. 234–54.

Margo, Robert (1992), 'Explaining the postwar suburbanization of the population in the United States: The role of income', *Journal of Urban Economics*, 31: 301–10.

Mieszkowski, Peter and Edwin S. Mills (1993), 'The causes of metropolitan suburbanization', *Journal of Economic Perspectives*, 7(3): 135–47.

Mills, Edwin (1979), 'Economic analysis of urban land-use controls', in Peter Mieszkowski and Mahlon Straszheim (eds), *Current Issues in Urban Economics*, Baltimore, MD: Johns Hopkins University Press, pp. 511–41.

Morris, Adele C. (1998), 'Property tax treatment of farmland: Does tax relief delay land development?', in Helen F. Ladd (ed.), *Local Government Tax and Land Use Policies in the United States: Understanding the Links*, Cheltenham, UK and Northampton, MA: Edward Elgar, pp. 144–67.

Nechyba, Thomas J. (1998), 'Replacing capital taxes with land taxes: Efficiency and distributional implications with an application to the United States economy', in Dick Netzer (ed.), *Land Value Taxation: Can It and Will It Work Today?*, Cambridge, MA: Lincoln Institute of Land Policy, pp. 183–204.

Nelson, Arthur C. (1986), 'Using land markets to evaluate urban containment programs', *Journal of the American Planning Association*, 52(2): 156–71.

Nelson, Arthur C. (1999), 'Comparing states with and without growth management: Analysis based on indicators with policy implications', *Land Use Policy*, 16: 121–7.

Nelson, Arthur C. (2000), 'Smart growth: urban containment and housing prices', *Journal of Housing and Community Development*, 57(5): 45–9.

Nelson, Arthur C., Rolf Pendall, Casey J. Dawkins and Gerrit J. Knapp (2002), *The Link Between Growth Management and Housing Affordability: The Academic Evidence*, Washington, DC: The Brookings Institution, Center on Urban and Metropolitan Policy.

Netzer, Dick (1998), *Land Value Taxation*, Cambridge, MA: Lincoln Institute of Land Policy.

Oates, Wallace E. and Robert M. Schwab (1997), 'The impact of urban land taxation: The Pittsburgh experience', *National Tax Journal*, 50: 1–21.

Orfield, Myron (1997), *Metropolitics*, Washington, DC: The Brookings Institution.
Orfield, Myron (1998), 'Conflict or consensus: Forty years of Minnesota metropolitan politics', *Brookings Review*, 16: 31–4.
O'Sullivan, Arthur (2000), *Urban Economics*, Boston, MA: McGraw-Hill.
Reschovsky, Andrew (1980), 'An evaluation of metropolitan area tax-base sharing', *National Tax Journal*, 33(1): 55–66.
Skidmore, Mark and Michael Peddle (1998), 'Do development impact fees reduce the rate of residential development?', *Growth & Change*, 29(4): 383–400.
Small, Kenneth A. (1997), 'Economics and urban transportation policy in the United States', *Regional Science and Urban Economics*, 27: 671–91.
Small, Kenneth A., Clifford Winston and Carol A. Evans (1989), *Road Work: A New Highway Pricing and Investment Policy*, Washington, DC: The Brookings Institution.
Tideman, Nicolaus (1998), 'Applications of land value taxation to problems of environmental protection, congestion, efficient resource use, population and economic growth', in Dick Netzer (ed.), *Land Value Taxation: Can It and Will It Work Today?*, Cambridge, MA: Lincoln Institute of Land Policy, pp. 263–76.
US Congress, Office of Technology Assessment (1995), *The Technological Reshaping of Metropolitan America*, OTA-ETI-643, Washington, DC: US Government Printing Office.
US Department of Housing and Urban Development (1999), *The State of the Cities 1999*, Washington, DC: author.
US Department of Transportation (1997), *Transportation Statistics Annual Report 1997*, Washington, DC: author.
Williams, Donald C. (2000), *Urban Sprawl*, Santa Barbara, CA: Contemporary World Issues.
Witte, Ann D., Howard J. Sumkam and Homer Erekson (1979), 'An estimate of a structural hedonic price model of the housing market: An application of Rosen's theory of implicit markets', *Econometrica*, 47(5): 1151–73.
Yinger, John (1998), 'Who pays development fees?', in Helen F. Ladd (ed.), *Local Government Tax and Land Use Policies in the United States: Understanding the Links*, Cheltenham, UK and Northampton, MA: Edward Elgar, pp. 218–33.

Index